RACE AND BIBLICAL STUDIES

RESOURCES FOR BIBLICAL STUDY

Editor
Davina C. Lopez, New Testament

Number 101

RACE AND BIBLICAL STUDIES

Antiracism Pedagogy for the Classroom

Edited by
Tat-siong Benny Liew and Shelly Matthews

 PRESS
Atlanta

Copyright © 2022 by SBL Press

All rights reserved. No part of this work may be reproduced or transmitted in any form or by any means, electronic or mechanical, including photocopying and recording, or by means of any information storage or retrieval system, except as may be expressly permitted by the 1976 Copyright Act or in writing from the publisher. Requests for permission should be addressed in writing to the Rights and Permissions Office, SBL Press, 825 Houston Mill Road, Atlanta, GA 30329 USA.

Library of Congress Control Number: 2022947216

Contents

Acknowledgments ix
Abbreviations xi

Introduction: Racism, Classroom Teaching, and Beyond
    Tat-siong Benny Liew and Shelly Matthews 1

Part 1. Naming Contexts

From Africa to Mesopotamia (Genesis 2:13–14) and from
India to Ethiopia (Esther 1:1b): How an Afro-Asiatic Biblical
Construction Was Twisted into a Eurocentric Claim
    Randall C. Bailey 25

Anachronistic Whiteness and the Ethics of Interpretation
    Denise Kimber Buell 43

Is the Hebrew Bible Racist? Diversity and Antiracist
Reading Practices
    Julián Andrés González Holguín 61

One Nation under God: Teaching Biblical Studies in the
Era of Religious Nationalism
    Sharon Jacob 81

Exegeting Racism: Before and after Hurricane Maria
    Jean-Pierre Ruiz 97

Staying Awake: Constructing Critical Race Literacy and
Reorienting Biblical Studies
    Abraham Smith 111

Part 2. Empowering Students

Pedagogies of Race and the Bible
 Eric D. Barreto 135

Teaching Vivaldi: Pedagogical Responses to the Work of
Claude M. Steele
 Greg Carey 151

Teaching through *Testimonio*: Latinx Biblical Studies and
Students as Knowledge Producers
 Kay Higuera Smith 171

An Intercultural Approach: Latinx Students, Exegesis, and the
Border Wall
 Francisco Lozada Jr. 187

Part 3. Reframing Contexts

Seeing Who's Not There: Velázquez's *Kitchen Maid with the
Supper at Emmaus*
 Sonja Anderson 205

Can the Biblical Subaltern Speak? A Case for Multiple
Historical Criticisms
 Haley Gabrielle 223

Reflections on Teaching the Bible and Black Lives
Matter in a Divinity School
 Wilda C. Gafney 241

"And I Will Give to You, and to Your Offspring after
You, the Land Where You Are Now an Alien": Kinship and
Land as Devices for Inclusive Pedagogies
 Roger S. Nam 259

A Pedagogy of Ethnic Prejudice in Matthew 15:21–28
 Wongi Park 275

Contributors 289
Modern Authors Index 291
Subject Index 297

Acknowledgments

We are grateful to Erin Beall of the Brite Divinity School for her expert assistance in editing this manuscript.

We thank Davina Lopez, editor of Resources for Biblical Study, for inviting us to submit the volume to this series. At SBL Press, we also thank Nicole L. Tilford and Bob Buller for their support of this project.

We appreciate the enthusiasm and work of our contributors. Without their essays, the idea for this volume would not have come to fruition.

Abbreviations

AB	*Anchor Bible*
AMAEJ	*Association of Mexican American Educators Journal*
AmPsych	*American Psychologist*
AT	*Anthropological Theory*
AThR	*Anglical Theological Review*
BASOR	*Bulletin of the American Schools of Oriental Research*
BCT	*The Bible and Critical Theory*
BibInt	*Biblical Interpretation*
B.J.	Josephus, *Bellum judaicum*
BTB	*Biblical Theology Bulletin*
C. Ap.	Josephus, *Contra Apionem*
C&P	*Culture & Psychology*
CBQ	*Catholic Biblical Quarterly*
CC	*Christianity and Crisis*
CEB	Common English Bible
ChrCent	*The Christian Century*
CLJ	*Community Literacy Journal*
CLR	*California Law Review*
CS	*Cultural Studies*
CTTA	*Counter Terrorist Trends and Analyses*
CurTM	*Currents in Theology and Mission*
DSCPE	*Discourse: Studies in the Cultural Politics of Education*
EAL	*Early American Literature*
EAQ	*Educational Administration Quarterly*
ERS	*Ethnic and Racial Studies*
EvRev	*Evergreen Review*
ExAud	*Ex Auditu*
FemT	*Feminist Theory*
FSJ	*The Foreign Service Journal*
GFACF	*Global Forum on Arts and Christian Faith*

HER	*Harvard Educational Review*
HLR	*Harvard Law Review*
HM	*Harvard Magazine*
HS	*Hebrew Studies*
HTR	*Harvard Theological Review*
Human	*The Human: Interdisciplinary Journal of Literature and Culture*
HWLJ	*Harvard Women's Law Journal*
ICC	International Critical Commentary
IJQSE	*International Journal of Qualitative Studies in Education*
ILR	*Iowa Law Review*
IOT	Issues of Our Time
JAfRel	*Journal of Africana Religions*
JBL	*Journal of Biblical Literature*
JFSR	*Journal of Feminist Studies in Religion*
JHE	*Journal of Higher Education*
JITC	*Journal of the Interdenominational Theological Center*
JLE	*Journal of Latinos and Education*
JNE	*Journal of Negro Education*
JRT	*Journal of Religious Thought*
JSJ	*Journal for the Study of Judaism in the Persian, Hellenistic, and Roman Periods*
JSNT	*Journal for the Study of the New Testament*
JTS	*Journal of Theological Studies*
LXX	*Septuagint*
MLR	*Michigan Law Review*
MRW	*The Missionary Review of the World*
Neot	*Neotestamentica*
NIB	Keck, Leander E., ed. *The New Interpreter's Bible.* 12 vols. Nashville: Abingdon, 1994–2004.
NIV	New International Version
NKJV	New King James Version
NovT	*Novum Testamentum*
NRSV	New Revised Standard Version
NTL	New Testament Library
Numen	*Numen: International Review for the History of Religions*
PC	*Palgrave Communications*
PCS	*Pedagogy, Culture & Society*
PF	*Peace and Freedom*

PM	*Practical Matters: A Journal of Religious Practices and Practical Theology*
Pss. Sol.	Psalms of Solomon
PT	*Poetics Today*
QT	*Qualitative Theory*
RelComp	*Religion Compass*
RelEd	*Religious Education*
RSV	Revised Standard Version
SA	*Small Acts*
SAm	*Scientific American*
SBLGNT	The Greek New Testament: SBL Edition
SCJ	*Sixteenth Century Journal*
SEÅ	*Svensk exegetisk årsbok*
SID	*Studies in Interreligious Dialogue*
SP	*Sociological Perspectives*
SPE	*Studies in Philosophy and Education*
SRev	*Southern Review*
TCR	*Teachers College Record*
TIP	*Theory into Practice*
TTR	*Teaching Theology and Religion*
UCLF	*University of Chicago Legal Forum*
UE	*Urban Education*
USQR	*Union Seminary Quarterly Review*
WCJT	*The Wabash Center Journal on Teaching*
WisC	Wisdom Commentary
WMJWL	*William and Mary Journal of Women and Law*
WSIF	*Women's Studies International Forum*
YLJ	*Yale Law Journal*

Introduction: Racism, Classroom Teaching, and Beyond

Tat-siong Benny Liew and Shelly Matthews

There is a poignant episode within Jhumpa Lahiri's (2003, 56–60) novel *The Namesake*. Following the Bengali tradition of giving each person two names (a "pet name" used by family and close friends during one's childhood and a "good name" to be used by people in the outside world), a couple of South Asian immigrants to the United States think that it is time for their US-born son to go by his formal name, Nikhil, instead of his pet name, Gogol, when he enters kindergarten. Despite their attempt to explain this practice to Mrs. Lapidus, the school's principal, they fail to convince her. Rather than seeking to understand what she does not know, the principal, whose last name in Latin means "stone," decides that it is right for her to keep using Gogol as the boy's name in school.

We begin with this episode because it captures in many ways the concerns of this volume. The admission of a racial and cultural Other into a school does not necessarily preclude an expectation or even imposition of unilateral adaptation. In fact, if politics is defined by who is given the time and space to see and to speak, then racial politics is undoubtedly present in a school and inside its classrooms (Rancière 2013, 8). Whiteness sees "no need for … a moment of quietude that encourages listening" (Yancy 2004, 12). In this episode, "the school stands as a metaphor for a mode of power that begins to declare that it knows how to place and recognize" different races and cultures (Ferguson 2012, 166–67). Finally, this story about a minor is fitting for our purposes because minoritization often involves a form of infantilization, through which adult students of color are belittled as dependents who lack the maturity to see independently or the capacity to speak sensibly (Lloyd 1990, 382; Bailey, Liew, and Segovia 2009, 6–8). Without awareness, sensitivity, and intentionality, teachers of biblical studies, especially those of the dominant culture, can easily stifle and stultify students of color in their schools and classrooms.

All teachers of biblical studies must remember (1) that the presence of diversity does not mean the absence of racism and (2) that we do not just teach materials but that we teach them to students (Liew 2016). Since the civil rights movements and the immigration laws of the 1960s, most of our classrooms have become diverse. For various reasons, including economic ones, schools have also accepted more international students. To teach students well, we must see them and listen to them, especially when they come from racial and cultural backgrounds that are different from our own. This statement does not deny the challenges that teachers of color often experience with white students "who are not accustomed to their leadership or embodied otherness in the classroom"; it only emphasizes the role and responsibility that we have as teachers to teach and teach well (Byron 2012, 108).

Education and Racial Management

We must remember that racism "is not only a personal ideology based on racial prejudice, but a *system* involving cultural messages and institutional policies and practices as well as the beliefs and actions of individuals" (Tatum 1997, 7). Education can, therefore, facilitate a form of domination "when the other forms…, the most spectacular and coded ones, beat a retreat" (Derrida 2002, 104). As Ngũgĩ wa Thiong'o (1986, 9) writes about the colonialization of Africa, "The night of the sword and the bullet was followed by the morning of the chalk and the blackboard." Those of us who live in the United States can also think of the boarding schools for Native American children in the late nineteenth century. These schools were not only "created by the military and operated under military authority," but also designed to "destroy children's Indianness" (Briggs 2020, 47–48). Craig Steven Wilder's (2013) study has shown "the troubled history" of higher education in the United States, involving not only indigenous erasure but also slavery. Although Jacques Derrida (2002, 2004; see also Haddad 2020) is focused on philosophical education, his point about the induction of students into a discipline as a colonial process is applicable to the teaching and learning of biblical studies. This is so because education takes place in many contexts within institutions that are not only "predominantly white" in demographics but also "dominantly white" in terms of history and culture (Pittman and Boyles 2019, 316).

In addition, schools are often supported by and subordinated to other powerful institutions, such as the state or civil society (Ferguson 2012,

9–11), so the teaching and learning of disciplines requires attention to all these institutions and their larger sociopolitical contexts (Derrida 2002, 23). English as a discipline "historically was used to rule, manage, and control the Indian Empire" in Asia (Sharpe 1993, 21; see also Viswanathan 1989). Another more recent but no less glaring example is the invention of area studies as a discipline in the university system by the US government in the 1940s and 1950s. Using research by area studies scholars, including the production and perpetuation of orientalist knowledge about the non-Western world and non-Western peoples, our state was able not only to intervene in but also to advance and benefit from the structuring of global power (Szanton 2004). The same is true of American studies, which was also "founded with government funding with the expectation that [the discipline] would, through an affirmative elaboration of the 'American character,' help advance the cultural Cold War" (Duclos-Orsello, Entin, and Hill 2021, 2).

Schools, as a part of the ideological state apparatuses (Althusser 1971, 127–86), have the power to "control meaning … preserve and distribute what is perceived to be legitimate knowledge … [and] confer cultural legitimacy on the knowledge of specific groups" (London 2002, 98). Through their repeated exposure to the so-called classics of the Western canon in schools, students are encouraged to forget their particularities by identifying with what they read and learn to become not only guardians of the Western tradition but also "good citizens" of a nation (Eng 1998). The very establishment of a canon is an act of evaluation through which some cultural products are elevated while others are relegated or rejected (Lloyd 1990, 380). One the one hand, we see this in Thomas Babington Macaulay's insistence in the 1830s that "the British Indian Government … should direct its attentions solely to promoting western knowledge" through the medium of English rather than "patronize 'Oriental' knowledges" (Seth 2007, 1). On the other hand, we also see the seduction that such a colonizing education offers in Derrida's (1998, 32–41) own experience, when he talks about a hyperbolic desire that he "also contracted at school" as an Algerian Jew, partly because the learning of other languages (such as Arabic, Berber, or Hebrew) was either not available or not encouraged: "As if I were its last heir, the last defender and illustrator of the French language … speak in good French, in pure French … 'more French than the French,' more 'purely French' than was demanded by the purity of purists" (47–49). These words of Derrida may resonate with some of our contributors and readers of color. Our desire might not be French, but we knew what it meant to be interpellated through what we read and studied into whiteness, which "circulates as an axis of power and identity around the world" (Rasmussen et al. 2001, 3).

What We Teach

Derrida's monolingualism speaks to the importance of curricular requirements and content materials, but it also speaks particularly to our role as teachers of biblical studies. One of the reasons Derrida (1998, 54) did not learn Hebrew growing up had to do with a "Christian contamination": "The churches were being mimicked, the rabbi would wear a black cassock, and the verger [chemasch] a Napoleonic cocked hat; the 'bar mitzvah' was called 'communion,' and circumcision was named 'baptism.'" One should not forget that the educational endeavors in Africa, the Americas, and Asia coming out of the North Atlantic were all attempts to simultaneously "civilize" and "Christianize."

Practices of racism and the invention of whiteness have long been linked with religion, particularly Christianity and the Bible (Heschel 1998, 2008; Goldberg 2003; Johnson 2004; Kidd 2006; Carter 2008; Jennings 2010). As Denise Kimber Buell and Caroline Johnson Hodge (2004, 251) argue, "the familiar idea that Christian identity renders ethnoracial differences irrelevant provides a problematic loophole for white scholars to deny or overlook the saliency of race." The ironic way this dismissal of racial difference ends up reinforcing whiteness can be seen in the pervasive image of a white Jesus (Blum and Harvey 2012) or in the persistent erasure of North Africa and West Asia from the geography of the so-called biblical world (Sadler 2007). Wongi Park (2021, 454) argues cogently that "whiteness as identity and method is fundamentally connected to an underlying Eurocentrism in the framework and sources of biblical scholarship." It is hard to deny the "racecraft" of biblical studies as a discipline: "a kind of fingerprint evidence that *racism* has been on the scene" (Fields and Fields 2012, 19, emphasis original).

Educators—with what they call explicit, implicit, and null curricula—have helped us realize that alongside what we deliberately teach, there are also important lessons we teach unintentionally or teach by what we leave out, so we can be reinforcing whiteness as the norm in many ways, wittingly or unwittingly (Kim-Cragg 2019). For example, since disciplinary power, as Michel Foucault (1995, 177, 202) explains, is "disindividualize[d]" and "everywhere," it is distributed over multiple sites, so whiteness as a norm is also present in the publishing industry just as it is present in the state and in schools. This explains why most introductory textbooks—with a few notable exceptions (e.g., Smith and Kim 2018)—are written by whites. If one adopts one of these as a main textbook and tries to supplement it with articles by biblical scholars of color, students quickly get the implicit signal, intended or not, of where the real authority lies. Once again, having a diverse representation can still end up reinforcing and regularizing the status quo of our discipline as dominantly white. The reinforcement of whiteness here is "something *educational*, something which happens to you 'at school,' but hardly a measure or decision, rather a pedagogical mechanism" (Derrida 1998, 37). Speaking from her own experience, Gay Byron (2012) points out that neither biblical scholars' academic research about race and the Bible nor their own experience of marginalization as racial/ ethnic minorities necessarily changes their pedagogical practice, partly because such integration requires reflection and intention. As teachers of biblical studies, most of us know and teach the process of canonization as one of politics and power. Why, then, can we not engage our students in understanding also the politics of course-material selection as well?

Pedagogical practices cannot be antiracist if they do not involve any kind of epistemological challenges that make room for other kinds of being and knowing (Ferguson 2012, 42, 51–52). Otherwise, pedagogical innovations, even or especially those that attend to racial difference, are only legerdemain that function to "blunt," "absorb," "contain," and "incorporate" any impetus for change (Omi and Winant 2015, 186). While the Jesus of the Synoptic Gospels is worried about putting "new wine" into "old wineskins" (Matt 9:16–17, Mark 2:21–22, Luke 5:36–38), we as teachers of biblical studies may need to pay more attention to the problem of packaging old wine in new wineskins. After all, that is what missionaries from the geopolitical West excel at when they talk about inculturating their specific version of the gospel in different cultures. We need vigilance so pedagogy will not become an alibi for not disrupting, not to mention rupturing, the dominantly white practices of biblical studies. We are particularly alarmed by a sobering question raised recently by our colleagues in American studies: "What if [our discipline] is defined not so much in the pages of the most cutting-edge publications, but through what happens in our classrooms?" (Duclos-Orsello, Entin, and Hill 2021, 6).

If education is not only about knowledge dissemination but also about knowledge production, then our classrooms must be spaces that enable the production of new knowledge without reproducing a white subject of the geopolitical West. For example, the Bible as canon fits with what Roland Barthes (1974, 4) calls "classic" or "readerly texts," which mean they "can be read, but not written." In other words, *classic* and *canonical* imply that these texts are exempted or "protected" from critique and change (Ferguson 2012, 39). If we are to produce knowledge, we will need to somehow help our students, of any race or ethnicity, to turn the Bible into what Barthes (1974, 4–5) calls "writerly texts": namely, texts that are not for our consumption but for our production of new writings, new texts, and new knowledge.

If our teaching of biblical studies for racial equity implies the opening up of new horizons, then it should not be merely about introducing readings from various minoritized perspectives, which can easily be consumed by students (including students of color) in essentialist ways. Without denying the importance of changing our habit of citation (Eng 1998; Liew 2008, 7–9), we need to do much more than to diversify whom we consider to be important or influential biblical scholars by adding scholars of color to a reading list for students or lifting up certain scholars of color as exemplary or even exceptional. We need to teach that racial difference is "infinitely plural," so we and our students must be willing to engage "the naming, unnaming, and renaming" of difference (Ferguson 2012, 176, 179). We also need to continue to undertake the genealogical work necessary to understand and teach how our discipline developed (e.g., Long 1997; Moore and Sherwood 2011), especially how race has factored in both its framework and practice (e.g., Kelley 2002; Park 2021, 435–56).

How We Grade

Given Foucault's interest in interrogating the process of subject formation, it is not surprising that his exposition of disciplinary power carries another important implication for our work as teachers of biblical studies: our role as graders, grade givers, and assessors. According to Foucault (1995, 190), disciplinary power works "to classify, … to determine averages, to fix norms." With what he calls "scales around a norm," Foucault shows how disciplinary power can "hierarchize individuals in relation to one another and, if necessary, disqualify and invalidate" (223). Looking back at the civil rights movement (particularly the demand of black and Puerto Rican students for reforms in admission policies and curricular designs) and three texts from the 1960s (John Gardner's [1961] *Excellence*; Clark

Kerr's [1963] *The Use of the University*; and June Jordan's "Black Studies: Bringing Back the Person"), Roderick Ferguson (2012, 76–102) shows how discourses of standards and excellence were developed and used by many in the academy for managing and limiting the presence of people of color, who are always already pathologized as lacking the capacity for educational advancements, in a long-standing and ongoing racist and colonial project. Framing education as a competitive and an individualist endeavor in the shape of a pyramid, an emphasis on excellence becomes "a technology of power" that "ingratiate[s] minorities by making ability not only a standard of incorporation but a mode of surveillance, exclusion, and measurement" (83, 86).

In addition to (1) whom we teach and (2) what we teach or do not teach, we need to consider how our evaluation or assessment of students can become an antiracist project rather than a racist project. Ferguson helps us think about not only the implications and consequences of extolling excellence but also the connection between our assessment practices and certain types of cultural ethos such as individualism or competition. In other words, what we need may not be simply more fair evaluation standards that can minimize the impact of teachers' racial bias, but something more transformative that changes the underlying cultural ethos of assessment—even or especially when traditional evaluation practices feel rational, natural, or normal.

Willie James Jennings's diagnosis of theological education is in many ways applicable to education in general. According to Jennings (2020, 31), the education project is a racist project driven by "the vision of the [white] self-sufficient man," who masters his discipline and controls everyone and everything around him. Comparing this vision to a plantation with a powerful owner surrounded by free women, children, and slaves, Jennings explains that education cultivates behaviors and relationships that are combative or perhaps even cutthroat in the name of academic standards or rigor, with participants trying to stay in the game by "outperforming" each other (77–104). As a result, we are "caught between an isolating individualism and … a soul-killing performativity aimed at the exhibition of mastery, possession, and control" (18). Through the shame and humiliation of grades and evaluation being handed out by teachers, many (especially people of color because of the racialized evaluation standards) get the signal that they do not belong. Instead, Jennings wonders whether we can envision an education project that emphasizes community and belonging to replace "a pedagogical imagination calibrated to forming white self-sufficient men" and commanded by an "exclusionary logic" (65, 66).

While Jennings does not give specifics on how we may concretize his vision of "an education in belonging" (see Jennings's subtitle) when we evaluate student performance, others have attempted to address the dominantly white practices of grading. Arguing that traditional, so-called quality-based grading practices not only produce "political, cultural, linguistic, and economic dominance for White people" but also "seek to exclude … by their nature and function … regardless of how we justify them or who uses them," Asao Inoue (2019, 8, 11) proposes an alternative: a labor-based grading model that promotes inclusive and equitable habits among teachers and students by evaluating students on the basis of how much labor they put in and whether their labor helps their classmates learn as well. Although Inoue's Marxist-informed proposal is focused on English writing courses in college (25, 28), many of our assignments for biblical studies involve writing, and there is no denying that a "white racial *habitus*" and a "white language supremacy" are both inherent in our current educational institutions and systems. At the same time, questions have been raised about whether evaluation by students' "*willingness to labor*" (247) may disadvantage students with disabilities or from underprivileged backgrounds who simply cannot afford to labor as much as others (Carillo 2021), especially given Inoue's (2019, 127) own acknowledgment that "we can only labor at the paces we can." This takes us back, of course, to attend to whom we teach: that is, the actual students who are present in our classroom, who may engage course materials and create knowledge in different way (Carillo 2021, 56–57).

We do not mention Inoue's and Carillo's work to endorse either but to show that we as teachers of biblical studies must also think about how our grading and evaluation practices can not only work for or against specific bodies but also may support or subvert certain types of racial ethos and cultural values. Expressions of quality and excellence may have a racist underside that we cannot ignore if we are serious about antiracist practices as teachers.

Contexts, Contours, and Contents

Contributors to this collection first presented their pedagogical concerns and practices in the Annual Meeting of the Society of Biblical Literature program unit Racism, Pedagogy, and Biblical Studies. They are diverse in race/ethnicity and gender; they also come from various institutional contexts and represent different stages in terms of teaching career. We are grateful for their enthusiastic responses when we reached out to them about putting their presentations into an anthology. Though varied in length and in focus, all their presentations, now revised in the form of essays, seek to interrogate racist assumptions and practices of teaching biblical studies.

We have organized these essays into three sections. The first section, "Naming Contexts," includes six essays, beginning with one by Randall C. Bailey, who prefaces his best practices for teaching against white supremacy with a fascinating tour of some of the key ways by which scholars have, wittingly or not, infused biblical studies with race and racism. He clearly delineates a concerted effort, across cartographic, artistic, and linguistic dimensions, to "de-Africanize and de-Asianize the characters and lands of the text" in service of white people's self-identification with the texts. With examples from both the Hebrew Bible and New Testament, Bailey reveals Europeanizing traditional interpretive moves, from racialization of the peoples of the biblical world to the creation of a Western trajectory with designations such as "ancient Near East" to the "translation gymnastics" employed to reverse the biblical binary wherein whiteness represents cursedness. Bailey therefore provides the reasoning, if not the urgency, behind the need for antiracist pedagogy before offering practical guidance.

After making the case for employing "anachronistic whiteness" as a lens to study the ancient Christian past, Denise Kimber Buell draws on Sara Ahmed's phenomenological approach to whiteness to situate the field and predominant approaches to biblical studies in relation to whiteness. She then offers examples of how critical attention to whiteness and its institutional and norming effects might enable us to encounter ancient notions of embodiment and early Christian practices, as well as ancient and modern debates about authority, including notions of canonicity and orthodoxy. Ending with a pedagogical example that juxtaposes Frank Yamada's reading of Gen 2–3 through the experience of Japanese Americans in the United States during World War II with readings of Gen 2–3 preserved in texts from Nag Hammadi, she raises questions of social context and scriptural authority. The task of reorienting away from whiteness, Buell concludes, is a call to, in James Baldwin's words, "do our first works over."

Julián Andrés González Holguín's essay considers the deployment of *diversity* in the academic space today. According to him, emphasis on diversity tends to treat the category of Other as monolithic, to thereby dehumanize the Other, and to blind even well-intentioned interpreters to ongoing enmeshment in oppressive global capitalism. Instead of offering a panacea-like use of diversity, Holguín builds on Michael Fishbane's notion of poesis to undergird the development of "a pedagogy of coexistence and compassion." This approach requires "the textualization of existence," with readers employing the ideals of Scripture into their lives in real, embodied ways. Such a way of reading and living, Holguín argues, is a critical endeavor, one that is necessary "to prevent the overformation of the text and its naive application." It will center the suffering in both texts and life, encourage continuing experimentation and midrash, disrupt prevailing narratives of scriptural formation and anamnesis, and challenge the dominance of neutrality in biblical studies. He concludes with a strong caution to scholars to beware of antiracist practices that may nevertheless reinscribe racist ideologies by their participation in a world permeated with racism.

Noting that nationalism and religious identities are useful lenses for exposing "religious supremacist thinking," Sharon Jacob tells a tale of the parallel ascendancy of racist and religious nationalism in both India and the United States. As in India, where *hindutva* serves as a political ideology seeking to make India a Hindu state at the expense of racial and religious minorities, so a Christocentric form of white religious nationalism in the United States marginalizes those outside the dominant race and religion. Jacob then turns this lens onto the book of Revelation, noting how this apocalyptic text often gestures toward a similar sort of nationalism, where John of Patmos envisions "a multilingual people transformed into a monolingual empire." In closing, she advocates for the importance of attending to religious nationalism in the biblical studies classroom—one that offers to students the opportunity to reflect critically on the politics of citizenship and belonging, and particularly on the role of language and linguistic racism, in the construction of empire.

Heeding the challenging statement of Vincent Wimbush in his 2010 presidential address to the Society of Biblical Literature that critical interpretation requires coming to terms with "the first contact—between the West and the rest, the West and the Others," Jean-Pierre Ruiz recounts the history of the colonization of Puerto Rico. Ruiz's essay offers up an investigation of the thoroughgoing racism that has colored the policies and attitudes of the United States toward Puerto Rico and its inhabitants from its takeover in 1898 until the present day. Engaging in an exegesis of that racism by focusing first on several images that date to the beginnings of the US colonization—images that vividly illustrate the depth and pervasiveness of racism and the policies and practices it fuels—Ruiz notes the most recent devastation of the island, by Hurricane Maria in 2017, and shows how the post-Maria appearance of a US president provides "a vivid example of the colonial condescension that continues to be typical of how the United States treats Puerto Rico." For Ruiz, these "deliberately racist policies and practices of colonial oppression" are supported by scriptural underpinnings.

In the final essay of this section on contexts, Abraham Smith argues that changes in the biblical studies classroom require awareness of the complexity of structural racism, and thus his essay begins by reviewing the history of the development of critical race theory and introducing important tools and concepts belonging to critical race theory. Understanding race as a construct, these tools and concepts include the construct of whiteness, racism as structural rather than individual, and differential racism as the means by which a number of racial groups are scripted against one another in the service of an exploitable workforce. Smith then moves to a number of suggestions for reorienting biblical studies "away from whiteness," calling for shifts at the institutional, disciplinary, and classroom level. He ends with a call for curricular transformation highlighting minoritized approaches, a critique of colonizing cartographies, and "deploying 'pedagogies from home' that interrogate the notion that knowledge emanates from a dominant culture."

The second section, "Empowering Students," has four entries. Questions of race, racism, and racialization in the biblical texts, in the guild and its methods, in pedagogies, and in the lives of students form the basis of Eric D. Barreto's reflections. His self-conscious musing that we might have "underestimated the ways biblical scholarship has misshaped public imaginations" serves as a call to biblical educators to take seriously identities, which he notes are shaped in and by colonialism, as "vibrant sites of reading, of imagination, and of the making of a people." In service of this belief, he offers five realistic and critical best practices for foregrounding Latinx students in biblical studies. Throughout Barreto insists on taking seriously biblical studies' role in colonization and complicity in the making of colonial subjects, while also pointing out that biblical studies itself is a colonized space. Ultimately, Barreto challenges his readers to see equality as realizable not through erasing differences but by embracing them.

Greg Carey's contribution is inspired by a faculty workshop at his institution devoted to discussing Claude M. Steele's book *Whistling Vivaldi:*

How Stereotypes Affect Us and What We Can Do, in which Steele attributes struggles of minoritized students to anxiety related to racist stereotypes and offers several principles for reducing that anxiety. These principles from Steele include fostering intergroup conversations, allowing students opportunity for self-affirmation, and assisting in the development of a narrative concerning the learning context that "explains their frustrations while projecting positive engagement and success in the setting." Carey then provides several specific examples of how he adapts Steele's principles to his teaching context, including how he manages first-day introductions, shapes writing assignments, and thinks about the grading process. He shares detailed steps of an exercise in film criticism and of how he sparks conversation by employing a collection of images of John the Baptist. Both exercises are designed to elicit the wisdom and expertise of each student through shared conversation.

After charting how the field of biblical studies has been racialized through its historic embrace of the (white) "myth of the West," Kay Higuera Smith advocates for a decolonized pedagogy that empowers students—especially students of color—to become confident in their capacities as knowledge producers. Here, she turns to the model, often used in Latinx critical theory, of the *testimonio*. Students of color in her class are assigned to write *testimonios* reflecting on their social-cultural geographic experience. Students from the dominant culture, ideally in partnership with students of color, are also asked to write testimoni*als* to reflect on their social and institutional location, but they need to do so by centering their partner's knowledge production. From this highly effective centering or recentering exercise, students move to careful readings of biblical texts. Higuera Smith helpfully lays out this pedagogical process step by step, before closing with additional sample teaching exercises inspired by concerns for social justice and transformation.

Building on his own work teaching biblical studies with an intercultural approach and leading travel seminars to the border wall between the United States and Mexico, Francisco Lozada Jr. presents a threefold method for engaging Latinx students, specifically, in biblical education: critically knowing oneself, knowing one's history, and knowing the Other. Foregrounding connectivity between the students with this method, Lozada encourages students to learn from their own experiences and those of their classmates in order to create space for cultural and biblical education, empathy, connection. This ethos is then embodied in the assignment to exegete the border wall as a text. Overall, Lozada's method strives to give Latinx students permission to challenge dominant (colonial) histories, racial hierarchies, and minoritization, especially of the self. Lozada connects these modern experiences to the biblical world, highlighting similar complexity, flux, and negotiations of identity—a similarity that makes it possible and necessary to take such aspects of modern identity seriously, even and perhaps especially in the biblical studies classroom.

Sonja Anderson's contribution is the first essay of the third and final section of this collection, "Reframing Contexts." Anderson offers a specific pedagogical exercise demonstrating how questions of race, gender, and class might be engaged critically and empathetically in biblical interpretation, noting that such engagement is especially crucial for nonwhite students in majority-white classrooms. Informed by art historian Jennifer Roberts on the importance of patience to the understanding of visual art, Anderson invites her students to patiently study Diego Velázquez's seventeenth-century painting *Kitchen Maid with Supper at Emmaus*. Among the many outcomes of this pedagogical exercise, Anderson notes that "the juxtaposition of image and text shows students how little information is conveyed by the text 'itself' and how much must be supplied by the reader" and how "making images of biblical characters ... involves decisions about race." Providing important exegetical context both for the Lukan Emmaus episode and for Velázquez's location in the slave-trading center of Seville, Anderson makes a passionate argument for reading Scripture with "vivid imagination."

Haley Gabrielle makes the case for dislodging traditional historical criticism as *the* single appropriate method in biblical studies and calls into question the traditional historical-critical approach as the only method for writing biblical history. She first surveys three alternative approaches to history writing that challenge the secular framing of traditional history: Walter Benjamin's "historical materialism," Saidiya Hartman's "critical fabulation," and M. Jacqui Alexander's "queer, decolonial, and transnational/women-of-color feminist approaches." Then Haley engages Gayatri Chakravorty Spivak as her primary interlocutor in reading the story of the enslaved girl in Acts 16:16. After elaborating Spivak's dilemma in writing about subaltern Indian women—wherein the nineteenth-century Hindu widow she studies cannot speak but is rather lodged between the discourses of imperialism and patriarchy—Haley argues that this subaltern figure in Acts is in a similar bind: caught between the discourses of "exclusivist Christianity," on the one hand, and "individualist feminism," on the other.

Wilda C. Gafney's personal situatedness—living and teaching in Fort Worth, Texas, during the initial stages of the Black Lives Matter movement—frames the content of her essay. Even as she began creating an ever-lengthening timeline of the extrajudicial killings of black people in America, Gafney also began crafting a course at the intersection of biblical studies and Black Lives Matter. The goal of the course was for every student to develop and to articulate "a functional Black Lives Matter hermeneutic," using Black Lives Matter's stated goals and commitments. In this course, Gafney and her students read Black Lives Matter in light of biblical texts and vice versa. With womanist praxis at the heart of the Black Lives Matter hermeneutic, Gafney shows how students wrestled with questions of race and ethnicity in the biblical world, analyzing which lives mattered then and there and which matter here and now, and how biblical texts must be challenged and read against in order to interpret any text through a Black Lives Matter hermeneutic.

Roger S. Nam explains how historical criticism, which still dominates both the guild and the biblical studies introductory curriculum, reifies whiteness and Western dominance in biblical studies. Focusing primarily on introductory biblical studies courses, Nam notes that other approaches are only offered as supplementary and of secondary importance—when presented at all. He concludes that "any inclusive pedagogies must interrogate the nearly exclusive primacy of historical-critical approaches to introductory classes" if we are to deconstruct hegemonic Eurocentric notions. The importance of such deconstruction, Nam argues, is both to avoid anachronistic readings of ancient texts and to prevent reinscription of white- and Western-dominant interpretations. Nam suggests that biblical studies educators employ ethnographic practices to challenge the deeply Western-oriented collective subconscious of the modern reader. By studying non-Western cultures and comparing their meaning-making and cultural practices with those of the ancient contexts, students can "access a wider range of meanings" for crucial biblical concepts such as kinship and land.

After identifying several challenges pertaining to teaching about racism in biblical studies at predominantly white institutions in general, Wongi Park focuses specifically on Matthew's story of the Canaanite woman (15:21–28) to offer up pedagogical strategies for using this pericope as a springboard for discussing race in this context. Park first invites his students to identify racial/ethnic markers that they see in the story and then works to unpack those markers. Typically, these discussions lead to awareness that Jesus exhibits ethnocentrism at best, and racism at worst, in this encounter. Park then situates this passage within the larger Matthean narrative, noting the tension between particularism and universalism in this gospel. The juxtaposition of the unflattering story of the Canaanite woman with the larger ethnocentric currents in Matthew leads Park to argue that "Jesus's mistreatment of the Canaanite woman is rather unremarkable in the scope of the gospel." His goal is to challenge the widespread notions among his students that Christianity is a universal religion, devoid of racial and ethnic bias.

Beyond Classroom Pedagogy

Although this volume is about classroom practices, we cannot emphasize enough the connection between our classrooms and larger institutional and societal dynamics. Even the best antiracist pedagogues will not be able to make much of a difference for students of color if they do not have enough financial and research support for their studies. To enter our classrooms, students today must show their passbooks—and also their passports if they are students of color. Unless and until the racist structures of our schools and of our society are transformed, changing our classroom pedagogy will not be enough. We are not saying this to discourage or belittle pedagogical reflection and renewal but to encourage and emphasize the need for all of us to set our sights wide. For example, can we push for institutional audits so we will know how our schools are doing in attracting and enrolling students of color? What about in recruiting and maintaining faculty and staff of color? Are numbers of students and faculty of color increasing, declining, or flatlining?

Talking about faculty of color, it is important for a school to have white faculty who teach in antiracist ways, but it is also imperative that a school hire faculty of color. According to Stefano Harney and Fred Moten (2013, 40), institutions of higher education are arguably the best exemplars of neoliberal asociality. Writing in the late 1960s with debates raging over university admission policies and the place of black studies, June Jordan (1969, 71) emphasizes the importance of community for black students and states, "We request Black teachers of Black studies. It is not that we believe only Black people can understand the Black experience. It is, rather, that we acknowledge the difference between reality and criticism as the difference between the Host and the Parasite." Jordan is suggesting here that students of color need more than good and thoughtful teachers, more than even teachers who are sympathetic to them and their experience. They need teachers who have walked where they walk, teachers who literally occupy the same position as they do in dominantly white schools, where they are not at home and are often pathologized as freeloading hangers-on.

Jordan's distinction between host and parasite points again to a larger question that goes beyond (1) admitting people of color as faculty and students and (2) adding minoritized materials to the curriculum. Using literary studies as a case study, Jodi Melamed (2011) shows how the issue of race for those in power can become only a means for achieving other purposes rather than the targeted end in itself, so demographic representation can be used to reinforce white culture and dominantly white institutions as the norm. That is also why Ferguson (2012) repeatedly raises the need for people concerned with racial equity in education to attend to racist structures that not only organize knowledge but also distribute power and resources. Without radical changes to the biblical studies guild and our schools as citadels of whiteness, our students of color will remain caught in the contradiction between the rhetoric of racial integration and the reality of racial insulation.

We also need to expand, or even explode, our concept of what it means to do and teach biblical studies. For instance, taking a clue from Lisa Lowe's (2015, 1) *The Intimacies of Four Continents*, which focuses on "the often obscure connections between the emergence of European liberalism, settler colonialism in the Americas, the transatlantic slave trade, and the East Indies and China trades in the late eighteenth and early nineteenth century," we can think about teaching biblical studies less in terms of communicating or making textual meanings of a biblical passage or book and more in terms of exploring relations that are not readily visible for students. These relations (whether in complicity with power, or resisting power, or both) can turn on different axes (e.g., temporal, geographical, racial, religious, or disciplinary), but reading and rendering them legible should have a twofold purpose: (1) to question "epistemicide" (Santos 2016), "*epistemological apartheid*" (Harrison 2016, 161, emphasis original), and knowledge formation (e.g., changing assumptions of what constitutes our scholarly repertoire as biblical scholars, particularly knowledge of academic studies of race and ethnicity) and (2) to effect social transformation (e.g., challenging both white supremacy and Christian triumphalism in biblical studies). While we love to talk about the Greco-Roman context as New Testament scholars, for example, we need to better research how Muslim scholars during the so-called Dark Ages translated and preserved much of what we know of that context, so we can understand that "the West as West, or the West as the world" is a fiction because many kinds of Western "institutionalisations are being produced by something that is being perpetuated outside of the West" (Spivak 1990, 5; see also Appiah 2018, 192–202).

Byron has also been trying to push biblical scholars to question or expand our conception of what constitutes the historical contexts of the biblical writings. With her research on Africa, particularly on Ethiopia, she challenges us to reconsider what count as relevant resources to study these writings (Byron 2009, 2016). Alternatively, one may, as Wimbush (2017) suggests, focus on helping students see various sociocultural phenomena, although they may seem far removed from the Bible, as effects entailing if not born of processes of scripturalization and racialization. In sum, we need to think of antiracist pedagogy in ways that far exceed the redesigning of syllabi, class activities, or course assignments. Aligning our teaching of biblical studies with an explicitly antiracist commitment necessitates a reconceptualization of the discipline of biblical studies because our discipline, being developed in modernity during the formation of the North Atlantic empire, is "an archive of colonial uncertainty" (Lowe 2015, 78) that seeks to disavow the racial and religious violence. This disavowal, which often works by isolating or simplifying a "cacophony" of complex relations (Byrd 2011), demands that we review and renew the discipline itself and not just how we teach the discipline. This must be our ongoing goal, even if it is not immediately legible or achievable in this volume.

Conclusion

The discipline of biblical studies, as a part of humanistic discourses, can be "used as a smokescreen for oppression, to divert attention away from discriminatory practices and identity-based patterns of segregation and exclusion" (Alcoff 2006, 290). At the same time, the recent fury over the 1619 Project and critical race theory indicates that the classroom can be a place that helps bring about personal and social transformation. We as scholars of the Bible should never underestimate the impact of our role as teachers, especially considering that most of our published books in biblical studies are not likely to sell more than a few hundred copies. At a time when white supremacists under the banner of Christian nationalism are once again becoming unabashed about their claim of superiority over and domination of other peoples, it is imperative and urgent that we spend time reflecting on the assumptions and practices of both our discipline and pedagogy so our guild and our classrooms can understand and repudiate racism and all the intersectional dynamics co-constituted with it. We must also remember that our pedagogical practices take place neither in vacuums nor with bolted doors. There is no impermeable membrane around biblical studies: it receives input and generates output in historically specific and sociopolitically complex ways.

Going back to the episode from Lahiri's *Namesake* with which we began this introductory essay, we as teachers should keep in mind that students who come into our classrooms can also help us learn, unlearn, and relearn if we remain open to listening to them. This reeducation is especially crucial for white teachers. Having said that, teachers of color, even those committed to resist white supremacy, can still stultify their students, including their students of color. A classroom as a teaching and learning community should mean that everyone in it, including the teacher, can potentially learn from other members. Sources and resources for learning and teaching can come from many unexpected places and persons, even those that are not institutionally or professionally legitimated.

Classrooms as communities are temporary, but the racial effects and affects that occur in classrooms can be long term. Teaching, like religion, is generative and worldmaking (Kondo 2018; Chuh 2021, 320, 324–25). The question is what kind of a world we are making for and with our students in and beyond our biblical studies classrooms.

Works Cited

Alcoff, Linda Martín. 2006. *Visible Identities: Race, Gender, and the Self.* New York: Oxford University Press.

Althusser, Louis. 1971. *Lenin and Philosophy and Other Essays.* Translated by Ben Brewster. New York: Monthly Review.

Appiah, Kwame Anthony. 2018. *The Lies That Bind: Rethinking Identity.* New York: Liveright.

Bailey, Randall C., Tat-siong Benny Liew, and Fernando F. Segovia. 2009. "Toward Minority Biblical Criticism: Framework, Contours, Dynamics." Pages 3–43 in *They Were All Together in One Place? Toward Minority Biblical Criticism.* Edited by Randall C. Bailey, Tat-siong Benny Liew, and Fernando F. Segovia. Atlanta: Society of Biblical Literature.

Barthes, Roland. 1974. *S/Z: An Essay.* Translated by Richard Miller. New York: Hill & Wang.

Blum, Edward J., and Paul Harvey. 2012. *The Color of Christ: The Son of God and the Saga of Race in America*. Chapel Hill: University of North Carolina Press.

Briggs, Laura. 2020. *Taking Children: A History of American Terror*. Berkeley: University of California Press.

Buell, Denise Kimber, and Caroline Johnson Hodge. 2004. "The Politics of Interpretation: The Rhetoric of Race and Ethnicity in Paul." *BibInt* 123:235–51.

Byrd, Jodi A. 2011. *Transit of Empire: Indigenous Critical Theory and the Diminishing Returns of Civilization*. Minneapolis: University of Minnesota Press.

Byron, Gay L. 2009. "Ancient Ethiopia and the New Testament: Ethnic (Con)texts and Racialized (Sub)texts." Pages 161–90 in *They Were All Together in One Place? Toward Minority Biblical Criticism*. Edited by Randall C. Bailey, Tat-siong Benny Liew, and Fernando F. Segovia. Atlanta: Society of Biblical Literature.

———. 2012. "Race, Ethnicity, and the Bible: Pedagogical Challenges and Curricular Opportunities." *TTR* 15.2:105–24.

———. 2016. "Black Collectors and Keepers of Tradition: Resources for a Womanist Biblical Ethic of (Re)Interpretation." Pages 187–208 in *Womanist Interpretations of the Bible: Expanding the Discourse*. Edited by Gay L. Byron and Vanessa Lovelace. Atlanta: SBL Press.

Carillo, Ellen C. 2021. *The Hidden Inequities in Labor-Based Contract Grading*. Logan: Utah State University Press.

Carter, J. Kameron. 2008. *Race: A Theological Account*. New York: Oxford University Press.

Chuh, Kandice. 2021. "Afterword." Pages 320–25 in *Teaching American Studies: The State of the Classroom as the State of the Field*. Edited by Elizabeth Duclos-Orsello, Joseph Entin, and Rebecca Hill. Lawrence: University Press of Kansas.

Derrida, Jacques. 1998. *Monolingualism of the Other; or, The Prosthesis of Origin*. Translated by Patrick Mensah. Stanford: Stanford University Press.

———. 2002. *Who's Afraid of Philosophy? Right to Philosophy 1*. Translated by Jan Plug. Stanford, CA: Stanford University Press.

———. 2004. *Eyes of the University: Right to Philosophy 2*. Translated by Jan Plug and others. Stanford: Stanford University Press.

Duclos-Orsello, Elizabeth, Joseph Entin, and Rebecca Hill. 2021. "Introduction: How Pedagogical Practice Defines American Studies." Pages

1–13 in *Teaching American Studies: The State of the Classroom as the State of the Field*. Edited by Elizabeth Duclos-Orsello, Joseph Entin, and Rebecca Hill. Lawrence: University Press of Kansas.

Eng, David L. 1998. "Queer/Asian American/Canons." Pages 13–23 in *Teaching Asian America: Diversity and the Problem of Diversity*. Edited by Lane Ryo Hirabayashi. Lanham, MD: Rowman & Littlefield.

Ferguson, Roderick A. 2012. *The Reorder of Things: The University and Its Pedagogies of Minority Difference*. Minneapolis: University of Minnesota Press.

Fields, Karen E., and Barbara J. Fields. 2012. *Racecraft: The Soul of Inequality in American Life*. New York: Verso.

Foucault, Michel. 1995. *Discipline and Punish: The Birth of the Prison*. Translated by Alan Sheridan. 2nd ed. New York: Vintage.

Gardner, John W. 1961. *Excellence: Can We Be Equal and Excellent Too?* New York: Harper & Row.

Goldberg, David M. 2003. *The Curse of Ham: Race and Slavery in Early Judaism, Christianity, and Islam*. Princeton: Princeton University Press.

Haddad, Samir. 2020. "Derrida on Language and Philosophical Education." *SPE* 40:149–63.

Harney, Stefano, and Fred Moten. 2013. *The Undercommons: Fugitive Planning and Black Study*. New York: Minor Compositions.

Harrison, Faye V. 2016. "Theorizing in Ex-centric Sites." *AT* 16.2–3:160–76.

Heschel, Susannah. 1998. *Abraham Geiger and the Jewish Jesus*. Chicago: University of Chicago Press.

———. 2008. *The Aryan Jesus: German Theologians and the Bible in Nazi Germany*. Princeton: Princeton University Press.

Inoue, Asao B. 2019. *Labor-Based Grading Contracts: Building Equity and Inclusion in the Compassionate Writing Classroom*. Fort Collins, CO: WAC Clearinghouse.

Jennings, Willie James. 2010. *The Christian Imagination: Theology and the Origins of Race*. New Haven: Yale University Press.

———. 2020. *After Whiteness: An Education in Belonging*. Grand Rapids: Eerdmans.

Johnson, Sylvester A. 2004. *The Myth of Ham in Nineteenth-Century American Christianity: Race, Heathens, and the People of God*. New York: Palgrave Macmillan.

Jordan, June. 1969. "Black Studies: Bringing Back the Person." *EvRev* 13:39–41, 71–72.

Kelley, Shawn. 2002. *Racializing Jesus: Race, Ideology and the Formation of Modern Biblical Scholarship.* New York: Routledge.

Kerr, Clark. 1963. *The Use of the University.* Cambridge: Harvard University Press.

Kidd, Colin. 2006. *The Forging of Races: Race and Scripture in the Protestant Atlantic World, 1600–2000.* Cambridge: Cambridge University Press.

Kim-Cragg, HyeRan. 2019. "The Emperor Has No Clothes: Exposing Whiteness as Explicit, Implicit, and Null Curricula." *RelEd* 114.3: 239–51.

Kondo, Dorinne. 2018. *Worldmaking: Race, Performance, and the Work of Creativity.* Durham, NC: Duke University Press.

Lahiri, Jhumpa. 2003. *The Namesake.* New York: Houghton Mifflin.

Liew, Tat-siong Benny. 2008. *What Is Asian American Biblical Hermeneutics? Reading the New Testament.* Honolulu: University of Hawai'i Press.

———. 2016. "Response to 'How We Teach Introductory Bible Courses': More to Be Done and More to Be Asked." *TTR* 19:145–47.

Lloyd, David. 1990. "Genet's Genealogies: European Minorities and the Ends of the Canon." Pages 369–93 in *The Nature and Context of Minority Discourse.* Edited by Abdul R. JanMohamed and David Lloyd. New York: Oxford University Press.

London, Norrel A. 2002. "Curriculum and Pedagogy in the Development of Colonial Imagination: A Case Study." *PCS* 10:95–121.

Long, Burke O. 1997. *Planting and Reaping Albright: Politics, Ideology, and Interpreting the Bible.* University Park: Pennsylvania State University Press.

Lowe, Lisa. 2015. *The Intimacies of Four Continents.* Durham, NC: Duke University Press.

Melamed, Jodi. 2011. *Represent and Destroy: Rationalizing Violence in the New Racial Capitalism.* Minneapolis: University of Minnesota Press.

Moore, Stephen D., and Yvonne Sherwood. 2011. *The Invention of the Biblical Scholar: A Critical Manifesto.* Minneapolis: Fortress.

Ngũgĩ wa Thiong'o. 1986. *Decolonizing the Mind: The Politics of Language in African Literature.* Portsmouth, NH: Heinemann.

Omi, Michael, and Howard Winant. 2015. *Racial Formation in the United States.* 3rd ed. New York: Routledge.

Park, Wongi. 2021. "Multicultural Biblical Studies." *JBL* 140:435–59.
Pittman, Amanda Jo, and John H. Boyles. 2019. "Challenging White Jesus: Race and the Undergraduate Bible Classroom." *RelEd* 114:315–27.
Rancière, Jacques. 2013. *The Politics of Aesthetics: The Distribution of the Sensible*. Edited and translated by Gabriel Rockhill. New York: Bloomsbury.
Rasmussen, Birgit Brander, Eric Klinenberg, Irene J. Nexica, and Matt Wray. 2001. "Introduction." Pages 1–24 in *The Making and Unmaking of Whiteness*. Edited by Birgit Brander Rasmussen, Eric Klinenberg, Irene J. Nexica, and Matt Wray. Durham, NC: Duke University Press.
Sadler, Rodney S., Jr. 2007. "The Place and Role of Africa and African Imagery in the Bible." Pages 23–30 in *True to Our Native Land: An African American New Testament Commentary*. Edited by Brian K. Blount. Minneapolis: Fortress.
Santos, Boaventura de Sousa. 2016. *Epistemologies of the South: Justice against Epistemicide*. New York: Routledge.
Seth, Sanjay. 2007. *Subject Lessons: The Western Education of Colonial India*. Durham, NC: Duke University Press.
Sharpe, Jenny. 1993. *Allegories of Empire: The Figure of Woman in the Colonial Text*. Minneapolis: University of Minnesota Press.
Smith, Mitzi J., and Yung Suk Kim. 2018. *Decentering the New Testament: A Reintroduction*. Eugene, OR: Cascade.
Spivak, Gayatri Chakravorty. 1990. *The Post-colonial Critic: Interviews, Strategies, Dialogues*. Edited by Sarah Harasym. New York: Routledge.
Szanton, David, ed. 2004. *The Politics of Knowledge: Area Studies and the Disciplines*. Berkeley: University of California Press.
Tatum, Beverly Daniel. 1997. *"Why Are All the Black Kids Sitting Together in the Cafeteria?" and Other Conversations about the Development of Racial Identity*. New York: Basic Books.
Viswanathan, Gauri. 1989. *Masks of Conquest: Literary Study and British Rule in India*. New York: Columbia University Press.
Wilder, Craig Steven. 2013. *Ebony and Ivy: Race, Slavery, and the Troubled History of America's Universities*. New York: Bloomsbury.
Wimbush, Vincent L. 2017. *Scripturalectics*. New York: Oxford University Press.
Yancy, George. 2004. "Introduction: Fragments of a Social Ontology of Whiteness." Pages 1–23 in *What White Looks Like: African-American Philosophers on the Whiteness Question*. New York: Routledge.

Part 1
Naming Contexts

From Africa to Mesopotamia (Genesis 2:13–14) and from India to Ethiopia (Esther 1:1b): How an Afro-Asiatic Biblical Construction Was Twisted into a Eurocentric Claim

Randall C. Bailey

I must begin this endeavor by claiming that this essay is really chronicling how I have learned, taught, and written about racism in the biblical text and in biblical interpretation. Thus it is somewhat autobiographical. It is also an expansion of the presentation I made on this subject for the Racism, Pedagogy, and Biblical Studies program unit at the Annual Meeting of the Society of Biblical Literature in 2017. I am glad that I am now given more space to pursue this subject in written form. I must also alert the reader that I have been an iconoclast for many years and have read texts in different ways from my discipline, my racial and gender groupings, and more specifically my own religious denomination. This explains why I have several humorous stories of the last time I was invited to preach in various pulpits across the United States due to my interpretations of biblical texts, as well as stories of translators often changing my interpretations of texts and being exposed by people present who were conversant in both languages and called them on it.

I also was examined by two presidents and three deans at my former institution in response to my teaching around issues of the Bible and sexuality. Most of the concerns were generated around how I showed exegetically in class that the narrator is claiming that Ruth and Boaz had sex on the threshing floor (Bailey 1992, 26–28). I was always intrigued that I was never reported for a queer reading of the song of Ruth. Perhaps the reporting students had stopped listening after I exegeted Ruth 3 and missed what I said when I returned to Ruth 1. These experiences always tickled me, as I left the classroom with students shaking their heads because of my lectures and my responses to their questions. In essence, while the NRSV translators obfuscate the sex in the narratives, my exegesis of these practices exposed such coverup translations. The same would be true in the ways I deal with issues of race and racism in the biblical text and in the history of translation and interpretation.

My readings regarding racism and the Bible, for the most part, grow out of my experiences of being a black male in the United States and of having lived on the rough side of the mountain. I note this in my article "They're Nothing but Incestuous Bastards" (Bailey 1994b). When I read a prepublication version of that article at the Annual Meeting of the Society of Biblical Literature, one of the noted scholars there stopped me and said, "You said you had lived in the outside group for most of your life. Which group was that?" I responded, "African Americans." He stated, "Oh, I didn't know you were of that group." This made me wonder whether there were other members of the guild who did not know from where I came. I never pursued with him whether that realization affected his view of my scholarship. Similarly, when I read another prepublication of that article at the Society for the Study of Black Religion, my critique of how African Americans had traditionally responded to the so-called curse of Ham landed me on many of their negative lists.[1] I guess I've been an equal-opportunity disruptor.

In another instance, a noted white male scholar was reading a paper on Ezra and Nehemiah. He argued that Ezra was a scribe and Nehemiah was an urban planner, so clergy should know how to relate to urban planners. When he got to the part about expelling the foreign wives and their children (Ezra 10:6–17, Neh 13:23–13), he noted, "Sometimes you just have to know who is in and who is out." During the question-and-answer period I noted, "It may be our differing social locations that have us looking at the expulsion of the foreign wives and their children differently. I have lived my life being on the outside, especially in this country and this guild, so your 'who's in and who's out' explanation makes that chapter even more problematic for me." I come to this subject, therefore, with a colored perspective (pun intended).

---

1. In essence the traditional argument of black scholars has been that Noah didn't curse Ham; he cursed Canaan, and being good Judeo-Christians we don't like Canaanites. My argument is that our history of chattel slavery problematizes a curse on Canaanites being slaves by virtue of birth (see Haynes 2007).

In this short treatment of the subject on teaching about racism and the Bible, I will address issues within the text as well as issues within the history of interpretation, sharing in the process how my growth on the subject as a scholar occurred and how concerns with this subject have affected my own teaching. I will talk about questions of geography and terminology as they relate to issues of race and the Bible. I will also explore how racism functions in relation to biblical interpretation in popular culture, especially in art. Finally, I will argue that, in addition to racist interpretations, the biblical text also contains problematic messages that are akin to racism. I must admit that my skills of teaching on this subject functioned well at times, and other times they did not function so well.

Racism, Bible, and Biblical Interpretation

I will begin with the definition of racism I will be using throughout this article: "Racism is a system of unequal power and privilege in which human beings are divided into groups or races, with social rewards being unevenly distributed to groups based on their racial classification. Variations of racism include institutionalized racism, scientific racism, and everyday racism" (Hill Collins 1998, 280). In this way one sees that there is a difference between racism and prejudice, since the latter does not imply sociopolitical structures but rather speaks to psychological and emotional responses. As I will argue, this definition makes it difficult to deal with the text as being racist, since either ethnocentrism or postcolonial, internalized oppression on the part of the writers of the text may be functioning, though there are texts that promote racist structures and policies. When one looks at interpretations of these texts, however, one can see more examples of racist interpretations. In other words, what we have here are biblical interpretations that are based on certain social constructs and policies.

When I taught at the Anglican College of the Transfiguration in Grahamstown, South Africa, the first time I was scheduled to preach was on Transfiguration Sunday. In that sermon I pointed out that Elijah and Moses appear to talk with Jesus in the text of Matt 17:3. During the lifetime of Jesus, however, Moses and Elijah were already dead. It appears, therefore, that Jesus is consulting the ancestors, most probably about the revolutionary activities he is to lead against the Romans, just as Moses had done with Pharaoh in Exodus and Elijah had done with Ahab in 1 Kings. Again, Moses and Elijah were already dead in the lifetime of

Jesus. I speculated that Deborah and Esther were also there meeting with Jesus, since the two other men mentioned in the narrative had a history of running away from trouble (see Exod 2, 1 Kgs 17). The patriarchal leanings of the narrator most probably caused the omission of the women. More importantly, though, this is a story of ancestral veneration right there in the text. Therefore, why did people believe the Christian missionaries who said that ancestral veneration was anti-Christian when it's in the text? I must confess that it was the experience of living in Africa for several months that opened *me* to such a reading and to other African notions affecting the biblical text.

While most of the students thought my exegesis made sense, many of the Zulus argued that the missionaries were right: their African religious concepts had to be rejected, and the transfiguration could not be a story of ancestral veneration. One can only imagine how they responded to my preaching on the postresurrection text as ancestral veneration, with Jesus having joined the ancestors. In other words, anti-African hermeneutics must be examined and questioned, especially since in the African colonies conquered by European nations conversion to Christianity was closely tied to socioeconomic advancement, and the Christian faith was introduced to the Africans bought and sold into this hemisphere. I have learned that an important practice of teaching about racism and white supremacy is to open avenues of discord, so students can raise questions about scholarly conventions and wisdom, many of which are grounded in supremacist teachings that the church and academy have willingly embraced.

Stories of the Origins of Ancient Israel and Judah

Let me turn to the national or racial identity of the people who made up the nation of Israel. The earliest such speculation is in Hos 11:1, from the eighth century BCE:

> When Israel was a child, I loved him,
>   and out of Egypt I called my son. (NRSV)

This synonymous parallelism equates "a child/my son," "I loved/I called," and "Israel/Egypt." The traditional interpretation of this passage is a reference to the exodus, the liberation event of enslaved Israelites being freed from bondage (see Wolff 1974, 198). The problem with this interpretation is that the liberation formula is "to bring out/lead out," with בוא and יצא in the *hiphil* (see Exod 3:10–11, 17; 6:11, 26; 12:17; 13:8, 14, 16; 16:6, 32; 18:1; 20:2; Lev 19:36; 22:13; 25:38; Deut 5:6; 6:12, 21; 7:8). Instead, we have in Hosea קרא in the *qal*. This is the verb for naming at birth (e.g., Gen 30:6, 8, 11). According to Hosea, Israel was originally an Egyptian subgroup that was named by YHWH. This makes sense, since Egypt was a major political force in the eighth century, and it was highly valued by ancient Israel. This is seen from the Solomonic administration having two positions, סופר and מזכיר (1 Kgs 4:3b), adopted from the Egyptian administrative style.

I recall that I came to this understanding of the passage while reading a first draft of an exegetical paper by an African student at the Interdenominational Theological Center. He had followed the commentaries on their interpretation of this unit as relating to the liberation of Israel from Egypt in Exodus. I pointed out to him these form-critical points of synonymous parallelism and the word study on קרא. I thought he would have welcomed this alternative interpretation, since he was now equipped with the skills to challenge secondary literature. When he submitted his final draft of his exegetical paper, I saw that he had stayed with the commentaries. I mentioned to him that I was not sure how things functioned in his country, but when one's professor in this country makes a suggestion on a student's first draft, the student considers it and then either adopts it if it makes sense or argues against it. In talking with him further, it became clear to me that he was uncomfortable with the idea that he might be following another African group, Israel, in the Bible after he had given up many of his African traditions and adopted Eurocentric constructs to become a Christian. He had given up too much for that. This also showed me why Eurocentric scholars might not be willing to explore this African backgrounding of ancient Israel. There was a strong anti-African bias in Eurocentric Christian exegesis, and that bias was cozy in the hearts of some in an historically black seminary.

If that is true in an historically black seminary, what do you think happens in historically white institutions? In a seminar I was taking as a seminary student on the minor prophets of the eighth century BCE, I asked, when we got to Amos 9:7a ("Are you not like the Ethiopians to me, O people of Israel?," NRSV), "Is that a positive or a negative statement?" The professor had his teaching assistant (a graduate student) do an impromptu fifteen-minute lecture on the location of Cush, ending with the conclusion that it was in Arabia and not in Africa. The professor, instead of using the graduate student's input to answer my question, then told me to stop raising questions that were not relevant to the seminar. In essence, issues of race were off the table in that seminary unless they were Europeanizing the people in the biblical texts. In the turn of the nineteenth to the twentieth century, European exegetes termed Cushites in the texts as slaves. This happened to the Cushite in David's army in 2 Sam 18 and to Ebed-melek in Jer 38. This racist hermeneutic was a staple in biblical scholarship (Bailey forthcoming). One of the positive aspects of teaching in an historically black theological seminary was being able to reclaim my earlier questions and to answer them in a better way than I was taught. The experience of being with a group of black biblical scholars for one week over three years, which resulted in the text *Stony the Road We Trod: African American Biblical Interpretation*, was invigorating and healed me from the racial abuse I had endured during seminary and graduate school (Felder 1991). Thus, in this publication I was able to argue that Amos's statement was a positive statement about the Cushites, who as Ethiopians were ancient Africans (Bailey 1991, 176; see also Rice 1978).

As noted before, the earliest claim of Israel's origins is found in Hosea, that Israel came from the south, specifically from Egypt. In the seventh century BCE, with Damascus a major military force, the Deuteronomist reformulated the story of the formation of the state by claiming that Israel didn't come from the south but rather from the north (Bennett 2008). One notes in the creedal statement in Deut 26:5b, "A wandering Aramean was my ancestor; he went down into Egypt and lived there as an alien" (NRSV). In this way there is agreement with the earlier claim of having been in Egypt, but the origin is now from the north and from Aram. I would argue that the switch of geographical location from Egypt to Aram was not racial but was tied to which nation held stronger political and colonial ties to the area of Israel and Judah. In essence, the major basis for location and self-identification was not race but (colonial) power.

In the sixth century BCE, with Babylonians in control of the empire, the Priestly writer again altered the myth of origins by claiming that they came from Ur of the Chaldeans: "Now these are the descendants of Terah. Terah was the father of Abram, Nahor, and Haran; and Haran was the father of Lot. Haran died before his father Terah in the land of his birth, in Ur of the Chaldeans" (Gen 11:27–28 NRSV). As Israel was under the control of another empire, it changed its narrative of origins as a way to connect it with the colonial empire under whose power it was controlled. It also appears that, on this level, this was not a racist shift. Rather, these moves were indicative of internalized oppression, of the colonized overidentifying themselves with their oppressors. To argue these as racist movements would also assume that ancient Israel and Judah were phenotypically of a race other than that of the ancient Egyptians, Arameans, and Babylonians. It is possible that ancient Israel and Judah were composed of people from all three racial/ethnic groups. One thing is certain, however: none of these groups were European.

Racism, Maps, and Biblical Geography

In teaching this approach one needs to help students with map work, identifying the geographical locations mentioned in the narratives as well as the way people looked in those areas at those times.

Working with the Bible maps in the back of their NRSV Bibles (student edition), I asked students to draw the land boundaries of this garden of Eden in Gen 2:10–14 (part of which forms the title of this article). This activity showed them several things. One was that the boundary went from ancient Cush—that is, ancient Ethiopia—to Mesopotamia. This one earthling is told to till this area from Cush to Mesopotamia but not to eat from the tree of knowledge, because he will die the day he does so (Gen 2:15–17). I often compared this social construction to slavery in the United States, where people were told to work the fields but could not learn how to read. In fact, were they found to have learned to read, they would be whipped or killed. I have no idea how some people could think this passage in Gen 2 is a description of paradise!

When students responded with a dogmatic reading of this text, I would respond with, "Yes, you could say that. Now, what words in the text support that reading?" When they couldn't do that, I would say, "Do you not see that you were detecting a problem embedded in the text? But dogma has taught you to ignore the problem by interpreting the text in line with church teachings. In essence, the church recognized the problem I have exposed in the text and tried to cover it up with a solution which had no grounding in the words on the page."

Returning to the geography lesson, I pointed out that not one European country could be found in these verses describing the garden in Gen 2. People inhabiting these lands were black and brown. They were not white.

When (what was called at the time) the Christian Education Unit of the National Council of Churches of Christ in the United States of America asked me to do Bible studies on a tour of the Holy Land for its denominational directors of Christian education, I divided them on the first night into three groups. Each group was to do an analysis of the Lukan birth narrative: one group was to do a gender analysis of the narrative, another a socioeconomic analysis, and the third a racial analysis. After twenty minutes, each group responded with their analysis. Groups 1 and 2 had reports ready, but group 3 didn't know how to do such an analysis. I told them we'd work on it later in the week.

We were lodged at Tantur, right on the border of Bethlehem and Jerusalem. On the day we were to travel to Qumran, a botanist on the staff gave us a lecture about flora and fauna that grew around the Dead Sea. In that lecture he noted there were certain flora that grew around the Dead Sea that only grew elsewhere in Africa.

I saw this as a teachable moment, so I jumped in and said, "So we are in Africa."

He responded, "No! We are in the Middle East!"

I said, "You said the only other place where these floras grew is in Africa. So, we must be in Africa if they are growing around the Dead Sea!"

"*No!* This is the Middle East!"

"I know the geopolitical construct which calls this 'Middle East,' so we won't think the Bible came out of Africa, but your science argues against the term 'Middle East.'"

"I told you, this is the Middle East!"

"So, you would jettison your science to keep that geopolitical construct?"

I then turned to the group and stated, "Now do you understand why the third group on the first night could not do a race analysis of the birth narrative?" We have been given intellectual constructs that relate to gender analysis and socioeconomic analysis of biblical texts. We have been trained in biblical scholarship to refer to this region as the "ancient Near East." East of where?

Racism and Terminology in Biblical Studies

This term, *ancient Near East*, rips the lands of the Bible out of their continental moorings of Africa and Asia. On my first trip to Ghana, whenever I heard people talking about the mythic West, I would remind them that Ghana was west of most European countries. They would look at me with the strange look to which I have become accustomed, but I was trying to make a point.

The terminology used in the discipline of biblical studies has argued, therefore, that we are not talking about Africa and Asia. Rather, we are talking about "proto-Europeans" or, as Charles Mills (1997) terms it, "off whites." In the same way, the depiction of the Persian Empire in Esther, "from India to Ethiopia" (Esth 1:1b NRSV), is a way in the text to argue that the Greeks were late to empire building (Dunbar 2019, 38; see also Bailey 2009).

In essence, the whole interpretive trajectory of Western Europe has turned the Bible into a Eurocentric book. In the same way, the argument of the so-called curse of Ham sees the Japheth folks to be proto-Europeans, the Shem folks kind of Asiatic, and the Ham folks Africans. It is amazing that Mr. and Mrs. Noah could give birth to three sons of different races. But this absurdity was necessary for not only justifying the African slave trade but also disavowing Israel's membership in that group. Again, the strategy is to lift the biblical Jews out of the African and Asian groupings and make them proto-Europeans.

At the same time, the term *anti-Semitic* is understood as against Jews but not against other nations in the listing of "the sons of Shem." Tying the term *Semitic* to Jews only results in the dismissal of other national origins noted in the line of Shem in the so-called Table of Nations (Gen 10:21–31) and in the lineage of Abram/Abraham (Gen 11:10–32). Similarly, since (1) Ishmael was born of Abram's rape of Hagar (Gen 16:4a, 16) and (2) the followers of Muhammad trace themselves back to Abraham through Ishmael, they also are Semites. The separation of European Jews from their Asiatic origins through Abram the Shemite established them as the only victims of anti-Semitism. On the basis of the Bible, however, an anti-Muslim rant by a politician in the United States is an anti-Semitic rant.

For a while I would get calls from local and national news persons during Black History Month in the United States (February) asking whether there was any biblical basis for claiming that Jesus was black. I also got calls when Minister Louis Farrakhan said that Jesus was black. When that happened, I would refer them to the genealogies of Jesus in Matt 1. They would usually respond, "But these were Jews."

"Right," I would respond. "But none of them were Europeans."

They would end the discussion and hang up. The word must have gotten out, because after two years they stopped calling me.

Similarly, one time when I was lecturing on "Ancient Africa and the Bible" in the United Kingdom, I was on a Sunday prechurch radio program. I mentioned some of these ideas, and the host said, "You aren't saying that Abraham and David and Solomon, etc., were black?" I responded, "I sure am!" That ended the interview, and I was led out of the studio. This white-supremacist tendency of interpretation is so very grounded in the minds of Christians and Jews that questioning it is enough to end discussion. I never did find out how that radio host filled out the rest of the twenty minutes, since I was scheduled to be interviewed by him for thirty minutes.

I have dealt with the sexual trope in Gen 12 before (Bailey 1994b). This is the story of Abram and Sarai going down to Egypt during a famine. He convinces her to pretend to be his sister in order to save his life. In essence, the text depicts the Egyptians as sexual degenerates. It is interesting to see how Rashi, the twelfth-century CE French Jewish exegete, dealt with this passage. He begins by explaining why Abram says to Sarai, "Now I know you are beautiful" (Gen 12:11). Didn't he know that before?

> Usually, because of the exertion of travelling a person becomes uncomely, but she has retained her beauty (Genesis Rabba 40.40). Still the real sense of the text is this ... I have long known that thou art fair of appearance: but now we are travelling among black and repulsive people brethren of the Ethiopian (Kushim), who have never been accustomed to see a beautiful woman. (Rosenbaum and Silbermann 1929–1934)

This reading by Rashi is important, for it shows how the Egyptians were understood to be black Africans. It also shows how Eurocentric white supremacy was well established in the eleventh century CE. It further shows how biblical Jews had become thought of as proto-Europeans. As we have seen, all the stories of origins of the ancient Israelites indicate that they came from either Egypt or Mesopotamia, neither of which was a part of Europe. Rashi's interpretation could be an evidence of how whiteness had become key to the spread of Judaism and Christianity in Europe.

Were I not trying to restrict my comments to the Hebrew Bible, I could say something of sexualizing and othering of gentiles. The writer of Ephesians says of them:

> Now this I affirm and insist on in the Lord: you must no longer live as the Gentiles live, in the futility of their minds. They are *darkened* in their understanding, alienated from the life of God because of their ignorance and hardness of heart. They have lost all sensitivity and have *abandoned themselves to licentiousness, greedy to practice every kind of impurity*. (Eph 4:17–19 NRSV)

But I don't want to overstep my bounds, even though this deutero-Pauline writer, who might have been an African like Paul, was issuing a counterattack on white folks.

Racism, Archaeology, and Biblical Art

Archaeology has sometimes been helpful in unmasking such troves, especially with information or descriptions of the local inhabitants in these areas. Other times archaeologists have created problems in the statues they have uncovered.

My wife and I were fortunate to be able to bring our children with us when the International Society of Biblical Literature meeting was held in Rome for the first time. They were in their early teens. The first time I took them to the United Kingdom, we went to the British Museum. I pointed out to them that the noses and lips on Egyptian statues had been broken off so that we wouldn't think these people were black. When we went to the Louvre, I pointed out the same thing happened in the Egyptian room. When we went to the Vatican's Egyptian room, however, our daughter said, "Look, Daddy, the noses and lips are on these statues." I asked, "And what do you see, Imani?" She said, "They look like my nose and lips." Not all European nations attempted to erase Africa and Africans from world history as they gained possession of these archaeological statues. One can use these statues and compare them with European arts of biblical characters to get students to ask, "From where and how did these Europeans get into the pictures?"

Consider Michelangelo's painting of creation on the ceiling of the Sistine Chapel. When I was there with my family years ago, my then fourteen-year-old son started pointing and said, "I know that picture. That's the finger of God going to the finger of Adam in creation!" I responded, "Yes, Omari, but I wonder what got Michelangelo to think that God was an old white man and that Adam was white?" At that point, people in the chapel started moving away from us. What is most sad to me about this story was that our son had been introduced to the picture in the children's chapel at the black Baptist church where we hold our membership. Again, like my African student, other black religious institutions buy into these white-supremacist artworks, even or especially when they are not based in the geographical realities of the biblical narrative.

It appears that artistic portrayals of biblical characters (including statuary and frescos), especially those in the Hebrew Bible, as proto-Europeans were essential to making the gospel of Jesus spread across the Roman

Empire and into the so-called Middle Ages. If the Great Commission of Matt 28 was to be accomplished, it needed to be done under the guise of white supremacy, as we have seen in Rashi.

The demonizing of black skin was also pushed through translation gymnastics of turning the Hebrew Bible curse—to "be made white as snow"—into a blessing. This was often done through the use of contorted exegesis, as in Isa 1:18–20, where אם is translated as "though" in the first two couplets and then "if" in the last two. In this way, to be made white as snow is turned from a prophetic judgment to a divine blessing (Bailey 1996). This construction is also seen liturgically, with dark purple being used for Advent and Lent but white for Christmas and Easter. In nonliturgical churches, the first Sunday of the month has the elements covered with white cloth and the clergy in white robes. This whiteness is used to signal that we are about to commune with God in full purity.

Though not related to a Hebrew Bible construct, in sixteenth- and seventeenth-century paintings of the magi, one of the three appears to be a black African. This inspired Langston Hughes to do his work on the "Brown King." When one looks at these paintings, however, the black one is always separated from the two European-looking ones and placed in the background, possibly singing, "If you miss me in the back of the bus, you can't find me nowhere; come on over to the front of the bus (someday) I'll be riding up there," as we sang in the civil rights struggle meetings of the 1960s. However, if, as the text in Matthew's Gospel states, the three kings came from the east and not from the northwest, how did the other two kings become Europeans?

Paintings by European artists play a significant role, therefore, in whitening the Bible. This is especially true with artistic portrayals of Jesus. Many of your former students who went into ordained ministries could tell you how their congregants would respond if they tried to replace the image of a European Jesus with a black or brown Jesus. The congregants would either object or just find the deposed white Jesus image and put it back, for we clearly couldn't be saved by a black man. This story could even be retold in African American churches.

We could look at the Hollywood movies of biblical stories. Their white-supremacist assumptions follow the same pattern as artwork. Ruth and Naomi and Boaz are all white; so is Esther in the movie *A Night with the King*, and Wanita Bynum would probably smack the black off anyone who claimed that Hadassah was a sister who gave it up that night to become queen (Bailey 2009). Yes, there are a few blacks in this film, but they are presented as slaves. In *Green Pastures*, an African American filmic representation of the Torah in the 1920s, not only is "de Lawd" black, but the sins that cause "him" problems are sex-obsessed black gamblers and smokers. Internalized oppression has a long history; just ask Ethiopians who, despite seeing the queen of Sheba as one of them, are more interested in claiming that she had sex with Solomon, got pregnant, and gave birth to Minelek I, their founder. In other words, they don't see the queen as the one who validated Solomon's wisdom in 1 Kgs 10 because he could pass her test with hard questions (Bailey 1991, 181). Rather, they are trying to validate themselves by connecting themselves to Solomon, whom they believe was white. This is how these white-supremacist constructs have captured and warped the minds of Africans and their descendants around the world. As I noted before with my Sudanese student exegeting Hos 11:1–7, many of us did not become Christian to join an ancient African group and religion.

Again, with the Great Commission in Matthew's Gospel having been carried out across the world, baptizing all, whether people wanted to be baptized or not, the arts fell in line with buttressing these racist perversions of the biblical text.

Racism in the Bible

We have been trained to follow readings and artwork that inject Eurocentric ideas into the biblical narrative, and we have been trained to see these constructs as normative and grounded in the text itself. We have often also trained our students to follow the discipline on these issues.

The problem, however, isn't just in the intellectual constructs we use to interpret biblical texts. The problem is also embedded in the text. When we look at maps of Paul's missionary journeys we often miss that Paul is always traveling north into Asia Minor and on to Rome. He never goes to Africa, south of his homeland. So the canon does not give us epistles to African nations as the gospel spread in that part of the world. Once the Ethiopian finance minister to the Candace returns home, the impact of Africa on the development of the faith is obliterated on the textual level (Smith 1994). As we read the Pauline and deutero-Pauline epistles we see the embrace of Roman philosophies and the rejection of African Israelite concepts. An important exercise is to have students look at the maps in the back of their study Bibles and explain what they see in these missionary journey maps and then, once they discover the nuance, have them discuss how such images affect them.

Similarly, the Deuteronomist lays out a chilling racist program in Deuteronomy, Joshua, and Judges, as I have argued in a celebratory response to Robert Allen Warrior's (1989) article "Canaanites, Cowboys, and Indians" (see Bailey 2005). In Deut 12 we have laws stating that the first thing one does in invading a land is to destroy the shrines and sacred articles of the Other. In Josh 2 there is an argument for finding collaborators from the Other to betray their own people. In Josh 9 the Gibeonites use trickery but end up becoming slaves of the invaders. In Judg 1 Caleb destroys Kiriath-sepher ("city of the book"), thereby destroying the Other's intellectual property. That is how one destroys a people and fully subjugates them. These are three of the most dangerous books in the whole biblical canon. Even enslaved Africans in plantations of the US South sang "Joshua Fit De Battle of Jericho," thereby identifying themselves with the invading subjugators. While there are some spirituals that connect different narratives to each other in a seditious manner, this particular spiritual wholly buys into this dangerous book in the canon (Bailey 1998).

On the other hand, the Priestly writer seems to have a more aggressive approach beyond the myth of origins. There is an anti-Egyptian polemic that runs through the Priestly narratives of Genesis and Exodus. For example, in the Table of Nations (Gen 10), the Priestly writer constructs a Shem, Ham, and Japheth division, with Egypt in the Ham line but Abram and his folks in the Shem line. In essence, the Priestly writer is arguing against both of the earlier narratives of origins, trying to tie the Abraham line with neither the south nor the north. In addition, in Gen 16:3, the Priestly writer claims that Abram married Hagar and thus moves the narrative away from the raping of a slave (Weems 1988).

In Gen 41:8, after waking up from a dream, Pharaoh assembles all Egyptian intelligentsia, *kemet*. They can't interpret the dream, but a young Hebrew boy, Joseph, is able to outsmart *kemet* and interprets the dreams. As a result of this, this young Abrahamic boy becomes the architect of Pharaonic wealth. In the Priestly plague narratives in Exod 6–10, there is a contest between *kemet* and Aaron and Moses, with Aaron debunking *kemet* (Bailey 1994a). In essence the Priestly school is fighting against the earlier Israelite view of highly evaluating ancient Egyptian wisdom. While this could be more a nationalist rendering by the writer, who is attempting to debunk the veneration of Egypt and replace it with veneration of the Babylonians, in today's constructs this would be viewed as a racist reconstruction.

By the same token, the Priestly writer highly sexualizes the Egyptians in the admonition to Israelites not to do like the Egyptians and Canaanites (those in the priestly Hamite line) do (Lev 18:1–5). These admonitions are followed by incest and other sexual laws, thereby implying that Egyptians and Canaanites do these things. As support for this sexualized claim, Ham, the progenitor of the Egyptians, is presented in Gen 9 as an incest practitioner (see Bailey 1994b). When we connect the use of sexual innuendo to discredit an Other with Ezek 23:19–21, a passage contemporaneous with the Priestly source, we see this same *Tendenz* at work. We see that there was a fixation on the Egyptian male genitals in ways similar to the myth of the big black dick. In this way we see one racist discursive strategy, as noted by Lillian Smith (1978) in her book *Killers of the Dream*: sexualizing the Other to dehumanize them and hence sanctioning the treatment of them as Other. As a result, the slave laws in Exod 21 and Deut 15 state that Israelite slaves will be slaves for seven years, while slaves of other nations will be slaves for life. Sexualization of the Other established a cheap, non-Israelite labor class, whose bodies and skills could be exploited to build the kingdoms of Israel and Judah. Such a system is not humane, and it provided a handy model to be adopted for chattel slavery in the United States centuries later (*pace* Gafney 2010, 49).

Conclusion

Racist readings of the Bible entail particular choices being made on geopolitical mapping, artworks, and standard terminologies. These were all designed to de-Africanize and de-Asianize the characters and lands of the text. As I have argued, this was part of an evangelizing strategy to get Europeans to buy into the biblical narratives and to see themselves in the book. As W. E. B. Du Bois (1947) has argued, the social contract with European universities consisted of creating terminologies and intellectual constructs to make the people getting rich from the slave trade not feel guilty about the blood money that was the basis of their wealth. In order for this to happen, Africans had to be dehumanized as property, kind of like the wife in the tenth commandment; belonging to the rich male, she is just like the house and field, ox, donkey, and male and female slaves (Exod 20:17). For the same reason, if Europeans were to be descendants of the biblical characters, biblical characters had to be made/constructed as white.

In teaching students on how to recognize and reject white-supremacist and racist strategies in biblical studies, we have to look at our own experiences in being trained in biblical studies. We also have to become aware of how the terminologies used in the discipline have been grounded in Eurocentric and white-supremacist constructs. In addition, we have to be cognizant of how biblical cartography has been skewed to chop ancient Africa and ancient Asia off the maps, so space and prominence can be given to southern Europe, especially Greece and Rome. We have to be aware that archaeologists often broke off the noses and lips of statues so they wouldn't be viewed as African. Similarly, the whole industry of biblical art has been designed with European sceneries and characters, most probably as a tool of evangelism, to get so-called pagan Europeans to adopt the religion that was spreading from the south and southeast. We have to be aware of biblical commentators who have used white-supremacist terminologies to comment on the biblical texts. Finally, we have to be self-aware of our own internalization of white-supremacist trends of interpretation. In these ways we can help sensitize students to the ways racism plays in biblical interpretation.

Works Cited

Bailey, Randall C. 1991. "Beyond Identification: The Use of Africans in Old Testament Poetry and Narratives." Pages 165–84 in *Stony the Road We Trod: African-American Biblical Interpretation*. Edited by Cain H. Felder. Minneapolis: Fortress.

———. 1992. "Doing the Wrong Thing: Male-Female Relationships in the Hebrew Canon." Pages 18–29 in *We Belong Together: The Churches in Solidarity with Women*. Edited by Sarah Cunningham. New York: Friendship Press.

———. 1994a. "And Then They Will Know That I Am YHWH: The P Recasting of the Plague Narratives." *JITC* 22:1–17.

———. 1994b. "They're Nothing but Incestuous Bastards: The Polemical Use of Sex and Sexuality in Hebrew Canon Narrative." Pages 121–38 in *Social Context and Biblical Interpretation in the United States*. Vol. 1 of *Reading from This Place*. Edited by Fernando F. Segovia and Mary Ann Tolbert. Minneapolis: Fortress.

———. 1996. "Wash Me White As Snow: When Bad Is Turned to Good." *Semeia* 76:99–113.

———. 1998. "The Danger of Ignoring One's Own Cultural Bias in Interpreting the Text." Pages 66–90 in *The Postcolonial Bible*. Edited by R. S. Sugirtharajah. Sheffield: Sheffield Academic.

———. 2005. "He Didn't Even Tell Us the Worst of It!" *USQR* 59:15–24.

———. 2009. "That's Why They Didn't Call the Book Hadassah! The Interse(ct)/(x)ionality of Race/Ethnicity, Gender and Sexuality in the Book of Esther." Pages 227–50 in *They Were All Together in One Place? Toward Minority Biblical Criticism*. Edited by Randall C. Bailey, Tat-siong Benny Liew, and Fernando F. Segovia. Atlanta: Society of Biblical Literature.

———. Forthcoming. "The Cushite in David's Army Meets Ebedmelek." In *Samuel Read through Different Eyes*. Grand Rapids: Eerdmans.

Bennett, Harold V. 2008. *Injustice Made Legal: Deuteronomic Law and the Plight of Widows, Strangers, and Orphan in Ancient Israel*. Grand Rapids: Eerdmans.

Du Bois, W. E. B. 1947. *The World and Africa: An Inquiry into the Part Africa Has Played in World History*. New York: Viking.

Dunbar, Ericka. 2019. "For Such a Time As This? #Us Too: Representations of Sexual Trafficking, Collective Trauma and Horror in the Book of Esther." *BCT* 15.2:29–48.

Felder, Cain Hope, ed. 1991. *Stony the Road We Trod: African American Biblical Interpretation*. Minneapolis: Augsburg Fortress.

Gafney, Wil. 2010. "Reading the Hebrew Bible Responsibly." Pages 45–51 in *The Africana Bible: Reading Israel's Scriptures from Africa and the African Diaspora*. Edited by Hugh R. Page Jr. Minneapolis: Fortress.

Haynes, Stephen R. 2007. *Noah's Curse: The Biblical Justification of American Slavery*. Oxford: Oxford University Press.

Hill Collins, Patricia. 1998. *Fighting Words: Black Women and the Search for Justice*. Minneapolis: University of Minnesota Press.

Mills, Charles W. 1997. *The Racial Contract*. Ithaca, NY: Cornell University Press.

Rice, Gene. 1978. "Was Amos a Racist?" *JRT* 35:35–44.

Rosenbaum, Morris, and Abraham M. Silbermann, eds. 1929–1934. *Pentateuch with Rashi's Commentary*. https://tinyurl.com/SBL03111a.

Smith, Abraham. 1994. "'Do You Understand What You Are Reading?' A Literary Critical Reading of the Ethiopian (Kushite) Episode (Acts 8:26–40)." *JITC* 22:48–70.

Smith, Lillian. 1978. *Killers of the Dream*. New York: Norton.

Warrior, Robert Allen. 1989. "Canaanites, Cowboys, and Indians." *CC* 49 (11 September): 261–65.

Weems, Renita J. 1988. *Just a Sister Away: A Womanist Vision of Women's Relationship in the Bible*. San Diego: LuraMedia.

Wolff, Hans Walter. 1974. *Hosea*. Translated by Gary Stansell. Philadelphia: Fortress.

Anachronistic Whiteness and the Ethics of Interpretation

Denise Kimber Buell

Whiteness was not a legible concept or set of embodied practices among the inhabitants of the early Roman Empire.[1] So, why invoke whiteness when discussing ancient constructions of identity? What do I mean by whiteness? This essay extends the prismatic approach I take in *Why This New Race: Ethnic Reasoning in Early Christianity*, an approach that modulates among three nodes: (1) our current locations and investments, political and cultural ones but also methodological and theoretical ones; (2) the histories of our fields in context and thus the ways in which the relatively recent past—meaning at least the last 150 years—informs how we approach the study of the ancient Christian past and our understandings of race, ethnicity, and religion; and (3) the ancient materials we engage to

---

This essay is an abridged version of Buell 2018. Used with permission. For their comments and suggestions on this essay, I thank Melanie Johnson-DeBaufre, Jacqueline Hidalgo, Jason Josephson, James Manigault-Bryant, Saadia Yacoob, Zaid Adhami, and Lloyd Barba. I also thank David Horrell for the opportunity to participate in the symposium in which an earlier version was presented, and Tat-siong Benny Liew and Shelly Matthews for the invitation to contribute to this volume.

1. Those who produced the texts and practices we retrospectively interpret as presaging or constituting early forms of Christianity did not have racial subjectivities, practices, and structures as we understand and inhabit them. Nonetheless, I and others have argued for the legitimacy of examining ancient formations of difference in relation to modern practices of race (see, e.g., McCoskey 2012; Buell 2005). My goal is neither to explore color symbolism in early Christianity, something Gay Byron has already done effectively, nor to explore color symbolism as it contrasts or resonates with the various meanings and forms of social organization that have arisen around imputed differences pertaining to skin color in medieval, early modern, modern, or current contexts. Both of these goals are important and, indeed, part of the transformation of biblical and early Christian studies that needs to continue (see Byron 2002; see also Eliav-Feldon, Isaac, and Ziegler 2009).

reconstruct meanings legible to us and putatively also to ancient audiences (see Buell 2005, 33).

Whiteness, anachronistic as it may be for antiquity, relates directly to the first two nodes. But we cannot undertake the third without the other two operating on us. In the United States and, in different ways, in the United Kingdom, Europe, Africa, Australia, and other parts of the globe, whiteness gets its embodied meanings in relation to the structures of power steeped in histories of settler colonialisms, modern slavery, Christian missionizing, and forms of white supremacy (including South African apartheid and US Jim Crow legal formations). Many scholars have written about whiteness, including from intersectional perspectives that attend to the mutual imbrication and production of race with gender, as well as to their contextual production in relation to religious, economic, and national formations.[2] For this piece, Sara Ahmed's (2007) article "A Phenomenology of Whiteness" serves as my point of entry and orientation. The critical study of race, including whiteness, has been developed especially in US contexts, but Ahmed, a British scholar based in the United Kingdom, demonstrates that the contemporary saliency of whiteness is not restricted to the United States.[3]

Ahmed eloquently states that whiteness is "real, material, and lived" as "an effect of racialization," "as an ongoing and unfinished history, which orients bodies in specific directions." Rather than an ontological given, whiteness is "received, or becomes given, over time" (Ahmed 2007, 150). She argues that "whiteness [is] a category of experience that disappears as a category through experience," which helps to explain why it so easily remains unarticulated or backgrounded on the one hand and, on the other, why it persists as an unmarked site for the marking of other bodies racialized as nonwhite. Indeed, one of the key insights of those writing about whiteness has been that many of us who are viewed as white or who view ourselves as white either do not view ourselves as having a race at all or speak about race as if it were really only about those viewed as nonwhites.

---

2. I cannot be exhaustive, but see, e.g., McIntosh 1989; Lipsitz 2006; Thandeka 1999; Harvey, Case, and Gorsline 2004.

3. I chose to foreground a British feminist scholar based in the United Kingdom because the symposium in which this essay was first delivered was in the United Kingdom. See also Ware and Back 2002 and the special issue of the journal *borderlands* 3.2 (2004) for critical whiteness studies from Australian, British, and North American perspectives.

As George Yancy (2012, 8) puts it, whiteness "functions, paradoxically, as that which signifies the 'superior' *race* while precisely obfuscating its status as *raced*.... Whiteness functions as a transcendental norm, as that which defines nonwhite bodies as different and deviant." When whiteness is the operative condition, he writes, "white bodies comport themselves with no particular need to see themselves *as white*" (2). We ought to expose white as a racialized formation and lift up the difficulties and possibilities in reorienting away from whiteness (see Ahmed 2004).

Individual reorientations of those of us habituated into whiteness are a necessary but not sufficient piece of the work to overcome racism and white privilege: "insofar as racism is a system that reproduces itself ... then only a major reorganization of society will address it, not simply a revision of personal attitudes where everything else remains the same" (Bernasconi 2005, 20). We may recognize explicit racism and reject it, but it is much more difficult to see and address implicit forms of racism that reinforce structural privileges that unequally advantage those of us racialized as white and disadvantage those racialized as people of color. Those of us raised to be white social subjects are "embedded within structures that privilege [us] against [our] will" and that do not change merely because we dislike or disavow racism (Yancy 2012, 8). *Thus, overcoming racism is not solely a matter of individual agency*. Such structural asymmetries and embodied habits are of course not restricted to racism and are enacted together with other social and material axes, including gender, sexuality, age, class, ability, and religious affiliation, which are neither static, nor completely arbitrary, nor fully in our control.

Whiteness operates through bodies as a set of capacities and limits in a context that both exceeds those bodies and requires things of them. Ahmed's piece helps me to understand better how my own embodied accumulation of experiences, as well as the institutional and social contexts in which I work and live, pose significant challenges to reorienting myself, even as a self-conscious feminist working to overcome racism, anti-Judaism, and Islamophobia. That is, Ahmed helps to connect the dots between whiteness as an effect of racialization produced in some *individual* bodies and the whiteness of *institutions* or *disciplines*, regardless of the demographic identifications its individual participants might avow or be assigned.

How does whiteness come to be? Ahmed (2007, 156) proposes, drawing on the work of Pierre Bourdieu and Maurice Merleau-Ponty, that "whiteness 'holds' through habits":

> [We] can think about the habitual as a form of inheritance. It is not so much that we inherit habits, although we can do so: rather the habitual can be thought of as a bodily and spatial form of inheritance.... If habits are about what bodies do, in ways that are repeated, then they might also shape what bodies *can do*.... The habitual body does not get in the way of an action: it is behind the action. I want to suggest here that whiteness could be understood as "the behind."... White bodies do not have to face their whiteness; they are not oriented "towards" it, and this "not" is what allows whiteness to cohere, as that which bodies are orientated around.

The terms *habit* and *inheritance* already make clear that whiteness is not simply a trait that individual bodies may manifest. Habituated bodies are formed in and shape larger contexts:

> Spaces also take shape by being oriented around some bodies, more than others. We can also consider "institutions" as orientation devices, which take the shape of "what" resides within them. After all, institutions provide collective or public spaces. When we describe institutions as "being" white, we are pointing to how institutional spaces are shaped by the proximity of some bodies and not others: white bodies gather, and cohere to form the edges of such spaces.... Whiteness is only invisible for those who inhabit it, or those who get so used to its inheritance that they learn not to see it, even when they are not it. Spaces are oriented "around" whiteness, insofar as whiteness is not seen. We do not face whiteness, it "trails behind" bodies, as what is assumed to be given. The effect of this "around whiteness" is the institutionalization of a certain "likeness," which makes non-white bodies feel uncomfortable, exposed, visible, different, when they take up this space. (Ahmed 2007, 157)

As this framing makes clear, whiteness is not reducible to skin color, even if that is what we use as shorthand. As I discuss below, to participate in New Testament studies means participating in institutional spaces oriented "around" whiteness.

An example from another discipline can help to set the stage for further discussion of New Testament and early Christian studies. Philosopher Robert Bernasconi (2005, 23) offers a productive articulation of how institutional and social contexts operate in and through individual bodies:

> Philosophers are largely in denial not only about the role of some of the most exalted philosophers in the history of racism and in preparing for other crimes against humanity, but also about philosophy's current

problems: the fact that philosophers in the United States are overwhelmingly white; the fact that Black philosophers, like women philosophers, often seem to have to leave philosophy for other disciplines in order to get a senior position; the fact that non-Western philosophy, although it is much sought after by undergraduates, is rarely taught and that graduate schools do not prepare new PhDs to teach it; and the fact that the philosophical canon alone in the humanities has not been revised to accommodate multiculturalism.

Invoking whiteness impels us to talk about what is rendered invisible by dominant interpretive approaches, including in New Testament and early Christian studies, so that academic disciplines and specific academic units might rethink their curricula, their pedagogies, and their modes of recruitment and mentoring in ways that transform not only the demographics of a field, institution, or department but its entire orientation.[4] In the case of biblical studies, this process is entangled with the ways that the Bible has been a vector for producing modern racial formations, including whiteness.[5]

I proceed in three parts, corresponding to the three prismatic nodes mentioned above. Part 1 discusses how whiteness offers a way to call attention to present concerns and challenges. Part 2 briefly discusses the histories of our academic fields and sociocultural and political landscapes. These sections thus attend to our current locations and the histories of our fields, the first and second nodes of my prismatic approach. In part 3, I offer an example of how examining whiteness opens up new possibilities to engage biblical and early Christian materials.

The Whiteness of New Testament and Early Christian Studies

The orientation of New Testament and early Christian studies is white not because all scholars in these fields are white; in the most recent survey

---

4. Bernasconi has helped to recruit and mentor especially African American doctoral students in philosophy, making his department at Pennsylvania State University worthy of a cover story in the *The Chronicle of Higher Education* (see Patel 2016).

5. See, e.g., Harrison 1990; Olender 1992; Lincoln 1999, 47–137; Perkinson 2004; Kidd 2006; Carter 2008; Hickman 2010; Jennings 2010; Vessey et al. 2011. Perhaps most obviously, monogeneticism carries with it a legacy of human creation from a common origin, if not a divine author; even polygenetics bears the shadow of the biblically informed alternative, formed as a counter to the monogenetic view.

of members of the Society of Biblical Literature, 85 percent of members described themselves as of European descent and 76 percent as male.[6] Instead, the orientation is white because of "the world that is inherited, or which is already given before the point of an individual's arrival," the histories and approaches of our fields, and the ways that students are disciplined into the field (Ahmed 2007, 153). Whiteness functions "as both norm and core, that against which everything else is measured, and as residue, that which is left behind after everything else has been named" (Frankenberg 1993, 238).

Think about the contemporary dynamics of biblical education and specifically what bodies of knowledge and skills are required (see Johnson-DeBaufre 2010, 319–53). Take language requirements. Those of us trained in New Testament studies, at least in most programs in the United States, must take Biblical Hebrew but not Aramaic; Septuagint may be on the menu but not Talmud; by not training students in languages and texts contemporaneous with the composition of the texts of the New Testament and the centuries in which early Christian formations were emerging, New Testament studies reinforces an old paradigm of late Judaism for the early Christian context even after most of us have rejected it. Syriac is gaining in vogue now, especially due to contemporary interest in Islam, but as Gay Byron (2009) notes, Ge'ez and Ethiopic history and traditions remain almost entirely out of view.

Moreover, the interpretive approaches within the study of the New Testament and early Christian history deemed most authoritative demand that interpreters distance themselves from any current commitments and structural constraints, which really means that some commitments and constraints are rendered invisible and acceptable, while others are hypervisible and a cause for suspicion or challenge. There is still an unmarked

---

6. Although commenting on membership in the major professional society for biblical studies rather than the specific demographics of PhD recipients, the 2015 Annual Report of the Society of Biblical Literature contains telling data on the gendered and racialized character of participation. The report summarizes: "A plurality of members is 31–50 years of age. Fewer than one in ten members is 30 years of age or younger.... About one in six members is over 65 years of age.... Nearly one-fourth of members are female, while 76.2% of members are male. Transgender records number 3 and account for 0.1% of membership.... Presently, 85% of members who claim to be United States citizens are of European descent, 3.8% are multiethnic, and 3.4% are of African descent. Members of Asian descent account for 2.3%, Latina/o descent totals 1.7%, and Native American, Alaska Native, or First Nation descent is 0.2%" (22).

category, "biblical interpretation," in distinction from, say, feminist or Latino/a biblical interpretation. As Jacqueline Hidalgo (2013, 121) rightly notes, "Academic fields at large, but perhaps biblical studies especially, are circumscribed by a certain politics of reading: the 'acceptable' canon of scholarly sources within any particular field, the authority that adheres to the reading of certain texts and not others, and the practices of authorization that surround and enable only certain ways of reading these texts."

Indeed, although "other ways of reading and other *politics* of reading" are possible and exist in biblical and early Christian studies,[7] there are very few doctoral programs in the United States in which students of all backgrounds are required to demonstrate competency in scholars, methods, or interpretive approaches associated with underrepresented groups, be they racially, sexually, religiously, or otherwise minoritized. In programs in the United Kingdom, Europe, and Nordic countries, doctoral students arrive with a dissertation project and thus do not even have the opportunity through coursework to engage alternative perspectives. Institutional structures thus have a deeply conserving effect on what count as authoritative knowledge frameworks.[8]

We see the effects of these habits also in our professional societies. Among the Society of Biblical Literature's program units, some have a visible interpretive approach (ideological criticism, LGBTQ hermeneutics, Paul and politics, feminist hermeneutics of the Bible) where others do not (Pauline Epistles, book of Acts, Gospel of Luke, etc.). Those for whom the unmarked units feel like home or the center of the field might do more to question the persisting homogeneity of the spaces in terms of approaches and questions entertained in them as well as in terms of whose embodied presences are taken for granted and whose bodies are viewed as adding diversity. The audience and panelists at these unmarked sessions are, not coincidentally, overwhelmingly white and male. Even with a recent upturn of interest in ethnicity in biblical studies in these unmarked sessions, the focus remains one in which contemporary racialized contexts are almost never mentioned, but instead biblical texts and contexts are discussed as if the current context has no bearing, with virtually no reference to the scholarship produced by those who more regularly present in other program units. Our citational practices reveal much about which interpretive

---

7. Hidalgo 2013, 121; she cites, among others, Dube 2001.
8. One might also look to the location of the institutions and publishing houses that continue to be viewed and counted as most prestigious.

approaches we value, and they function to transmit generationally a narrow genealogy of legitimate voices (I use the reproductive imagery deliberately); too often these citational practices erase voices that are not white.

The persisting underrepresentation of male-identified scholars from ethnic and racial groups other than European as well as female-identified scholars of all racial and ethnic groups has not gone unnoticed, as evidenced by long-standing institutional groups such as the Society of Biblical Literature's Underrepresented Racial and Ethnic Minorities in the Profession Committee and the Status of Women in the Profession Committee, as well as many specific Society of Biblical Literature program units (e.g., African American Biblical Hermeneutics, Asian and Asian American Hermeneutics, Latino/a and Latin American Biblical Interpretation, Feminist Hermeneutics of the Bible). Given the historic and persisting inequities of race and gender in the academy, program units that focus on marginalized and minoritized approaches and perspectives continue to play a vital role in the field; nevertheless, the existence of these committees and program units is not sufficient to alter the whiteness of biblical and early Christian studies.

It is thus of crucial importance to attend to what is habitual and routine in our methods and approaches and not only to the body count of who gets PhDs, appointments, tenure, and promotion. That is, attention to who participates at the undergraduate, graduate, and faculty levels in New Testament and early Christian studies matters, but always in the context of the very shapes and orientations of the spaces, physical and intellectual, in which this work unfolds. Reorienting the fields of biblical and early Christian studies is an undertaking that also requires deep engagement with the histories of our interpretive approaches and willingness to adopt new perspectives.

Inheritances:
The Construction of the Fields of Biblical and Early Christian Studies

Higher criticism developed especially in Germany to study biblical texts and histories so as to make them objects of scientific investigation rather than simply to reinforce dogma; even so, the research results also functioned to support goals for contemporary theological and political reforms. These studies often transpose contemporary concerns about intra-European or intra-American identifications and rights into biblical studies.[9]

---

9. See especially Heschel 1998; Kelley 2002; Johnson 2004.

Even with a methodological insistence on historical rupture, studying biblical pasts held the promise to inform the present home context, including the meaning and place of religion in relationship to racial and national identifications in North America and Europe.[10]

Early Christian studies was also seen as relevant for understanding relationships between metropole and colonies, especially in the context of Christian missionary efforts. As Elizabeth Clark (2011, 154), has shown, when church history emerged as a subfield in the late nineteenth century, its proponents viewed "church history [as] essential for training missionaries for the Orient"; as Union Theological Seminary Professor Roswell Hitchcock put it in 1872–1873 in his course notes, church history should be used to inform contemporary attempts to convert to Christianity "Heathen, Moslems, and Jews" (cited in Clark 2011, 154). Sydney Cave (1919, 1–2), a Christian missionary writing at the turn of the twentieth century, claims that "any one familiar to some extent with the writings of the early fathers of the Church will feel, if he lives in India, that he is living in a world surprisingly like theirs.... Books such as Harnack's *Expansion of Christianity* ... would, *mutatis mutandi*, serve, far better than any missionary reports would, to describe the religious situation in India today." As Sylvester Johnson has shown, African American preachers Henry McNeal Turner and Edward Blyden argued for racial unity between African Americans and Africans as descendants of Ham while insisting on a stark gap between civilized Christians and degenerate uncivilized heathens. At the same time, they also struggled with the fact that the racial uplift they argued was made possible through conversion to Christianity did not erase or resolve racist treatment of both Africans and African Americans (Johnson 2004, 73–108, esp. 75–91; see also Johnson 2015).

But it is not simply that scholars have composed histories of early Christians in modern historical contexts that are racialized and interconnected with modern religious movements. It is also that these historical narratives correlate the racialized bodies of colonized and formerly enslaved peoples as well as the (usually) white bodies of colonizers with the kinds of bodies who received and promulgated forms of early Christian teachings and practices. Many reconstructions of early Christian history echo modern racial discourse when they depict early Christianity as a movement with a single origin that, even if aspirationally universal, risked

---

10. For a careful analysis on emergent nationalisms, see Moxnes 2012.

contamination from Greeks and other "heathens," from Jews, as well as from impure insiders, framed as "heretics."[11]

If non-Christians, whether framed as "Jews" or "heathens," have been racialized as problematic others in modern Christian missionary efforts, we should be attentive to how Christian belonging is correspondingly racialized, not simply akin to whiteness but, in Europe and North America, sometimes as whiteness. In North America, this working out of whiteness has a specifically Protestant dimension, as the majority of scholars of Christian origins were Protestants whose characterization of Roman Catholicism often portrayed its adherents as embodying a degenerate form of Christianity, an argument correlating with nineteenth-century social and political rhetoric about the racial and ethnic differences among European immigrants to the United States. The excellent work on how various European immigrants to the United States became white, including various Catholic immigrants and Jews, could benefit from further examination of the coconcealing and coconstituting relations of race and religion.[12]

Moreover, to decenter rather than recenter whiteness, those in New Testament and early Christian studies need to engage more deeply with work that has already been undertaken to highlight the multiple ways that people outside academia have interpreted, ignored, used, and refracted biblical texts and historical narratives.

Reencountering Ancient Sources

Invoking whiteness does not simply concern the present or recent past. Our interpretive approaches allow us to ask and produce knowledge about antiquity. To attempt to understand ancient materials and their legibility and impact within their contexts of production and circulation is always an exercise in imagination and an act in and of the present. There is no

---

11. See Buell 2005, 10–29; 2014. In discussions of conversion to Christianity in the nineteenth century, race and religion are frequently positioned as contrasting concepts, either to disable arguments for conversion of certain racialized groups or to insist that conversion cannot alter social inequities deemed to be racially based, as Sander Gilman (1993), among others, has shown for late nineteenth-century Germany, Sylvester Johnson (2004) for nineteenth-century American Christianity, and Gauri Viswanathan (1998) for nineteenth- and twentieth-century India.

12. Gil Anidjar (2008, 28) makes this important point about religion and race as "coextensive and, moreover, co-concealing categories." See also Brodkin 1998; Frye 1998; Roediger 1999.

lens we can use that lacks a prescription.[13] Using explicitly contemporary lenses enables us to encounter the strangeness of antiquity and potentially reorient our relation to the present and future.

Unlike *gender* or *ethnicity*, terms that scholars have accepted as viable for ancient Greek, Roman, Jewish, and Christian materials, *race* and certainly *whiteness* jar as anachronistic. But gender, ethnicity, and religion are no less anachronistic than race or whiteness if we mean that our discursive and material productions of these concepts differ significantly from ancient formations. Attention to whiteness may be illuminating for how we approach ancient texts and reconstructions of the past.[14]

Historical-critical approaches to the New Testament in their early articulations have functioned especially as a way for some European Protestants to authorize their own visions of true Christianity over and against both institutionalized forms of contemporary Protestantism and Catholicism (see, e.g., Smith 1990), not to mention over against those identified as anything other than Christian. An insistence on the gap between the past and present goes hand in hand with the argument that New Testament writings offer a site for recovering the path from which original Christianity strayed. Such approaches align Christian origins with a racialized logic of essential essences (Buell 2005, 1–29).

This history of historical criticism may make it tempting to assert that whiteness, as it has been inherited and inhabited, including in Christian theology, is merely a kind of deforming infection to an otherwise blameless Christian essence. For Yancy (2012, 5, 4) and many others, "Christian theology and whiteness ... are incompatible," and whiteness should be viewed as a kind of "structural sin." We see a version of this also in J. Kameron Carter's (2008) work, which diagnoses racialized and protoracist thinking as symptomatic of Christian heresy, thereby insisting that there is an orthodox and thus authentic core of early Christianity available to antiracist Christians today to reactivate.

The universalizing claims and aspirations we see in New Testament and early Christian writings are usually hailed as the key evidence to assert the essential nonracism or even antiracism of Christianity. I have argued, in contrast, that the universalizing claims and aspirations in these ancient

---

13. To make this point, Elisabeth Schüssler Fiorenza (1992, 1) cites Audre Lorde's (1978, 94) poem "Contact Lenses."
14. The original version of this essay contains a second example (see Buell 2018, 159–61).

sources are fully compatible with defining belonging in Christ as entering into membership in a people, with acquisition of new ancestry and concomitant inheritance rights for gentiles. Furthermore, the possibility of belonging in Christ simultaneously communicates an implicit, if not explicit, assertion of the problem for those who fail to take up this membership (Buell 2005, 138–65; 2009). My arguments are compatible with Victor Anderson's (2012, 196) point that "the gospel of Jesus is a scandalous gospel that carries within itself its own history of supersessions, which mimetically join Christology and whiteness; for the gospel of Jesus is good news for some and bad news for others."

This double-edged and ambivalent legacy is one that demands interpretive approaches show their work in any reconstruction. One way to do so is to stress the stakes of interpretation and the context of production. As Frank Yamada (2009, 115) has compellingly argued, the experience of Japanese Americans in the United States during World War II offers a productive lens to read Gen 2–3; this juxtaposition highlights not original sin or fall but rather "a setting of mistrust and control, marked by the arbitrary command of a suspicious ruling authority." I teach early Christian interpretations of Gen 2–3, and specifically Nag Hammadi interpretations of Gen 2–3, alongside Yamada's work to reorient our approaches to interpreting early Christian materials and reconstructing the varieties of early Christian perspectives.

Many of my students find it difficult to make sense of how Nag Hammadi texts such as the Hypostasis of the Archons and the Secret Revelation of John read Gen 2–3 so as to refute the legitimacy of the one who commands Adam not to eat of the fruit of the tree of knowledge (see Meyers 2007 for English translations of these texts). Many of my students find these texts alienating and opaque because they are unfamiliar and noncanonical. Their noncanonical status makes some students suspicious of them before even beginning to read, since these texts have typically been classified as heretical or heterodox.

After discussing these ancient texts in class, I assign Yamada's essay, which centers the experiences of Japanese American Christians interred in detention camps such as Manzanar in the United States during World War II to frame his interpretation of Gen 2–3. Yamada notes that the disobedient humans in Genesis are not in fact put to death by God, as threatened, but are instead cursed and exiled from the garden. He notes that "when interpreters align their perspective with the divine point of view, human disobedience, which is usually equated with sin, creates a rift between God and humanity" (Yamada 2009, 113). But, in contexts including the experience of Japanese Americans' internment by their own government, we can ask whether "ruling authority is justified in suppressing humanity's initiative, especially in the name of state security" (114). As Yamada points out, the Genesis narrative makes clear that, despite the threat of death and the imposed exile, humanity continues to thrive.

On the one hand, Yamada's essay helps students of all backgrounds to imagine the kinds of social contexts that might have produced readings of Gen 2–3 such as appear in Nag Hammadi texts, thus serving to undermine conventional historical narratives that render the texts products of elite heretics. Yamada (2009, 108) notes that "the tree of the fruit of the garden of good and evil functions initially as a way to distinguish between the divine and the human" and that this "prohibition not to eat from the tree … is arbitrary," a use of power to maintain—and I would suggest create— distance between the gods and humans. It resonates with the arbitrariness of racial and ethnic distinctions deployed in the process of declaring Japanese Americans intrinsically suspect in the name of preserving "American" loyalty during World War II.

On the other hand, juxtaposing these readings of Gen 2–3 also illuminates theological and ontological differences between them. Unlike the Nag Hammadi texts, which offer an alternative, singular divine source of authority outside the text of Gen 2–3, Yamada's essay shows that the very aspiration for a singular, totalizing authority—divine or otherwise—is one that racially minoritized groups and individuals have good reason to question. The majoritized ought to be just as skeptical.

By modulating between specific historical or contemporary contexts and reading communities and ancient texts, I am calling attention to what is true of all biblical interpretation: it is located, situated, and partial. But majoritized forms of biblical studies continue to position the goal and ideal of biblical studies as a rejection or minimizing of these frames—a move that I see as aligned with perpetuating whiteness as normative, regardless of the embodiment of those who participate in the guild. To counter this, we need to expand biblical studies to include the production and interpretations of the Bible in specific contexts over time, so that the borders between New Testament and early Christian history no longer hold, so that the borders between New Testament and reception history no longer hold.[15]

---

15. It is precisely in this spirit that much white feminist and racially and ethnically minoritized scholarship has been produced over the last four decades. One important institutional form this has taken is in the Institute for Signifying Scriptures, created by

Conclusion: The Price of the Ticket

"White people are not white: part of the price of the white ticket is to delude themselves into believing that they are" (Baldwin 1998, 835). With these powerful words, James Baldwin stresses the amnesia required of those who have become white in America, that white Americans cannot afford to confront the reasons for our presence in America and the losses this transition has entailed. At the same time, he rightly connects this amnesia with additional costs, borne especially by those of African descent: "I know very well that my ancestors had no desire to come to this place; but neither did the ancestors of those who require of my captivity a song. They require of me a song less to celebrate my captivity than to justify their own" (842). Baldwin refers to his own Christian upbringing, to the exhortation to "do our first works over," as a practice that white Americans do not observe, a practice that would call whiteness into question.

Reorienting away from whiteness in New Testament and early Christian studies would require those of us in these fields to do our first works over in the sense of reassessing the costs of our dominant methodologies and transforming them in conversation with ones already available in minoritized, feminist, and other marginalized scholarship. This work is part of much larger transformations needed in academia (see Ahmed 2012).

My home institution has an institutional commitment to diversifying the student body, faculty, and staff, defining diversity in the historical context that has produced patterns of underrepresentation that persist in US higher education, especially by gender, race, ethnicity, and socioeconomic factors. These efforts are most likely to be successful when academic units first have done the work to consider the values of their respective curricular areas: to ask why they consider certain methods, frameworks, questions, and content to be vital and others to be elective; to consider which pedagogies are recognized as valuable and effective and why; both to discuss what they currently do well and to educate themselves about new trends in their field(s), especially those directions being developed by scholars from groups still underrepresented in the field(s). Such work

---

Vincent Wimbush (2012; Wimbush, Lalruatkima, and Reid 2013), whose own scholarship offers a vital roadmap. The Society of Biblical Literature's Semeia Studies series is also an important publishing venue for scholars using interpretive approaches that offer important alternatives for biblical and early Christian studies.

is vital for reorienting us away from the institutional structures and habits that sustain whiteness.

Works Cited

Ahmed, Sara. 2004. "Declarations of Whiteness: The Non-performativity of Anti-Racism." *borderlands* 3.2.
———. 2007. "A Phenomenology of Whiteness." *FemT* 8.2:149–68.
———. 2012. *On Being Included: Racism and Diversity in Institutional Life*. Durham, NC: Duke University Press.
Anderson, Victor. 2012. "The Mimesis of Salvation and Dissimilitude in the Scandalous Gospel of Jesus." Pages 196–211 in *Christology and Whiteness: What Would Jesus Do?* Edited by George Yancy. New York: Routledge.
Anidjar, Gil. 2008. *Semites: Race, Religion, Literature*. Stanford, CA: Stanford University Press.
Baldwin, James. 1998. "The Price of the Ticket." Pages 830–42 in *Collected Essays*. New York: Library of America.
Bernasconi, Robert. 2005. "Waking Up White and in Memphis." Pages 17–25 in *White on White/Black on Black*. Edited by George Yancy. Lanham, MD: Rowman & Littlefield.
Brodkin, Karen. 1998. *How the Jews Became White Folks and What That Says about Race in America*. New Brunswick, NJ: Rutgers University Press.
Buell, Denise Kimber. 2005. *Why This New Race: Ethnic Reasoning in Early Christianity*. New York: Columbia University Press.
———. 2009. "Early Christian Universalism and Modern Forms of Racism." Pages 109–31 in *The Origins of Racism in the West*. Edited by Miriam Eliav-Feldon, Benjamin Isaac, and Joseph Ziegler. Cambridge: Cambridge University Press.
———. 2014. "Challenges and Strategies for Speaking about Ethnicity in the New Testament and New Testament Studies." *SEÅ* 49:33–51.
———. 2018. "Anachronistic Whiteness and the Ethics of Interpretation." Pages 149–67 in *Ethnicity, Race, Religion: Identities and Ideologies in Early Jewish and Christian Texts, and in Modern Biblical Interpretation*. Edited by Katherine M. Hockey and David G. Horrell. London: T&T Clark.
Byron, Gay L. 2002. *Symbolic Blackness and Ethnic Difference in Early Christian Literature*. New York: Routledge.

———. 2009. "Ancient Ethiopia and the New Testament: Ethnic (Con)texts and Racialized (Sub)texts." Pages 161–90 in *They Were All Together in One Place? Toward Minority Biblical Criticism.* Edited by Randall C. Bailey, Tat-siong Benny Liew, and Fernando F. Segovia. Atlanta: SBL Press.

Carter, J. Kameron. 2008. *Race: A Theological Account.* Oxford: Oxford University Press.

Cave, Sydney. 1919. *The Religious Quest of India: Redemption Hindu and Christian.* London: Milford.

Clark, Elizabeth A. 2011. *Founding the Fathers: Early Church History and Protestant Professors in Nineteenth-Century America.* Divinations. Philadelphia: University of Pennsylvania Press.

Dube, Musa W., ed. 2001. *Other Ways of Reading: African Women and the Bible.* Atlanta: Society of Biblical Literature.

Eliav-Feldon, Miriam, Benjamin Isaac, and Joseph Ziegler, eds. 2009. *The Origins of Racism in the West.* Cambridge: Cambridge University Press.

Frankenberg, Ruth. 1993. *White Women, Race Matters: The Social Construction of Whiteness.* Minneapolis: University of Minnesota Press.

Frye, Matthew Jacobson. 1998. *Whiteness of a Different Color: European Immigration and the Alchemy of Race.* Cambridge: Harvard University Press.

Gilman, Sander. 1993. *The Case of Sigmund Freud: Medicine and Identity and the Fin de Siècle.* Baltimore: Johns Hopkins University Press.

Harrison, Peter. 1990. *"Religion" and the Religions in the English Enlightenment.* Cambridge: Cambridge University Press.

Harvey, Jennifer, Karin A. Case, and Robin Hawley Gorsline, eds. 2004. *Disrupting White Supremacy from Within: White People on What We Need to Do.* Cleveland: Pilgrim.

Heschel, Susannah. 1998. *Abraham Geiger and the Jewish Jesus.* Chicago: University of Chicago Press.

Hickman, Jared. 2010. "Globalization and the Gods, or the Political Theology of 'Race.'" *EAL* 45:145–82.

Hidalgo, Jacqueline M. 2013. "The Politics of Reading: US Latinas, Biblical Studies, and Retrofitted Memory in Demetria Martínez's Mother Tongue." *JFSR* 29:120–31.

Jennings, Willie James. 2010. *The Christian Imagination: Theology and the Origins of Race.* New Haven: Yale University Press.

Johnson, Sylvester A. 2004. *The Myth of Ham in Nineteenth Century American Christianity: Race, Heathens, and the People of God*. New York: Palgrave.

———. 2015. *African American Religions, 1500–2000: Colonialism, Democracy, and Freedom*. Cambridge: Cambridge University Press.

Johnson-DeBaufre, Melanie. 2010. "Mapping the Field, Shaping the Discipline: Doctoral Education as Rhetorical Formation." Pages 319–53 in *Transforming Graduate Biblical Education: Ethos and Discipline*. Edited by Elisabeth Schüssler Fiorenza and Kent Harolds Richards. Atlanta: Society of Biblical Literature.

Kelley, Shawn. 2002. *Racializing Jesus: Race, Ideology and the Formation of Modern Biblical Scholarship*. London: Routledge.

Kidd, Colin. 2006. *The Forging of Races: Race and Scripture in the Protestant Atlantic World, 1600–2000*. Cambridge: Cambridge University Press.

Lincoln, Bruce. 1999. *Theorizing Myth: Narrative, Ideology, and Scholarship*. Chicago: University of Chicago Press.

Lipsitz, George. 2006. *The Possessive Investment in Whiteness: How White People Profit from Identity Politics*. Rev. and expanded ed. Philadelphia: Temple University Press.

Lorde, Audre. 1978. *Black Unicorn: Poems*. New York: Norton.

McCoskey, Denise Eileen. 2012. *Race: Antiquity and Its Legacy*. London: Oxford University Press.

McIntosh, Peggy. 1989. "White Privilege: Unpacking the Invisible Knapsack." *PF* (July/August): 10–12.

Meyers, Marvin, ed. 2017. *The Nag Hammadi Scriptures: The International Edition*. San Francisco: HarperOne.

Moxnes, Halvor. 2012. *Jesus and the Rise of Nationalism: A New Quest for the Nineteenth-Century Historical Jesus*. London: Tauris.

Olender, Maurice. 1992. *The Languages of Paradise: Race, Religion, and Philology in the Nineteenth Century*. Translated by Arthur Goldhammer. Cambridge: Harvard University Press.

Patel, Vimal. 2016. "Diversifying a Discipline." *The Chronicle of Higher Education*, 27 March. https://tinyurl.com/SBL03111b.

Perkinson, James. 2004. *White Theology: Outing Supremacy in Modernity*. New York: Palgrave Macmillan.

Roediger, David R. 1999. *The Wages of Whiteness: Race and the Making of the American Working Class*. London: Verso.

Schüssler Fiorenza, Elizabeth. 1992. *But She Said: Feminist Practices of Biblical Interpretation.* Boston: Beacon.

Smith, Jonathan Z. 1990. *Drudgery Divine: On the Comparison of Early Christianities and the Religions of Late Antiquity.* Chicago: University of Chicago Press.

Society of Biblical Literature. *Society Report.* November 2015. https://tinyurl.com/SBL03111c.

Thandeka. 1999. *Learning to be White: Money, Race, and God in America.* New York: Continuum.

Vessey, Mark, Sharon V. Betcher, Robert A. Daum, and Harry O. Maier, eds. 2011. *The Calling of the Nations: Exegesis, Ethnography, and Empire in a Biblical-Historic Present.* Toronto: University of Toronto Press.

Viswanathan, Gauri. 1998. *Outside the Fold: Conversion, Modernity, and Belief.* Princeton: Princeton University Press.

Ware, Vron, and Les Back. 2002. *Out of Whiteness: Color, Politics, and Culture.* Chicago: University of Chicago Press.

Wimbush, Vincent. 2012. *White Men's Magic: Scripturalization as Slavery.* Oxford: Oxford University Press.

Wimbush, Vincent, with Lalruatkima and Melissa Renee Reid, eds. 2013. *Misreading America: Scriptures and Difference.* Oxford: Oxford University Press.

Yamada, Frank. 2009. "What Does Manzanar Have to Do with Eden? A Japanese American Interpretation of Genesis 2–3." Pages 97–117 in *They Were All Together in One Place? Toward Minority Biblical Criticism.* Edited by Randall C. Bailey, Tat-siong Benny Liew, and Fernando F. Segovia. Atlanta: Society of Biblical Literature.

Yancy, George. 2012. "Introduction: Framing the Problem." Pages 1–18 in *Christology and Whiteness: What Would Jesus Do?* Edited by George Yancy. New York: Routledge.

Is the Hebrew Bible Racist?
Diversity and Antiracist Reading Practices

Julián Andrés González Holguín

When the interpretation of the Hebrew Bible does not address questions of the existential quest for meaning and the struggle for freedom, it participates in undermining the public worth of racially differentiated bodies. Marginalized readers are articulating their sense of the Hebrew Bible's historical context and the xenophobic impact of its interpretations against themselves (people of color, women, LGBTQ+ individuals, and the elderly) in light of the contemporary terrors, anxieties, and fears of living in a racist society. They interrogate our thinking process about racism, because racism reproduces itself in ever new permutations. Racism's manifestation takes a variety of forms, and racism is expressed in a variety of modes (academic, legal, cultural, political). Modernity, the field of discourse and rationality that makes racism possible, remains the same (Goldberg 1993, 41–60).[1]

Diversity as Antiracist Strategy

Diversity, understood as the mix of difference to evade the structural, political, and economic questions posed by racism, has become a theological platform in the struggle against racism's diverse and complex manifestations. The idea is that we are better able to address racism when diversity is a core value for seminaries and seminarians. Diversity is supposed to help students see how interpretation is not monolithic in construction, expression, and practice. Through diversity, we could exit the power structure that creates whiteness and blackness. However, the creation of nuanced

---

1. For a definition of modernity as a field of discourse, see Bauman 1992, xv.

identities at the institutional and individual level occurs in a manner consistent with the expectations of global capitalism. Theological schools create curricula and pedagogical strategies that fail to engage the logic of racism and the co-optation of diversity within the economic system. Alain Badiou's (1994, 14) reflections on global capitalism may reveal the problem with what we do in biblical interpretation: "Capital demands a permanent creation of subjective and territorial identities in order for its principle of movement to homogenize its space of action; identities, moreover, that never demand anything but the right to be exposed in the same way as others to the uniform prerogatives of the market." In other words, global capitalism does not limit the proliferation of interpretive voices. Instead, its hegemony welcomes and produces fragmented and multiculturalist scholarly and ecclesial subjectivities to the point that almost any interpretation is valid, except, of course, the one that challenges the current patron of all others—global capitalism (Worthington 2015, 20).

Therefore, biblical studies should not just provide another voice in a spectrum of difference. Struggles for liberation demand more than adding another voice to the mix. Diversity is not a matter of adding the invisible ones as addenda to the European-centered historical method. In this vital work, the practice of interpreting the Hebrew Bible may not afford replications of "the corporatist model of diversity that encourage respect, inclusion, and fair treatment without a concomitant desire to tackle the more difficult conversation about the roots of racial conflict and injustice" (Fisher-Steward 2016, 458). Neither is the solution a methodological inversion—one in which the values of the oppressed group dominate—because it would devolve into another power play to master interpretation and being dogmatic.

I argue that diversity is about two related notions. First I will address the deconstructive perspective.[2] This is the hermeneutical orientation that questions the pattern onto which the biblical drama is rendered applicable to today's context. It entails the critical reading of the Hebrew Bible to interrogate its authority and ability to define and express freedom for those who suffer. An emancipatory political exegesis is not enough because such an approach repeats the meaning of existence that needs overcoming: namely, the assimilation of minorities into dominant cultural identities. Simple oppositionality as a guiding principle to interpretation is insuffi-

---

2. I will develop the constructive perspective in the next section.

cient because it inevitably presupposes and reinstates the very racial configurations it is expressly committed to challenging.

Diversity becomes patronizing and tokenistic when predominantly white, patriarchal theological institutions and churches embrace the multiplicity of interpretations and yet resist their message or remain inactive and reject efforts to stand against racism at all levels: curricula development, pedagogical practices, community life, and the public square. It is not enough in antiracist education to push toward the general appreciation of the beauty of the Other by demonstrating how cultures appropriate the Hebrew Bible. As the history of orientalism shows, an appreciative study of cultures is another form of domination, making the Other aesthetically exceptional and offering affirmation from a dominant cultural perspective as if that appreciation were a surprise (Ceballos 2019).

Diversity becomes oppressive when a historical examination of the biblical tradition works to illustrate the logic of the past to confirm our belief that the present rests on profound intentions and immutable necessities. This genealogical approach to history justifies the suffering of those on the margins of the logic of redemption. A historical sense should confirm our existence among countless other possibilities of being in the world without a landmark or a point of reference (Burnett 2000) to argue that our interpretation of the Hebrew Bible is the only official and authoritative one. In other words, a historical analysis of the Hebrew Bible does not provide certainty or lays bare the rational unfolding of ancient Israelites' drama to be superseded by the Christian era and the New Testament. Recognizing that a dominant epistemological center no longer holds and never really did, supersessionism reveals itself as racist doctrine because it is the effort to establish fictive lines of purity between the Christian and Jewish traditions. Judaism became the antithesis to and corruption of all that was good and wholesome in nineteenth-century Western society and Christianity (Heschel 1998, 75). Whiteness and its production of racialized bodies work under the same supposition (Carter 2008, 30, 82).[3] It is dehumanizing because it is a regime of knowledge and self-understanding that feeds itself by conquering others, subsuming into its logic what is visible

---

3. The term *whiteness* defines a regime of political and economic power for arranging the world, as the outcome of a cultural and legal structure and political and economic identification with rulership and privilege. In class terms, it implies social superiority, political control, and economic privilege (see Mignolo 2005; Wallerstein 1974–1989).

and sayable. Racism is implemented by negating the principle of equality or consciousness to women, blacks, workers, and others. Therefore, racism is patriarchal, xenophobic, sexist, and classist in its manifestations.

In the increasing number of movements for liberation, including the rising awareness and activism for environmental restoration, interpreting the Hebrew Bible cannot be but a political exercise. It recognizes people at the margins practicing a hermeneutical task that reckons with the reality of humanity and the divine in their diverse manifestations. It is political because it rejects the logic of racism by questioning the modern tyranny structured in terms of the binary: lives that are considered human and have rights against those without rights and therefore expendable (Agamben 1995, 51–54).

The tyranny plays itself out and reproduces its dehumanizing consequences through narratives of origin, such as the creation account in Gen 3, where gender inequality is the modality through which the divisions within the social order articulate themselves. Therefore, political exegesis is a crisis-centered exegesis that deploys interpretation as an instrument to enable more effective action by the promotion of relentless criticism of texts and their interpretations as well as by self-criticism of interpretive communities (Aichele, Miscall, and Walsh 2009, 388). We need a political criticism that unmasks whiteness, which, as the norm to measure humanity and the world, tyrannically dehumanizes and divides people in terms of obedient bodies (usually depicted as female) and (male) bodies to be obeyed.

The intersection between the Hebrew Bible and political exegesis highlights the fluidity of the text as it encounters communities of readers from different sociopolitical realities. This fluidity facilitates the continuous adoption of characters and changes of events in the biblical drama with issues in our modern world. Identification is an ongoing process, necessary to make the ancient texts relevant to situations of today's world, but it bears significant risks. For example, Robert Allen Warrior's (2006) "A Native American Perspective: Canaanites, Cowboys, and Indians" asserts that every story of liberation is also a story of colonizing other people. In a ready identification of the exodus story, readers may use the text as an excuse for their pet theory (Pixley 1987; Levenson 2000) that promises to fix all the problems humanity faces in the twenty-first century without paying attention to Warrior's insight on the dualism of the exodus story. Warrior's work demonstrates the naive assumption of early Latin American liberation theology that did not pay attention to the co-optation within basic ecclesial communities. These communities also desired to benefit from the economic system that oppressed them. The lack of awareness of desire and its limits stands in opposition to the struggle for equality, making each member of the communities an oligarch in *potentia* and a *little* capitalist.

Warrior's critique raises the question of the Hebrew Bible's capability to articulate liberation for oppressed communities when the imagination of the biblical text overdetermines their language. A critical reading of the Hebrew Bible cannot be evaded because one can read it within the theological grammar of the Christian faith, and yet do so in a way that sanctions and even sanctifies, in Michel Foucault's (1971) terms, "the order of things."[4] For example, the marriage metaphor in the book of Hosea imagines liberation as resisting the feminine in the quest to seize the consciousness of manhood as the realm of freedom. Hosea 1–3 portrays God as a faithful husband and Israel as a faithless wife. The metaphor represents the liberated self as the mode of right agency and emancipated identity as male. Theological problems for present-day women become apparent when the husband's strategy is a series of physical and psychological punishments against the wife, as described in Hos 2. Therefore, gender-ordered freedom is not freedom at all because gender-predicated and -ordered power always requires its reproduction, its reiterated assertion. Otherwise, its power ceases. The notion of freedom in the marriage metaphor needs a logic of determination that at once discounts the freedom such necessity dictates.

The problems described above do not mean that we should discard the Hebrew Bible and the task of interpretation. Still, they do underline the requirement of caution and intellectual rigor before we claim the text and our interpretive practice as liberating or resembling any form of an existence freed from racialized categories. All hermeneutical approaches

---

4. A classic example of this position is Basil of Caesarea, whose argument justifies slavery by a problematic theology of creation (see Carter 2008, 237). In current philosophical studies, Giorgio Agamben (1995) has shown how theology as a discourse buttresses the political economy, its social order, and the ongoing need for the figure of the *homo sacer*. In biblical studies, I take Agamben's insights to demonstrate how the imagination in modern biblical studies is surreptitiously complicit in how the self comes to be forged in the furnace of the sacred, sacrificial, and therefore sanctifying violence of sovereign power. The social order is maintained by an economy of sacrifice informed by a Christian religious discourse of the primeval family (see González Holguín 2018).

are part of the modern discourse or its postmodern critique, thus infused with the category of race. The practice of interpretation can help outline a pedagogy of coexistence and compassion to address racist ideologies.

Toward a Pedagogy of Coexistence and Compassion

The constructive notion of diversity is about the ethical exercise manifested in the embodiment of practices of interpretation that provide a perspective into the realm of God as a table where justice and peace, based on the respect for the tiniest differences, are its hallmarks.[5] It is the exercise of remaking the world and the self in what Michael Fishbane (1998, 2–4) calls "poesis," the creative act of interpretation that "attempt[s] to textualize existence by having the ideals of (interpreted) Scripture embodied in everyday life." The modern self and subjectivity are formed through a racializing process, which Foucault (1988, 146) calls a violent subjection to the notion of freedom in modernity. The textualization of existence requires a midrashic exegesis by which the interpreter enters into the world of the Hebrew Bible to reconstitute the self (Fishbane 1998, 106–10), being aware of the binary whiteness/blackness and the racialized gender conventions associated with it. In other words, it is a new technology of the self, or a performance of existence that reimagines, through a critical engagement with the Hebrew Bible, how to be in the world. For example, the In[heir]itance Project seeks to recontextualize biblical tales in urban America, using a range of dramatic approaches to create plays that bring communities together. Its goal is to plant openness, generosity, and awareness of others and to counter the usual claim of ownership of the Scriptures for purposes of division, condescension, and judgment (Merwin 2018).

The interpretive task also consists of making visible what is hidden and getting what is only audible as noise to be heard as speech. This orientation is especially important to reveal the omissions, additions, and rearrangements that occur in the art of translation. A standard part of translational rewritings is to omit chunks of primary sources, sometimes because they are held to be unacceptable or irrelevant to the receiving audience. A political reading of the Hebrew Bible should ask the questions, Why did a translator omit some aspects of the Hebrew text, add some of them,

---

5. See Lim 2017 for a proposal to embody diversity in the context of predominantly white institutions.

and rearrange others? What is the translator's ideological standpoint, and what informs it? The answers to these questions usually reveal a theological stance. An exemplar in this task is Wilda Gafney (2013, 2017), who has consistently outlined how her work and practice build on a critical analysis of the racist practices in translating and interpreting the Hebrew Bible, as well as the connections of these practices to the broader cultural and racial climate of the United States. For example, in the first two verses of the Hebrew Bible, God is described using masculine and feminine verbs. However, "in translation and tradition God became virtually exclusively male. The gendering of God's spirit as feminine calls for the feminine pronoun, yet generations of sexist translations have gotten around this by religiously avoiding the pronoun altogether" (Gafney 2017, 19–20).

The essential task is the *critical reading* of the Hebrew Bible to prevent the overformation of the text and its naive application on current struggles against racism. By *critical*, I mean three things. First, it involves an ideological critique of how the Hebrew Bible has traditionally been read to explain how racism permeates academic/scholarly and ecclesial/liturgical interpretations. These interpretive traditions become stereotypes that hold the logic of racism in place, because we pass from generation to generation this knowledge as dominant and authoritative. For example, *The Genesis of Liberation: Biblical Interpretation in the Antebellum Narratives of The Enslaved* (Powery and Sadler 2016) investigates how African Americans developed methodologies that allowed them to create alternative narratives about themselves to participate in the political project of Western civilization, which used the Scriptures to enslave them. This work demonstrates that without a critical distancing from and then oppositional reengagement with reading traditions, teaching the Hebrew Bible becomes a unarticulated but effective way to oppress. Ideological commitments and rhetoric belie the conceptual network in which the teaching itself is constituted.

Second, the Hebrew Bible becomes a psychological weapon of social and physical annihilation. Readers learn racialized stereotypes and apply them to the Hebrew Bible without much time to unpack and critique them (Kelley 2002).[6] Race, like gender, shapes reading of the Hebrew Bible by quietly insisting on some seemingly neutral historical approaches to the

---

6. Kelley traces the impact of philosophical currents in the nineteenth and twentieth century to biblical studies, and demonstrates their links to racism.

task of interpretation. A faithful reading, however, connects interpretation with *suffering* and the voices of those suffering, instead of simply underlining the injustice of who gets to be neutral and who does not. The centrality of suffering opens the possibility of countermemories, that is, alternative ways of identification with the Hebrew Bible that reappraise the washing, silencing, and erasing reading strategies of the dominant white heterosexual culture. For example, "Painted Eroticism: Sex and Death in Cain and Abel's Story" (González Holguín 2021) traces the visual history of Gen 4:1–16 and demonstrates how eroticism is part of the semantical potential of the story. These graphical representations contribute to decentering dominant white heterosexual models of subjectivity and spirituality that emerged within the written history of interpretation. They predominantly argue that Abel is the model of faith and suffering, and Cain is the paradigmatic representation of evil.

The Hebrew Bible itself could be considered a prototype of countermemory, because it is a mythical-historical narrative that counters the hegemonic one told by the oppressors of ancient Israelites.[7] Its multitude of theological voices is a struggle against external sovereign forces—to speak theologically, of *anamnesis*—of remembering in a certain way. Therefore, countermemories prompt us to reevaluate diversity, to become aware of the constraints of the logic of racism, and to move toward an intercommunal pedagogy of coexistence. This pedagogy challenges racial, gender, and class essentialism in the interpretation of the Hebrew Bible for religious communities, theological discourses, and the broader culture. Essentialism is characterized by the applicability of whiteness into other ways of being in the world. It is a form of reductionism by which the white, hetero-

---

7. Two caveats to this possibility. First, the distinction between Israelite and Canaanite, or later Jew and gentile, which is critical in Israel's prototypical self-identification as a counterhistorical people. The mythical story of the biblical drama can inspire liberation or resistance from empire history. Alternatively, it can invest the logic of the imperial oppressors and convert the story of struggle into a discourse of the superiority of Jewish identity, thus becoming hegemonic itself. Second, Israel defined itself as a collective in contrast to its oppressors, using the ancient Near East model of the vassal treaty. Israel's theological adaptation of the Assyrian covenant took the oppressor's political model and transformed it to express resistance. However, this hybrid model creates ambivalence. It is supposed to blunt power's sharp edge and to shift its oppressive expression; however, it does so by assuming some of the hierarchical aspects of power. Therefore, the text reflects both an impulse to undermine the colonial presence and the desire to be like the colonizer.

sexual, middle-class men perspective becomes the norm, or pure expression of thought, experience, and emotions. The result of essentialism is the reduction of different forms of oppression to addition problems. Therefore, the lives of racially differentiated bodies are fragmented before being subjected to analysis (Bartlett, Rhodesia, and Grossman 2013, 784–85). Global capitalism takes advantage of essentialist interpretations and creates insularity while maintaining a notion of diversity. A diverse insularity, also known as multiculturalism, becomes the ground for tyranny, because it reduces the multicultural condition to formal singularities segregated into separate segments. In the words of Stuart Hall (2000, 213), it results in "the subaltern proliferation of difference."

Finally, by critical, I mean continuous experimentation in the process of interpreting the Hebrew Bible. Political exegesis underlines that the Hebrew Bible is a contested ground of identity, a site of struggle of whom we take ourselves to be to other ways of being in the world. Experimentation upsets the oppositional logic that is at work in how racism operates, because it offers the possibility to create meanings, ceaselessly moving between the limits of tradition and what it excludes. Experimentation embraces diversity, is suspicious of readings that have become universal and generalized, and focuses instead on the variability of how readers make interpretations and appropriate the Hebrew Bible to their sociopolitical contexts. We walk a fine line between making our interpretation an absolute moral principle and a plain indifference to the text. Although a moral system and its related ethical discussions are necessary as communities read the text, so also is its shattering to counterbalance the transformation of our interpretations into self-security and diversity into racist hierarchical orders.

In other words, experimentation is a tradition of wrestling with the Hebrew Bible, following the Jewish heritage of reading the Tanak. As the old proverb puts it: "Two Jews, three opinions." The name *Israel* means one who "wrestles with God." From Jacob's battle with the angel to post-Holocaust Jewish scholars wrestling with mass murder during the Nazi era, the Jewish tradition is rich in calling God to task over human suffering and experienced justice (Laytner 1990). Experimentation is a fundamental part of the biblical tradition: what we call innerbiblical exegesis, or how parts of the Hebrew Bible reinterpret or allude to other texts. This practice moves outside the text into the study of reception history. It examines how later readers and communities engage with commentaries, art, poetry, and homilies spanning the millennia and across religious traditions, ranging from classical rabbinic and early Christian typological interpretation to postmodern, feminist, postcolonial, and ecocritical commentaries among others.

Wrestling with the Hebrew Bible also becomes a strategy for staying in relation with and not discarding the Hebrew Bible; this is analogous to the struggle of the prophets. They brought urgent and compassionate critique to bear on the evils of their day, which they also struggled to understand themselves in their context. Countermemories are prophetic speech because they help us rupture the static and unifying aura of white hegemonic imagination.

The stories of the ancient Israelites, who were politically and militarily dominated but tried to endure against all the odds, may help create and maintain a critical attitude of resistance and engagement with the Hebrew Bible and its power of identification and imagination for struggles of liberation. The Hebrew Bible's refusal to escape from pain and misery by indulging in dogmas, doctrines, or abstract systems of philosophy underlines that interpretation unfolds under the shadows of death, dread, and despair of ancient Israelites who searched for human and divine love, dialogue, and justice. These old stories may also be used to enter into current battles in which communities' life is at stake.

Therefore, using the lens of tragedy and terror to understand the drama in the Hebrew Bible may yield the most thoughtful reflections and depiction of the limits of critical intelligence in confronting our worldly existence. The text's acute sense of inconsistency, contradiction, suffering, and violence highlights human experience and grounds a hermeneutic of compassion for each of us.[8] We learn in suffering to recognize the humanity of others, and this acknowledgment is the beginning of any struggle. The tragic perspective into our reality ignites and keeps alive the fight for liberation. This can be summed up in Theodor Adorno's dictum: "The need to let suffering speak is the condition of all truth" (cited in Cornell 1992, 13).

In a world of racial tyranny in which political and religious leaders express ethnoracial disdain of one sort or another, the intellectual work of interpreting the Hebrew Bible is political, because it deploys interpretation

---

8. See González Holguín 2018 for an example of an engagement with the biblical text that underlines these characteristics in the story of Cain and Abel and connects its analysis with questions of existence in the twenty-first century around the topic of global migration.

to advance the interest of the most dispossessed and degraded in society. This is an impossible identification, because no individual would want to pronounce it on themselves. It involves a choice to identify with the bodies beaten to death in the name of white supremacy. Biblical studies discourse should discover itself as a discourse of tragedy and terror, in which the centrality of suffering may help to identify and resituate critically and ethically the intellectual production toward pervasive power structures through which the logic of racism works. In doing so, the very character and goals of interpreting the Hebrew Bible will be transformed. It is the neutral mode of reading, a heritage of modernity's emphasis on a self-interested, autonomous, and rational subject, that keeps biblical studies entangled with racism. This disposition suspends the demands of the current situation, including the constraints of social and economic necessity. It maintains the art of biblical interpretation as a play-world that raises problems for the pleasure of solving them; these problems do not arise out of a world in crisis, and they don't impose any urgency on the ends interpretation proposes. Therefore, reading the Hebrew Bible (un)wittingly justifies a history of Western expansionism and the (re)creation of racist discourses with the biblical text.

The Hebrew Bible has been deployed by colonial societies to dispossess people of their land and cultures and to racialize populations and their spiritualities. Given this devastating legacy, many people do not consider the Hebrew Bible as worth their time. It remains a question as to whether the discourse of biblical interpretation can relinquish the current power structures that shape its practice, exit the whiteness/blackness binarism, enter a decolonial space of reading and imagination, and divest the foundational text from all Euro-Christian racist discourse of the past few centuries. This space arises from the everyday practices of people in their worlds of pain, suffering, poverty, and death. It is fraught with questions. Who can inhabit this space, and on what grounds can someone stand to undertake this critique? How can nonwhite intellectuals live in the in-between world of academic production and the material reality of crisis and death? How may critical biblical scholarship be innovative enough to exit the prevalent racism of the discipline? How does one identify that which can be discarded from that which can be reconfigured? How do practitioners of this alternative space expose the logic of racism now in its gendered and classist-inflected modalities? The paradox is that a critical reading of the Hebrew Bible is framed and expressed by the very terms it takes as its critical object. This linguistic fact demonstrates that antiracist pedagogies and interpretations are forced into the narrowing confines of comprehensibility already determined by modernity as a discourse. It reduces the choices of resistant readings to imposed social and cultural values being represented in dominant approaches to the Hebrew Bible. However, forgetting the everyday consequences of racism in people's realities of death and poverty reinforces the whiteness that reigns as the invisible structure of biblical interpretation (Kelley 2002, 3–4), and how it continues to function as a discourse of death.

Teaching Tactics from a Biblical Scholar

I invite you to practice a hermeneutics of coexistence and compassion, which constructs multivalent and multidimensional interpretations. It articulates the complexity and diversity of identification and appropriation of the Hebrew Bible for communities in the twenty-first century. Such critical analysis of texts and traditions underlines the political and ethical dimension of biblical interpretation and could become a catalyst, capturing readers' imagination and drawing them out to address racism: the pure and simple rejection of the Other—that is, the transmogrification of the racially differentiated either into monsters or into the rationality defined by white standards and norms, ways of knowing and being, thinking and doing. This transmogrification causes people to lose their capacity to grieve in public and reduces them to wordless victims (Butler 2004, 35–37). For example, immigrants are workers stripped of their names, never perceptible as such. They appear as perpetrators of an inexpiable offense and the cause of a problem calling for a consensus solution. As a problem and target of hatred, immigrants suffer a spiral of lost political subjectivity (like the *homo sacer*, included by their exclusion), and they become a horrible threshold of people who can be killed with impunity.

As a biblical scholar writing and teaching in a school of theological education, I am aware of the responsibility to help students engage the Hebrew Bible sensibly, considering the increasingly visible racism in our society, particularly through government policies, police brutality, and social media. Teaching texts that are received canonically underlines the critical task of addressing the current struggles for liberation that shape the context in which students interpret the Hebrew Bible. My teaching is characterized by the following: (1) an analysis of received reading traditions of the Hebrew Bible to identify and analyze racist assumptions within the discipline, (2) a centering of biblical characters who have been at the margins in biblical studies but who are central to readers of color and those of diverse sexualities and different embodiments and mobilities, (3) a commitment to help students draw connections between current circumstances of struggles for liberation and a biblical text's literary and historical contexts, and (4) a reading that continually picks apart and then weaves the text back together to avoid excessive identification, because familiarity breathes inattention. Theological formation and ecclesial reading practices often quiet and domesticate the hermeneutical possibilities of the Hebrew Bible to address racism, turning it into an object of habitual regard. This process of socialization and acculturation leads Stephen Prothero to argue that to study the Scriptures in the Christian tradition is no longer a suitable means for developing and refining religious intelligence among churchgoers in the United States. There is a gap between faith and knowledge. American Christianity has gravitated toward an evangelical religion of the heart where the emphasis is on loving Jesus and having a relationship with him, but rarely if ever on knowing something about the rich and historical traditions associated with their sacred texts (Prothero 2008, 6–25).[9] The question that must be addressed is: What does it mean to practice the art of biblical interpretation from within the current crises in which communities' lives and the restoration of earth is at stake?

Looking for marginalized places and characters in the Hebrew Bible that invert the traditional values of intelligibility is central to the task of interpretation (González Holguín 2015, 2018, 2021). It is the practice of looking at the minor characters in the stories, the silent voices who don't really get to be represented by the narrator. It is a highly imaginative reading that does not explain the interpretive complexity of texts in terms of what is most straightforward, most elementary, and most evident, but in terms of what is most confused, obscure, disorganized, and haphazard. It is essential to hold space for angrier readings that are reacting to the dominant voices in biblical scholarship, living with the text in its picked-apart state, as ugly and uncomfortable as that may be. This state helps students stay in touch with the everyday realities of people and highlights our peculiar wrestling with appearance and reality, opinion and knowledge, illusion and truth, and the collective struggle for a decent society.

---

9. The counterargument is that mainstream denominations are lost in their traditions, incapable to address an audience with little to no knowledge or interest in mainstream traditions. In other words, they keep preaching to the choir.

I understand the danger of cynicism in dwelling on such critical readings rather than on beautiful syntheses that reweave texts and traditions. However, a brilliant synthesis can risk failure to honor the trauma of those harmed by the text and its interpreters. To remain longer with the text is like continually singing a good Latin American bolero;[10] it creates melancholic yet melioristic indictments of the misery created by racist structures and prejudices without concealing the wounds inflicted or promising permanent victory. With their slow tempo and unhurried melody, songs such as "Bésame Mucho" and "Solamente Una Vez" describe life's suffering briefly made bearable by love.[11] As listening to a bolero, critically and constantly appropriating the Hebrew Bible may lead us through our contemporary inferno with love and sorrow, but not cheap pity or promise of ultimate happiness.

Leaving Racism Behind?

A hermeneutic of coexistence and compassion also impels practitioners of biblical interpretation to reveal how the very operation of power within our immediate work contexts (academy, classroom, church) is an integral component of our production. This strategy puts us in a double-bind situation because, while linking the critical production with the fundamental and structural overhaul of societal institutions and global capitalism, we often remain financially dependent on them. Our task as critical readers of the Hebrew Bible and its interpretations to address racism is simultaneously progressive and co-opted. To face the hegemonic power of global capitalism is not an easy task. It implies antagonism, rejection, and dissensus. However, it also includes fascination and ambivalence toward white cultural and ideological values. We may struggle against racism through our task of biblical interpretation. At the same time, we are also part of the economic system from which we benefit. While the consequences of

---

10. Latin-American bolero has its roots in Cuban music in the early twentieth century (see Bigott 2018, 19–27).

11. The English version for "Solamente Una Vez" is "You Belong to My Heart." It was written by Ray Gilbert for the Disney animated film *The Three Amigos*. One line reads: "Only once in my garden / hope did shine / the hope that brightens / the road of my loneliness." This song has been recorded and played in varied settings. It describes the intensity of love when couples sway together to its soothing, wistful melody, holding on to each other lest love end and loneliness win the day.

the current economy are widespread and intolerable, most of us actually understand so little about the ways it affects our lives that we continually contribute to its consequences in the world. It is not simply that we decide to involve ourselves in this crisis through our teaching and scholarship but that we are already, by what we do and fail to do, participating in it. Our academic production remains restless and wandering. It may dissent and critique, but it is parasitic because its existence depends on the continuation of the economy and of racism.

This parasitical fact deeply delimits the taking up of race as an organizing theme to antiracist pedagogical practices. The invocation of race is fraught with danger because it is at once implicated in the possibility of producing and reproducing racist interpretations. Although race is conceptually open to antiracist mobilizations, the impacts of racism on the origin and development of the modern field of biblical studies—including its definition, organization, and goals (Kelley 2002; Carter 2008)—delimit our potential resistance through an invocation of race. It can be mobilized to antiracist purposes but, at best, only as a short-term and contingent strategy. Otherwise, antiracist pedagogical practices of reading the Hebrew Bible may likely reinscribe elements of the very presuppositions they are committed to ending, making the results of any pedagogy ambivalent and ambiguous.

To exit racism requires an exact appreciation of the price we must pay to detach our intellectual production and way of being in the world from it. It assumes that we are aware of the extent to which racism insidiously is embedded in the world. It implies a knowledge that allows us to think against and beyond racism but also be mindful of that which remains racist afterwards. We must determine the extent to which our antiracist practices are possibly one more trick of racism directed against us, at the end of which racism stands, motionless, waiting to meet us again, telling us that any declared victory over it perpetuates its presence. Racism has been an efficient system, crafty and resilient to the power of critique by emphasizing a superficial appropriation and celebration of multicultural approaches to the Hebrew Bible, or by rerouting one's rightful anger into the ambivalence of mere colorblind conditions.[12] Therefore, being able to exit its logic is easier to state than to achieve. It is not the case that biblical

---

12. This expression reinscribes the relative invisibility, or anonymity, of the presence of racism adapting to the wake of the postcolonial and global systems.

scholars' intentions are in any way disingenuous, deficient, or inadequate to address racism. The problem resides on the level of discourse and of materiality rather than individual intentions. On these levels, modernity, its philosophical breakthroughs, and its frameworks continue to shape and haunt biblical studies. We must insist that the interpretation of the Hebrew Bible is racist not merely because of the racial composition of the biblical scholars. The interpretation of the Hebrew Bible may be racist because of the function it plays in producing and reproducing, constituting and effecting racially shaped discursive spaces and material realities with real-world implications regarding accesses and restrictions, inclusions and exclusions, conceptions and modes of representation. To the extent that the interpretation of the Hebrew Bible operates to exclude or privilege in or on racial terms, and insofar as its interpretations circulate in and reproduce a world whose meanings and effects are racist, the work will remain compromised.

The hermeneutical task of interpreting the Hebrew Bible should begin from the beginning. It must not forget the context of dread, death, and despair that created the text and which the text reflects. This perspective neither excludes nor opposes the traditional historical approaches to the interpretation of the Hebrew Bible. It points to the need for an overhauling of the interpretive task to address racialized biblical discourse and the hegemonic power of whiteness, because our views of the past usually reflect modern dreams and desires. This reading must address the existential concerns of humanity in the postcolonial, postmodern, post-European age; it must confront the legacy of oppression and racism that shaped the task of interpreting the Hebrew Bible in the last two centuries; and it must challenge the ideological underpinnings of our anachronistic projections on antiquity. Social movements such as Black Lives Matter and political pressure from outside theological institutions and churches are vital so that the political exegesis of the Hebrew Bible does not degenerate into mere lethargic accommodation or sheer indifference, preyed on by the temptations of intellectual merit and pride. Perhaps the power of social movements outside the church can limit the self-arrogation of those within the church and the academy of biblical studies to command significant social and political resources. There is no guarantee that the pressure will yield the results we want for the practice of interpreting and teaching the Hebrew Bible to address a racist society. Still, without the pressure, the status quo will remain the same or regress.

Works Cited

Agamben, Giorgio. 1995. *Homo Sacer: Sovereign Power and Bare Life.* Translated by Daniel Heller-Roazen. Stanford, CA: Stanford University Press.
Aichele, George, Peter Miscall, and Richard Walsh. 2009. "An Elephant in the Room: Historical-Critical and Postmodern Interpretations of the Bible." *JBL* 128:383–404.
Badiou, Alain. 1994. *Saint Paul: The Foundation of Universalism.* Stanford, CA: Stanford University Press.
Bartlett, Katharine T., Deborah L. Rhodesia, and Joanna L. Grossman. 2013. *Gender and Law: Theory, Doctrine, Commentary.* 6th ed. New York: Wolters Kluwer.
Bauman, Zygmunt. 1992. *Intimations of Postmodernity.* London: Routledge.
Bigott, Luis Antonio. 2018. *Historia del Bolero Cubano.* Caracas: Fondo Editorial Ipasme.
Burnett, Fred. 2000. "Historiography." Pages 106–12 in *Handbook of Postmodern Biblical Interpretation.* Edited by Andrew K. M Adam. Duluth, GA: Chalice.
Butler, Judith. 2004. *Precarious Life: The Powers of Mourning and Violence.* New York: Verso.
Carter, J. Kameron. 2008. *Race: A Theological Account.* New York: Oxford University Press.
Ceballos, Manuela. 2019. "Questions of Taste: Critical Pedagogy and Aesthetics in Islamic Studies." Pages 22–34 in *Teaching Islamic Studies in the Age of ISIS, Islamophobia, and the Internet.* Edited by Courtney M. Dorrol. Bloomington: Indiana University Press.
Cornell, Drusilla. 1992. *The Philosophy of the Limit.* New York: Routledge.
Fishbane, Michael. 1998. *The Exegetical Imagination: On Jewish Thought and Theology.* Cambridge: Harvard University Press.
Fisher-Steward, Gayle. 2016. "To Serve and Protect: The Police, Race, and the Episcopal Church in the Black Lives Matter Era." *AThR* 99:439–59.
Foucault, Michel. 1971. *The Order of Things: An Archaeology of the Human Sciences.* New York: Pantheon.
———. 1988. "The Political Technology of Individuals." Pages 145–62 in *Technologies of the Self: A Seminar with Michael Foucault.* Edited by

Luther H. Martin, Huck Gutman, and Patrick H. Hutton. Amherst: University of Massachusetts Press.

Gafney, Wilda C. 2013. "It Does Matter if You're Black or White, Too-Black or Too-White, But Mestizo Is Just Right." Pages 43–52 in *Jewish And Black Biblical Interpretation*. Edited by David Nelson and Rivka Ulmer. River Road, NJ: Gorgias.

———. 2017. *Womanist Midrash: A Reintroduction to the Women of the Torah and the Throne*. Louisville: Westminster John Knox.

Goldberg, David T. 1993. *Racist Culture: Philosophy and the Politics of Meaning*. Cambridge: Blackwell.

González Holguín, Julián Andrés. 2015. "Lev. 24:10–23: An Outsider Perspective." *HS* 56:89–102.

———. 2018. *Cain, Abel, and the Politics of God: An Agambenian Reading of Genesis 4:1–16*. New York: Routledge.

———. 2021. "Painted Eroticism: Sex and Death in Cain and Abel's Story." *BibInt* 29:1–24.

Hall, Stuart. 2000. "The Multi-cultural Question." Pages 209–41 in *Un/settled Multiculturalisms: Disporas, Entanglements, Transruptions*. Edited by Barnor Hesse. London: Zed.

Heschel, Susannah. 1998. *Abraham Geiger and the Jewish Jesus*. Chicago: University of Chicago Press.

Kelley, Shawn. 2002. *Racializing Jesus: Race, Ideology and the Formation of Modern Biblical Scholarship*. New York: Routledge.

Laytner, Arson. 1990. *Arguing with God: A Jewish Tradition*. Northvale, NJ: Aronson.

Levenson, Jon. 2000. "Liberation Theology and the Exodus." Pages 215–30 in *Jews, Christians, and the Theology of the Hebrew Scriptures*. Edited by Alice Ogden Bellis and Joel Kaminsky. Atlanta: Society of Biblical Literature.

Lim, Swee Hong. 2017. "What Is the Right Kind of Worship … if You Want North American Congregations to Sing Global Songs?" *GFACF* 5:48–57. https://tinyurl.com/SBL03111d.

Merwin, Ted. 2018. "Sacred Texts As a Stage For Community Building." *The New York Jewish Week*, 1 May. https://tinyurl.com/SBL03111e.

Mignolo, Walter. 2005. *The Idea of Latin America*. New York: Routledge.

Pixley, Jorge V. 1987. *On Exodus: A Liberation Perspective*. Maryknoll, NY: Orbis.

Powery, Emerson B., and Rodney S. Sadler Jr. 2016. *The Genesis of Liberation: Biblical Interpretation in the Antebellum Narratives of The Enslaved*. Louisville: Westminster John Knox.

Prothero, Stephen. 2008. *Religious Literacy*. New York: HarperCollins.

Wallerstein, Immanuel. 1974–1989. *The Modern World-System*. 3 vols. New York: Academic.

Warrior, Robert Allen. 2006. "A Native American Perspective: Canaanites, Cowboys, and Indians." Pages 235–41 in *Voices from the Margin: Interpreting the Bible in the Third World*. Edited by R. S. Sugirtharajah. New York: Orbis.

Worthington, Bruce. 2015. "Introduction." Pages 3–20 in *Reading the Bible in an Age of Crisis: Political Exegesis for a New Day*. Edited by Bruce Worthington. Minneapolis: Fortress.

One Nation under God: Teaching Biblical Studies in the Era of Religious Nationalism

Sharon Jacob

> National consciousness, instead of being the all-embracing crystallization of the innermost hopes of the whole people, instead of being the immediate and most obvious result of the mobilization of the people, will be in any case only an empty shell, a crude and fragile travesty of what it might have been.
> —Frantz Fanon, "On National Culture"

Nation, as Benedict Anderson (2006, 124) reminds us, is an "imagined political community—and imagined as both limited and sovereign." Constructs of nation and nationalism rely on binary definitions that promote the supremacy of one group over and above another. Florian Bieber demonstrates the ways in which a dichotomous ideology of nation and nationalism promotes a citizenry of supremacy. Bieber (2018, 520) writes: "Nationalism is best understood as a malleable and narrow ideology, which values membership in a nation greater than other groups (i.e. based on gender, parties, or socio-economic group), seeks distinction from other nations, and strives to preserve the nation and give preference to political representation by the nation for the nation." Although Bieber makes a good point regarding the ways nationalism as a narrow ideology constructs its superiority based on gender, economics, and so on, he leaves out an important category: religion. More recently, citizenship has come to be defined by religion, thereby promoting a kind of supremacy.

In this essay I will look at the rise of religious nationalism and the redefinition of citizenship in the American and Indian contexts. As a Christian Indian immigrant living in the United States for more than twenty years, I have felt suspect in both contexts. In both contexts, my religious and racial otherness impedes my ability to fully belong to either, making me a perpetual outsider. I bring this outsider lens into the classroom when I teach New Testament texts. The use of nationalism and religious identity as lenses to interpret biblical texts helps students uncover religious supremacist thinking and deconstruct the ways in which dichotomous interpretations can otherize people and nations. I should note, however, that conversations about religious nationalism are incomplete if they do not deal with the ways racist language is used to describe those who belong to other religions.

India First

The open embrace of nationalism by some countries has led to the privileging of certain religious identities. For the purposes of this paper, I will focus on two contexts, the United States and India. Recent years have seen a deliberate push toward an India that benefits a Hindu national identity with little to no room for secularism. In his essay "Christian Indians and Sharing Cultures: Key Insights and Lessons in the Context of Indian Nationalism," Joseph Daniel (2017, 78–79) writes that "*Hindutva* seeks to define Indian culture in terms of Hindu values at the expense of India's age-old secular or pluralist values and milieu. It is highly critical of secular policies and its agenda is to make India a theocratic Hindu nation." However, we must draw a stark distinction between *hindutva* and Hinduism. *Hindutva*, as author Sudha Ramachandran (2020, 16) explains, is a political ideology that sees Indian culture through an exclusively religious lens and aims to make India a Hindu state. Hindutva was introduced by Vinayak Damodar Savarkar in his work *Hindutva: Who Is a Hindu?* A Hindu, Savarkar (1969, 84, 119, 129–31, 133–34) argues, is one who regards the subcontinent in personal terms, has descended from parents who are Hindus, and considers the land to be holy. Arvind Sharma (2002, 22), in his essay "On Hindu, Hindustan, Hinduism, and Hindutva," explicates this further, noting, "These then constitute the three 'essentials of Hindutva—a common nation (Rashtra), a common race (Jati) and a common civilization (Sanskriti).'" Race, in other words, is intertwined with nation and civilization.

Toward the end of 2019, the Indian government passed the Citizenship Amendment Act (CAA). Under the act, minorities who had experienced persecution in Pakistan, Bangladesh, and Afghanistan could be required to swear an oath of Indian citizenship. This act targeted Hindu,

Sikh, Parsi, Jain, Christian, and Buddhist religious minorities (Shankar 2020). Almost immediately, it was evident that the ruling party (also known as the Bhartiya Janata Party, or BJP) had conveniently overlooked Muslims and explicitly used religion as a political qualification. Prime Minister Narendra Modi framed it as a noble gesture that welcomed oppressed Hindus from neighboring majority Muslim nations (Shankar 2020). In similar fashion, the Trump administration prioritized the entry of Christian refugees into the United States, with Donald Trump stating, "If you were a Muslim you could come in, but if you were a Christian, it was almost impossible and the reason that was so unfair—everybody was persecuted, in all fairness—but they were chopping off the heads of everybody but more so the Christians. And I thought it was very, very unfair. So we are going to help them" (Burke 2017). The privileging of certain religious identities in both the United States and India must be analyzed in terms of race as well as religion.

Religious minorities living in India such as Christians and Muslims have never been "true Indians." Savarkar (1923, 113) argues, "Hindus are the only true Indians as their pitrbhu (fatherland) and punyabhu (holy land) are in India. Muslims and Christians, however, could not be considered Indian as their holy lands were not in India but in 'far off Arabia or Palestine.'" Indian Christians and Indian Muslims are suspect and their patriotism questioned even when they have actively participated in serving their country in freedom movements and the armed forces.

We witness a similar form of distrust and alienation within the context of the United States. Whether it is attacks on former President Barack Obama's birthright (Zurcher 2016), or Trump openly challenging the judgment of a federal judge in Indiana because he was Mexican (Wolf 2018), or blaming Asian Americans for the inappropriately termed "Chinese virus" (Donaghue 2020), the distrust and suspicion toward racialized bodies is also rooted in a narrow idea of American culture. Religious and racial minorities in both the Indian and American contexts are depicted as belonging to a fundamentally different culture that can never become a part of the national fabric. Simply put, Indian, Muslim, and Asian Americans are assumed by the way they speak, dress, eat, look, and pray to be the cultural other, no matter their origins. The categories of religion and race are often used to create perpetual outsiders in contexts where nations either overtly or covertly give predominance to one religious identity over others.

Along with the Citizenship Amendment Act (CAA), India also conducted the National Register of Citizens (NRC), which is pertinent to only Indian citizens and is used to identify and exclude noncitizens. Such censuses put forth by a nationalist government create a new category of "doubtful citizens" who have to prove their Indian citizenship (Shankar 2020). It is important to note that under the CAA and NRC, birthplaces and birthrights needed to be proven in light of the Hindu *rashtra*. Daniel (2017, 83) writes, "*Hindutva* means 'Hindu-ness'—a quality or characteristic that those who are not Hindu by religion may possess, as long as their culture and lifestyle is Hindu in form and substance. The inherent idea is that there is an innate Hindu quality in the practice of any religion once it makes its home in the Indian subcontinent." Thus, one could argue that the CAA and NRC were put in place for religious, especially Muslim, minorities to prove their Indianness or *Hinduness* over other identities. In other words, the task of creating a Hindu-supremacist *rashtra*/nation was now in motion. When the CAA and NRC are read alongside Savarkar, it is clear that these policies are about determining one's *jati* or race solely by birth certification (Sharad 2020). Hence, in India, religion and race are now so entwined that any distinction seems improbable.

Defining India as Hindu creates an unstable and revocable citizenship; next comes a populist takeover of space. The Babri Masjid (mosque) was demolished on 6 December 1992. For those minorities who witnessed this day, there was an almost immediate shift in the culture of India; this was when we came to realize our true place in what we had known to be our motherland.[1] A quick recounting will suffice: In 1992, Hindutva activists demolished the Babri Masjid, believing that it was originally the site of a Hindu temple torn down by King Barbar in 1528. As Ramachandran (2020, 16) describes it, "the Ramjanmabhoomi movement pledged to 'liberate' a site in Ayodhya in Uttar Pradesh, which it argued was where Hindu deity Ram was born. It maintained that a temple that once existed there was torn down by Mughal King Babar in 1528 A.D., who built a mosque, the Babri Masjid in its place." The aim was to reclaim Hindu roots by reestablishing sacred ground.

To certify this annexation, the Supreme Court in November 2020 handed the disputed land to Hindus for their temple: "Hindutva scored another victory in November last year, when India's Supreme Court handed the disputed Babri Masjid/Ramjanmabhoomi site in Ayodhya to

---

1. Sudha Ramachandran (2020, 17) writes, "The mosque's demolition and the horrific violence it triggered across India polarised the society and politics along communal lines."

Hindus for construction of a temple there" (Ramachandran 2020, 19). This verdict legitimized the violence that took place almost twenty-eight years earlier and furthered the marginalization of Indian Muslims. Moreover, a special court acquitted all thirty-two men and women charged with inciting the clashes that led to the mosque's destruction (Ellis-Petersen 2020). It is hard not to view these decisions as a legitimation of Hindutva ideology, support for a Hindu *rashtra*, and the demoralization of religious minorities.

One might think such events are sufficient for a new India, but these are only the early steps (Pandey and Arnimesh 2020). The next is to officially declare India a holy land for Hindus. The current government and the prime minister, who takes pride in the slogan "India First," laid the foundation for the Ram Mandir at the disputed site (BBC 2020). In a speech, Prime Minister Narendra Modi declared, "'I believe that this grand Ram temple to be built in Ayodhya, like the name of Shri Ram, will reflect the rich heritage of Indian culture. I believe it will inspire the entire humanity till eternity." He urged "attendees to chant 'Jai Siya Ram'" and said, "This chant is not just echoing in Ayodhya but in the entire world" (Shah and Khan 2020).

The temple, Modi reminded his audience, will be a sacred place that devotees, or Ram *bhakts*, from everywhere will visit. Inspired by Christian and Muslim sacred sites, India has now begun the construction of a temple that will serve as a sacred site for all Hindus. Hence, the third tenet of *hindutva* has come to fruition and is a stark reminder to minorities that our citizenship and sense of belonging are now at the mercy of a religious and racial supremacist ideology.

America First

While India under the current administration privileges one racial and religious identity, recent years in the United States have brought white Christian nationalism to the fore. Dennis McDaniel (2020) notes, "Returning America to greatness meant asserting 'Christianity' and 'Christian values' as the guiding principles of American life, rescuing them from the continual assault of modernity." Although this synonymity between Christianity and the American empire is not new, recent events demonstrate how this close relationship openly promotes a Christocentric nationalism. On 1 June 2020, peaceful protestors who were gathered in Washington, DC, to protest the police killing of George Floyd and other African Americans were tear-gassed and cleared out of the area with brutal force so that Donald Trump could pose with a Bible in front of Saint John's Episcopal Church (Warren 2020). The use of such symbolism by this administration played on race and religious supremacy. As the dominant religion in the United States, Christianity takes on the lens of the dominant race, a white lens, thereby constructing America as both a Christian and a white nation. Jason Mahn (2016, 32), in his chapter, "Unpacking Christian Privilege," explicates this point: "Being a member of a majority group allows people to ignore questions about their own identity—how it shapes them and how it confers certain advantages." Countries such as India and the United States are often blind to how the majoritarian religiosity intersects with race and caste to create a toxic environment for marginalized subjectivities.

Furthermore, Mahn (2016, 33) writes, "The assertion of 'colorblindness' results in an automatic privileging of the norm (which, with respect to race in the United States, means 'white')." Similar to colorblindness, I contend that countries such as India and the United States engage in a form of *religious blindness* that privileges dominant religious identities and fails to understand the experiences of religious minorities. While not all people belonging to the dominant Hindu or Christian religions in either of these contexts marginalize religious minorities, we must acknowledge the privilege that comes with belonging to a dominant religious identity. Peggy McIntosh (1989, 11) writes: "Privilege sometimes costs us the clarity of vision needed to see what we're doing, and how even in our resistance, we sometimes play the collaborator." Thus, when religiously dominant identities coincide with racially dominant ones, white Christian nationalism results. Mahn (2016, 37) makes this connection, noting that he has "undertaken this excursion in the problem of white privilege because of how well it aligns with the experience of being identified as a Christian in the United States today." Thus, being both Christian and white in America can lead to blindness of one's privilege.

Another aspect of religious nationalism is its reliance on a muscular definition of religion that is a conscious attempt to overshadow the ways in which Christianity and Hinduism have been viewed in the past. In her book *Jesus and John Wayne: How White Evangelicals Corrupted a Faith and Fractured a Nation*, Kristin Kobes Du Mez (2020, 4) points to the ways in which white evangelical Christianity assigns masculinity to the image of Jesus:

For evangelicals, domestic and foreign policy are two sides of the same coin. Christian nationalism—the belief that America is God's chosen nation and must be defended as such—serves as a powerful predictor of intolerance toward immigrants, racial minorities and non-Christians. It is linked to opposition of gay rights and gun control, to support for harsher punishments for criminals, to justifications for the use of excessive force against black Americans in law enforcement situations, and to traditionalist gender ideology.

Thus, nationalism built on religion and race also favors masculinity and a form of deep aggression and patriarchy. This form of white nationalist, muscular Christianity shows disdain for a Christianity that speaks of humility, loving one's neighbor, and turning the other cheek. Instead, this theology views apology as weakness and sees cruel dehumanization of the Other, even helpless immigrant children forcibly separated from their parents at the border, as strength (Gamboa 2020).

Similarly, Ram from the ancient Indian epic the *Ramayana* has also undergone a muscular transformation in recent times. Often equated with *ahimsa* and nonviolence, Hinduism deliberately eschews such benevolence under *hindutva* influence. Sikata Banerjee (2003, 168), in her essay "Gender and Nationalism: The Masculinization of Hinduism and Female Political Participation in India," points out, "This image rooted in a notion of masculinity defined by attributes such as decisiveness, aggression, muscular strength, and a willingness to engage in battle, is opposed to a notion of femininity that is defined by traits such as weakness, non-violence, compassion, and a willingness to compromise." Ram is often depicted as the Maryada Purushottam, loosely translated "ideal man." Growing up in India, I saw the figure of Ram as a humble and good man who was unafraid to make sacrifices for the good of the people. This image of Ram, a favorite in the widely read Amar Chitra Katha comics, has now become hypermasculine hero complete with a ripped male body. Banerjee (2003, 173) observes: "In BJP posters, Ram's muscles ripple as he towers over a Hindu temple protecting it against aggressors. The disengaged, androgynous, divine Ram has become a masculine Hindu warrior."

The transformation of both Jesus and Ram exemplifies how nationalism is not only about religion and race but also gender. Regrettably, as with white nationalist muscular Christianity, the Kashtriya Hindu masculine, national ideal is taking root in the Indian context. Both dismiss religious calls for nonviolence, peace, and love of neighbor. Statements such as "America First" and "India First" transmit exclusivist racial, religious, and gender preferences, leading me to wonder, How can one teach the Bible in such contexts?

Nations First: Revelation 7:9–17 and One Nation under God

Revelation 7:9–17 gestures to a national vision of divine empire where people from all the nations, tribes, and languages gather before the Lamb and cry out in one voice and in one language. Speaking in one voice signifies this imperial nation is stable, fixed, and homogeneous. Although the book of Revelation never uses the word *nationalism*, the text nevertheless articulates a nationalized vision of a sovereign empire of God.[2] John of Patmos, the author of Revelation, presents a divine empire as an alternative to Rome.[3] However, when interpreted through the lens of nationalism, this vision demonstrates the ways in which assimilation of nations is used to progress an imperial agenda.[4] Giles Deleuze and Félix Guattari (1987, 76), in their book *A Thousand Plateaus: Capitalism and Schizophrenia*, comment on the role of the kind of language in Rev 7:9–17: "Language is not made to be believed but to be obeyed, and to compel obedience." Language functions as a tool of obedience in Rev 7:9–17: it recognizes various nations but only insofar as they comply by replacing their native language with the official language.

Revelation 7:9 says: "After these things I looked, and behold, a great multitude which no one could number, of all nations, tribes, peoples, and tongues, standing before the throne and before the Lamb, clothed with white robes, with palm branches in their hands" (NKJV). This verse, when read through the lens of religious nationalism, promulgates a cultural

---

2. Anderson (2006, 124) defines a nation as "an imagined political community—and imagined as both inherently limited and sovereign."

3. Susan Garrett (1998, 469) points out in her commentary, "Some of the book's most important symbols use feminine imagery. The new Jerusalem is envisioned as 'coming down out of heaven from God, prepared as a bride adorned for her husband' (21:2). At the opposite extreme, the city of Babylon (a symbolic name for Rome) is portrayed as a whore who is 'holding in her hand a golden cup full of abominations and the impurities of her fornications.'"

4. Anderson (2006, 125) argues that a nation is imagined as a community "because, regardless of the actual inequality and exploitation that may prevail in each, the nation is always conceived as a deep, horizontal comradeship. Ultimately it is this fraternity that makes it possible, over the past two centuries, for so many millions of people, not so much to kill, as willingly to die for such limited imaginings."

assimilation of various nations through language and dress. As Håkan Ulfgard (1989, 73) interprets this vision in his book *Feast and Future: Revelation 7:9–17 and the Feast of the Tabernacles*: "The symbolic figure 144.000 is thus best understood as representing the people of God *in its totality* without racial or other distinction, and the juxtaposition of the 144.000 and the great multitude as in some way expressing the typical New Testament perspective of *already–not yet*." While I see Ulfgard's point, language and dress become the precise markers that not only set the nations apart from others but also construct them as exclusive and special in their proximity to the divine.

The emergence of nation-states speaking in the dominant language is performative of what Partha Chatterjee terms "linguistic nationalisms."[5] The unity of a nation is signified through language. In his essay "The Language of the Apocalypse," Allen Dwight Callahan (1995, 457) observes, "The author of the Apocalypse writes in the language of the eastern Roman empire, modified in a provincial dialect. Drawing lexically and syntactically on Hebrew and Aramaic its base is nevertheless the language of the dominant." Writing in the language of the dominant gestures to the political stance the author makes in his text. The desire to participate and perform the language of the empire, even with an accent, never ceases to end or be forgotten. The use of nationalism as a lens exposes the ways in which John of Patmos envisions the great multitude speaking in one voice, assimilated in body and language before the throne and the Lamb. In John's vision, the multilingual nations sing praises to the new emperor, and "they cry out in a loud voice." Although the text never explicitly states what language all these nations cry out in, the song that they sing suggests uniformity. The vision, then, is of a multilingual people transforming into a monolingual empire. Deleuze and Guattari (1987, 101) write, "The unity of language is fundamentally political. There is no mother tongue, only a power takeover by a dominant language that advances along a broad front, and at times swoops down on diverse centers simultaneously."

---

5. Describing the three models of nationalism that emerged, Partha Chatterjee (2006, 126) writes, "The second 'model' was that of the linguistic nationalisms of Europe, a model of the independent national state which henceforth became 'available for pirating.'"

The ability to speak in the language of the empire confers power, domination, and identity by "facializing" the Other.[6] Thus, enforcing an official language can be viewed as a form of facializing on a global scale. Speaking in the language of the empire is a political and racial act. To speak in the language of the empire signals not only assimilation, as noted above, but also the facialization of a multitude. The subjectivity of the nations, tribes, and people in the text of Rev 7:9–17 is brought into existence in verses 10–11, which read: "And they cried out in a loud voice: 'Salvation belongs to our God, who sits on the throne, and to the Lamb.' All the angels were standing around the throne and around the elders and the four living creatures. They fell down on their faces before the throne and worshiped God" (NIV). The faceless nations, people, and tribes gathered before the throne and the lamb, facialized through imperial language, immediately fall on their faces before the throne and worship God. Deleuze and Guattari (1987, 181) write, "The deterritorialization of the body implies a reterritorialization on the face; the decoding of the body implies an overcoding by the face." The multitude falling to their faces becomes the moment where their diverse bodies, hidden under a homogenous garb, are reterritorialized on their faces as they all shout in unison, singing praises to the throne. This moment is the culmination, where the faces of the multitude hidden before the throne are "facialized" before John of Patmos. Speaking in the language of the empire works in two ways: first, by speaking in the language of empire the empire is able to grasp the "other" by making the strange seem familiar, and second, such speaking creates aspirations of equality.

The desire to create a singular nation out of a multitude demonstrates how national belonging is often depicted as a divine right. As a result, those nations that assimilate into the vision of John of Patmos in Rev 7:9–17 are viewed as superior and therefore deserving of divine favor. Such a form of religious nationalism also invokes a form of supremacy that must be critically interrogated and deconstructed. Thus, it is important to read Rev

---

6. I draw on the term *facialization* from chapter 7 of Delueze and Guattari's book *A Thousand Plateaus*. In their chapter "Year Zero: Faciality," Deleuze and Guattari (1987, 179) connect language and face, noting, "A language is always embedded in the faces that announce its statements and ballast them in relation to the signifiers in progress and subjects concerned. Choices are guided by faces, elements organized around faces: a common grammar is never seperable from a facial education. The face is a veritable megaphone."

7:9–17 from both a historical-critical and religious nationalist lens, wary of any claims to racial and religious supremacy.

Teaching the Bible in the Era of Nationalism

Over the past few years, the world has witnessed a rise of nationalism in global contexts. Florian Bieber (2018, 519) writes, "From the election of Donald Trump to Brexit, the nationalist policies of the Japanese Prime Minister Shinzō Abe, his Indian counterpart Narendra Modi and the Turkish president Recep Tayyip Erdoğan, the success of far-right parties in Italian, German and Austrian elections in 2017 and 2018, nationalism appears to be on rise globally." Thus, my employment of religious nationalism as a hermeneutical lens to read and interpret biblical texts brings to the surface a nuanced perspective on conversations around race in classroom settings. The connection between nationalism and religion to white supremacy begins with a question on the politics of belonging. Specifically, my aim is for students learning to read and interpret biblical texts to reflect on the politics of citizenship and the meaning of belonging to certain nations over others. Such discussions often point to the strategic ways in which citizenship of certain countries is also connected to an ideology of supremacy with regard to race and economics.

Conversations around citizenship and the politics of belonging often lead to one or more students pointing to the myth of American exceptionalism and its connection to whiteness and Christianity. As a class, we then ponder the question of how one belongs to a particular nation. Since this class often takes place in the United States, we begin with the simple question of how an immigrant, a foreigner, a person belonging to another nation becomes American. The answers to this question often vary; however, in my experience the one answer that most students tend to settle on is language. In particular, students point out that learning the language, which in the case of the United States would be English, is an important first step of citizenship. Once this observation is made, we shift our attention to Rev 7:9–17, our text of the day.

Our discussion centers on language as an important identity marker that is also effectively used to discriminate native speakers from nonnative speakers. Often in our conversations, students reflect on the way accents are also used to create a sense of hierarchy. I then introduce the concept of linguistic racism (Friedland 2020) and ask my students to imagine the multitude in Rev 7:9–17 speaking Greek with an accent, and I ask how that would play into their belonging to new vision perceived by John of Patmos.[7] This leads to larger discussion around white supremacy in language and the idea that speaking in certain languages is constructed as beneficial ideologically, politically, and economically. Although the author of Revelation hopes to construct a scene of reverence and worship, our readings on postcolonial interpretations of Revelation enable us to take a nuanced approach. Conversations arise about what it means to have a national or official language and how to some extent our bodies are facialized or recognized if we speak in the language of the empire.

Speaking in the language of the empire, whether it is English, in the case of America; Hindi, in the case of India; or Greek, in the case of the book of Revelation, contributes to a linguistic assimilation. At the same time, one cannot and must not ignore the ways in which speaking the language of the empire is often used to create a hierarchy and a supremacist thinking wherein those unable to speak in the imperial language are unable to access success and belong to the empire. Nationalism as a hermeneutical lens is important because it makes students aware that politics of belonging and engaging in white systems of power often move beyond skin color. The desire to belong to a nation through language is a powerful ideological tool that contributes to white-supremacist thinking.

Conclusion

When one reads Rev 7:9–17 through the lens of religious nations, a theme of oneness and proximity to the divine emerges. The American Pledge of Allegiance, declaring we are "one nation under God," resembles the election manifesto of the Bharatiya Janata Party, which interprets Indian nationalism as "one nation, one people, and one culture."[8] In Rev 7:9–17, John of Patmos makes a similar claim: a polyglossia is to become one nation that gathers before the throne. National oneness highlights the ways in which nationalism privileges certain religious and racial identities. At the same time, this particular national identity is often divinized and is effectively at odds with any claims to inclusivity. Biblical texts, when read critically, can

---

7. I draw on this article to introduce students to the concept of linguistic racism for our discussion.

8. Banerjee (2003, 172) writes, "The manifesto goes on to interpret nationalism as based on the idea of 'one nation, one people, and one culture.' One may ask what will be the basis of this monolithic nation?"

help us become aware of religious, racial, and national supremacy. Lenses such as religious nationalism help readers become aware of the ways in which conversations of citizenship are often grounded in racial and religious supremacy, promoting and privileging the unity of oneness. Read with and through a religious nationalist lens, Rev 7:9–17 is a constant reminder that underneath the façade of oneness lies the plurality of nations, people, and languages. Beneath the white and saffron robes of a so-called national identity appears a diversity that is unified in its heterogeneity. In other words, rather than focusing on the unity presented through the singular color of clothing used to cover the diversity of the citizens living in nations, it is time to define unity not through the lens of assimilation and homogeneity but rather through the lens of heterogeneity and diversity—thus reclaiming and uncovering a national identity that embraces a unified diversity with respect to race, religion, and cultural identities.

Works Cited

Anderson, Benedict. 2006. "Imagined Communities." Pages 123–25 in *The Post-colonial Studies Reader*. Edited by Bill Ashcroft, Gareth Griffiths, and Helen Tiffin. 2nd ed. New York: Routledge.

Banerjee, Sikata. 2003. "Gender and Nationalism: The Masculinization of Hinduism and Female Political Participation in India." *WSIF* 26:167–79.

BBC. 2020. "India PM Modi Lays Foundation for Ayodhya Ram Temple amid Covid Surge." 5 August. https://tinyurl.com/SBL03111k.

Bieber, Florian. 2018. "Is Nationalism on the Rise? Assessing Global Trends." *Ethnopolitics* 17:519–40.

Burke, Daniel. 2017. "Trump Says US Will Prioritize Christian Refugees." CNN Politics, 27 January. https://tinyurl.com/SBL03111f.

Callahan, Allen Dwight. 1995. "The Language of the Apocalypse." *HTR* 88:453–70.

Chatterjee, Partha. 2006. "Nationalism as a Problem." Pages 126–27 in *The Post-colonial Studies Reader*. Edited by Bill Ashcroft, Gareth Griffiths, and Helen Tiffin. 2nd ed. New York: Routledge.

Daniel, Joseph. 2017. "Christian Indians and Sharing Cultures: Key Insights and Lessons in the Context of Indian Nationalism." *SID* 27.2:77–94.

Deleuze, Gilles, and Félix Guattari. 1987. *A Thousand Plateaus: Capitalism and Schizophrenia*. Translated by Brian Massumi. Minneapolis: University of Minnesota Press.

Donaghue, Erin. 2020. "2,120 Hate Incidents against Asian Americans Reported during the Coronavirus Pandemic." *CBS News*, 2 June. https://tinyurl.com/SBL03111g.

Du Mez, Kristin Kobes. 2020. *Jesus and John Wayne: How White Evangelicals Corrupted a Faith and Fractured a Nation*. New York: Liveright.

Ellis-Petersen, Hannah. 2020. "India's BJP Leaders Acquitted over Babri Mosque Demolition." *The Guardian*, 30 September. https://tinyurl.com/SBL03111h.

Friedland, Valerie. 2020. "The Sound of Racial Profiling: When Language Leads to Discrimination: The Problem Isn't with the Speech Itself but with the Attitudes That Interpret Speech." *Nevada Today*, 16 June. https://tinyurl.com/SBL03111i.

Gamboa, Suzanne. 2020. "Trump Administration's Child Separations a 'Moral Stain'—and a Voter Issue." *NBC News*, 22 October. https://tinyurl.com/SBL03111j.

Garrett, Susan R. 1998. "Revelation." Pages 469–74 in *Women's Bible Commentary: Expanded Edition*. Edited by Carol A. Newsom and Sharon H. Ringe. Louisville: Westminster John Knox.

Mahn, Jason A. 2016. *Becoming a Christian in Christendom: Radical Discipleship and the Way of the Cross in America's "Christian" Culture*. Minneapolis: Fortress.

McDaniel, Dennis. 2020. "US Christian Nationalism Is Far from Christianity, Authors Argue.," *National Catholic Reporter*, 15 April. https://tinyurl.com/SBL03111l.

McIntosh, Peggy. 1989. "White Privilege: Unpacking the Invisible Knapsack." *PF* (July/August): 10–12.

Pandey, Neelam, and Shankar Arnimesh. 2020. "RSS in Modi Govt in Numbers—Three of Four Ministers Are Rooted in the Sangh." *The Print*, 27 January. https://tinyurl.com/SBL03111m.

Ramachandran, Sudha. 2020. "Hindutva Violence in India: Trends and Implications." *CTTA* 12.4:15–20.

Savarkar, Vinayak Damodar. 1923. *Hindutva*. New Delhi: Bharti Sahitya Sadan.

———. 1969. *Hindutva: Who Is a Hindu?* Bombay: Veer Savarkar Prakashan.

Shah, Pankaj, and Arshad Afzal Khan. 2020. "At Bhoomi Pujan, PM Modi Likens Mandir Campaign to Freedom Movement." *Times of India*, 6 August. https://tinyurl.com/SBL03111n.

Shankar, Soumya. 2020. "India's Citizenship Law, in Tandem with National Registry, Could Make BJP's Discriminatory Targeting of Muslims Easier." *The Intercept*, 30 January. https://tinyurl.com/SBL03111o.

Sharad, Arpita. 2020. "Fearing CAA and NRC, Citizens Line Up for Birth Certificates." *Times of India*, 6 March. https://tinyurl.com/SBL03111p.

Sharma, Arvind. 2002. "On Hindu, Hindustan, Hinduism, and Hindutva." *Numen* 49:1–36.

Ulfgad, Håkan. 1989. *Feast and Future: Revelation 7:9–17 and the Feast of the Tabernacles*. Stockholm: Almqvist & Wiksell.

Warren, Michael. 2020. "Trump Risks Potential Backlash from Evangelicals with 'Tone-Deaf' Bible Photo-Op." CNN, 3 June. https://tinyurl.com/SBL03111q.

Wolf, Z. Byron. 2018. "Trump's Attacks on Judge Curiel Are Still Jarring to Read." CNN Politics, 27 February. https://tinyurl.com/SBL03111r.

Zurcher, Anthony. 2016. "The Birth of Obama 'Birther' Conspiracy." BBC News, 16 September. https://tinyurl.com/SBL03111s.

Exegeting Racism:
Before and after Hurricane Maria

Jean-Pierre Ruiz

This would have been a substantially different essay if I had simply filled in the outline I had completed before 20 September 2017. September 20 was the day Hurricane Maria made landfall in Puerto Rico as a Category 4 storm, the first Category 4 hurricane to make landfall on the island since Hurricane San Ciprian in 1932. Making landfall only weeks after Hurricane Irma had affected the island, Maria was the second most destructive hurricane to strike Puerto Rico, second only to Category 5 Hurricane Felipe Segundo in 1928. Years after Maria, the situation on the ground in Puerto Rico remained a nightmare as a result of inadequate relief and reconstruction efforts but also because of the earthquakes that began to afflict the island on 6 January 2020. Thousands of Puerto Ricans were made homeless, taking refuge in shelters from the ongoing seismic activity.

What has the situation in Puerto Rico to do with the theme of this essay? Consider this: Frances Negrón-Muntaner (2017; see also Lluveras 2017) reports that when CNN's Jake Tapper asked Senator Bernie Sanders "if he thought President Donald Trump's punishing response to hurricane-ravaged Puerto Rico had something to do with 'race or ethnicity,' Sanders hesitated a bit but ultimately said, 'We have a right to be suspect.'" Sanders could not have been any more understated about the thoroughgoing racism that has colored the policies and attitudes of the United States toward its territory from 1898 until the present day. In my contribution to this volume, I will engage in an exegesis of that racism by asking us to consider several images dating to the beginnings of the United States' colonization of Puerto Rico, images that vividly illustrate the depth and pervasiveness of that still-persistent and still-destructive racism.

Reimaging Race in Puerto Rico after 1898

"School Begins" is a cartoon that was published in *Puck*, a magazine of political satire published in the United States from 1871 to 1918. It took its name from the character in Shakespeare's comedy *A Midsummer Night's Dream*, and its motto, "What fools these mortals be," from act 2, scene 3. Drawn by Louis Dalrymple, this cartoon appeared on pages 8 and 9 of the 25 January 1899 issue, published only a few weeks after the signing of the Treaty of Paris, which formally ended the Spanish-American War. Under the terms of the treaty, Spain ceded Cuba, Guam, the Philippines, and Puerto Rico to the United States. The caption reads, "School Begins. Uncle Sam (to his new class in Civilization): Now, children, you've got to learn these lessons whether you want to or not! But just take a look at the class ahead of you, and remember that, in a little while, you will feel as glad to be here as they are!" The cartoon itself depicts Uncle Sam in a one-room schoolhouse, with four unkempt and ill-behaved children seated on a bench in front of his desk, cowering before the pointer that Uncle Sam wields threateningly as he scowls over them, his eyes bulging behind his spectacles. From left to right, the children are identified as Philippines, Hawai'i, "Porto Rico" (an older variant spelling), and Cuba. Seated behind them at individual desks—with the class ahead of them—are several rows of older children. Neatly dressed and well-behaved, they are reading quietly and undisturbed from books that are labeled Texas, California, Alaska, Arizona, and New Mexico.

Fig. 1. Louis Dalrymple, "School Begins," *Puck*, 25 January 1899.

Seated to the left of the door, isolated from the rest and drawn with a sad expression—as though being give a time-out by Uncle Sam—is a Native American, who holds what appears to be a spelling primer upside down, while an African American stands on a ladder washing the classroom window and a Chinese boy stands outside the door looking into the schoolroom.

Hawai'i is seated in the front row between the Philippines and Puerto Rico, while Alaska is seated next to Arizona among the older children on the back row, because the United States purchased Alaska from Russia in 1867, while Hawai'i was annexed to the United States in 1898. It was as a result of the devastation wrought by Hurricane San Ciriaco in August 1899 that Puerto Ricans first emigrated to Hawai'i. Unemployed men were recruited as laborers by the owners of sugarcane plantations and were transported to Hawai'i under conditions that were so awful that many sought to escape when the ships that carried them docked at intermediate ports on the way (Whalen 2005; see also López 2005). The ongoing pattern of depopulation of Puerto Rico and labor outmigration to the mainland of the United States that continues to the present day had its start at the very beginning of the United States' colonization of the island.

The cover of the book on Uncle Sam's desk reads "U.S.—First Lessons in Self Government," and the note under the book is a roster that reads, "The new class—Philippines, Cuba, Hawai'i, Porto Rico." The poster above and to the left of the door reads, "The Confederated States refused their consent to be governed; But the Union was preserved without their consent," while the blackboard reads, "The consent of the governed is a good thing in theory, but very rare in fact.—England has governed her colonies whether they consented or not. By not waiting for their consent she has greatly advanced the world's civilization.—The U.S. must govern its new territories with or without their consent until they can govern themselves."

The depiction of white Uncle Sam teaching a lesson in civilization to his newest and darkest pupils with a textbook titled *First Lessons in Self-Government* leads to the inevitable assessment question. What became of Uncle Sam's entering class of 1898 with respect to the learning goal of self-government? At the head of the class, Cuba's independence was recognized by the United States in May 1902, and the Philippines became independent on 4 July 1946. Hawai'i became the fiftieth state of the United States on 21 August 1959. Puerto Rico remains a colony of the United States, with a curious official status as an unincorporated territory of the United States. It is officially an *estado libre asociado*, a "free associated state" that is neither a state nor free to determine the nature of its association with the United States. In 1902 the Supreme Court of the United States ruled, "We are therefore of the opinion that the island of Porto Rico is a territory appurtenant and belonging to the United States, but not part of the United States within the revenue clauses of the constitution" (*Downes v. Bidwell*, 182 U.S. 244, 287; see Neuman 2015).[1] This means that after four centuries as a Spanish possession and more than a century under the control of the United States, Puerto Rico holds the sad distinction of being the world's oldest colony (Monge 1997). The status referendums that have taken place in which the population of Puerto Rico has been asked to express their preference vis-à-vis the island's status (1967, 1993, 1998, 2013, and 2017) have all been nonbinding, with the ultimate responsibility for adjudicating Puerto Rico's status in relation to the United States residing not with the people of Puerto Rico but with the United States Congress, where Puerto Rico has only one, nonvoting representative.

In *Downes v. Bidwell*, a case heard by the Supreme Court of the United States in 1902 that dealt with the question of the extent to which the provisions of the Constitution of the United States extended to Puerto Rico and its inhabitants, Associate Justice Henry Billings Brown wrote:

> It is obvious that in the annexation of outlying and distant possessions grave questions will arise from differences in habits, laws and customs of the people, and from differences of soil, climate and production, which may ... be quite unnecessary in the annexation of contiguous territory inhabited only by people of the same race, or by scattered bodies of native Indians. (*Downes v. Bidwell*, 182 U.S. 244, 287 [1902]; cited in Román 2010, 120)

Associate Justice Brown went on to opine:

> If those possessions are inhabited by alien races, differing from us in religion, customs, laws, methods of taxation and modes of thought, the

---

1. Charles R. Venator-Santiago (2017) explains, "In Downes, the court was asked to rule on the constitutionality of a tariff on goods trafficked between the island of Puerto Rico and the mainland imposed by the Foraker Act, a territorial law enacted to govern Puerto Rico in 1900. Opponents of the tariff argued it violated the Uniformity Clause of the Constitution, which barred tariffs on goods trafficked within the United States. A majority of the justices, however, concluded that Puerto Rico was not a part of the U.S. for the purposes of the Uniformity Clause and affirmed the tariff. In effect, the U.S. treated Puerto Rico as a foreign country."

administration of government and justice, according to Anglo-Saxon principles, may for a time be impossible; and the question at once arises whether large concessions ought not to be made for a time, that, ultimately, our own theories may be carried out, and the blessings of a free government under the Constitution extended to them. (*Downes v. Bidwell*, 182 U.S. 244, 287 [1902]; cited in Román 2010, 120)

Clearly, the court ruled that Puerto Rico was the sort of possession that was "inhabited by alien races, differing from us in religion, customs, laws, methods of taxation and modes of thought," so that Puerto Rican citizenship, conferred on Puerto Ricans by the Jones-Shafroth Act of 1917, amounted to second-class citizenship. To this day, doubt about the status of Puerto Ricans as citizens of the United States is pervasive. In a May 2016 poll, 41 percent of those surveyed did not believe that this was the case. Worse still, 40 percent of Hispanics living in the United States did not believe that Puerto Ricans were citizens of the United States (Frankovic 2016).

I am not an attorney, but exegeting the racism in *Downes v. Bidwell* is a no-brainer, if I may resort to a nonacademic colloquialism. So also is it a no-brainer to diagnose the egregious racism in the cartoon "School Begins." If that were not enough, though, let us take a look at two more political cartoons. The first is "Holding His End Up," which appeared in the *Philadelphia Inquirer* in 1899. The caption reads: "John Bull: 'It's really most extraordinary what training can do. Why, only the other day I

Fig. 2. "Holding His End Up," *Philadelphia Inquirer*, 1899.

thought that man unable to support himself.'" Here, as in "School Begins," there is a comparison of the incipient colonial project of the United States with British colonialism, albeit more indirect. The quotation in the caption of "Holding His End Up" is attributed to John Bull, who was a fictitious personification of the United Kingdom.

This cartoon portrays Uncle Sam as a circus strongman clad in the stars and stripes and standing on a platform with "Army and Navy" written on its base. Striking a pose with arms extended, he holds a figure identified as the Philippines in his right hand and the Ladrones Islands (the Marianas) in his left, holding up the otherwise unclothed figures by their underpants (holding *their* ends up, as it were). "Porto Rico" balances on Uncle Sam's right arm, while linking arms with Hawai'i, who is balanced on Uncle Sam's head, while linking arms with Cuba, who is balanced atop Uncle Sam's left arm. Like "School Begins," this cartoon illustrates the "white man's burden," as Rudyard Kipling's poem calls it, a responsibility to civilize the peoples they colonized who once belonged to Great Britain, handed on to the United States with the territories it acquired in 1898. In the caption, John Bull expresses admiration at how far the military prowess of the United States has come, the effects of training putting to rest his earlier worries that the United States was not strong enough to support itself. Around the platform stand figures that represent the nations of Europe, looking up with admiration at Uncle Sam's performance.

Another cartoon, this one by Victor Gilliam, is explicitly titled "The White Man's Burden (Apologies to Rudyard Kipling)." Appearing in *Judge* magazine in April 1899, this cartoon draws the connection between the colonial projects of Britain and the United States even more clearly, with John Bull leading the way up the mountain peak of civilization, overcoming the rocky obstacles of brutality, vice, superstition, ignorance, oppression, and barbarism. Uncle Sam follows his lead, and each carries on his back a wicker basket full of each nation's colonial subjects, who are depicted—as they also are in "School Begins" and "Holding His End Up"—in grotesquely and overtly racist ways. Cartoons such as these reflect views like that expressed in an 1885 article by John Fiske titled "Manifest Destiny." He writes, "The work which the English race began when it colonized North America is destined to go on until every land on the earth's surface that is not already the seat of an old civilization shall become English in its language, in its religion, in its political habits and traditions" (Wagenheim and Wagenheim 2013, 90).

Fig. 3. Victor Gilliam, "White Man's Burden," *Judge*, 1899.

Mapping and Missionizing the Colonial Other after 1898

The last image for our consideration here is not a political cartoon but a map of the island. The map is found in historian Samuel Silva Gotay's (1998, 111) important study of Protestant Christianity in Puerto Rico from 1898 to 1930, in a chapter titled "La invasion misionera protestante en 1898: Primeras trincheras" ("The Protestant Missionary Invasion in 1898: First Trenches"). The map reflects the outcome of gatherings such as a meeting that took place in New York not long after the invasion by the United States. At that meeting, representatives of several Protestant denominations gathered around a map of Puerto Rico and "prayed that God would help them to enter into Puerto Rico in such a way that there would never be any missionary conflict on the island" (Gotay 1998, 112, my translation). The map is the outcome of efforts to avoid missionary conflict by carving up the island into zones of influence for the missionary endeavors of the various denominations. Drafted during the war, it calls to mind the sort of map that would be used by military commanders to plot their strategy and to deploy their forces to different parts of the battlefield.

There was wide support for military action by the United States against Spain in its colonies. Kal Wagenheim and Olga Jiménez de Wagenheim (2013, 91) tell of how, on 4 July 1898, from the pulpit of the Central Presbyterian Church of Brooklyn, "The Rev. J. F. Carson read from the Holy Bible, 'And Joshua took the whole land, and the land rested from war.' He sermonized that 'the high, supreme business of this Republic is to end Spanish rule in America, and if to do it that it is necessary to plant the Stars and Stripes on Cuba, Puerto Rico, the Philippines, or Spain itself, America must do it.'" That same night in a Presbyterian church on Fifth Avenue in Manhattan, Rev. Robert McKenzie declared, "God is calling a new power to the front. The race of which this nation is the crown, is now divinely thrust out to take its place as a world power" (Wagenheim and Wagenheim 2013, 91–92). If a Presbyterian pastor in Brooklyn could invoke the book of Joshua in support of a biblically warranted expansionism by the United States, Puerto Ricans could be cast as latter-day Canaanites.

The US government relied on the efforts of the Protestant missionaries to Puerto Rico because, as Gotay points out, there could be no loyalty to the political institutions of the United States without the religious foundations that grounded them ideologically. In the words of a 7 March 1900 letter from the United States' commissioner of education, "education that contemplates a change in the native language [from Spanish to English] implies a change of religion [from Catholicism to Protestantism] and a complete change of the people's body of traditions" (Gotay 1998, 111, my translation). This strategy to colonize not only the bodies but the souls of Puerto Ricans to render them compliant was part and parcel of the military strategy of the United States. On 18 October 1898, the island's first military governor of the United States, General John R. Brook, commanded Jesuit Father Thomas Sherman, chaplain to the fourth regiment of Missouri Volunteers, to conduct a survey of the island's religious situation (*New York Times* 1911). He left the very next day and presented his report on 30 September. In that report, he concluded that "the state of religion in Puerto Rico is very unsatisfactory," going on to say, "The Church had been so united with the [Spanish] state and so identified with it in the eyes of the people that it shares in the hatred which the people generally feel toward the Spanish regime" (Gotay 1998, 198).

In a brief article summarizing Sherman's report, the 13 January 1899 issue of *The New York Times* reported, "Father Sherman says the people of the island are docile and kindly disposed toward Americans. He does not speak in favorable terms of the state of religion and education on the island, and says the state of morality of the people is not very good. The prevailing religion is Roman Catholic, but Father Sherman says that very few are more than Catholic in name." It should be said that Sherman's own father was Civil War Union Army General William Tecumseh Sherman (Durkin 1959). Aside from that, it seems perplexing that a Catholic priest would have strengthened the case for Protestant missionary efforts in Puerto Rico through his report at a time when anti-Catholicism was rampant in the United States, especially given his own reputation for eloquent oratory that took on the anti-Catholicism that went hand in hand with nativist antiimmigrant sentiments.

In addition to what Sherman had to say about the condition of Puerto Rican Catholicism, what Protestant missionary journals had to say about the people of Puerto Rico mirrored in words the racism portrayed in the cartoons we have considered. In a contribution to the April 1900 issue of *The Missionary Review of the World*, titled "Puerto Rico under the United States," the Reverend J. M. McElhinney (1900, 270) of Rochester, New York, writes of his arrival in Puerto Rico that "Our boat had hardly reached the dock when the flies and white-clad Puerto Ricans assailed us in about equal numbers."

He goes on to report:

> The mature Puerto Rican stands as erect as an Indian, slight in frame, thin in flesh, with large feet and small head. Being the product of the negro [sic] and the Spanish races, he has eliminated the coarseness of the one and the weakness of the other and has retained the straight nose, mild, black eye, and rich olive skin. The young men are agile and the young women well shapen and attractive. (270)

He also observes,

> Eighty-seven percent of the people are unable to read or write; sixty-five per cent are said to be of illegitimate birth.... Girls at twelve and thirteen years of age are generally wives and mothers. The little children of poor seldom wear clothing of any sort. Their food, after they are weaned, is the same as that given to mature persons. Excessive use of bananas by children under five is seen in the distended abdomen, arising from lack of proper nourishment and producing what is called the "banana stomach." ... The children have a short and cheerless childhood.... It is noticed that the children seldom sing. In fact, it is a land without songs. (270–71)

A land without songs? In Puerto Rico, nothing could be further from the truth, except perhaps under the traumatic circumstances of a neocolonial transposition of Ps 137, for "How can we sing in a land that is still not our own?"

McElhinney's colonizing gaze is relentlessly demeaning, infantilizing, and primitivizing. To him, Puerto Ricans were fallen savages, immoral and incapable of keeping their sexual instincts under control, and entirely lacking in the virtues of civilized people, unable even to provide adequate and appropriate clothing and nourishment for their children. Yet when it comes to his description of United States' Protestant missionary activity on the island, his tone takes a remarkable shift, seriously accentuating what he regards as the positive impact of that strategic initiative: "Perhaps in no other field in recent times has there been such ready response to the Macedonian cry as from Puerto Rico. The Episcopalians, Methodists, Presbyterians, Congregationalists, Baptists and Disciples have established among them one or more mission stations with services both in English and Spanish" (McElhinney 1900, 275).

As for the extent to which efforts were made to generate popular buy-in to the Protestant missionary initiative, consider the exercise called "Uncle Sam's Little Children," written by Amy Brain Taylor, published in the *Sunday School Times* on 24 January 1903 and then reprinted in the March 1915 issue of the *Missionary Review of the World* ("Uncle Sam's Little Children" 1915).[2]

To borrow a turn of phrase from Simone de Beauvoir, one is not born but rather becomes a racist. "Uncle Sam's Little Children" inculcates not only its intended objective, showing "the scope of home missions." It also very effectively inculcates racist attitudes that go hand in hand with the sort of Christianity the missionaries brought with them to Puerto Rico. Consider these verses:

> Have you ever heard of the children
> That uncle Sam can claim,
> And how we are trying to tell them
> The story of Jesus' name?
> "Of such is the kingdom of heaven,"
> Our Lord Jesus Christ has said;
> He wants not only the white ones,
> But the black, the brown and the red.

Later on, the doggerel continues:

> In the seas to the south of the homeland,
> Porto Rico and Cuba both lie;
> There are thousands of little dark children,
> "Oh, send us the Gospel!" they cry.

---

2. I am especially grateful to my colleague, theologian Carmen Nanko-Fernández, for bringing this to my attention.

The civilizing power of the gospel—in English—for which the doggerel claimed that they clamored, would bring the "thousands of little dark children" of "Porto Rico" and Cuba into the "great Shepherd's fold" and would simultaneously make them docile subjects of Uncle Sam. Of Uncle Sam's four littlest children, those adopted in 1898, "Porto Rico" and Cuba, were the responsibility of the home missions. As for "Uncle Sam's little children" in Hawai'i and the Philippines, a footnote in the *Missionary Review* explains, "The work in the Hawai'ian Islands is largely under the care of the Hawai'ian Evangelical Association ... and the work in the Philippines is under the care of the Foreign Boards" ("Uncle Sam's Little Children" 1915).

Uncle Sam Redux

There have appeared and there continue to appear overwhelming numbers of heart-rending images of post-Maria Puerto Rico in digital and print media. Yet, at least for *this* Puerto Rican living in the diaspora, the most disturbing of all is not an image of a ruined home or of people lined up to get potable water for themselves or fuel to power their generators. It is instead an image taken on 3 October 2017, just two weeks after the storm, of the president of the United States tossing rolls of paper towels into an apparently grateful and appreciative crowd. "There's a lot of love in this room," Donald Trump said (Vitali 2017). The image echoes in so many ways the images we have exegeted today, "School Begins," "Holding His End Up," and "The White Man's Burden." In the photo that most unsettles me, a latter-day Uncle Sam in every respect except for the outfit doles out goodies to a noisy horde of impoverished-but-grateful-and-enthusiastic natives.

Knowing the backstory of this carefully staged photo op makes the image even more upsetting and renders it an even more vivid example of the colonial condescension that continues to be typical of how the United States treats Puerto Rico. First of all, this president of the United States has claimed that his two favorite books are the Bible and *The Art of the Deal*. On 20 January 2017, Trump took the oath of office with his left hand resting on two Bibles—one used by Abraham Lincoln at his first inauguration in 1861, and the other given to him during childhood by his mother in 1955, a visible endorsement of the Good Book's place in the national mythology and in its most important public liturgies (McCann 2017).

Trump's 3 October photo op was staged at Calvary Chapel of Puerto Rico, an evangelical church located in Guaynabo, a municipality that is part of the San Juan metropolitan area. The church was founded by Dan Crespo, a New York–born Puerto Rican, the son of parents from the island. In the late 1990s, Crespo moved to Puerto Rico, where he planted Calvary Chapel in Caguas. Crespo has since returned to the United States as pastor of a sister church to Calvary Chapel in Rochester, New York. His moves to and from the island are typical of comings-and-goings by both Puerto Ricans born on the island and those members of the diaspora who were born on the mainland of the United States, the so-called *vaivén* (Calvary Chapel Puerto Rico n.d.). Crespo's successor, Calvary's current senior pastor, is Jason Dennett. On Calvary's website, Dennett shares:

> I came to Puerto Rico with the U.S. military, as a non-christian, [*sic*] in 1997. After having completed a personal 2 year investigation of the historical, scientific, philosophical, and prophetic evidence for the Bible, and the dedicated friendship of a Christian, I finally gave my life to Christ in August of 1998 at the age of 20. I have had the privilege of walking with Him ever since. (Calvary Chapel Puerto Rico n.d.)

A non–Puerto Rican who arrived in Puerto Rico with the armed forces of the United States and who gave his life to Christ on the island—an interesting coincidence in the light of the beginnings of the United States' involvement with Puerto Rico in 1898—Pastor Dennett now presides over a church where the preaching is in English, and Spanish speakers must use headphones to listen to the simultaneous translation, and where the website is English-only. It would have been very difficult for Trump to find a less Puerto Rican space anywhere in Puerto Rico—except perhaps for a military installation of the United States—than Calvary Chapel in which to stage his hurricane relief photo op.

Conclusion

In his 2010 Society of Biblical Literature presidential address, Vincent Wimbush (2011, 9) set the following challenge before the members of this society:

> There can be no critical interpretation worthy of the name, without coming to terms with the first contact—between the West and the rest, the West and the Others—and its perduring toxic and blinding effects and consequences. The challenge remains for this Society and all collectivities of critical interpreters in general to engage in persistent and

protracted struggle, not symbolic or obfuscating games around methods and approaches, to come to terms with the construal of the modern ideologization of language, characterized by the meta-racism that marks the relationship between Europeans and Euro-Americans and peoples of color, especially black peoples.

Taking up the challenge that Wimbush set before the Society of Biblical Literature calls for us to reckon seriously with the fact that in an 1898 sermon a Presbyterian pastor in Brooklyn invoked the book of Joshua to advocate the extension of Manifest Destiny to "plant the Stars and Stripes on Cuba, Puerto Rico, the Philippines, or Spain itself," and that in 1903 children in the United States were taught to recite,

> In the seas to the south of the homeland,
> Porto Rico and Cuba both lie;
> There are thousands of little dark children,
> "Oh, send us the Gospel!" they cry.

Far from being embarrassing artifacts of the views of only a few, views that advocated a road not chosen, they represent the scriptural underpinnings of deliberately racist policies and practices of colonial oppression that continue to take their tragic toll on the people of Puerto Rico more than a century later.

Works Cited

Calvary Chapel Puerto Rico. N.d. "About Us." https://tinyurl.com/SBL03111t.

Durkin, Joseph T., SJ. 1959. *General Sherman's Son: The Life of Thomas Ewing Sherman, S.J.* New York: Farrar, Straus & Cudahy.

Frankovic, Kathy. 2016. "Americans' Limited Awareness of Puerto Rico or Its Crisis." YouGov America, 17 May. https://tinyurl.com/SBL03111u.

Gotay, Samuel Silva. 1998. *Protestantismo y política en Puerto Rico, 1898–1930: Hacia una historia del protestantismo evangélico en Puerto Rico.* 2nd ed. San Juan: Editorial de la Universidad de Puerto Rico.

Lluveras, Lauren. 2017. "Is Racial Bias Driving Trump's Neglect of Puerto Rico?" The Conversation, 18 October. https://tinyurl.com/SBL03111v.

López, Iris. 2005. "Borinkis and Chop Suey: Puerto Rican Identity in Hawai'i, 1900 to 2000." Pages 43–67 in *The Puerto Rican Diaspora:*

Historical Perspectives. Edited by Carmen Teresa Whalen and Víctor Vásquez-Hernández. Philadelphia: Temple University Press.
McCann, Erin. 2017. "The Two Bibles Donald Trump Used at the Inauguration." *New York Times*, 18 January. https://tinyurl.com/SBL03111w.
McElhinney, J. M. 1900. "Puerto Rico under the United States." *MRW* 23 (April): 270–75. https://tinyurl.com/SBL03111x.
Monge, José Trias Monge. 1997. *Puerto Rico: The Trials of the Oldest Colony in the World*. New Haven: Yale University Press.
Negrón-Muntaner, Frances. 2017. "The Crisis in Puerto Rico Is a Racial Issue. Here's Why." *The Root*, 12 October. https://tinyurl.com/SBL03111y.
Neuman, Gerald E. 2015. *Reconsidering the Insular Cases: The Past and Future of the American Empire*. Cambridge: Harvard University Press.
New York Times. 1911. "Father Sherman in Asylum." 21 September.
Román, Ediberto. 2010. *Citizenship and Its Exclusions: A Classical, Constitutional, and Critical Race Critique*. New York: New York University Press.
"Uncle Sam's Little Children." 1915. *MRW* 38 (March): 220.
Venator-Santiago, Charles R. 2017. "Are Puerto Ricans American Citizens?" *US News & World Report*, 3 March. https://tinyurl.com/SBL03111aa.
Vitali, Ali. 2017. "Trump Throws Paper Towels to Hurricane Victims in Puerto Rico." NBC News, 3 October. https://tinyurl.com/SBL03111ab.
Wagenheim, Kal, and Olga Jiménez de Wagenheim, eds. 2013. *The Puerto Ricans: A Documentary History*. 5th ed. Princeton: Wiener.
Whalen, Carmen Teresa. 2005. "Colonialism, Citizenship, and the Making of the Puerto Rican Diaspora." Pages 7–9 in *The Puerto Rican Diaspora: Historical Perspectives*. Edited by Carmen Teresa Whalen and Víctor Vásquez-Hernández. Philadelphia: Temple University Press.
Wimbush, Vincent L. 2011. "Interpreters—Enslaving/Enslaved/Runagate." *JBL* 130:5–24.

Staying Awake: Constructing Critical Race Literacy and Reorienting Biblical Studies

Abraham Smith

Introduction

While a call for wakefulness has long appeared in African American arts and letters, the idea of staying awake is *en vogue* again (Smith 2020). In many of its recent iterations, though, the call resounds to generate the political consciousness and literacy capacity deemed necessary to create a revolution against state-sanctioned or state-supported violence against all black people. To generate that political consciousness, the hashtag #StayWoke, one of the more recognizable hashtags of the Black Lives Matter Global Network and the larger Movement for Black Lives, was developed. It appears frequently in social media, from Twitter, Tumblr, and Instagram accounts to Facebook. Furthermore, the hashtag #StayWoke appears in the title of actor/activist Jesse Williams's documentary on the Black Lives Matter movement: "#StayWoke: The Black Lives Matter Movement" (Richardson and Ragland 2018, esp. 44).[1]

---

1. By now, most of us are familiar with the origins of the slogan #BlackLivesMatter, the BlackLivesMatter Global Network, and the larger coalition known as the Movement for Black Lives. Briefly, in July 2013 and in the wake of the 2013 acquittal of neighborhood watch volunteer George Zimmerman for the 2012 vigilante shooting death of seventeen-year-old Trayvon Martin in Sanford, Florida, Alicia Garza posted on Facebook "a love letter to black people" (Ransby 2018, 5). One of Garza's friends, Patrisse Cullors (now Patrisse Khan-Cullors), then created the hashtag #BlackLivesMatter. With the aid of a social media platform built by Opal Tometi, moreover, all three women began to promote the slogan as well as to ponder how to develop a

While the exact origin of the use of the term *stay woke* is disputed, the meaning of the expression is clear. It is "a political consciousness type of being awake" (Richardson and Ragland 2018, 43). Thus staying woke means to remain vigilantly conscious or politically aware of the contradictions of US society. It means to have the consciousness and capacity to recognize the "complexity of oppression" and to know why it is so insidiously difficult to contend against (Hill 2016, xxii). It means to keep our eyes open in the fight for full equity and to recognize the embeddedness of unequal relations of power, especially in an age when so many of today's "strange fruit" (whether trans people or unarmed black and brown children, women, and men) have had their lives choked out or gunned down at the hands of the police or vigilantes.

I would argue, though, that the *capacity* to contend against the "complexity of oppression" and therefore to be awake requires a type of critical race literacy that is attuned to the shape-shifting machinations and mutations of oppression. Accordingly, with this essay, I suggest that the phrase stay woke today is particularly helpful in discussions about educational classrooms and beyond because the capacity to address the complexity of oppression demands first an awareness of the operations of that complexity, especially so in a society that still purports to be colorblind (or race-conscious-negligent). That is, any effort to address the structural inequities in our society demands first that we actually *see* them and that we

---

movement around the slogan. Not until 2014, after police officer Darren Wilson killed eighteen-year-old Michael Brown with two shots to the head and let his body lie on the street for four hours in Ferguson, Missouri, however, did the hashtag gain popularity on Twitter and Facebook, as thousands of mostly young people protested everywhere, especially in Ferguson, where protesters and the press braved the local police's use of military-grade weaponry (see Ince, Rojas, and Davis 2017, esp. 1819). From its modest beginnings with a hashtag in 2013, the Black Lives Matter movement has blossomed into an intergenerational global network with over forty chapters, with a basic set of guiding principles, and with a leadership model that eschews the traditional reliance on either "heterosexual, cisgender males" or a "singular leader" (Cooper 2015). Instead, it embraces a wider framework that also includes women, transgender people, and gays and lesbians. Still, there were other groups responding to the deaths of young blacks. From those groups along with the Black Lives Matter movement and a variety of supportive organizations, there arose then the coalition of organizations now known as the Movement for Black Lives. Thus, the Movement for Black Lives is an umbrella term that includes the Black Lives Matter movement and multiple other groups at the local and national levels.

see the actors who participate in the continuation of those inequities. So, while drawing on the Movement for Black Lives' emphasis on being politically awake as a necessary beginning point for changing society, this essay deploys some of the concepts and tools of critical race theory to enhance our capacity to see the intricacies and complexity of racism in our educational institutions.

Toward that goal, I will proceed in two steps. First, I offer a brief history of critical race theory and a lexicon of its principal concepts and tools in an effort to enhance the critical race literacies that must be known to stay awake. Second, I turn to institutional, disciplinary, and pedagogical matters related to biblical studies to consider how biblical studies' professionals might rely on such literacies to address the real and changing mutations of racism in our institutions of higher education.

Critical Race Literacies

In truth, the forces of oppression are complex. Those forces are more quotidian than they are quixotic. They are more perennial than they are peculiar. The trauma they cause to the human spirit is best described not as an exceptional puncture wound but as an everyday pummeling that dispels hope, defers dreams, and disheartens the drive of those who live daily on the undersides of society in the United States. How then do we fight such forces? One set of concepts and tools to help us understand the "complexity of oppression" is critical race theory.

History of Critical Race Theory in US Educational Institutions

What is critical race theory? How did it emerge? How did it widen its parameters to examine the educational arena as well? Critical race theory is a theoretical-political interventionist project with a distinctive heritage, heart, and hope. Its *heritage*, as noted by Cornel West (1995), emanates from precursors or pioneers such as Robert Cover and A. Leon Higginbotham Jr. The pivotal writings for the movement's foundation, though, were the provocative analyses of Derrick Bell (the first tenured African American Harvard Law School professor) and Alan Freeman (a white SUNY-Buffalo Law School professor). The former's "interest convergence" thesis showed that many of the changes in the civil rights era came because the interests of whites (needing to spare any tarnishing of the United States' international image as a place of freedom during the Cold War era) converged with the interests of African Americans (needing civil rights reforms) (Bell 1976, 1980). The latter's "narrow conception of violation" thesis stated that most of the civil rights cases settled by the liberal Warren US Supreme Court focused only on the individual intent of a perpetrator of discrimination, not on the effects or outcomes of the discrimination on the victims (Freeman 1978).

Despite its disparate threads, the distinctive *heart* of critical race theory—and what marks it as different from critical legal studies—is a spirited, engaged critique of the liberal notion that meritocracy is a neutral category unaffected by legal systems of racial privilege.[2] As such, in agreement with critical legal studies, critical race theory denies the notion of a neutral legal system (Brown and Jackson 2013, esp. 12–13). Departing from critical legal studies, however, critical race theory also critiques the notion of racism as an intentional, irrational, and individual aberration from an otherwise neutral legal system (Delgado 1991, esp. 1393–96).[3] Furthermore, the law school professors who first met at a 1989 Madison, Wisconsin, workshop to develop critical race theory measuredly opposed the liberal discourse of the civil rights movement—not the inspirational energy of the movement nor even some of the effective social gains of the movement, but the presupposition that the gaining of formal equality or the end of visible, sinister, and crude apartheid marked a new postracial moment in which race neutrality would be seen as an ideal between the extremes of white supremacy, on the one hand, and black nationalism, on the other.[4]

---

2. According to Adrienne Dixson (2018, 233), "CRT emerged as a response to the limitations of the class-only analysis by Critical Legal Scholars (CLS), who engaged a [neo-] Marxist critique of U.S. jurisprudence.... While not abandoning class as an explanatory factor, CRT scholars believed that the law played a specific role in reifying (and was often responsible for) racial subordination and inequity."

3. According to Joe Feagin (2020, 13), "[The] bigot-causes-discrimination view is, like other mainstream views, generally oriented to individual or small-group processes and does not substantially examine the deep structural foundation in which such acts of racial discrimination are regularly imbedded."

4. On those attending the workshop (including Derrick Bell, Kimberlé Crenshaw, Richard Delgado, and Patricia Williams, to name a few), see Brown and Jackson 2013, 21 n. 1; see also Delgado and Stefancic 2001, 12. On the social gains of the civil rights movement (for example, formal equality) and the role of the civil rights movement as a source of inspiration for critical race theory despite the latter's critique of the implicit liberalism that underwrote the legal foundations of the civil rights movement, see

According to West (1995, xi), the *hope* of critical race theory is to change society so that the rule of law is positioned to "serve liberation rather than domination." As such, although Bell (1992, ix), one of the principal founders of critical race theory, advocated racial realism—the idea that "racism is an integral, permanent, and indestructible component of this society"—critical race theory does not seek only to understand how white supremacy historically developed or merely how it has deployed legal discourse to subordinate distinctive outgroups historically and in contemporary contexts (Gillborn 2006, 26). Rather, the objective of critical race theory is to change "the vexed bond between law and racial power" (Crenshaw et al. 1995, xiii; see also Gillborn 2006, 26).

Furthermore, while critical race theory began as a critique of US jurisprudence, it has also influenced other fields, such as women's studies (Wing 1997), sociology (Aguirre 2000), and, for our purposes, education. According to the editors of *Critical Race Theory Matters: Education and Ideology*, the use of critical race theory in a "call ... to educational activism" ostensibly began with the work of two scholars, Gloria Ladson-Billings and William Tate (Zamudio et al. 2011, 8). The two educational theorists published a paper read at the American Educational Research Association in *Teachers College Record* in 1995 (Ladson-Billings 2017, vii). The two scholars deemed the call relevant because they recognized (1) that race was yet a "salient factor in U.S. society in general and in education in particular" and (2) that "race ... was undertheorized in education" (Dixson and Rousseau Anderson 2017, 1; see also Ladson-Billings and Tate 1995, esp. 50). As they challenged education specialists to analyze race and racism within the parameters of critical race theory, "an intellectual movement rooted in American jurisprudence scholarship," they also "challenged scholars to examine more closely the ways that seemingly race-neutral policies and practices served to reinforce and reify education in inequity" (Dixson and Rousseau Anderson 2017, 1).

The initial work of these two scholars, though, was exclusively applied to a K-12 context. In the wake of their work, others have explored higher education using the lens of critical race theory (Patton 2016, esp. 316). Using critical race theory, for example, Susan VanDeventer Iverson argues that many college and university diversity plans

---

Crenshaw et al. 1995, xiv–xv. On the basic tenets of critical race theory, see Zamudio et al. 2011, 11–40. For a projection of the next steps needed by critical race theory in a so-called postracial climate, see Cho 2009.

camouflage power differentials because the creators of such plans (mostly contracted consultants) presuppose whiteness as the norm, people of color as deficient, and diversity as a competitive market commodity (Iverson 2007). Other scholars—with an eye on the creation of a positive, healthy racial climate—deploy critical race theory to explore the presence of microaggressions (such as microassaults, microinsults, and microinvalidations) for African American or Latina/o/Latinx college and university students (Solórzano, Ceja, and Yosso 2000; Yosso et al. 2009).[5] To expose what Edward Taylor labels as "widespread historical illiteracy" (or the mistaken view that higher education has always been available and accessible for African Americans), Shaun Harper, Lori Patton, and Ontario Wooden (2009, esp. 392; see also Taylor 1999) deploy critical race theory to chart the initial denial of African American participation in higher education and then the constant progressive and regressive policies that aided or blocked African American access to higher education from the post–Civil War era on. Informed by critical race theory, Victor Ray (2019, 88) argues that college desegregation never was "a simplistic morality tale," with universities coming to repentance for the errors of their past. Instead, much remains unchanged. Many buildings still carry the name of a slaveholder. Curricula—despite the gallant effort of Native American studies, black/Africana studies, and Latinx studies programs—have remained mostly intact. Gatekeeping exams—albeit relaxed during the COVID pandemic because universities need bodies enrolled in their institutions—still underestimate potential and allow admissions committees to claim plausible deniability when they fail to admit blacks and other minorities into their programs (Ray 2019, 89–96).

---

5. Yosso et al. (2009, 664) argue that a positive racial climate features (1) "the inclusion of Students, Faculty, and Administrators of Color"; (2) "a curriculum reflecting the historical and contemporary experiences of People of Color"; (3) "programs to support the recruitment, retention, and graduation of Students of Color"; and (4) "a mission that reinforces the institution's commitment to diversity and pluralism." On microaggressions or "subtle, innocuous, preconscious, or unconscious degradations, and putdowns" that cumulatively "contribute to diminished mortality, augmented morbidity, and flattened confidence," see, for example, Pierce 1995, esp. 281. On the various types of microaggressions, see Sue et al. 2007, esp. 274. On the impact of racial microaggressions, see Ledesma and Solórzano 2013.

As we will see, moreover, the work of jurisprudence scholars and educational theorists suggests key terms and tools that must be known if we are to become literate in understanding the work of race and racism.

Mapping Key Concepts and Tools in Critical Race Theory

Presupposing that race is a social construction that has been and still is an effective force in society, critical race theory not only defines race and the racist structures through which racism operates. Critical race theory also seeks to demystify racial ideologies and to clarify the insidiousness of racism with select conceptual prisms that show the importance of antiracist activism in the fight against racism. What, then, are critical race theory's key concepts and tools?

To begin, *race* is a social construction. As critical race theory specialists Richard Delgado and Jean Stefancic (2001, 9) note, "race and races are products of social thought and relations. Not objective, inherent, or fixed, they correspond to no biological or genetic reality; rather, races are categories that society invents, manipulates, or retires when convenient." Thus, notwithstanding the dizzying array of racial taxonomies proposed by race scientists from the Enlightenment to the present, racial classification still is biologically indefensible, a "cultural construction superimposed upon already selected features of human variation" (Kidd 2006, 8–10). To argue that race as a biological determinant is bankrupt, however, is not tantamount to an acceptance of "vulgar constructionism," that is, to a denial of the *performative* force of or consequences of racialized thinking (Smith 2006, 92).

Next, we must understand not just race but *racial structures* and *racism*. According to Eduardo Bonilla-Silva (2018, 8), ever since the dawn of the use of the term *race* in human history, racial structures or racial social systems have "awarded systemic privileges to Europeans (the peoples who became 'white') over non-Europeans (the peoples who became 'nonwhite')." To speak about racial structures (or a system of "social relations and practices"), though, is not to speak merely about what we may call prejudice or a psychological hostility, though such hostility may be ingredient to the larger structural forces of oppression or to what Feagin (2020, 4; see also Bonilla-Silva 2018, 8) calls "the white racial frame—the dominant racial frame that has long legitimated, rationalized, motivated, and shaped racial oppression and inequality in this country." The assumption that racism just equals bias or prejudice, though, denies the structural nature of racism and makes it an individual's blatant or latent psychological disposition to a racial group with no regard for an analysis of white privilege based on a white person's location in society.[6] Rather, *racism* is the enforcement of a social hierarchy of status, means, and goods through physical, legislative, and juridical force—that is, through a systemic infrastructure—on the basis of essentialist race classification systems (Kelley 2002, 16–17).

Furthermore, in accordance with market needs, the dominant order racializes outgroups differently over time. Thus, some critical race theorists refer to the concept of *differential racism*, namely, "the ways the dominant society racializes different minority groups at different times, in response to shifting needs such as the labor market" (Delgado and Stefancic 2001, 9–10). This is the perspective assumed by critical race theory scholar Natalia Molina (2014, 9) in her work *How Race Is Made in America*. Avoiding the pitfalls of examining racialized groups in an isolated fashion, she looks at the racialization of Mexicans in the United States in the larger relational context of other racialized groups such as African Americans, Asian Americans, and white Americans. In so doing, she shows the power of racial scripts—those enduring, recycled fictions or stereotypes (such as claims of laziness, sexual irresponsibility, or drug dependency) that the dominant order imposes on one outgroup after another for the sake of controlling an "exploitable work force" (10; see also Delgado and Stefancic 2001, 9–10).

For racism's assignment of privilege and enforcement of a racial hierarchy to be accepted, moreover, it also needs ideology. Thus, a quest for an understanding of the fundamentals of the complexity of oppression also requires a knowledge about racial ideology. *Racial ideologies* are the so-called master narratives that are used to justify or oppose the assignments of privilege through racialized structures. They are assumed as the commonsense narratives that justify whether one agrees with or contends against the racial status quo (Bonilla-Silva 2018, 9).[7]

---

6. On how prejudice or "affective dispositions may be manifest or latent," see Bonilla-Silva 2018, 7.

7. According to Richard Delgado (1989, 2413; cited in Zamudio et al. 2011, 12), a master narrative is "the bundle of presuppositions received wisdoms, and shared understandings against a background of which legal and political discourse takes place. These matters are rarely focused on. They are eyeglasses we have worn for a long

Among the racial ideologies that critical race theory demystifies, *three* are prominent. The first myth is that of meritocracy (Laughter 2013), which assumes "a level playing field," a bootstrap philosophy of success, and a view of education as "the great equalizer" (Zamudio et al. 2011, 12).

A second myth is liberalism's notion of universal equality. Liberalism promises an ideal of equality for all (i.e., every individual), but the ideal does not match the "concrete inequality" that minoritized groups have faced from the historical past and in the contemporary present (Zamudio et al. 2011, 16).[8]

The third myth is the myth of colorblindness, which "suggests that today everybody enjoys equal treatment without regard to race. The notion of colorblindness is a product of interrogating the many ways that race and racism play out in contemporary society to reproduce ongoing social inequality" (Zamudio et al. 2011, 21). Such a perspective overlooks interpersonal and institutional forms of racism because it assumes racism works as a matter of intentionality rather than impact (30).[9] It assumes that civil rights movement legislation was enough and that the removal of blatant, egregious forms of racism is all that is necessary (21). It does not

---

time.... We use them to scan and interpret the world and only rarely examine them for themselves."

8. Liberalism itself is one of the foundations of Western, capitalist societies. As it has worked in the United States, for example, liberalism has always been tied to two concerns—"individual political and property rights," with both understood as a masculinist ideal, that is, "the rights of man" (Zamudio et al. 2011, 15–16). Some scholars, such as Samuel Bowles and Herbert Gintis, would even say that "universal liberal schooling developed to prepare students not for promised expanded opportunities but for the exploitative needs of a capitalist economy. While liberal educational reformers believe that education provides a means to equalize the disparities of wealth and poverty by providing individuals with the opportunity to compete and rise to their natural potentials, the Marxist perspective of Bowles and Gintis posits that schools in fact reproduce the inequalities of the broader society. The organization of schools into a hierarchy—the instruction of some pupils in technical and operational skills, the emphasis on obedience and authority, and the reproduction of the liberal ideology designed to accommodate the capitalist economy rather than to challenge it—structures education to serve the profit imperative of capitalism rather than to serve the egalitarian purpose of the personal development of students" (Zamudio et al. 2011, 18).

9. Imani Perry and others have asked us to look beyond intent. Perry (2011, 9) argues that we must "think of race in a way that takes us beyond the notion of intent as being necessary for the existence of racial discrimination."

look at the role of earlier state-sponsored doctrines of discrimination that produced social inequality: the country's initial "'separate and unequal' doctrine" and its "'separate but equal' doctrine with its Jim Crow policies that obtained thereafter (i.e., the absence of anti-discrimination laws, state rights' claims that allowed states to exercise unequal treatment, and safety and wage law exclusions for occupations dominated by people of color such as farm workers and maids)" (27). It ignores how the GI Bill of Rights was structured as an affirmative action plan for whites (27).

Nor do proponents of a colorblind United States society consider how the wealth of whites was built up through "a history of exploitations"— whether in housing (through race-based affirmative action for whites in suburbs) or educational opportunities (such as a largely race-based allocation of educational resources in suburban schools versus urban schools, where black and Latinx students attend, and reservation schools, where Native American students attend; Zamudio et al. 2011, 27, 29). Finally, some persons actually promote an active form of "colorblind racism" designed to: (1) "obscure the privilege of whiteness," and (2) to "reverse the gains of the Civil Rights Movement by attacking race-based programs designed to provide historically oppressed groups access to social resources in general, and education in particular" (29).

Even with these concepts, the impact of racism may be difficult to detect. Thus, critical race theory often refers to three other conceptual tools that expose racism's power. One tool is *critical white studies*. The objective of white studies is not simplistically to critique white individuals. It is a critique of the white racial frame. It also calls attention to the social construction of whiteness and the value assigned to it. Indeed, one reason that some whites think they live in a colorblind society is that they do not see how historically whiteness became a property or a unit of value.[10] As this country developed, "whiteness was constructed as a precondition to claiming the rights of liberal society," whether one speaks of political rights or property rights (the latter meaning the right to possess or own land) (Zamudio et al. 2011, 33). No matter how much class works elsewhere, it has always been tied to race in the United States, and thereby race became a basis for establishing a hierarchy of people groups. Whiteness, though a construct, was naturalized as if it were an ontological thing by

---

10. According to Cheryl Harris (1993, 1731), "the law has accorded 'holders' of whiteness the same privileges and benefits accorded holders of other types of property."

which one group had value and other groups defined binarily as nonwhite (whether they were Native Americans, African Americans, or Mexicans) were deemed as inferior. Even when such groups have attained a small measure of rights, what typically follows is that laws and practices mutate to ensure the inviolability or exclusivity of the value of whiteness—as seen in the case of the racialization of Mexicans, US immigration policies, and the race-based white affirmative action programs of New Deal and Fair Deal legislation (31–34).

A second tool is *intersectionality*. Intersectionality is a concept that presupposes "the multiple ways that structures of privilege and disadvantage intersect in individual lives" (Zamudio et al. 2011, 37). Thus, critical race theory advocates avoid using a "single-axis framework" that overlooks "multidimensionality," whether the multidimensionality features a "person's status identity" or the same person's "performance identity" (38).[11] Intersectionality theory also introduces strategies to avoid the microaggressions faced by those who are cornered as if their performative identities should match their status identity based on a certain marker of identity. Such strategies may include an appreciation of "funds of knowledge" or "pedagogies of the home" that minorities "learned in their homes or communities as possible forms of resistance" (39).

A third tool is *counterstory telling*. According to critical race theorists, counterstories are necessary to show the cracks in the foundations of the "sincere fictions" (Feagin 2020, 11). This is indeed what the Black Lives Matter movement and Movement for Black Lives have done. In using social media to tell a different story, they question the justice of a country in which "one in every three black male babies born in this century is expected to be incarcerated" (Stevenson 2014, 15).

Of course, counterstories may work on multiple levels, as the case of intersectionality studies has shown. So, given that initially the names of black men and boys killed by police or vigilantes received prominent

---

11. According to Delgado and Stefancic (2001, 10–11), "No person has a single, easily stated, unitary identity. A white feminist may also be Jewish or working class or a single mother. An African American activist may be male or female, gay or straight. A Latino may be a Democrat, a Republican, or even black—perhaps because that person's family hails from the Caribbean. An Asian may be a recently arrived Hmong of rural background and unfamiliar with mercantile life or a fourth-generation Chinese with a father who is a university professor and a mother who operates a business. Everyone has potentially conflicting, overlapping identities, loyalties, and allegiances."

attention without giving due attention to the black women and girls who suffered equally from state violence, the Chicago-based Black Youth Project 100 (BYP100) began to "publicize the case of Rekia Boyd after the 2015 acquittal of Dante Servin, the Chicago cop who fatally shot her in 2012" (Ransby 2018, 150). Furthermore, in association with a black feminist call for a 21 May 2015 Day of Action "to remember women and girls who had been victims of violence," a local chapter of Black Youth Project 100, one based in New York, created the hashtag #JusticeforReka and #JusticeforAllBlackWomenandGirls (Ransby 2018, 151). Likewise, Kimberlé Crenshaw (who coined the term *intersectionality*) created the hashtag #SayHerName to frame the Black Lives Matter discussion more distinctly on women and girls, such as "Sandra Bland, Rekia Boyd, Tanisha Anderson, Aiyana Stanley-Jones, and many others whose stories are often disregarded" (Richardson and Ragland 2018, 46).

Biblical Studies and Critical Race Literacies: Reorienting Institutions, Disciplines, and Classrooms Away from Whiteness

In "A Phenomenology of Whiteness," critical race theory scholar Sara Ahmed (2007, 152–55) sees whiteness as an orientation, an inheritance of proximities with other like bodies that are similarly habituated. Furthermore, in many instances, whiteness goes unmarked and becomes the invisible center from which yet other bodies then become marked as deviant (157). If we wish to denormalize this often unmarked whiteness, then, what is necessary at all levels is to perform practices that make possible what Denise Kimber Buell (2018, 151) has called "reorienting away from 'whiteness.'"

Reorienting Institutions

Ahmed (2007, 157) views institutions as "orienting devices, which take the shape of 'what' resides in them." To change these institutions, then, requires movement away from the institutionalization of whiteness or away from the orientation and normalization of spaces to white privilege. Helpful nods in that direction could be: (1) to develop bilingual websites that make institutional spaces more welcoming, (2) to reject the typical "anything but racism" mantras used to explain away the experiences of students of color (Ledesma and Calderón 2015, 214), (3) to avoid "deficit" tropes that discursively suggest that students of color are "unprepared" (215, 217),[12] (4) to admit that "normative conceptions of merit" actually falter in the face of the hard fact that whites are admitted into graduate programs of study over Asian Americans even when the latter have equal or better "standardized academic records" (216), and (5) to change the names of school buildings that quietly but horrifically sanction a racist past.[13]

Reorienting Disciplines

Reorienting away from whiteness also entails changing the disciplines of religious studies and of biblical studies. As Richard Newton (2020, 4–6) argues, multiple disciplinary canons must be changed, including the "center/periphery model" that reveled in deploying such categories as the "uncivilized" or "heathens" for those at the periphery, the so-called standard textbooks that largely promote a white male perspective on theories of religion, and a notion of Scripture that reduces the term "to specific instantiations—often Christian and biblical." Buell (2018, 153–54) insists that the whiteness of our disciplines is not just—even if at all—about the demographics in the membership of the Society of Biblical Literature. Instead, she draws on Ahmed to argue that the discipline itself is "'white' because of the 'world that is inherited, or which is already given before the point of an individual's arrival'" (Buell 2018, 154; see Ahmed 2007, 153). That world habitually often overlooks the importance of some languages, some noncanonical texts, and some methodologies, especially those methodologies that specifically mark themselves such as "feminist or Latino/a biblical interpretation" (Buell 2018, 154)—and the list could be extended.

In their critique of dominant criticism, which, in Buell's terms, could be seen as a world of whiteness, Randall C. Bailey, Tat-siong Benny Liew, and Fernando F. Segovia (2009, 26, 29, 31) also speak about the need to rupture the notion of "the objective-universal optic," expand the scope of biblical studies to include "the social-cultural frameworks of Africa or the

---

12. Such tropes smack of "culture of poverty" notions that blamed generations of poverty on behavior, not on societal structures (Lewis 1966).

13. At the University of Alabama, for example, the names of at least two buildings have been changed because those buildings were named for persons who tried to justify slavery with the Bible (as in the case of Basil Manly) or to support the notion of black inferiority with pseudoscience (Josiah Nott) (see Pinarski 2020).

religious frameworks of Hinduism and Buddhism," and interrogate criticism itself to make it more self-critical.

All of these changes could reorient the discipline away from the view that the discipline as it has historically been constructed is simply natural or normal. To the contrary, the discipline's construction as an objectivity-based discourse that then denies the value of social location thoroughgoingly whitewashes the truth that all methodologies develop out of social locations.[14]

All methods are "culturally contextualized" (Segovia 2008, 24). Form criticism depends heavily on Hermann Gunkel's importation of the Brothers Grimm German folk collection. Narrative criticism is firmly rooted in humanistic thinking and in moral psychology (Frow 1986, 228; Hunter 1983, 229). Reader-response criticism in the United States draws heavily on the ideas of individualism.[15] Wolfgang Iser's (1974) reader-response theory, in association with the Constance School of Aesthetic Reception, depends heavily on phenomenology. Sociocultural criticism, which arose hard on the heels of the civil rights era and other liberation movements that emphasized social structures of oppression and enhanced a more self-reflective consciousness, draws heavily from the social sciences and anthropology (Horsley 1994, 2). To portray the discipline thus as a disinterested study—uninterested in social location—is disingenuous. It is tantamount to a denial of the discipline's own historicization in a way that mimics some white persons' denial of their own privileged markers of whiteness.

Reorienting Classrooms

Reorienting away from whiteness also entails changing how we teach, from our curricula and cartographies to the conceptual coinage by which we speak about our subject matter. With respect to our curricula, we may need

---

14. As Wayne A. Meeks has noted, for example, "Modern NT studies marched onto the field in the train of historicism" (Meeks 2010, 60). He also avers that historicism or "the science of history was a weapon of liberation. It was bequeathed to us by those who had engaged in the hard-fought struggles of Reformation, Enlightenment, and the Modernist–Fundamentalist controversies" (2010, 60). The Protestant Reformation's *sola scriptura* (scripture alone) principle, for example, gave rise to the democratic study of Scripture and to an interest in the historical meaning of Scripture (see Baird 1992, xvi–xix).

15. That is, reader-response criticism in the United States creates a largely essentialist and unified reader while avoiding the liberation emphasis of the radical political discourses of the 1960s (see Mailloux 1989, 51–52).

wholesale changes that steer us away from a putative theory-practice divide, which appears to give prestige to the former. Rather, as Manning Marable (2005, 7) implies with regard to black/Africana studies—and the same could be applied to biblical studies—a prescriptive goal is "scholarship with collective struggle, social analysis with social transformation." Both are necessary.

Likewise, Musa Dube (2007, 125) has argued that theological studies in academic institutions needs a "curriculum transformation," that is, a transformation that would take seriously the ways in which our pedagogy perpetuates the view that some approaches—for example, "Latin American and Hispanic, Asia and Asian American, African and African American, Native American and Palestinian"—are deemed derivative or peripheral, while other approaches are deemed central. Thus, constructing syllabi that tell a counterstory about what is valuable in biblical studies—by including black queer biblical studies, womanist biblical approaches, and an unhomogenized variety of African biblical studies—reorients what is possible in the biblical studies classroom.

With respect to our cartographies, we must acknowledge that maps are conceptual instruments that organize knowledge, cultural products that assign value, and the constitutive means by which spaces are created, reified, contested, or otherwise negotiated by cartographers. Maps thus may be used to colonize, as indeed they were used to do so in the seventeenth and eighteenth centuries (Moran 2002, 168). The type of map deployed in a publication already assigns a cultural value to its type over other possible mapping traditions, where maps may be construed through cosmological mandalas (as in Hindu cultures), song lines (as among indigenous Australians), or charcoal sketches (as among Koreans and the Japanese) (Cosgrove 2005, 30). Furthermore, maps convey an implicit ideology. Clarice Martin (1989) notes, for example, the modern ideological bias of those biblical atlases that omit the "region south of Palestine and Egypt." Likewise, Randall Bailey (1991) notes that many modern maps de-Africanize what we now know as Africa by referring to "African territories" as "the Near East." Rodney Sadler argues, moreover, that the designation of "biblical lands" as "the Near East" or "the Middle East" reflects a Eurocentric orientation. He writes, "It is only from a European orientation that these imprecise designations have meaning" (Sadler 2007, 25).[16]

---

16. In agreement about such designation is Philip J. King (1983, xi), who writes, "With unbecoming provincialism, they [Western geographers] divided that vast

With respect to our conceptual coinage, our pedagogical frames must create spaces for a new linguistic currency. One way to do so is to create a larger canvas from which students may be able to integrate what they already know with the study of biblical texts. In critical race theory, this is a form of deploying "pedagogies from home" that interrogate the notion that knowledge emanates from a dominant culture. If students already know hip-hop, why not deploy hip-hop poetics—the distinction between a sample (separating an evoked musical tradition from its roots and broad thematic development) and a remix (expanding on the broad thematic development of an evoked musical tradition for the sake of relevance)—to explain the uses of the exodus tradition in the Hebrew Bible and beyond (Fentress-Williams 2010)? If students already are familiar with Latinx communities' understanding of *destino*, why not let them deploy that term to explain the divine imperative on the character Jesus in Luke's Gospel (Bordas 2012, 196)? If students already know jazz, why not allow them to describe the undisputed Pauline texts as vintage jazz Paul and the disputed Pauline texts as jazz-fusion Paul? Such turns to pedagogies from home decentralize decades-long terminologies that certify a singular (often white) currency as a norm or standard to which all other groups must concede to speak properly about biblical studies.

Conclusion

The world has seen many a philosopher or prophet who reminded others to wake up or to stay awake. There was the first-century CE seer John, whose language about a call to *metanoia* in the prophetic edicts of Revelation (2:1–3:22) and the stern call "Come out of [Babylon], my people" (18:4) may have been calls to wake up, calls to a change in consciousness lest the seven churches of the Roman province of Asia buy into the polite fictions of domination. There was nineteenth-century muckraker journalist Ida B. Wells, who frequently used wakefulness diction in her writings to shake public sentiment in the United States from its stupor with respect to the injustice and heinousness of lynching (Murry 1998, 121). There was the Rev. Dr. Martin Luther King Jr. (1986, 269), the Georgia seer who delivered his "Remaining Awake *through* a Revolution" sermon at the

---

expanse [of so-called non-Western lands] into three parts—Near, Middle, and Far East—in reference to their own perspective."

National Cathedral in Washington, DC, to rouse the US public from its slumbering contentedness, its benumbed, desensitized, and anesthetized response to the human rights revolutions that were taking place within it and all around it in the 1960s. Then came the Black Lives Matter movement and Movement for Black Lives, which have told all of us to *stay woke*. If we develop the literacy to stay awake, if we reorient biblical studies, and if we thus deliver at least some persons from self-delusional sincere fictions, we may be able to create a more just and a more equitable society for everyone—for not only the Michael Browns and the Matthew Shepards and the Mya Halls and the George Floyds and the Breonna Taylors but also for you and for me (Feagin 2020, 11).

Works Cited

Aguirre, Adalberto, Jr. 2000. "Academic Storytelling: A Critical Race Theory Story of Affirmative Action." *SP* 43:319–39.
Ahmed, Sara. 2007. "A Phenomenology of Whiteness." *FemT* 8:149–68.
Bailey, Randall C. 1991. "Beyond Identification: The Use of Africans in Old Testament Poetry and Narratives." Pages 146–84 in *Stony the Road We Trod: African American Biblical Interpretation*. Edited by Cain Hope Felder. Minneapolis: Fortress.
Bailey, Randall C., Tat-siong Benny Liew, and Fernando F. Segovia. 2009. "Introduction: Toward Minority Biblical Criticism: Framework, Contours, Dynamics." Pages 3–43 in *They Were All Together in One Place? Toward Minority Biblical Criticism*. Edited by Randall C. Bailey, Tat-siong Benny Liew, and Fernando F. Segovia. Atlanta: Society of Biblical Literature.
Baird, William. 1992. *History of New Testament Research*. Minneapolis: Fortress.
Bell, Derrick. 1976. "Serving Two Masters: Integration Ideals and Client Interests in School Desegregation Litigation." *YLJ* 85:470–517.
———. 1980. "*Brown v. Board of Education* and the Interest Convergence Dilemma." *HLR* 93:518–33.
———. 1992. *Faces at the Bottom of the Well: The Permanence of Racism*. New York: Basic Books.
Bonilla-Silva, Eduardo. 2018. *Racism without Racists: Color-Blind Racism and the Persistence of Racial Inequality in America*. 5th ed. Lanham, MD: Rowman & Littlefield.
Bordas, Juana. 2012. *Salsa, Soul, and Spirit*. San Francisco: Berrett-Koehler.

Brown, Kevin, and Darrell D. Jackson. 2013. "The History and Conceptual Elements of Critical Race Theory." Pages 9–22 in *Handbook of Critical Race Theory in Education*. Edited by Marvin Lynn and Adrienne D. Dixson. New York: Routledge.

Buell, Denise Kimber. 2018. "Anachronistic Whiteness and the Ethics of Interpretation." Pages 149–67 in *Ethnicity, Race, Religion: Identities and Ideologies in Early Jewish and Christian Texts and in Modern Interpretation*. Edited by Katherine M. Hockley and David G. Horrell. New York: Bloomsbury, 2018.

Cho, Sumi. 2009. "Post-Racialism." *ILR* 94:1589–1649.

Cooper, Brittney. 2015. "11 Major Misconceptions about the Black Lives Matter Movement." *Cosmopolitan*, 8 September. https://tinyurl.com/SBL03111ac.

Cosgrove, Denis. 2005. "Mapping/Cartography." Pages 27–33 in *Cultural Geography: A Critical Dictionary of Critical Concepts*. Edited by David Atkinson, Peter Jackson, David Sibley, and Neil Washbourne. London-Tauris.

Crenshaw, Kimberlé, Neil Gotanda, Gary Peller, and Kendall Thomas, eds. 1995. *Critical Race Theory*. New York: New York University Press.

Delgado, Richard. 1989. "Storytelling for Oppositionists and Others: A Plea for Narrative." *MLR* 87:2411–41.

———. 1991. "Review Essay (Recasting the American Race Problem): A Review of *Rethinking the American Race Problem* by Roy L. Brooks." *CLR* 79:1389–1400.

Delgado, Richard, and Jean Stefancic. 2001. *A Critical Race Theory: An Introduction*. 3rd ed. New York: New York University Press.

Dixson, Adrienne D. 2018. "'What's Going On': A Critical Race Theory Perspective on Black Lives Matter and Activism in Education." *UE* 53:231–47.

Dixson, Adrienne D., and Celia K. Rousseau Anderson. 2017. "Introduction: Critical Race Theory and Education: Singing a New Song." Pages 1–8 in *Critical Race Theory: All God's Children Got a Song*. Edited by Adrienne Dixson, Celia K. Rousseau Anderson, and Jamel K. Donnor. New York: Routledge, 2017.

Dube, Musa W. 2007. "Curriculum Transformation: Dreaming of Decolonization in Theological Studies." Pages 121–38 in *Border Crossings: Cross-Cultural Hermeneutics*. Edited by Devadasan N. Premnath. Maryknoll, NY: Orbis.

Feagin, Joe R. 2020. *The White Racial Frame: Centuries of Racial Framing and Counter-Framing*. New York: Taylor & Francis.
Fentress-Williams, Judy. 2010. "Exodus." Pages 80–88 in *The Africana Bible: Reading Scriptures from Africa and the African Diaspora*. Edited by Hugh Page Jr., Randall C. Bailey, Valerie Bridgeman, Stacy Davis, Cheryl Kirk-Duggan, Madipoane Masenya (Ngwan'a Mphahlele), Nathaniel Samuel Murrell, and Rodney S. Sadler Jr. Minneapolis: Fortress.
Freeman, Alan D. 1978. "Legitimizing Racial Discrimination through Antidiscrimination Law: A Critical Review of Supreme Court Doctrine." *MLR* 62:1049–1119.
Frow, John. 1986. "Spectacle Binding: On Character." *PT* 7:227–50.
Gillborn, David. 2006. "Critical Race Theory and Education: Racism and Anti-racism in Educational Theory and Praxis." *DSCPE* 27:11–32.
Harper, Shaun R., Lori D. Patton, and Ontario S. Wooden. 2009. "Access and Equity for African American Students in Higher Education: A Critical Race Historical Analysis of Policy Efforts." *JHE* 80:389–414.
Harris, Cheryl. 1993. "Whiteness as Property." *HLR* 106:1709–91.
Hill, Marc Lamont. 2016. *Nobody: Casualties of America's War on the Vulnerable, from Ferguson to Flint and Beyond*. New York: Atria.
Horsley, Richard A. 1994. *Sociology and the Jesus Movement*. New York: Continuum.
Hunter, Ian. 1983. "Reading Character." *SRev* 16:226–43.
Ince, Jelani, Fabio Rojas, and Clayton A. Davis. 2017. "The Social Media Response to Black Lives Matter: How Twitter Users Interact with Black Lives Matter through Hashtag Use." *ERS* 40:1814–30.
Iser, Wolfgang. 1974. *The Act of Reading: A Theory of Aesthetic Response*. Baltimore: Johns Hopkins University Press.
Iverson, Susan VanDeventer. 2007. "Camouflaging Power and Privilege: A Critical Race Analysis of University Diversity Policies." *EAQ* 43:586–611.
Kelley, Shawn. 2002. *Racializing Jesus: Race, Ideology and the Formation of Modern Biblical Scholarship*. New York: Routledge.
Kidd, Colin. 2006. *The Forging of Races: Race and Scripture in the Protestant Atlantic World, 1600–2000*. Cambridge: Cambridge University Press.
King, Martin Luther, Jr. 1986. "Remaining Awake through a Great Revolution." Pages 268–78 in *A Testament of Hope: The Essential Writings and*

Speeches of Martin Luther King, Jr. Edited by James Washington. San Francisco: Harper.

King, Philip J. 1983. *American Archaeology in the Mideast: A History of the American Schools of Oriental Research.* Philadelphia: American Schools of Oriental Research.

Ladson-Billings, Gloria. 2017. "Foreword: The Evolving Role of Critical Race Theory in Educational Scholarship." Pages vii–x in *Critical Race Theory: All God's Children Got a Song.* Edited by Adrienne Dixson, Celia K. Rousseau Anderson, and Jamel K. Donnor. New York: Routledge.

Ladson-Billings, Gloria, and William Tate. 1995. "Toward a Critical Race Theory of Education." *TCR* 97:47–68.

Laughter, Judson C. 2013. "'I Am My Brother's Keeper; I Am My Sister's Keeper': Rejecting Meritocracy and Embracing Relational Pluralism." Pages 13–24 in *Contesting the Myth of a "Post-racial" Era: The Continued Significance of Race in U.S. Education.* Edited by Dorinda J. Carter Andrews and Franklin Tuitt. New York: Lang.

Ledesma, Maria C., and Dolores Calderón. 2015. "Critical Race Theory in Education: A Review of Past Literature and a Look to the Future." *QT* 21:206–22.

Ledesma, María C., and Daniel Solórzano. 2013. "Naming Their Pain: How Everyday Racial Microaggressions Impact Students and Teachers." Pages 112–27 in *Contesting the Myth of a "Post-racial" Era: The Continued Significance of Race in U.S. Education.* Edited by Dorinda J. Carter Andrews and Franklin Tuitt. New York: Lang.

Lewis, Oscar. 1966. "The Culture of Poverty." *SAm* 215.4:19–25.

Mailloux, Stephen. 1989. *Rhetorical Power.* Ithaca, NY: Cornell University Press.

Marable, Manning. 2005. "Living Black History: Resurrecting the African-American Intellectual Tradition." Pages 3–13 in *The New Black Renaissance: The Souls Anthology of Critical African-American Studies.* Edited by Manning Marable. Boulder, CO: Paradigm.

Martin, Clarice. 1989. "A Chamberlain's Journey and the Challenge of Interpretation for Liberation." *Semeia* 47:105–35.

Meeks, Wayne A. 2005. "Why Study the New Testament?" *NTS* 51:155–70.

Molina, Natalia. 2014. *How Race Is Made in America: Immigration, Citizenship, and the Historical Power of Racial Scripts.* London: University of California Press.

Moran, Joe. 2002. *Interdisciplinarity.* London: Routledge.

Murry, Linda O. 1998. *To Keep the Waters Troubled: The Life of Ida B. Wells*. New York: Oxford University Press.

Newton, Richard. 2020. "Racial Profiling? Theorizing Essentialism, Witness, and Scripture in the Study of Religion." *RelComp* 14:1–15.

Patton, Lori D. 2016. "Disrupting Postsecondary Prose: Toward a Critical Race Theory of Higher Education." *UE* 51:315–42.

Perry, Imani. 2011. *More Beautiful and More Terrible: The Embrace and Transcendence of Racial Inequality in the United States*. New York: New York University Press.

Pierce, Chester M. 1995. "Stress Analogs of Racism and Sexism: Terrorism, Torture, and Disaster." Pages 277–93 in *Mental Health, Racism, and Sexism*. Edited by Charles V. Willie, Patricia P. Rieker, Bernard M. Kramer, and Bertram S. Brown. Pittsburgh: University of Pittsburgh Press.

Pinarski, Phil. 2020. "UA Renames Buildings Named after Former President, Slave Supporter." CBS42, 13 November. https://tinyurl.com/SBL03111ad.

Ransby, Barbara. 2018. *Making All Black Lives Matter: Reimagining Freedom in the Twenty-First Century*. Oakland: University of California Press.

Ray, Victor E. 2019. "The Still Furious Passage of the Black Graduate Student." Pages 88–103 in *Intersectionality and Higher Education: Identity and Inequality on College Campuses*. Edited by W. Carson Byrd, Rachelle J. Braun-Bevel, and Sarah M. Ovink. New Brunswick, NJ: Rutgers University Press.

Richardson, Elaine, and Alice Ragland. 2018. "#StayWoke: The Language and Literacies of the #BlackLivesMatter Movement." *CLJ* 12:27–56.

Sadler, Rodney S., Jr. 2007. "The Place and Role of Africa and African Imagery in the Bible." Pages 23–30 in *True to Our Native Land: An African American New Testament Commentary*. Edited by Brian K. Blount. Minneapolis: Fortress.

Segovia, Fernando F. 2008. "The Bible as a Text in Cultures: An Introduction." Pages 23–30 in *The Peoples' Bible*. Edited by Curtiss Paul DeYoung, Wilda C. Gafney, Leticia Guardiola-Saenz, George E. Tinker, and Frank Yamada. Minneapolis: Fortress.

Smith, Abraham. 2020. "Staying Awake: Ida B. Wells-Barnett and the Central Challenges of Ethical Leadership." Pages 82–91 in *I Wish Someone Had Told Me: Equity for Women in the Church*. Edited by Alfie Wines. Monroe, LA: Equity for Women in the Church.

Smith, Andrea. 2006. "Dismantling the Master's Tools with the Master's House: Nativist Feminist Liberation." *JFSR* 22:85–97.

Solórzano, Daniel G., Miguel Ceja, and Tara J. Yosso. 2000. "Critical Race Theory, Racial Microaggressions, and Campus Racial Climate: The Experiences of African American College Students." *JNE* 69:60–73.

Stevenson, Bryan. 2014. *Just Mercy: A Story of Justice and Redemption*. New York: Random House.

Sue, Derald W., Christina M. Capodilupo, Gina C. Torino, Jennifer M. Bucceri, Aisha M. B. Holder, Kevin L. Nadal, and Marta Esquilin. 2007. "Racial Microaggressions in Everyday Life: Implications for Clinical Practice." *AmPsych* 62:271–86.

Taylor, Edward. 1999. "Critical Race Theory and Interest Convergence in the Desegregation of Higher Education." Pages 181–204 in *Race Is … Race Isn't: Critical Race Theory and Qualitative Studies in Education*. Edited by Laurence Parker, Donna Deyhle, and Sofia Villenas. Boulder, CO: Westview.

West, Cornel. 1995. "Foreword." Pages xi–xii in *Critical Race Theory*. Edited by Kimberlé Crenshaw, Neil Gotanda, Gary Peller, and Kendall Thomas. New York: New Press.

Wing, Adrien Katherine, ed. 1997. *Critical Race Feminism: A Reader*. New York: New York University Press.

Yosso, Tara J., William A. Smith, Miguel Ceja, and Daniel G. Solórzano. 2009. "Critical Race Theory, Racial Microaggressions, and Campus Racial Climate for Latina/o Undergraduates." *HER* 79:659–90.

Zamudio, Margaret M., Caskey Russell, Francisco A. Rios, and Jacquelyn L. Bridgeman. 2011. *Critical Race Theory Matters: Education and Ideology*. New York: Routledge.

Part 2
Empowering Students

Pedagogies of Race and the Bible

Eric D. Barreto

Race is a central concern in the teaching of the Bible. That is the overarching claim of this essay. First, I will contextualize this claim in light of the larger demographic and scholarly realities of the guild of biblical studies, which is still coming to terms with the deep racialization of the discipline, the training of its scholars, and the pedagogies biblical scholars have embraced. To illustrate these realities, I will outline how readings of the story of the Ethiopian eunuch in Acts 8:26–40 reflect the pernicious racialized perspectives that biblical scholarship must now deconstruct. Next, we will focus on one particular minoritized community in order to illustrate the implications of these preliminary findings. Latinx students in the biblical studies classroom are one potent case study of how our discipline and teaching alike might be transformed and renewed by the presence, perspectives, and stories of our students.

In some ways, a claim that race is a central concern in the teaching of the Bible should seem rather uncontroversial. More and more, scholars have come to see that race is not just *a* factor among others but determinative in our discourses, our work, our shared histories, and even the very shaping of our identities as scholars, teachers, and, yes, people.[1] Much to the discipline's detriment, however, biblical scholars have lagged in recognizing this critical insight in various ways.

First, the demographics of the membership of the Society of Biblical Literature remain perniciously homogeneous, let alone the demographic makeup of professors of Bible. For comparison's sake, in terms

---

1. On race and/in theological education, see Jennings 2020. In biblical studies particularly, see inter alia Brett 1996; Buell and Johnson Hodge 2004; Byron 2002; Hockey and Horrell 2018; Kelley 2002; Nasrallah and Schüssler Fiorenza 2009; Powery and Sadler 2016; Sechrest 2010.

of the overall population of the United States, 13.4 percent are African American and 18.5 percent are Latinx, while whites make up 60.1 percent (United States Census Bureau 2020). It is important to share this data publicly and clearly. As Gallup notes, "The typical American estimates the percentages of blacks and Hispanics in this country to be more than twice as high as they actually are" (Carroll 2001). The 2016 Society of Biblical Literature Society Report notes, "Of all respondents who provided ethnicity data, 3.5 percent are multiethnic. 87.9 percent are of European descent, and 5.3 percent are of African descent. Members of Asian descent account for 5.1 percent, Latina/o descent totals 3.6 percent, and Native American, Alaska Native, or First Nation descent is 1.7 percent. Native Hawaiian or Oceanian descent is 0.2 percent" (Kutsko 2016, 26).[2] The numbers are equally sobering when looking at the professional rank of faculty members in the Association of Theological Schools in the United States and Canada. In 2016, there were a total of 3,452 full-time faculty members. Of those, 263 or 7.6 percent self-identify as black, 148 or 4.3 percent as Latinx (Association of Theological Schools in the United States and Canada 2016–2017, table 3.1). These numbers do not tell the whole story, since more than a third of minoritized faculty serve in what Association of Theological Schools labels "predominantly racial/ethnic schools" (Association of Theological Schools in the United States and Canada 2016–2017, graph 3C).[3]

These statistics only account for faculty, of course. The numbers among Association of Theological Schools students are actually quite different, with minoritized students the only growing demographic in Association of Theological Schools schools. In fact, as Juan Martínez (2014) has written in reference to the 2040 inflection point when the United States will have a majority minority population,

> that turning point might occur even sooner in the context of theological education. It is already the case that the non-white constituency in

---

2. I am left wondering whether Gallup's findings would be reflected if we asked members of the Society of Biblical Literature to estimate the racial composition of their own guild. I suspect that most members of the Society of Biblical Literature would overestimate the number of people of color within the Society of Biblical Literature's membership.

3. As a side note, I would encourage us all to remember and deploy these numbers when the inevitable lament arises from students or colleagues who decry the difficulties of the job market for white males in particular. The job market is broken, to be sure, but not in the way too many seem to assume.

many of the fastest-growing seminaries is near the 50 percent mark or even past it. And seminaries with declining enrollments tend to have proportionally larger white student populations. If the trends charted in these two studies continue, white students could account for less than 50 percent of the general seminary population sometime during the 2020s.

These massive demographic changes are not off in some distant future. They are the present for theological educators, to be sure, but also for all of us who are members of the Society of Biblical Literature.

Moreover, the guild's most widely recognized work—its members' reading, teaching, and writing about the Bible—tends to lean away from the insights of race and racism. Many biblical scholars dismiss these issues or face them on a surface level, rarely plumbing the depths of how the grammar and ideology of biblical studies are racialized through and through. Considerations about race are too rare within doctoral programs in Bible. Those who see race as a determinative factor in our work remain marginalized, but this view is one that the guild and our students need to acknowledge more than ever.

Racial animus is unavoidable in recent days, even in the biblical studies classroom. In fall 2016, I taught a course I regularly teach on Race, Ethnicity, and the New Testament. Yet another deadly encounter between a police officer and a black man sparked protests in Charlotte early in the semester. Given the content of the course, it was quite natural to discuss how this latest event intersected with our studies. But it was the result of the presidential election in November of that year that most shaped my teaching that semester. During the class session that week, we created space to hear one another mourn and worry. In particular, it was my students of color, especially women of color, who relished the recognition that their pain was a matter worthy of conversation in a seminary classroom. Let me say too that this course on race and ethnicity was not the only one in which I discussed what it meant to be in the midst of theological education after the election and what that election result revealed about our lingering racial rifts. In my Greek class, I shared with my students that the worries they might be feeling were real and welcome in my classroom. I also told them that we should continue to study this ancient language not as a distraction from the real racial questions pressing on us but because I believed (and I continue to believe) that learning Greek would prove to be a vital tool in the work of racial justice in their future ministries.

In addition, I wrote the following a few years ago in the wake of the 2015–2016 academic year, an academic year framed for me by the protests in Ferguson, Missouri, and Baltimore, which followed from more instances of police misconduct against black men.

> My own reflections on teaching #Ferguson are shaped by the new class I'm teaching at the moment. My colleague and I have two semesters to introduce Scripture, its theological import, and the wide diversity of those who have read and loved and (sometimes) misused these texts for generations.
>
> In the class, I teach Scripture in all its complexities. These texts evade easy answers and bear the most significant questions we can conjure. These texts narrate moments of liberation alongside tragedies. These texts have inspired the marginalized to speak prophetically, but these texts have also been aligned with the cruelest forms of dehumanization. In other words, these texts contain stories of hope and stories of despair. These texts have fueled liberation and oppression. How then do we learn from the insights and mistakes of the past and present? How do we help communities extend the stories of God's moving in the midst of those people who seek to follow God?
>
> I hope to teach my students that the application of Scripture to these contemporary matters is neither mechanical nor simple. But what is equally true is that these living words of God can breathe life into communities stifled by oppression. Scripture is a powerful source of imagination, an imagination for a world turned upside down.
>
> I can't avoid thinking and teaching about Ferguson and its aftermath. If our theology cannot speak in Ferguson, then I can't help but wonder if our theology is worthy of its name and, even more importantly, worthy of the God we yearn to follow. And if we teachers don't equip our students to speak in places like Ferguson and if we don't invite them to do so even now, then our pedagogies will leave us poorer as a people and a church.
>
> In short then, Ferguson is revelatory. It betrays pedagogies that are not up to the task and belies theologies merely posing as God's living word. Are we up to the task? Can we teach in such moments? We can, and we must.

And yet too much of our work and, yes, too much of our teaching does not grapple with how biblical imaginations have misshaped popular notions of race, how readings of Scripture have fed racist imagination, how our teaching has too often embodied and modeled a denial of particularity that generates racial injustice. These concerns only grew during Donald

Trump's presidency, because of its appeals to white nationalism and its widespread support by white Christians.

Therefore, let's ask: What if biblical studies and our teaching of the Bible are in need of a radical intervention? Such an intervention would not be completely novel or innovative, for a dedicated number of minoritized scholars have been drawing our attention to these questions for quite some time. Such an intervention would not be an intrusion on a field of study that has long grappled with questions of racial identity without calling them as such. Such an intervention would prove challenging to us all, for it identifies the frailties at the heart of the scholarly and pedagogical enterprises captured under the banner of the Society of Biblical Literature.

Again, race is an imperative category of analysis for biblical scholars and pedagogues of biblical literature alike. A vital implication overflows from this argument. Racism is a threat to the teaching and scholarship of the Bible, but we have yet to diagnose fully the pernicious presence of this threat.

My contention embraces two key assumptions:

1. We have been taught a lie in this culture that the source of racial injustice is the very existence of race. The concomitant distortion is that erasing particularity in various forms is the path away from racial inequities. I dispute these facile notions. The particularity of the scholar, the particularity of the biblical authors, the particularity of our students: these are not just subject matter for our study but the sites around which we might reimagine the discipline and our teaching.

2. I approach these questions as a theological educator, someone who is committed to the preparation of leaders of faith communities of many kinds. My own scholarship is committed to writing and research that enhance the work of faith communities to do the work of God's justice. I want to be clear, therefore, that my comments are not just rooted in a commitment to a particular guild. They are, to be sure, but they are also shaped by my commitments to a theological enterprise. That theological enterprise has to take seriously the fact that theological education will have to come to grips with our complicity in bringing us to this political moment. Clearly, theological educators have taught a God of fear, hopelessness, and violence. We have taught a God who preserves white normativity. At the same time, theological education has also formed prophetic leaders who are already naming the lies of power, empire, and colonialism, as well as embodying the truth of the Christian gospel. We have taught a God of grace, resurrection, and shalom. To which form of theological education will we commit? I want to continue pressing

that question from the perspective of the biblical studies classroom at a seminary.

To illustrate these arguments, I want to take two approaches. First, I will draw on a text in Acts as an example of the way racialized thinking is present in our scholarship and thus shapes our pedagogies. The story of the encounter between an unnamed eunuch of Ethiopia and Philip (Acts 8:26–40) illustrates quite well a malady at the heart of our discipline and our teaching. In various ways, scholars have named (or not), recognized (or not), exegeted (or not) the Ethiopian eunuch's complex racial and gendered identity. As I sketch the contours of this malicious problem, I hope I can also help us think about what our responses as teachers and scholars might be.

Second, I will highlight the particular opportunities and struggles scholars of the Bible confront when teaching one community of students in particular: Latinx students. Thinking about such particular students, I will point to best practices in teaching that centralize and nuance the importance of racial and ethnic identities in biblical studies. In the complex negotiation of ethnic identity we can see among Latinx students, teachers of the Bible learn something of the complex pedagogies that ought to accompany our work as biblical scholars.

On Race and Eunuchs: What Scholars Notice about Acts 8:26–40

That Luke communicates any concern about ethnicity in Acts 8:26–40 is dismissed offhand by Hans Conzelmann (1987, 68): "Luke certainly has no geographical or ethnological interest in the area." A more subtle but equally problematic example is Robert Tannehill's (1990, 109) treatment of the passage; he devotes only one sentence to the Ethiopian's ethnicity: "When told that a man was Ethiopian, people of the ancient Mediterranean world would assume that he was black, for this is the way that Ethiopians are described by Herodotus and others." Tannehill here neglects to elaborate on what importance, if any, this recognition adds to the narrative; he does not even mention what role Ethiopia might have played in an ancient person's imagination. These are just a pair of examples, excluding the commentaries that do not breathe a syllable about the black man narrated in these pages of Scripture (e.g., Kurz 2013, 145–49).

One final commentator on this pericope demonstrates well the need for a new pedagogical and scholarly approach to race in biblical studies: "A reasonable case can be made for seeing this narrative as being about the reaching of those from the parts of Africa that were at or beyond the borders of the Empire, those that were at the ends of the earth. Indeed, this story is about the reaching of these sorts of people of color apparently before the gospel comes to what we call Europe today" (Witherington 1997, 29). There is much to wonder about in this quote. In what way can we talk about borders in antiquity? In what way is the category "people of color" helpful as a notion in historical analysis of antiquity? How quickly might we elide "the borders of the Empire" with powerful political structures today? That is, how do students of this text place themselves in the narrative? Should they place themselves in the othered space of Africa and beyond the borders or at the center of the world the exegete assumes? Who exactly is the "we" at the end of this quote? Though clearly sensitive to contemporary *concerns* about race, there is insufficient analysis of the *significance* of race, such as its meaning and its historical legacies.

In contrast, African American commentators in particular have helped clarify the racial dimensions of this text. The work of Clarice Martin (1986, 1989) takes pride of place in bringing attention to the racial dimensions of this narrative. More recently, Margaret Aymer (2012, 541) contends,

> For African American readers, Acts 8 also represents a New Testament rarity: the presence and power of black-skinned people within the narratives of the New Testament. "Rarely is it admitted" in academic scholarship "that the Ethiopian eunuch is a *recognizable black African from ancient Nubia.*" This omission, no less than imperialism or patriarchy, continues to perpetuate oppressive contemporary readings of this narrative.

As Willie Jennings (2017, 83) has recently written, "[The Ethiopian eunuch's] difference is marked by his origin in Ethiopia, the outer limits of the known world, and is even signified by his blackness. His difference is also marked by his sexuality, neither unambiguously male nor female." To these interpreters dealing with race, we could well add other attempts to read the complexities of the Ethiopian eunuch's gendered identity (e.g., Burke 2013; Villalobos 2011; Wilson 2015). That is to say, even as we deal with these significant questions, we have yet to touch on intersectional concerns about gender and sexuality!

The contrast in interpretation and the situatedness of the interpreters could not be clearer. Can we imagine that attention would have been brought to bear on questions of the Ethiopian eunuch's race were it not for scholars and teachers whose very identity was reflected in the pages of the

Bible? Would an ethnically homogenous guild have reached these conclusions? Here we also must press questions about what counts as *excellence* in biblical studies. Regardless of one's methodological approach, can a reading of the Ethiopian eunuch that does not account for the racial, gendered, religious identities of this figure meet standards of excellence?

The pedagogical and scholarly questions before us are manifold and well beyond the scope of this brief essay. I would lift at least four areas of analysis in sore need of attention. First, in our teaching and research alike, we must broach questions about race and the biblical texts. In what ways did race function in antiquity? How might our analysis of ancient Judaism or Judaisms expand and be more precise if we thought along racial lines alongside notions of religion? How might the presence of racialized persons in antiquity help unearth the complexities of these ancient texts? Second, critical questions remain to be asked about race and biblical interpreters (e.g., Tupamahu 2020). In what ways have racialized ideologies pervaded the guiding assumptions and epistemologies of the discipline (e.g., Horrell 2017)?[4] Can *methods* be racist? Or is racism a problem only because of people who use the methods? Can *interpretations* be racist, or is only their impact racist? Third, these two initial sets of questions meet in queries about our pedagogical commitments. How do we teach these texts in light of both the complexities of antiquity and the traditions of scholarship that have shaped us? An article in the *New Republic* wondered whether historians have a race problem, noting the misuse of medieval historical scholarship among white-supremacist groups (Livingstone 2017). The guild of biblical studies may not be at the crosshairs of this political moment in quite the same way, but perhaps we have underestimated the ways biblical scholarship has misshaped public imaginations. After all, it has happened before, during the Third Reich (Heschel 2008).[5] Fourth, what about race and students in our classrooms? How do our contemporary questions and hopes and anxieties about racial identities shape how and why we read these texts? What exegetical legacies have shaped and misshaped the communities where these texts are read as holy writ?

---

4. Horrell's work here is a prime example of the kind of work in which white scholars might engage alongside minoritized scholars.

5. In addition, I am reminded of a display in Berlin's Topography of Terror museum in 2017, noting the ways Martin Luther's ideas and works were used in the rise of the Nazis. That exhibit included a number of well-known names in biblical studies; biblical scholars were not always on the right side of this tragic history.

These are significant questions to pursue. How we might answer them is only complicated by the wide diversity of students we teach as biblical scholars. Thus, I want to turn my attention to one specific set of students in order to illuminate a way toward a more inclusive, aware, and excellent approach to biblical studies.

Colonial Subjects? Latinx Students in Biblical Studies Classrooms

What might it mean if the first dates and places we taught in biblical studies classrooms were not Jerusalem in the year 70 CE or the Babylonian exile in the sixth century BCE? What if we centered instead the Caribbean in 1492, Havana Harbor in 1898, or even Puerto Rico in September 2017? That is to say, what might it mean to center the contemporary contexts of coloniality, the times and the places in and during which colonial powers shaped Latin America, the Caribbean, and the Latinx students learning in our classrooms? What if, as scholars and teachers, we are not required to make a choice? What if the choice between Jerusalem and San Juan, between Babylon and the borderlands, is not a binary option?

The presence, perspectives, stories, and agency of Latinx students in biblical studies classrooms can help clarify certain underlying assumptions many teachers have regarding the worth and purpose of biblical studies. In other words, even as we discern together the best pedagogical practices for Latinx students in the biblical studies classroom, we might also learn something about the discipline and the pedagogies embedded within our commitments and practices in the classroom. Specifically, biblical studies is not just a study of ancient texts, ancient peoples, ancient places, or ancient thoughts; it is an inquiry into how the pluriform diversities of today (re)construct and (re)imagine how we read the literature of the Bible in diverse contexts. That is to say, in teaching Latinx students, we might also catch a glimpse of an emerging telos for the discipline. What if Latinx students in our classrooms are colonial subjects whom we can help become critical creators of communities of transformation? What if, at the very same time, Latinx students in our classrooms can help to transform us, their teachers, to become far more aware of the coloniality of our discipline?

Prior to turning to some of the best practices I would like to highlight, I want to contextualize my own comments and the particular Latinx perspective from which they emerge. I am writing as a child of Puerto Rico. I lived there until I was nine years old and then moved to several states in my adolescence and now through my adult years. I have not lived in Puerto Rico since we first moved, but that place remains at the center of my sense of identity. The story of Puerto Ricans, however, is not identical to those stories emerging from other parts of Latin America. My comments below came from the particularity of my own journey. In light of that particularly, I highlight five pedagogical practices that foreground the concerns of Latinx students in the biblical studies classroom.

1. *Learn, acknowledge, contextualize the diversities of Latinx communities.* Among the most important assumptions that still need to be challenged is that there is *a singular* Latinx experience, that a single story covers over the breadth of culture, history, and even language that draws together Latinx communities. We are a diverse people thrust together by some parallels; we are also extraordinarily diverse. In order to teach Latinx students, therefore, it is necessary to heed their diverse stories without imposing assumptions too often voiced in the popular imagination about immigration experiences, for instance. In short, not all Latinx students, their parents, or communities are immigrants. Puerto Ricans have been citizens of the United States since 1917, and a number of Latinx communities in the borderlands literally had the border cross over them and their communities in the wake of the Mexican-American War. At the same time, stories of migration, of the loss of home, of moving from one place to another are common in these various communities even as their experiences vary.

In addition, not all Latinx students speak Spanish. Some students will not have learned Spanish formally. Some will be adept in a hybrid Spanglish. Some will come from communities that speak Portuguese. Some will have learned any of a number of indigenous languages. In short, if our teaching assumes a clear baseline of experiences that link Latinx communities, we will fall short in meeting students where they are, and instead we will fall into mere caricatures that will do more harm than good in our classrooms. No one Latinx student can represent the whole of Latinx experience. This is especially vital to remember when, in many contexts, there may only be one or a few Latinx students embodying Latinx experiences. Our teaching simply cannot expect or, worse, demand that these students do work that belongs only to the teacher. The Latinx student's job is not to volunteer to teach their classmates or to serve as an object lesson for majority-culture classmates.

2. *Learn, acknowledge, contextualize the realities of cultural hybridity.* To further add complexity to the multiplicities found with Latinx commu-

nities, teachers will also have to contend with the cultural hybridity many Latinx students will be negotiating. Some Latinx students have grown up in communities full of connections to their families' places of origin. Others may find themselves isolated in majority cultures. Both kinds of students will have had to negotiate majority-dominated spaces in order to arrive in most of our classrooms. That is to say, our students will have learned what it means to be Latinx in white-dominant spaces, and they have developed a set of practices to negotiate these various spaces. Moreover, Latinx students will also have had to negotiate their gender and/or perception of their gender, their sexuality and/or perceptions of their sexuality. Latinx students span the breadth of genders and orientations. Similarly, Latinx students span the ways race is understood and embodied in the United States in particular. Black Latinx communities will have confronted the uneven treatment with which the justice system and policing in the United States afflict black bodies. Latinx who can pass as white may have confronted questions about the authenticity of their identities. The legacies of *blanquiamento* found in many Latin American contexts have valorized whiteness and denigrated blackness among many Latinx students. Again, as teachers, we cannot make any singular assumptions about the experiences Latinx students bring to the classroom; nor can we forget that these same students have likely grown quite adept at making their way through majority-culture spaces. In sum, we may not know the depth of adaptability and pain Latinx students feel without carefully listening to them and without carefully educating ourselves about the complexity of Latinx experiences in the United States.

3. *Learn, acknowledge, contextualize the religious contexts that nourish Latinx communities.* Similarly hybrid and complex are the various religious contexts that Latinx students might bring into the classroom. The same lesson holds here. One cannot make sweeping assumptions that Latinx students will be Roman Catholic or Pentecostal or any particular Christian tradition. Here too, hybrid belief systems may be in play as Latinx students may have negotiated their way through a number of religious communities or none at all. Moreover, Latinx students may have been nurtured in communities where syncretism was embraced, where various forms of religious practice merged together in ways perhaps uncommon in majority cultures in this country. So, again, we ought not to make assumptions, or simply impose our assumptions about orthodoxy or other clear demarcations between this religious tradition and that one. I was reminded of these blurry lines with the death in 2019 of Walter Mercado, a Puerto Rican

astrologer and TV personality whose influence could be felt from Catholic to Pentecostal households, no matter what other convictions might be voiced in these traditions about astrology or even about Mercado's bold performance of gendered norms. Latinx religiosity contains multitudes. For that reason, teaching biblical studies, no matter the context, requires care as we draw all our students into critical and thoughtful reading practices around the Bible.

4. *Learn, acknowledge, contextualize the contributions of Latinx biblical scholars in the larger context of minoritized interpretation.* The first three practices have focused on the variegated needs and contexts of Latinx students. The last two turn to us, their teachers. This best practice requires some of us to do some extra reading. If we aspire to teach Latinx students, then we must become deeply conversant with Latinx biblical scholarship. We must teach the literature and not just treat it as an afterthought in the last week of a course; instead, we need to put it at the center of the courses we teach (e.g., Hidalgo 2017). I do not think there is a way around this. To be sure, the diversity of identities we will find among Latinx students may mean that these same students will likely gravitate to a variety of methods and approaches. But no matter how such students choose to approach the discipline, it will be vital in their education to hear voices that in some way echo their experiences, their cultures, and their hybrid realities. This means the need for teachers to understand that Latinx approaches are related to but not identical to Latin American approaches. This means us coming to understand the origins of Latinx biblical scholarship in the earliest work of Latinx theologies (Aponte and De La Torre 2020). This means our coming to understand the diversity of methods and approaches currently embraced by Latinx scholars. This means us grappling with a difficult reality; not all Latinx scholars are engaged in Latinx biblical scholarship. Moreover, this means our learning how readings of the Bible in nonacademic contexts precede and continue to nourish current academic approaches. Last, this means the need for teachers to contextualize Latinx biblical scholarship alongside other forms of minoritized biblical scholarship (see Bailey, Liew, and Segovia 2009). This means us teaching all our students that minoritized biblical scholarship is not a competition among minoritized groups but, at its best, is a collaborative and interwoven endeavor.

5. *Support a rising generation of Latinx scholars.* This last practice is certainly tricky in a tenuous higher education context, but I think it is a vital practice to encourage and mentor a rising generation of Latinx bibli-

cal scholars. I feel a consistent tension in the profession. On the one hand, the job market in higher education is such that it is both ethical and wise for doctoral programs to be far more judicious in how and how many students are admitted into their programs. It is also ethical and wise to be honest with students hoping to pursue doctoral education about the complex prospects we and they face. It is right to name the current crises in theological education and higher education alike. On the other hand, I worry that the first instinct of so many biblical scholars is to dissuade each and every eager student from pursuing doctoral studies. In my work with the Hispanic Theological Initiative, I see the deep need for multiplying and amplifying the voices of Latinx scholars precisely in this moment. Moreover, the high barriers to enter our particular discipline mean that students have to start learning ancient languages quite early in their education. If we dissuade every student from pursuing doctoral studies, then the membership and leadership of Society of Biblical Literature will remain perniciously homogeneous. I am not certain I know what this looks like, but I'm certain that, even in the midst of so much change in higher education, we will need many more Latinx biblical scholars in our midst. Such scholars will not emerge without careful, thoughtful, and intentional mentoring from us in our biblical studies classroom. Not every gifted student—not even every gifted Latinx student—ought to become like us in profession and vocation, but I'm left wondering how we can transform our discipline without the presence and voice of Latinx scholars in higher education and theological education, even or perhaps especially during a time of multiple crises.

In short, teachers of the Bible must come to grips with the diversities embedded within what too many assume is a homogenous Latinx context. We need to wrestle with the emotional weight of cultural hybridity. We need to learn from the diverse religious orientations Latinx students bring with them into the classroom. We need to teach the discipline fully instead of continuing to teach only the usual suspects of biblical studies. We must teach the breadth of the discipline, including Latinx biblical scholars in the context of other minoritized scholars and scholarship. And we must find a way to nurture a generation of Latinx scholars even in the midst of challenging realities in higher education.

We might summarize all these best practices around one critical insight. There is no generic, universal reader of the Bible. Similarly, no Latinx student is a generic, universal representative of a mottled community. Latinx identities are forged and earned in the midst of colonial realities. Such identities are vibrant sites of reading, of imagination, and of the making of a people. If we aim to teach students who have been nurtured by these communities, then we have no choice but to ask even more fundamental questions about the presumptions of pedagogy and scholarship in which we were nurtured and which many of us continue to practice.

There is, therefore, one critical prerequisite to these pedagogical best practices. Our pedagogies must take fully into account the colonial legacies of biblical studies as a discipline—how biblical studies has facilitated the making of colonial subjects and how biblical studies itself is a colonial subject. First, biblical studies has too often been complicit in the making of margins, in the labeling of the outsider and the powerless. From the conquest of the Americas to the rationalization of an economy of slavery, from the policing of communities of color to the separation of families at the border, the reading of the Bible has too often been a complicit partner in injustice. Equally true is that oppressed communities have also turned to these same texts with imagination, resilience, rage, and hope to imagine beyond the colonial possibilities imposed by the powerful (e.g., Bowens 2020). Too often we have been consumed by the former and neglected the latter. Thus, second, the discipline must realize more fully that biblical studies is itself a colonial subject. It is a subject of study nurtured at the heartbeat of colonial imaginations that have left the scars of conquest on bodies, landscapes, and epistemologies alike. It is insufficient to teach in our classrooms the injustices of the past; our classrooms must also peel back the embedded assumptions, the deadly epistemologies and methodologies that have not faded with time but continue to consume colonial subjects today.

As I stated in the beginning of this essay, race is an imperative category of analysis for biblical scholars and pedagogues of biblical literature alike. To analyze fully these implications will take far more work, analysis, and repair, particularly in this moment of racial foment. As both teachers and scholars, we bear significant responsibilities; even more significant may be the influence we might have through our teaching and scholarship.

Works Cited

Aponte, Edwin David, and Miguel A. De La Torre. 2020. *Introducing Latinx Theologies*. Rev. ed. Maryknoll, NY: Orbis.

Association of Theological Schools in the United States and Canada. 2016–2017. "Annual Data Tables." Association of Theological Schools: The Commission on Accrediting. https://tinyurl.com/SBL03111ae.
Aymer, Margaret. 2012. "Acts." Pages 536–46 in *Women's Bible Commentary*. 3rd ed. Edited by Carol A. Newsom, Sharon H. Ringe, and Jacqueline E. Lapsley. Louisville: Westminster John Knox.
Bailey, Randall C., Tat-Siong Benny Liew, and Fernando F. Segovia, eds. 2009. *They Were All Together in One Place? Toward Minority Biblical Criticism*. Atlanta: Society of Biblical Literature.
Bowens, Lisa M. 2020. *African American Readings of Paul: Reception, Resistance, and Transformation*. Grand Rapids: Eerdmans.
Brett, Mark G., ed. 1996. *Ethnicity and the Bible*. Leiden: Brill.
Buell, Denise Kimber, and Caroline Johnson Hodge. 2004. "The Politics of Interpretation: The Rhetoric of Race and Ethnicity in Paul." *JBL* 123:235–51.
Burke, Sean D. 2013. *Queering the Ethiopian Eunuch*. Minneapolis: Fortress.
Byron, Gay L. 2002. *Symbolic Blackness and Ethnic Difference in Early Christian Literature*. New York: Routledge.
Carroll, Joseph. 2001. "Public Overestimates U.S. Black and Hispanic Populations." Gallup, 4 June. https://tinyurl.com/SBL03111af.
Conzelmann, Hans. 1987. *Acts of the Apostles*. Translated by James Limburg, A. Thomas Kraabel, and Donald H. Juel. Edited by Eldon Jay Epp with Christopher R. Matthews. Philadelphia: Fortress.
Heschel, Susannah. 2008. *The Aryan Jesus: Christian Theologians and the Bible in Nazi Germany*. Princeton: Princeton University Press.
Hidalgo, Jacqueline M. 2018. *Latina/o/x Studies and Biblical Studies*. Leiden: Brill.
Hockey, Katherine M., and David G. Horrell, eds. 2018. *Ethnicity, Race, Religion: Identities and Ideologies in Early Jewish and Christian Texts, and in Modern Biblical Interpretation*. London: T&T Clark.
Horrell, David G. 2017. "Paul, Inclusion and Whiteness: Particularizing Interpretation." *JSNT* 40:123–47.
Jennings, Willie James. 2017. *Acts*. Louisville: Westminster John Knox.
———. 2020. *After Whiteness: An Education in Belonging*. Grand Rapids: Eerdmans.
Kelley, Shawn. 2002. *Racializing Jesus: Race, Ideology, and the Formation of Modern Biblical Scholarship*. New York: Routledge.
Kurz, William S. 2013. *Acts of the Apostles*. Grand Rapids: Baker.

Kutsko, John F. 2016. "2016 Report." Society of Biblical Literature. https://tinyurl.com/SBL03111ag.

Livingstone, Josephine. 2017. "University History Departments Have a Race Problem." *The New Republic*, 25 October. https://tinyurl.com/SBL03111ah.

Martin, Clarice. 1986. "The Function of Acts 8:26–40 within the Narrative Structure of Acts: The Significance of the Eunuch's Provenance for Acts 1:8c." PhD diss., Duke University.

———. 1989. "A Chamberlain's Journey and the Challenges of Interpretation for Liberation." *Semeia* 47:105–35.

Martínez, Juan. 2014. "It's Already 2040 at a Seminary Near You." Center for Religion and Civil Culture, 2 April. https://tinyurl.com/SBL03111ai.

Nasrallah, Laura, and Elisabeth Schüssler Fiorenza, eds. 2009. *Prejudice and Christian Beginnings: Investigating Race, Gender, and Ethnicity in Early Christian Studies*. Minneapolis: Fortress.

Powery, Emerson B., and Rodney S. Sadler Jr. 2016. *The Genesis of Liberation: Biblical Interpretation in the Antebellum Narratives of the Enslaved*. Louisville: Westminster John Knox.

Sechrest, Love L. 2010. *A Former Jew: Paul and the Dialectics of Race*. London: T&T Clark.

Tannehill, Robert. 1990. *The Narrative Unity of Luke Acts: A Literary Interpretation*. Vol. 2. Minneapolis: Fortress.

Tupamahu, Ekaputra. 2020. "The Stubborn Invisibility of Whiteness in Biblical Scholarship." Political Theology Network, 12 November. https://tinyurl.com/SBL03111aj.

United States Census Bureau. 2020. "Quick Facts, United States." https://tinyurl.com/SBL03111ak.

Villalobos, Manuel. 2011. "Bodies *Del Otro Lado* Finding Life and Hope in the Borderland: Gloria Anzaldúa, the Ethiopian Eunuch of Acts 8:26–40, *y Yo*." Pages 191–221 in *Bible Trouble: Queer Readings at the Boundaries of Biblical Scholarship*. Edited by Teresa Hornsby and Ken Stone. Atlanta: Society of Biblical Literature.

Wilson, Brittany. 2015. *Unmanly Men: Refigurations of Masculinity in Luke-Acts*. Oxford: Oxford University Press.

Witherington, Ben. 1997. *The Acts of the Apostles: A Socio-rhetorical Commentary*. Grand Rapids: Eerdmans.

Teaching Vivaldi:
Pedagogical Responses to the Work of Claude M. Steele

Greg Carey

Several years ago, the faculty at Lancaster Theological Seminary devoted its end-of-year faculty workshop to exploring Claude M. Steele's (2010) *Whistling Vivaldi: How Stereotypes Affect Us and What We Can Do*. Our school has committed itself to antiracist work within the curriculum and beyond. Like most schools that share this commitment, we know the frustration of mixed success. We have attracted more diverse students, slightly diversified our full-time regular faculty, significantly diversified our board of trustees, and measurably transformed our reading lists and course content. Students appreciate the efforts and come to our school in part because of them, yet they also report concerns about structural racism at various levels of seminary life. More pointedly, it remains the case that students who encounter various forms of academic distress are more likely to be black or brown than white. We assume the fault is institutional.

I know our situation is hardly unique.

Over the years I have invested significant formal and informal work, on my own and with my Lancaster Seminary colleagues, to becoming more effective in helping all students succeed, with particular attention to the needs of minoritized students. It matters that I am a tenured full professor who is white. This work has included lots of reading, participation in a two-year Wabash Center workshop, procuring a Wabash Center grant to bring a consultant to Lancaster Seminary, publishing occasionally on the Wabash Center blog, taking online seminars, participating in the Society of Biblical Literature's Racism and Pedagogy program unit, and participating in workshops with my Lancaster colleagues. More than any other resource I have encountered, Steele's work has inspired me to believe that I could take practical steps that would foster greater racial equity in my teaching. I have adapted Steele's insights more fully than I have any other resource. I have modest hope that these innovations have aligned my classroom teaching toward equity.

Steele's book directly addresses the struggles of minoritized students, attributing them to *stereotype threat*. Stereotype threat involves that anxiety that attends performing a task when one belongs to a group identified as having deficiencies in that area. For example, white Princeton University students who were told their success at miniature golf reflected their natural athletic ability performed less well than their white peers who did not receive that instruction. Giving the same instruction to black students had no effect on their success compared to black students who received no such instruction. What hindered black students was being informed that their golf task measured "strategic sports intelligence" (Steele 2010, 8–10).

Psychologists credit the lower performance of white students who think they are measuring natural athletic ability and the lower performance of black students—at Princeton, no less—who think they are measuring strategic sports intelligence to stereotype threat. Stereotypes into which we all are socialized tell white students they have relatively low natural athletic ability and black students they have relatively low intellectual aptitude. This is the case even for students who have proven track records of success. According to Steele, stereotype threat so heavily weighs on our minds that we perform below our capacities when it applies to us.

Steele offers several principles for countering stereotype threat, some of which I have attempted to adopt. These include (Steele 2010, 216):

- "By changing the way you give critical feedback, you can dramatically improve minority students' motivation and receptiveness."
- "By simply fostering intergroup conversations among students from different backgrounds, you can improve minority students' comfort and grades in a setting."
- "By allowing students, especially minority students, to affirm their most valued sense of self, you can improve their grades, even for a long time."
- "By helping students develop a narrative about the setting that explains their frustrations while projecting positive engagement and success in the setting, you can greatly improve their sense of belonging and achievement—which if done at a critical time could redirect the course of their lives."

Steele also discusses another principle that has proven critical to my work as a teacher: students experiencing stereotype threat benefit from teaching that emphasizes the process of learning and improving rather than a vague notion of ability. Here he draws on studies that distinguish between "incremental" theory, which sets forth learning as a process that occurs in increments, and "fixed" theory, the "either you have it or you don't" assumption concerning intelligence and ability (Steele 2010, 168). I interpret this framework to mean that "students experiencing stereotype threat best learn when learning is experienced as an incremental process everyone experiences together."

Prior to encountering Steele's work, I already framed some of my teaching according to these principles through intuition. Having read Steele, I have developed new assignments and teaching practices in order to apply these insights. I believe it is essential to set the tone for a course right from the start, literally in the first few minutes of the first class session, and then to follow through with concrete practices throughout the term.

Context is everything. Lancaster Theological Seminary is a small ecumenical school affiliated with the United Church of Christ. The school values explicit commitments to LGBTQ inclusion and to creating an antiracist learning environment. We achieve mixed success concerning our antiracism work, as one would expect from an historically white institution, but we do have concrete measures in place to support that work. The courses I will discuss here feature serious interaction with authors who represent a broad range of social positionings: when introducing a new author, I generally display their picture and provide a brief biographical sketch. Our school hosts master's degree classes in separate weekday and weekend/hybrid curricula. A typical class will have between ten and fifteen students. Our student body generally consists of just over 30 percent students of color, most of whom are black, and about 20 percent LGBTQ—categories that overlap. The average age of our master's degree students is just under forty, with clusters of younger and older students.

Setting the Tone, Part 1: Interpreting in Context

I teach three required courses at my institution, two of which I design and teach alone. The latter two are Introduction to the New Testament and Interpreting in Context. Students take Interpreting in Context during their first academic year and Intro to New Testament during their second. Interpreting in Context invites students to reflect critically concerning how the process of interpretation applies to many facets of religious leadership, from pastoral care to administration, theology to biblical interpretation. Almost never do I have more than twenty students in a class section, a factor that enhances the effectiveness of these strategies.

As soon as the time arrives to begin the first class session, I introduce the name of the class and my name, then immediately invite students into a brainstorm process. We do no introductions, through most students already know one another, and the paper syllabi remain in front of me. We do not pray. I ask students: "Suppose you walk into a hospital room as an authorized religious leader. How many actions of interpretation will you perform in just the first few minutes?" I invite students to offer only one insight at a time, and we build a list of their contributions. Routinely students begin with the individual patient and their needs and begin to account for factors such as family dynamics, race, class, and the student's own identity. Occasionally students will extend their range to account for the institutional medical setting and broader social realities. As we conclude, I share that the conversation echoes the point of the course: religious leaders frequently perform complex interpretive work; the students are already skilled at doing so; and the course aims to help them become both more self-aware and more fully equipped in interpretive resources. Ideally, the exercise fulfills several aims set forth by Steele: (1) students with diverse identities meet on common ground and learn from one another, (2) students' sense of self is affirmed as their contributions to the discussion demonstrate their competence and wisdom, and (3) learning is presented as a process in which everyone can participate and everyone benefits.

Introductions, the Syllabus, and Pass/Fail Grading

After this opening exercise, we go through the ordinary first-day-of-class rituals: an opening prayer, survey of the syllabus, and more proper introductions. During the introductions, I ask students to name one thing they think they are good at, again emphasizing the diverse competencies present in the classroom and providing an opportunity for early interaction. I point out that I do have advantages as an instructor, given that I have spent more time with the questions and resources related to our subject matter, but that in real life each person in the class has their own areas of competence, all of which may bear on our common work.

This period also involves going over the default grading setting for all the courses I teach: pass/fail. I explain that students may have good reasons for requesting letter grades and that they are entitled to receive them. I also indicate that pass/fail courses have the same standards for receiving credit that letter-graded courses have. Passing a pass/fail course is no easier than passing a course with conventional letter grades. I also explain why I prefer pass/fail grading over letter grades. I began using pass/fail grading about fifteen years ago in response to suggestions from experts in educational ministry, but Steele's work has helped me appreciate and articulate it in more helpful ways.

First, I suggest that letter grades tend to place an evaluation on students' abilities in a narrow range of skills rather than on the learning they accomplish or the competencies they demonstrate. That point allows me to promise that I value students' learning above all else. By laying this out, I aim to foster an incremental learning mindset rather than a static assessment of students' talent.

Second, I alert students that my approach to learning and assessment may differ from the ones they have experienced previously. I use the model of coaching, which is about developing students' capacities, helping them become more self-aware and building on strengths while shoring up deficits.

> Let's think about coaching. Serena Williams may be the most accomplished tennis player in history. Do we think her coach says, "Wow, Serena—great shot!"—two hundred times per practice session? More likely, her coach says things like, "Have you noticed what your opponents do when you charge the net off your backhand?" Or, "When you serve to the forehand court, why not try turning your left toe a little more outward?" Maybe her coach observes a relative weakness and sets up some drills to work on it, or maybe her coach helps her build a strategy that maximizes her strengths.

The idea of this talk is to help students visualize the difference between coaching and traditional grading. Both involve assessments of strengths and weaknesses; however, while traditional grading offers a thumbs-up versus thumbs-down assessment of a particular moment in time, coaching involves an ongoing learning process and helps students evaluate themselves.

Third, one effect of pass/fail teaching is that my comments on student work will rarely focus on how "good" students are at academic work. Instead, my comments will focus on what students have to say, what they do well, and where their work could improve. I try to begin my comments by engaging not the quality their performance but the substance of what the student has to say. I also include questions aimed to encourage the student to think more deeply about the subject, to imagine how they might follow up on the work they have already done, or to consider alternative possibilities.

Fourth, I warn students that they may wonder whether they have passed an assignment. Therefore, I assure them that if an assignment does not represent passing work, or if it barely represents passing work, I will inform them directly, and they will receive an opportunity to revise it and resubmit it. Our common focus is on learning, after all. I assure students that I am accountable for students' grades and that I record actual grades for their assignments; therefore, if a student is in jeopardy of failing the course, I will reach out to them as soon as possible. Otherwise, a student for whom I record an A will receive feedback that may look similar to that received by a student for whom I record a C.

The *Maltese Falcon* Exercise

Individual class sessions in my institution last either 130 minutes for our weekday curriculum or 180 minutes on weekends. In either case, on the first day I reserve the final 45–50 minutes for an exercise in film criticism. The exercise involves a clip from the 1941 film *The Maltese Falcon*, which is based on the 1930 novel by Dashiel Hammett. The film stars Humphrey Bogart in film noir mode, and the scene in question introduces the character of Joel Cairo, played by Peter Lorre. The scene is available for streaming via YouTube and lasts just over three minutes (Movieclips 2012).

The only characters in the scene are Cairo, Bogart's Sam Spade, and Spade's administrative assistant, Effie Perine, played by Lee Patrick. The scene does not directly address race, nor is race a primary focus of the exercise. All the characters present as white, though Joel Cairo's ethnic identity is enigmatic. Cairo speaks English with a marked but unidentifiable accent, and he carries three passports: Greek, French, and British. I often think I might look for an updated sample, one in which race or ethnicity figures more prominently, but the clip has its own advantages. Although it is a classic in the canon of American filmmaking, few students have seen it already. *The Maltese Falcon* is old enough that contemporary students will experience its cultural strangeness in important respects. A little historical and cultural criticism will come into play. Moreover, in my experience all of our students, including international students, have a fairly level playing field when performing this exercise. Lancaster Seminary's explicit commitment to affirm the sexual orientation and gender expression of all members of the community opens some freedom to discuss this scene, and sexual orientation and gender expression figure prominently in the exercise. Finally, I have enjoyed so much success with the exercise—students seem genuinely to enjoy it—that I am reluctant to try alternative material.

The exercise uses the representation of gender and sexuality on the part of Joel Cairo primarily, but also of Sam Spade, as a means of teasing out several dimensions of interpretation. The exercise demonstrates that students already possess multiple skills in critical interpretation; that a group will bring forth more insight than will single individuals; that a group can host reasonable debate concerning a cultural artifact by appealing to reasoned processes of interpretation; that interpretation invites patient, detailed attention; and that experts (in this case film critics) can contribute to our reasoning process without overpowering our own insight. In short, the exercise counters stereotype threat by inviting everyone into a critical conversation and honoring their contributions.

If we have time, I add one more layer of preparation before we view the clip. I invite students to identify one instance in which they debated a work of art—a song, film, story, painting—with someone else. I ask them to think without speaking out. Then I invite one, two, or at most three students to share their experiences. In transitioning to the film clip, I name that we participate in interpretive conversations all the time. I ask the group: "How does that kind of private conversation differ from the work of public interpretation?" Public interpretation, I suggest, involves being self-aware of our thought processes, being able to explain our judgments to persons who may not share our assumptions, and being able to understand the reasons other people provide. We might even change our minds!

First Pass

I introduce the film clip with minimal information: I identify the film and its date, note the novel it's based on, and identify it as film noir with two major actors. Then I ask students to focus on one thing: How does the scene portray Joel Cairo? What conclusions do they draw concerning him from this short scene?

After we view the scene, I invite students to identify Cairo's character traits, one student and one trait at a time, without any explanation. I inform them that we'll discuss their suggestions later, but first I will simply record the traits they name. I record the suggested traits on the board.

The next step involves drawing out students' reasons for their contributions. At this point I add another section to the board. Most student observations attend to the surface level of the scene: what characters say and do, what they wear, and so forth. These are no less valuable or important than are any other insights. For example, I might ask a student who calls Cairo "shady" to explain what Cairo does that is shady. Then the student might explain that Cairo carries three passports; another might observe that he maintains furtive eye contact; another that he speaks to his concerns indirectly. A second cluster of observations is generally shorter: it involves techniques of filmmaking such as music, lighting, camera perspective, and pacing. We specifically name the distinction between the first and second classes of observations. A third set of observations is usually the shortest, involving cultural and historical information pertinent to 1941 that might not apply today. At this point of the exercise, I help students identify that, while we may not do so with critical awareness, we routinely appeal to different kinds of evidence when we talk about interpretation. I share that being self-aware and critical in doing so is an essential part of the course, as is expanding the set of interpretive resources from which we draw.

In describing this exercise, I have so far withheld a key element. I want to receive and discuss as many student insights as possible to this point. Some disagreement is generally helpful. But I secretly hope a student will say something about the presentation of Joel Cairo's gender or sexuality. In my experience, one of three things happens: First, sometimes no one offers a comment related to gender or sexuality. When that happens, I ask whether anyone had made such an observation but chose not to share it. On the one or two occasions when that has happened, one or more students has shared that they did make such a judgment but chose not to share it with the class. We discuss that choice. Second, quite often a student will offer a judgment that draws just short of explicit reflection: they might say Cairo is weak, vain, or even effeminate. Finally, sometimes a student will just say it: "I think he's gay." That explicit judgment elicits discussion without any help from me as instructor: some students are surprised, and a few disagree. We discuss the reasons for the students' judgment. Now we're ready for our second pass with the clip.

Second Pass

At this point, our common conversation involves the presentation of Cairo's sexual orientation. I instruct students that we will watch the clip again and invite them to pay special attention to the representation of Cairo's sexuality and gender performance.

Students report that this second viewing is fun. I suspect our institution's pro-LGBTQ ethos creates space for this to be so. Students respond audibly to several clues, many of which reflect the conventions and constraints of 1941 filmmaking. Some particularly stand out to students. Before admitting Cairo to Sam Spade's office, Effie presents his business card: it smells of gardenia. Lilting music accompanies Cairo's entrance into the room. Cairo's dress is extremely formal, including opera gloves, a top hat, and a pinky ring. Some students observe that Cairo caresses his opulent umbrella handle with his lips during the scene. And, of course, Spade physically overpowers Cairo despite the fact the Cairo is holding a pistol. We list these observations and others, leaving most—but, significantly, not all—students convinced that he is represented as gay. Beyond Cairo's dress, speech, and conduct, some students also observe the effect of camera angles and pacing in the presentation of Cairo's queerness.

After we view the scene a second time, I share my own experience. I watched *The Maltese Falcon* in the late 1980s and loved it, but Cairo's sexual orientation did not cross my mind. I'd grown up in a conservative social environment in which I knew literally no one who was openly gay, lesbian, bisexual, or transgender. After all, polling shows that between 1993 and 2013, the percentage of Americans who reported having close friends or relatives who were gay or lesbian climbed from 22 percent to 65 percent (Cox, Navarro-Rivera, and Jones 2014), a massive change in social perception. It also happens to track with my own experience of watching *The Maltese Falcon* right around 2013, roughly twenty-five years after my first viewing. I relate that, in 2013, it immediately struck me that Cairo was gay. I also share that I pursued the question by reading queer film criticism, where Cairo is frequently discussed (Russo 1987, 94; Spöhrer 2016; Barrios 2003, 187–88).

I then share that, while Cairo's sexuality is not explicitly named in the 1941 film, it is explicitly named in the 1930 novel. How does that kind of background information, known in biblical studies as historical criticism, influence our assessment of Cairo?

We are now ready to discuss the work of interpretation at another level. In addition to the surface factors of speech, dress, and action, we have seen how the art of filmmaking contributes to Cairo's characterization. But now other factors are on the table. One is cultural change: if my perception of the character changed over twenty-five years, how much has changed concerning homosexuality and its representation since 1941? Some students will be aware of the "Hays Code," the conventions by which all American films sublimated sexuality, particularly queer sexuality. Many students will know that gayness was conventionally associated with effeminacy and physical weakness in 1941 and that gay men were generally regarded as untrustworthy, stereotypes that remain in play today. We discuss the role of historical and cultural awareness in interpretation, and we reflect on how the work of experts can add nuance to our interpretive work. Again, I explicitly name the capacities and insights students already bring to the conversation, including the benefits of interpreting in community.

If we have time, we watch the clip a third time.

Third Pass

The third pass reinforces the value of group conversation and of consulting with expert interpreters. I do not consider it essential, but I do believe it is valuable. After we discuss the second viewing, I add a layer: some film critics suggest that Spade, the character played by that icon of masculinity Humphrey Bogart, is portrayed as bi-curious. I am embarrassed to confess that I cannot find the sources that persuaded me of this interpretation. However, the discussion of this question decidedly follows lines I encountered several years ago.

This suggestion almost always activates students: rarely does a single student find it persuasive, even after the second viewing. So, we watch again with Spade's bi-curiosity in mind. By the end of the process, the class is almost always divided on the question—again, a good thing.

Students who perceive complications in Spade's sexuality gravitate toward several data points. First, they observe a new detail when Effie hands Cairo's calling card to Spade: Spade sniffs the card, and Effie knowingly replies, "Gardenia." Then Spade says, "Quick, darling. In with him." Is the scented card a point of attraction or amusement?

Second, while Cairo suggestively rubs the tip of his umbrella against his lips and caresses it with his fingers, the view shifts from Cairo's front to an angle that views Spade over Cairo's right shoulder. While the umbrella tip resides at Cairo's lips, visible from behind, Spade places his cigarette on his own lips and takes a deep drag. In other words, Spade mirrors Cairo's suggestive behavior. Indeed, Spade was holding his cigarette paper to his tongue as Cairo entered the room.

Finally, Spade overpowers Cairo. Cairo has just frisked Spade, patting him on the posterior, when Spade rapidly disarms him. Three things happen at this point. The camera angle looks up at Spade, emphasizing his size advantage. The pace of action slows down, as Spade presses Cairo backward. No words are exchanged. A sly smile crosses Spade's lips, a characteristic expression in the film, as Spade savors the moment before he knocks out Cairo with one punch and draws a trickle of blood from Cairo's lips.

At this point, I remind students that film directors have a near-infinite range of choices and that little in a scene happens by chance. I further suggest that students will find more data on the question if they watch the entire film. (In a later scene, a female character slaps Cairo, Spade stops Cairo from striking her in retaliation, Cairo objects, and Spade replies, "When you're slapped, you'll take it and like it!" Then Spade slaps him three more times.)

These exercises—from the initial question about a hospital encounter, to putting forth coaching as a metaphor for instruction, to the *Maltese Falcon* conversation—all specifically aim to mitigate stereotype threat according to Steele's recommendations. They draw on the wisdom of each individual student, bringing the entire group into conversation with one another. They demonstrate that every student already has some expertise with respect to the subject matter. They set the tone that learning entails a process of growth rather than a static measure of students' innate ability. Again, this exercise works well in our setting, where conversations about gender and sexuality occur in a relatively safe environment and occur at many points in students' experience.

Setting the Tone, Part 2: New Testament Introduction

Lancaster Seminary's ten-week required New Testament survey happens fast, so getting off to a good start is essential. In important ways, the opening session resembles that of Interpreting in Context. We begin with a quick opening exercise meant to draw out students' interpretive wisdom. I then introduce the syllabus, emphasizing the reasons for the default pass/fail grading approach and the instruction as coaching metaphor. Here I briefly discuss the opening exercise, then address two formal graded assignments that occur early in the term: a field report that is due at the beginning of second week and the interpretive essay, our version of the familiar exegesis paper.

As with Interpreting in Context, the opening exercise in Introduction to the New Testament precedes opening session rituals such as prayer and introductions. I e-mail all enrolled students prior to the first class session, attaching a copy of the syllabus and inviting them to bring a Bible to class. When it is time for class to start, I welcome everyone, tell them what we will accomplish in the first session, and then ask them to open their Bibles to Mark 1. Before I read Mark 1:1–11, I invite students to focus on the figure of John the Baptist. Having read the passage, I turn their attention to a slideshow projected onto the board. I inform students that the slideshow includes six images of John and his ministry, none of them specifically keyed to Mark's Gospel. We will slowly work through the six, then go back through them in reverse. A final slide presents a collage of all six images in order to jog students' memories. Before starting the sequence, I share the prompt: "Which image most resonates with Mark's portrayal of John?"

The six images are quite diverse in their interpretations of John, their cultural settings, and the physical representation of people.

The first is a photograph of actor David Morris portraying John. Dressed like John, he stands in a river and gestures as if he is preaching, perhaps inviting a response from an unseen audience.

The second is an icon of John from the website of Holy Cross Melkite Church, a Greek Orthodox church in Placentia, California. John assumes the familiar iconic posture of blessing, and he is marked with a halo. His staff culminates in a cross. His unconventional dress is subdued, but his hair is wild.

The third is taken from Eliza Codex 17, a sixteenth-century Ethiopic biblical manuscript. Jesus stands in the water while John, who is larger than Jesus, places a hand over Jesus's head in blessing. Here too John holds a staff that culminates in a cross.

The fourth is an image from contemporary artist Jack Baumgartner. It portrays John's face and hands as if John were blowing a woodwind instrument. Dynamically moving water surrounds John's face. A dove proceeds from John's breath. Jesus is absent from this image.

The fifth is Leonardo da Vinci's 1519 *St. John the Baptist*. A portrait of the prophet alone, John smiles demurely, a camel-hair garment over one shoulder, while his uncovered arm points heavenward. John looks youthful in this image, perhaps a teenager.

Finally, we view *Sermon of St. John the Baptist* by Pieter Bruegel the Elder, an example of sixteenth century Flemish Renaissance art. This painting stands out among the images because John and Jesus are difficult to identify, as they are surrounded by a great crowd, the river far behind them. John stands well off-center in a preaching pose, while Jesus stands with arms folded in a nearly white garment, as if he were prepared for baptism. Students have never been able to identify Jesus on the screen due to his size within the slide.

After showing and reshowing the images, I proceed through the series from the first image through the last. For each image I ask students to speak up if they chose the one currently on the screen, and I invite them to explain their selection. Never do I criticize a student's selection. In each case we draw out how the image draws on Mark's story, including matters of selection and focus. Each image, after all, zooms in on some details while omitting others.

Having worked through the images and having heard from most students, I lead the class in reflecting how all acts of interpretation do just what the students have done. We observe how both artists and students participate in the interplay of selection, emphasis, and contextualization. When students draw on historical-critical details, we discuss that. When students observe aspects of Mark's account that appear in none of the images or ways in which the images intersect with our contemporary social realities, we dwell on those things. As we conclude the exercise, I offer suggestions very much like those from the *Maltese Falcon* exercise: we all bring interpretive skills to the conversation; all interpretations are partial and have some merit; interpretation is perspectival; and so forth.

Often I will add an observation from the experts, the tradition of academic biblical commentary. I will suggest, "Why do we assume that John's baptism is about individual repentance? What if John is preparing Israel to repent in preparation for God's eschatological redemption?" I cannot recall having a student who had already been exposed to this interpretation, a commonplace among scholars. The point of posing this question is, as with the Joel Cairo scene, to hint toward the value of attending to professional interpreters.

Interpretive Essay

Like many other theological schools, Lancaster asks students to compose an interpretive essay. The essay asks students to develop a focused interpretation of a biblical passage, covering basic interpretive questions along the way. It requires a very modest level of library work.

Students appreciate that the interpretive essay comes in three stages. Stage 1 requires students to compare translations and the notes attached to the NRSV and to observe, in complete sentences, any significant differences among the translations or significant issues presented by the NRSV notes. Most Lancaster students do not take biblical languages, so we do not encourage them to resolve these issues. This stage also requires students to identify and explain the boundaries for the passage they select—we note there are no absolute right or wrong answers—and to assess both the internal structure of the passage and its relationship to the larger biblical book in which it occurs.

The key to stage 1 is that we want students to read the passage closely on their own, drawing their own observations while paying little or no attention to the opinions of experts. We ask students to identify a likely focus of their study moving forward.

Stage 2 introduces bibliographic work, as students share the specific and substantive contributions of just three secondary sources, then write a brief abstract of the final stage. As with other exercises we have discussed, stage 2 models seeking input from experts—but only on the foundation of the students' own interpretive insights.

Students discuss one another's stage 2 submissions in guided small group conversations, with no more than five students per group. In this capacity students take the instructor's seat. I provide questions for the review process, and individual authors are to remain silent, unless called on, while other students assess their work. In this class session every student takes the role of instructor, at once helping their peers and learning from the work of their peers. Students show high levels of appreciation for this process.

In stage 3 students articulate their focused interpretation, including a thesis statement and supporting argument, in only twelve hundred to fifteen hundred words. Stage 3 is due two weeks before the end of the term so that students have time to submit revisions if necessary.

The interpretive essay process is designed to foreground students' agency. They begin by applying their own interpretive skills, and they participate in the review of one another's work. The three-stage process and the opportunity to revise the final assignment, if necessary, underscore that learning is a process, not a static accomplishment.

The Field Report

At the beginning of week 2, students submit a field report. I inform them that every student who simply completes the assignment will earn a grade of 100 percent. I also tell them they are unlikely to submit an excellent assignment, as they will continue developing the capacities necessary for the assignment throughout the course. Currently the field report and class discussion related to it occur in our online learning platform, Moodle.

Here are the directions for the field report, taken from the course syllabus:

> Your field report will contribute to one of the Moodle discussion forums in Week 2. It should be no longer than 500 words. Please write in complete sentences. The goal of this report is to reflect on the assumptions and use of the Bible in the faith communities represented in our classroom.
> 1. Base your report on a worship service you have attended in your own primary religious tradition.
> 2. Where and when did you attend worship?
> 3. Did the worship service include the reading of a sermon text—or perhaps a set of sermon texts? What text(s)?
> 4. Assess how the sermon you heard related to the primary biblical text that was referenced. Below are some common options for your reference, but trust your judgment. Once you've assessed how the sermon relates to biblical texts, reflect some more. Sermons embody certain assumptions about the Bible, what the Bible means, and how the Bible can function in the church. In this case, what might those assumptions be?

The field report introduces students to the diverse interpretive communities represented in the classroom. Each student represents their own religious tradition, and all students encounter the findings of other students. I attach to the syllabus a framework by which students may evaluate their own traditions and those of others. That framework, called "Mapping Interpretations," appears as an appendix to this paper.

I developed the field report prior to encountering *Whistling Vivaldi*. In large part the assignment adapts a framework proposed by Norman K. Gottwald in "Framing Biblical Interpretation at New York Theological Seminary: A Student Self-Inventory on Biblical Hermeneutics." That inventory appears in multiple publications. I have found that the field report addresses several of the proposals advanced by Steele. Early in the course, it affirms the wisdom of each student's interpretive tradition, relativizing all of them. It encourages students who represent very different social experiences and ecclesial traditions to learn from one another. Finally, it presents our common learning as a process in which everyone can participate.

Conclusion

When one contributes to a volume on pedagogy, especially a volume that addresses racism, the task suggests assuming the position of an expert. By no means have I arrived as a teacher or as an activist. Nor have I gained the competence to assess the effectiveness of these interventions in a meaningful way. Our school's course-evaluation forms include a question concerning how effectively courses address diversity, and these two courses receive positive responses. Nevertheless, the challenges that first motivated me to seek resources for antiracist pedagogy remain present in my classrooms. In this paper I am sharing how one rubric, the work of Steele, has given me hope that the effects of my teaching better align with my aspirations.

Appendix: Mapping Interpretations

Consciously or unconsciously, biblical interpreters generally adopt a variety of interpretive strategies. Their choices range from how we identify texts for interpretation, to the kinds of questions we ask of those texts, to the fields of meaning to which we gravitate.

In many faith communities, particular modes of interpretation go unspoken and untaught, as do the kinds of meaning we expect from the Bible. These things seem natural to us—until we encounter other ways of reading.

By this point in your education, you have encountered quite different examples of interpretation. By now we might have become self-aware of our own interpretive habits. We might also be able to articulate how the communities that have formed us compare with and relate to other interpretive communities.

The following chart presents some of the interpretive options we encounter. It does not exhaust the range of possibilities. Nor are the various options exclusive of one another. Most of the time they mix and mingle in search of suitable matches like desperate characters in *Sex in the City* or *Insecure*.

As you review these tables, consider what you might add, subtract, or correct. Think about the interpretive spaces in which your faith communities are most at home, and ask yourself whether your interpretive workout needs to strengthen different muscles.

What Text?	
The Bible is largely ignored or is used for reference to other themes.	The primary unit of meaning is a biblical passage or pericope.
The interpreter focuses on a word, a phrase, or a verse.	Several biblical passages are related to one another in order to create meaning.
	The interpreter identifies a topic, then seeks passages that speak to that topic.

Locating Meaning	
The interpreter takes account of multiple translation possibilities.	The interpreter takes account of the text's literary context within a whole biblical book or part of a book.
The interpreter takes account of the text's design, structure, or genre.	The interpreter takes account of the social, cultural, and historical context of the texts.
The interpreter takes account of the text's prehistory by using source, form, or redaction criticism.	The interpreter places the text within a larger canonical context.

Location, Location, Location	
The interpreter addresses the text to the particular cultural moment.	The interpreter self-consciously (or unconsciously) relates the text to the interpretive concerns of particular affinity groups (e.g., feminist, womanist, queer, migrant, postcolonial, class identities, ethnic or racial identities).

The interpreter relates the text to a specific religious (denominational?) tradition.	The interpreter draws on the history of the text's interpretation.
The interpreter relates the text to a particular congregation or community.	

Codes: What Matters?	
Moral: Interpretation tells people how they should behave.	Communal: Interpretation fosters the self-understanding and practice of a community.
Social/political: Interpretation finds significance in the connection between the text and culture or politics.	Individual: Interpretation primarily bears on the lives of individuals or families.
Doctrinal: Interpretation stresses the text's theological implications with respect to a standard theological topic.	Evangelistic: Interpretation calls people to the life of faith, either as individuals or as an invitation to a religious community.
Devotional/inspirational: The interpretation brings the text to bear on the audience's spiritual life. It may offer a lesson or an insight. It may also foster a spiritual modality such as inspiration, encouragement, or comfort.	Reorientation: Interpretation subverts common assumptions and invites its audience to a new way of perceiving and relating to the world.

Works Cited

Barrios, Richard. 2003. *Screened Out: Playing Gay in Hollywood from Edison to Stonewall.* New York: Routledge.

Cox, Daniel, Juhem Navarro-Rivera, and Robert P. Jones. 2014. "A Shifting Landscape: A Decade of Change in American Attitudes about Same-

Sex Marriage and LGBT Issues. Executive Summary." PRRI, 26 February. https://tinyurl.com/SBL03111al.
Hammett, Dashiel. *The Maltese Falcon*. New York: Knopf, 1930.
Movieclips. 2012. "The Maltese Falcon (2/10) Movie CLIP—Joel Cairo (1941) HD." YouTube, 3:01. https://tinyurl.com/SBL03111am.
Russo, Vito. 1987. *The Celluloid Closet: Homosexuality in the Movies*. Rev. ed. New York: Harper & Row.
Spöhrer, Markus. 2016. "Homophobia and Violence in Film Noir: Homosexuality as a Threat to Masculinity in John Huston's *The Maltese Falcon*." *Human* 6 (June): 56–71.
Steele, Claude M. 2010. *Whistling Vivaldi: How Stereotypes Affect Us and What We Can Do*. IOT. New York: Norton.

Teaching through *Testimonio*: Latinx Biblical Studies and Students as Knowledge Producers

Kay Higuera Smith

The ideological assumptions and discursive norms of the academic field of biblical studies have to change in order to address contemporary demographic and institutional concerns. Most importantly, its practitioners must acknowledge its ideological roots in Hegelian, existential, and of course white, European Enlightenment rationality, as well as its framing within a colonialized, racialized ideological tradition. What is becoming clear is that, despite all our training, we cannot avoid our philosophical and epistemic assumptions shaping the urgent questions we bring to our research and our teaching. These assumptions are not value neutral. In the case of biblical studies, there is good evidence that we are reinforcing racialized norms within our guild and, by extension, our classrooms. This, in turn, creates hostile environments for students who may not operate within those norms. Given the large number of students who may not resonate with those norms, it is incumbent on those of us who teach in the classroom to disrupt and challenge those norms.

Shawn Kelley (2002) identifies many of the racialized, colonialized, and orientalist assumptions that frame the intellectual genealogy of our discipline. He has brought attention to narratives that have been corrected to some extent but that have not been sufficiently interrogated as to their power to shape and underwrite contemporary epistemological assumptions. One example of such assumptions is the predilection toward epistemic binaries that is well documented in the academic field of biblical studies. Such binaries as those between Jewish (or Pharisaic) particularity and Christian freedom were widely assumed well into the late twentieth century. Kelley brings to light the colonializing nature of these binary constructions and shows how, in the twentieth century, existentialist assumptions took up and reinforced the same binaries. Such assumptions underwrite the interpretive claims of many of our fathers of biblical studies, and Kelley shows how the interpretive choices that grew out of these epistemologies were racialized. In this, he demonstrates how the intellectual genealogy of racism finds its way into some of the categories we use despite our best intentions.

Kelley, writing in 1999, seemed to recognize presciently how crucial it is to perform a critical analysis of epistemic assumptions when evaluating critical biblical scholarship. Today, some twenty years after Kelley wrote, we live in a time in which the importance of such analyses seems to be widely accepted; nevertheless, at the time of its writing, Kelley's work did not receive the attention it deserved. He argues that, in line with their intellectual genealogy, the premier biblical scholars of the twentieth century constructed certain value systems based on existential notions of authenticity, which they then introduced into the study of the New Testament. The category of authenticity, he argues, by definition introduces aesthetics into the equation. For this reason, to employ authenticity in evaluating ancient religious historical figures and actors ipso facto underwrites an epistemology that legitimizes a binary us/them taxonomy of social identity. That is, it pits those who authentically lived out their identities—in the case of the scholarship, generally those who were Greek—against the inauthentic and particularistic Jews or so-called Orientals. This then gets played out in value-laden assumptions about cultures. In our field, the normativity of Western European epistemological assumptions is assumed, implying that other epistemologies are either deviant or lacking. This shapes not only how we reconstruct the world of the New Testament but also how we interact with other religious traditions.

Kelley cites Ernst Renan, Ferdinand C. Baur, and Georg W. F. Hegel at length to demonstrate how the idea of the myth of the West became inscribed into Western ideologies and, by extension, into the field of biblical studies. Hegel (1953, 11–12, as cited in Kelley 2002, 49) offers an insight into this mythic understanding:

> The Orientals do not know that the spirit (*Geist*) is free (*frei*) in itself, or that man is free in himself. Because they do not know it, they are not free. They only know that "one" is free.... This "one" is therefore a despot, not a free man, not a man. The consciousness of freedom (*das Bewußtsein der Freiheit*) arose among the Greeks, and therefore they

were free.... Only the Germanic (*die germanischen Nationen*) nations have in and through Christianity achieved the consciousness that man *qua* man is free, and that freedom of the spirit (*die Freiheit des Geistes*) constitutes his very nature.

The myth of the West, which Edward Said (1979, 1993) has famously mapped out, has shaped the way seventeenth- through twenty-first-century biblical scholars have interpreted Scripture. This myth includes the assumptions that Western Enlightenment thinkers are able to achieve objective rationality in their interpretation of the Bible and that Western epistemologies underwrite more trustworthy claims about meaning than do other epistemological formulations.

In the twentieth century, Rudolf Bultmann carried forward this tradition by employing the category of existentialism to reinforce the binary, now reconceptualized as the binary between authenticity and inauthenticity. Bultmann substituted Hegel's *Geist* for the existentialist category of authenticity. In this construction, ancient Judaism represented slavish inauthenticity, while Jesus's message instituted the authenticity that led to freedom. Referring to the Jesus of the Synoptic Gospels, Bultmann (2007, 11, emphasis original) presented Jesus as an existentialist prophet: "*He in his own person signifies the demand for decision*, insofar as his cry, as God's last word before the end, calls men to decision. Now is the last hour; now it can be only: either—or! Now the question is whether a man really desires God and His reign or the world and its goods; and the decision must be drastically made."[1] For Bultmann, existential authenticity drove his aesthetic evaluations of various characters and events in the biblical era.

Against this existential call to embrace authenticity drastically, Bultmann (2007, 11, as cited in Kelley 2002, 143) contrasts the inauthenticity of ancient Judaism:

> As interpretation of the will, the demand, of God, Jesus' message is a great *protest against Jewish legalism*—i.e. against a form of piety which regards the will of God as expressed in the written Law and in the Tradi-

---

1. To be sure, Bultmann was a member of the Confessing Church, which vigorously challenged the Nazi regime. However, see Baranowski 1999, who has demonstrated how the members of the Confessing Church themselves espoused anti-Jewish sentiments. Their concern, according to the editor, Robert P. Ericksen, primarily was to ensure the autonomy of their churches, not to protect the Jews.

tion which interprets it, a piety which endeavors to win God's favor by the toil of minutely fulfilling the Law's stipulation[s].

In this way, Bultmann operated within the ideological framework of the long history of marking Jews as backward, obsolete, and slavish. Rather than using those categories, however, Bultmann assigned to Jewish people the same aesthetic judgment of inauthenticity that he had to ancient Judaism—an aesthetic judgment that he needed in order to construct Jesus as embodying the kind of existential authenticity, and hence superior value, he saw in him. "Sin," Bultmann (1960, 133, as cited in Kelley 2002, 145) argues, "is the care, boasting and confidence of the man who forgets his creatureliness and tries to secure his own existence. It reaches its acme in the Jew." At the same time, however, Bultmann was also asserting the superior value of his own constructions of meaning over against others based on his assiduous attention to Western Enlightenment modes of discourse. By introducing such aesthetic values into his reading of the ancient texts, Bultmann perpetuated this racializing discourse.

Only recently are some students in PhD and seminary programs being asked to evaluate critically how the norms of historical-critical and literary-critical scholarship, which emerged within this ideological framework, have in turn constructed racialized environments in the classroom.

Lindsay Pérez Huber is one scholar who recognizes the way knowledge gets constructed in the classroom in general. Pérez Huber (2009, 649) introduces pedagogical models that seek to disrupt binary categories: "The notion of authenticity is a concept rooted in a Eurocentric perspective where dichotomies dominate logical reasoning and where the question of authenticity directly relates to the contestation of truth." Once one introduces a value-laden category such as authenticity in evaluating the legitimacy of interpretations, then that category reinforces racialized interpretations. Pérez Huber's argument is that we must take seriously the epistemological categories we introduce into our pedagogy. Many of them result in racialized classroom environments. Given how this history has played out in the academic study of the Bible, we in this field need to be especially diligent in examining our own assumptions, for we have been guilty of creating such racialized environments for centuries.

The epistemological assumptions that have shaped the guild of biblical scholars result in our collectively replicating a racialized and racializing social identity. All we have to do is look around at any Society of Biblical Literature conference, and such an assumption seems to be self-ratifying, given the small number of black, indigenous, and people of color in our midst.² The good news is that things are beginning to change. Moreover, along with the change of faces will come challenges to the unstated epistemic norms of our academic tradition.

Another reason these norms must change is that our students are changing. Forty percent of my undergraduate students are Latinx. Many students express to me a desire to see Latinx professors in the classroom. They lament that they spend four years in college and often do not encounter a single Latinx professor within their major. This is certainly borne out in biblical studies. When Jacqueline Hidalgo (2019, 178) of Williams College carried out a survey of Latina biblical scholars in 2019, she was only able to identify a total of sixteen Latinas teaching biblical studies in the United States, out of the thousands of biblical scholars currently in the field.³ It will be many years before my young Latina students see women like themselves in the role of biblical studies professor. Male Latinx professors are also severely underrepresented (Society of Biblical Literature 2019).

How, then, do I teach my undergraduate Latinx students in a way that inspires and opens up possibilities to them, and reinforces their own sense of justice and representation when there are so few role models? I do so with the following assumptions that underlie my own pedagogy. I also will discuss here the pedagogical and curricular changes I am making or have made to work through these assumptions.

1. *Students must be involved in their own knowledge production.* In the past, I taught biblical studies by employing the classic historical-critical and literary-critical models. I threw in some contextual and critical approaches, but the structure of my assignments remained mostly unchanged. I teach at an eight-thousand-student evangelical Christian university in the Wesleyan tradition. This tradition offers us institutional

---

2. According to the "SBL 2019 Member Data" report, of the current Society of Biblical Literature members who are faculty and who report having been born in the United States, 3 percent identify as of Latin American descent; 3 percent as African American; 4 percent as Asian; 2 percent as Native American, Alaska Native, or First Nation; and 0.2 percent as Native Hawaiian or Oceanian. Against those numbers, 87 percent identify as of European or Caucasian descent.

3. Given the total numbers in the "SBL 2019 Member Data" report, this breaks down to less than 0.7 percent of faculty in the United States, as not all Latina faculty were born in the United States.

space to challenge the fundamentalist, neo-Reformed models of other evangelical institutions. However, the broader constituencies behind and before the university—its donors, its board, and the audience to which its graduates will go forth—rarely understand those distinctions.

In our institution, it is a general-education requirement that all undergraduate students take three biblical studies courses. The first is a course that introduces students to the Hebrew Bible. The second course, which I, among many, teach, introduces students to the New Testament. For the third, students may choose to study a book from either the Hebrew Bible or the New Testament. Our approach traditionally has been literary critical—what some call inductive biblical studies. It is ideologically driven by positivist, modernist assumptions such as that if you follow a certain method, you will get at the meaning that is most plausible for ancient hearers of the texts. At the least, my colleagues and I know better than to locate the objective meaning of the text in authorial intent. Nevertheless, those who employ this approach sometimes claim to seek to develop responsible biblical interpretations. On one level, the sentiment is commendable, because our philosophy is to challenge the naive, precritical approaches of many white evangelical churches. Because three biblical studies courses are general-education requirements, in the vast majority of our classes, all the way through the three hundred level, we may not have a single major. Our hope as a department is that we give students the tools to read critically and to exegete texts for themselves, taking into account genre, context, and lexical meaning. In the last five years, we have added a contextual-critical requirement to the first two introductory courses.

On another level, however, despite having made real progress over the last few years in convincing our faculty of the importance of minoritized biblical criticism, we, as a group (with some notable exceptions among full-time faculty), still tend to teach in a way that assumes all of the classic assumptions of the modernist study of the Bible. We continue to reinforce the assumption that skilled biblical scholars are able to efface their subjectivity in order to challenge successfully their own preassumptions and the assumption that to do so is of value. This modernist paradigm internalizes colonialist assumptions about the objective authority of the Western producer of knowledge, and it is still operational.

Fortunately, after ten years of aggressive hiring of faculty of color, it is no longer the case that, when I teach Biblical and Philosophical Hermeneutics at the undergraduate senior level, the students look at me with incredulity and ask, "Why hasn't anybody taught me this before?" Now, thanks to the excellent work of most of my colleagues, my students understand that the modernist paradigm is itself an ideological production. They know its limitations; it remains for me to teach them the theoretical and philosophical underpinnings that legitimize such a production.

I would like to see changes in our pedagogy that operate across the board, however, and not just among a select few faculty. The capacity for students to be involved in their own knowledge production depends on the text of the Bible making sense to them in their own sociocultural worlds. This, of course, is antithetical to the classic pedagogy of the academic study of the Bible. With the value it places on effacing one's own social identity, it trains us to distance ourselves from our current lived experience. This is precisely the opposite of the approach I now employ, which I elaborate below. I must admit, it has taken a little getting used to, and I have to push myself because I was so deeply socialized into the norms of the guild. Part of me worries that I am reinforcing students in a precritical approach that sees the Bible as nothing more than an extension of themselves. But, as we have learned, we cannot cognize any work or text unless we can re-cognize/recognize something familiar in that text. Therefore, I am pushing forward with this approach, hoping that I can add a self-evaluative component as well to address that risk. Thus, my first move is to embrace an approach that makes explicit the claim that meaning production is a function of the interpreter, the text, the interpreter's social group, and the interpreter's salient social identity norms.

To accomplish this goal, I have made some changes in my two hundred-level general-education New Testament introduction course. First, I start right off the bat by foregrounding contextual, gender-critical, and critical race theoretical approaches in constructing meaning. I do not compartmentalize these topics or save them until later in the course. Rather, I center them from the beginning. Second, in order to counteract the defensiveness that such an approach might elicit among white students, I tell them at the outset that I assume that all white students in this classroom are allies, cocreators of meaning, or coconspirators in reading the Bible in a way that is life giving for those who have felt its power to silence in other contexts. That is, I let the white students know that I assume the best of them. They like that I trust them, and thus they do not respond with defensiveness. This approach has worked. I have not received any hostility from white students since adopting it.

Once we have laid this groundwork, and very early in the course, the students' first assignment is a *testimonio*/testimonial. In this assignment, one student of color partners with a student from the dominant culture, if possible. Both of them, independently, first reflect on their own collective identity. I spend some time in class helping them identify collective identity as the identity that emerges from the collection of stories, narratives, social memories, anecdotes, jokes, and memes told around family gatherings or in intimate conversations with older family members. I discuss weak group identity versus strong group identity and urge the students to consider their own social identity in light of the collective social memory of their social-cultural and geographic experience.

Once they have reflected on their own collective narratives and memories, they read through the entire book of Luke, jotting down any passages that jump out at them in light of this social memory. Then they meet with their partner and compare and contrast what jumps out for each of them. Later in the semester, they do the same exercise with the book of Acts.

After that meeting, they write their *testimonios*/testimonials. A *testimonio* is a pedagogical tool employed in Latinx-critical and, more specifically, Chicana-critical theory. The purpose of *testimonio* is to allow students from minoritized communities, especially women, to locate themselves as authoritative knowers. As a pedagogical tool, *testimonio* allows the writers to reflect on how their own social-historical space is crucial and valuable for producing meaning (Martínez et al. 2017, 41).[4] Through this assignment, students see that I affirm and legitimize their own production of knowledge. They then begin to recognize and assert their own agency and authority as knowledge producers. They also begin to acknowledge the ways certain remembered events or memorialized histories not only have shaped them in how they produce meaning but also are legitimate spaces out of which meaning can be produced. This is a crucial revelation for them as they engage reading the Bible.

Testimonio, though, is more than just a pedagogical tool for all students. As it has developed in the discourse, it assumes that the *testimonialista* is someone whose social-historical experience has been that of disenfranchisement, marginalization, or silencing—particularly, but not exclusively—as a woman. It allows the *testimonialista* to express the pain of those experiences as she may have internalized them while growing up in such spaces and to recognize both that her individual ways of meaning

---

4. See also Pérez Huber 2009, 643, for a variety of ways that the approach is understood.

making are legitimate and that they are bound up with her collective ways of meaning making.

My dilemma in creating this assignment was in how to handle the students from white, dominant-cultural spaces. For this I thank Leticia Guardiola-Saenz for giving me the idea of the testimoni*al* as a way to include the dominant-culture students but also allow them to enter into the space of their partners empathetically. I instruct those students also to think of their racialized, gendered, institutional space, but to do so in relation to the space of their partners. Thus, in the process of the assignment, they have to center their minoritized partners' knowledge production. This allows them to perceive how those disenfranchised social spaces produce important and distinct meanings in interpreting the Bible that the dominant-culture students have never considered. The minoritized student writes a *testimonio*; the dominant-culture student writes a testimoni*al*—a testimonial of how they themselves understand the biblical text in a new light after engaging with their partner's *testimonio*. In both cases, however, I ask them to consider the roles of social power, social identity, and race, class, gender, and ability in how those discourses shape meaning.

This has been a wonderful exercise both for myself and the students. Let me give you just a couple of examples of how students' collective memories have shaped their reading of texts. One student, who was a bicultural Latinx/African American, found that the passages that jumped out at him focused on healing and care for the neglected. He related that he had an aunt who took in three cousins from a broken family, so he read the stories of healing through the lens of his aunt's actions.

Another student, an Anglo-European, noted that his *testimonio* partner, who was Latina, had a much harder time than he did when reading Luke 9:60. There Jesus says, "Let the dead bury their own dead. But you, go and proclaim the reign of God" (NRSV). This command did not stand out to the Anglo-European student. But his Latina partner found it difficult, he reported, because of the importance of family in Latinx culture. For her, to leave one's family, especially at a time of grief and mourning, seemed harsh and cruel. The Anglo partner, on the other hand, admitted that he had glossed over the command when he had read the text, even though he too cared about his family. This was an eye-opener for him.

For the most part, not surprisingly, it was female students for whom the Mary/Martha story and the unequal treatment of women (Mary, Elizabeth, Mary Magdalene, the women at the tomb, etc.) jumped out. There was only one male, student, Filipino and raised by a single mother, who noted a woman character, in this case Elizabeth, in light of her role in naming John. Not one other male student mentioned the female characters in Luke.

That same young Filipino male, though, wrote, "I think no matter what perspective I am reading the book of Luke from I will always have the same experience and reflections, no matter my race, gender, or social location." Yet he had noticed no other female character, nor, for instance, disabled characters; nor had he made any comment about the different social locations of Jews and gentiles in Luke, in which ethnicity played a role. After we reflected on these observations in class, he later noted in an online threaded discussion post how the exercise had taught him that his assumption that he had no social location was in itself evidence that he had internalized a particular social narrative as one who grew up in predominantly white spaces, especially white church spaces.

Students discovered on their own, and reported later in the threaded discussion, that when it came to status differences in Luke, students of color found themselves much more likely, in contrast to their dominant-culture partners, to perceive those differences as social and economic, or class-based. The Anglo-European students, on the other hand, tended to assume that the differences were merely a function of different religious sensibilities. Class or social hierarchies, for the most part, were invisible to them.

For instance, one student of color appreciated a line in the Magnificat, Luke 1:53, where Mary proclaims that God has "sent away the rich." This student interpreted that phrase as an affirmation of people who are not from a wealthy class. Another student, an Asian first-generation student in the United States, who reported that he had grown up with constant food insecurity, wrote in his *testimonio*: "It sounds/feels selfish to say, but for my family, if we couldn't afford groceries or make rent, it felt like if someone were to tell us, 'Hey don't worry about that stuff. Jesus loves you!' it would just be offensive and annoying." For that student, Jesus's words not to worry (Luke 12:22–31) did not connect. He wrote, "I would need to follow a God who actually cares and hurts with us in our earthly struggles." Only one such observation was forthcoming from an Anglo-European student. The rest overlooked these social and class factors.

This reaction reflected a common pattern, which was that students of color tended to associate *themselves* with the marginalized characters in Luke, while Anglo-European students—especially the female ones—

tended to associate themselves with *Jesus*, whom they then associated as the one caring *for* the marginalized. All the students reacted visibly to this insight as students themselves pointed out this disparity in class.

One student who was bicultural mentioned that the theme of insider/outsider jumped out at them, with their white identity able to relate to the insider and their minoritized identity able to relate to the outsider. For them, this distinction was economic (rich = insiders; poor = outsiders). Their reaction contrasted with their Anglo-European partner, who, along with the other Anglo-European students, saw the distinction between insiders and outsiders not as economic but as faith-based (disciples = insiders; Pharisees = outsiders).

Only one Anglo-European student (a woman and a social work major) put herself among those who have an obligation to be aware that they are part of a privileged class, a class who has more; hence, she argued, they must recognize that more will be expected of them. This kind of thinking apparently never occurred to the others.

Finally, one student of color compared the stories in which Luke depicts Pharisees repeatedly questioning Jesus with the way police and other guardians of the culture in society often question or second-guess people of color and their motives or abilities. This student connected with Jesus not as the one rescuing the marginalized but as the one being marginalized by the religious elite through rhetorical games and honor/shame challenges.

Here are some final comments directly from the students:

> Bringing in my own life experience and personal perspective to how I view a book of the Bible is not something I am used to. Being half white and half Filipino is something that has changed the way I view society in the world I live in, and I now realize that it can also affect the way I view the Bible. Usually, I just see the books of the Bible as "old" stories that are things of the past that have elements in them that I can maybe apply to my life. However, I have realized that it is more than the stories affecting my life; it is also my own life affecting the stories. (Anonymous, 23 September 2019)

Another student, freed from the stigma of mentioning their culturally bound life memorial events, wrote: "Being completely cured [from seizures] a month before my quinceañera was a blessing from Jesus. It was a month filled with joy knowing how Jesus cares about us and I truly felt his presence in my life" (Anonymous, 22 September 2019).

This exercise has been a success in accomplishing my course goal of ensuring that the students become confident producers of their own knowledge about the Bible. As we go on to work through careful readings of the text of Luke-Acts, I find that (1) they are much more comfortable with intersectional, multivalent readings of the text; (2) they are freer to bring themselves into the text; and (3) they make assertions about interpretations with much greater confidence.

In order to attain cultural competence, we can no longer avoid introducing students to such concepts as critical race theory, institutional poverty, and injustice. This will require us to include readings from the social sciences, history, critical theory, and even criminal justice and legal theory. This is my first foray into changing pedagogies in an introductory class.

Here are some other assumptions on which I am working. I have based these assumptions on the desiderata Michael Dantley and Linda Tillman (2007, 23) suggest in their article "Social Justice and Moral Transformative Leadership."

2. *Students must learn about the nature of social institutions in their broader contexts.* In teaching about the ancient Mediterranean, I intend to incorporate assignments in which students research poverty in the ancient Mediterranean and connect it to the institutional structures that sustained ancient Greco-Roman power systems. So, one assignment looks like this:

- Read Luke 16:19–17:2 (the story of Lazarus and the rich man). Reread pages 31–36 in Mark Allan Powell (2018), *Introducing the New Testament*, "Social Systems and Cultural Values," where he discusses wealth, poverty, and taxation in the Roman system.
- Reflect on the system and institutional factors that might have led to Lazarus's poverty and ill health.
- Retell the story of Lazarus and the rich man, incorporating into the story how these systemic factors may shape the meaning of the story.

3. *Students must learn to identify and critique marginalizing behaviors and predispositions within institutions and institutional readings.* Here is an assignment I have incorporated:

- Read Acts 10–11.
- What is the purpose of Peter's dream?
- How has your church interpreted this story?

- How might we read the story differently if Peter's identity as a practicing Israelite Jew were validated?
- What effect, if any, has your church's interpretation had in how readers of the Bible think about social identity in their church contexts?

4. *Students must commit to affirming counterhegemonic narratives.* Here is an assignment I have incorporated:

- Read Luke 1:46–55 (the Magnificat).
- Write a short paragraph reflecting on how this story was conveyed to you as a child, whether through sermons or Sunday school lessons. If you were not raised in a church environment, write on how the person of Mary of Nazareth was conveyed to you through cultural narratives.
- Rewrite Mary's hymn as a counterhegemonic narrative in light of the political and economic situations of the ancient Mediterranean under Rome.
- Rewrite Mary's hymn as a counterhegemonic narrative in light of the political and economic situations prevalent in the United States currently.

5. *Students must translate rhetoric into civil rights action.* Here is an assignment that I might incorporate:

- Read this article on faith-rooted organizations: Friedman 2014.
- In conjunction with the Center for Student Action, the Student Center for Reconciliation and Diversity, or the Center for Service Learning, sign up for ten hours of service learning with one of the following organizations:
  - The Immigration Resource Center of the San Gabriel Valley (n.d.). Volunteer opportunities:
    - volunteer work in the office
    - translation services
    - collecting supplies for immigrant families
  - Clergy and Laity United for Economic Justice (n.d.)
  - Volunteer for faith-rooted organizing for justice for
    - prisons
    - per diem workers

- women's economic rights
- Offer aid for asylum seekers
  - This might include walking a picket line with workers, joining a delegation to visit a city hall meeting or a congressperson's office, or writing letters to constituents
- Write a four-page reflection paper on the justice work that you completed and how it relates to your reading of Luke or Acts. Highlight particular passages in those biblical books that you have found relevant in your work for civil rights action.

This kind of work runs completely counter to how I was trained, but it runs right in line with what I believe to be morally right and just. To be sure, I still teach my students historical-critical and literary-critical approaches. But I do not believe that my job is done until I have been able to walk alongside students who have learned to make the Bible their own—a task that, at one time, I saw as the opposite of what I wanted to accomplish.

Works Cited

Baranowski, Shelley. 1999. "The Confessing Church and Antisemitism: Protestant Identity, German Nationhood, and the Exclusion of the Jews." In *Betrayal: German Churches and the Holocaust*. Kindle ed. Edited by Robert P. Ericksen and Susannah Heschel. Minneapolis: Fortress.

Bultmann, Rudolf. 1960. *Existence and Faith: Shorter Writings of Rudolf Bultmann*. Translated and edited by Schubert M. Ogden. New York: Meridian Books.

———. 2007. *Theology of the New Testament*. Vol. 1. Translated by Kendrick Grobel. Repr., Waco, TX: Baylor University Press. (Orig. 1951)

Clergy and Laity United for Economic Justice. N.d. https://www.cluejustice.org/.

Dantley, Michael, and Linda Tillman. 2007. "Social Justice and Moral Transformative Leadership." Pages 19–34 in *Leadership for Social Justice: Making Revolutions in Education*. 2nd ed. Edited by Catherine Marshall and Maricela Oliva. Boston: Allyn & Bacon.

Friedman, Stan. 2014. "Faith-Rooted Organizing: A Conversation with Alexia Salvatierra." The Evangelical Covenant Church. https://tinyurl.com/SBL03111ay.

Hegel, Georg W. F. 1953. *The Philosophy of History*. Pages 1–158 in *The Philosophy of Hegel*. Translated by Carl J. and Paul W. Friedrich. Edited by Carl J. Friedrich. New York: Modern Library.

Hidalgo, Jacqueline M. 2019. "Latina Diversity and Difference in Biblical Studies." Pages 175–92 in *Women and the Society of Biblical Literature*. Edited by Nicole L. Tilford. Atlanta: SBL Press.

Immigration Resource Center of San Gabriel Valley. N.d. "What You Can Do." https://tinyurl.com/SBL03111an.

Kelley, Shawn. 2002. *Racializing Jesus: Race, Ideology and the Formation of Modern Biblical Scholarship*. New York: Routledge.

Martínez, Vanessa Lina, Ma. Eugenia Hernandez Sanchez, Judith Flores Carmona, and Yvonne P. El Ashmawi. 2017. "*Testimonio* Praxis in Educational Spaces: Lessons from *Mujeres* in the Field." *AMAEJ* 2:38–53.

Pérez Huber, Lindsay. 2009. "Disrupting Apartheid of Knowledge: *Testimonio* as Methodology in Latina/o Critical Race Research in Education." *IJQSE* 22:639–54.

Powell, Mark Allan. 2018. *Introducing the New Testament: A Historical, Literary, and Theological Survey*. 2nd ed. Grand Rapids: Baker Academic.

Said, Edward. 1979. *Orientalism*. New York: Vintage Books.

———. 1993. *Culture and Imperialism*. New York: Vintage Books.

Society of Biblical Literature. 2019. "SBL 2019 Member Data." https://tinyurl.com/SBL03111ao.

An Intercultural Approach: Latinx Students, Exegesis, and the Border Wall

Francisco Lozada Jr.

Introduction

This essay is a reflection on teaching Latinx students in biblical studies classes from an intercultural approach, an approach that emphasizes making meaningful connections between students' identities and what they are learning.[1] This notion of connectivity between teacher and student is the thread woven throughout my pedagogy. At the same time, the act of stitching pieces of my pedagogy together promotes the value of inclusion of identities, whereby students can define and construct their own self-understanding. Conversely, it also challenges white privilege, which assumes that all students learn as white students.[2] Given this moment

---

1. The nomenclature *Latinx* in this essay signifies all genders among Latinos/as/xs. The descriptor is not fixed, and depending on one's geographical location, generational identity, or ethnic heritage, the term may or may not be used by a person to whom it refers. Other descriptors may include *Hispanic*, *Latinos*, or *Latinas*, for example. It is a term, albeit problematic, pointing to all groups of "people of Latin American descent" living in the United States, including indigenous and African populations (see Salinas and Lozano 2017).

The first part of this essay was delivered at the Annual Meeting of Society of Biblical Literature on 25 November 2019 in San Diego, California, under the Society of Biblical Literature program unit Racism, Pedagogy, and Biblical Studies. The focus of the session was Best Practices for Latinx Students in Our Biblical Studies Classrooms. Even though this essay is driven by my experience of teaching Latinx students, anyone can draw on these pedagogical strategies for developing practices that connect teachers and the lived experience of students.

2. See Esteban-Guitart and Moll 2014; Moll et al. 1992. Both essays explore how to connect family and community resources to make meaning and to construct identity.

in history—when vulnerable communities are experiencing cases of the COVID-19 virus disproportionately higher than white society, along with the challenge to systemic racism advanced by Black Lives Matter, and migrant children are being detained or returned alone to their home countries—teachers, I believe, have a responsibility to reflect on those pedagogical strategies that advance equity of learning.

However, before beginning, a brief discussion of my previous and current teaching contexts is in order. Since 1994, I have taught at three academic institutions. Most of my experiences emanate from the most recent two. I taught at a Catholic liberal arts university, the University of the Incarnate Word, what the federal government calls a "Hispanic-serving institution." A Hispanic-serving institution is defined as a college or university with 25 percent or more undergraduate Latinx full time–equivalent student enrollment. I currently teach at Brite Divinity School, whose Latinx student full-time equivalent is well below 25 percent, but I have had various Latinx master's and doctoral students over the course of the last thirteen years.[3] For sure, these latter Latinx students have been quite diverse, ranging across the myriad of Latinx identities and cultures, sexualities, genders, economic classes, ethnic/racial heritages, and religious identities, with the biblical text seen as foundational in one way or another to their theological and religious outlook.

It is important to keep in mind that just because I taught and teach Latinx students at these institutions and am myself Latino—of Puerto Rican descent—does not mean I can speak for all Latinx students or professors. Of course, we (I use the pronoun cautiously) Latinx teachers can never speak inclusively for all Latinx communities, though we self-identify

---

As for these scholars, this essay is driven by an equity agenda that suggests that Latinx experience and history are resources for learning. *White* is a social construction defined differently throughout the United States' history and defined by what they were not (e.g., black, Asian, Native American, Latinxs). Here it refers primarily to Anglo-Saxons, incorporating Irish, Italian, Catholic, and Jewish Americans over time (see Masuoka and Junn 2013, 17).

3. I might add that my student assistant for the last two years is Latinx (a master of divinity student at Brite). This particular relationship also contributes to my reflections in this essay. For instance, rather than keeping learning contained in the classroom between teacher and student, a shared Latinx experience or understanding (for non-Latinx teachers) between teacher and student can broaden the learning experience outside the classroom. Over time, it can be anchored by a *confianza* (mutual trust) between teacher and student (see Moll et al. 1992, 133–34).

as Latinx and are signified as Latinx from inside and outside the group (Lozada 2017, 21–39). At the same time, while I cannot speak for Mexican Americans in the Southwest or Cuban Americans in Florida, whose particular experiences I do not exactly share, I can speak to the experiences of racialization, marginality, and other concerns that I have experienced along with them as a collective community.[4] Furthermore, as a heterosexual male middle-class Latinx educator, I cannot speak, for example, for queer Latinx folks or for Latinx women, but I can speak self-reflectively from the politics of my own location about the issues of marginality as ethical, political, and ideological, which implicate the social relations we all share in the classroom. One final note before I move to the theme itself: Many of us may have never had a Latinx biblical professor. I was not one of those students. I was very fortunate to have a Latinx doctoral professor, so besides the practical teaching experiences I have had with Latinx students over the years, I also draw from the experiences I have had with my graduate director in and out of the classroom.

In this essay, I reflect critically on certain practices in my courses, from teaching introductory courses in early Christian literature and origins, Johannine literature, Galatians, the history of hermeneutics, and various courses in cultural hermeneutics. I am also informed by three borderlands travel seminars with students (some of whom are Latinx) at Brite, to the borders of El Paso, Texas, and Nogales, Arizona. Even though the travel seminar is not a biblical studies course per se, my approach to it is hermeneutical. We study texts such as the history of the Southwest, we study readers such as the migrants themselves, and we study readings such as policies. And like all the components of this narrative communication model, they are constructions by those of us in the class. An intercultural approach to teaching, I contend, aids in helping Latinx students—and all students for that matter—see the relevance between who they are and what they are learning. To support this line of thinking, I explore three propositions regarding practices that contribute to making

---

4. On the one hand, the United States sees Puerto Ricans as not foreign because they are its colonized subjects, but on the other, they are foreign in how the United States treats them as expendable. This domestic foreignness is reflected in President Trump's reported remarks after Hurricane Maria devastated the island of Puerto Rico: "Can we sell the Island? You know, or divest of that asset?" (Shear 2020). See Saito 2019 regarding how foreignness is one link among others that connects Puerto Ricans with other immigrant communities and ethnic/racialized communities.

this connectivity happen: know yourself, know your history, and know the Other. What follows these three pedagogical axioms is a conversation about the traditional exegesis (or interpretation) paper in relationship to the border wall—the physical barrier between the United States and Mexico.[5] This latter part serves as a glimpse into what is meant by an intercultural approach to teaching.[6]

Self-Introspective Teaching Practices

Know Yourself

Over the years, I have come to believe that knowing yourself in a critical fashion is a good practice for Latinx students (of all genders) in our biblical studies classrooms. Knowing yourself here refers to recognizing or consciously accepting my minoritized status and marginalized agenda associated with the Latinx community. Such a recognition is important to allow a space for Latinx students to embrace their own identity and community if they so choose, and also provides them an entry point where self-assertion—a rhetorical move made by many minoritized scholars in interpretation—challenges the dominant mode of interpretation's repression of identity in the interpretative process.

Thus, my entry point into the history and literature of early Christianity is often the disclosure of my Latinx particularity among other identity formations. This decision to disclose comes with anxiety. A mental anguish that remains present today is the constant tension to

---

5. Having visited the border wall on many occasions, the term *barrier* or *border fence* is probably a better one. As Reece Jones confirms, the style of fencing varies depending on the terrain and location. Most of the fencing consists of tall metal bars crisscrossed with a mesh metal design to allow the wind and light to go through but making it very difficult for people (and animals) to walk through (Jones 2017, 32–43). The term *exegesis* I do find problematic. The term divides the task of interpretation into two separate questions: "What did it mean?" and "What does it mean?" The term *interpretation*, which I prefer, brings them together as one. For the sake of convenience, I will use the term *exegesis* since most readers and students in biblical studies and/or theological studies understand this term.

6. While this essay is focused on how to connect with Latinx students in the field of biblical interpretation, the topic resonates with Fernandez 2014. In this volume, see an excellent essay on the life of a Latina in the teaching profession: Martell-Otero 2014.

assimilate to the dominant or dominantized society. Assimilation, for me, is the incorporation into a community or society through a one-sided process of adaptation (Castles and Miller 2009, 247). This notion of assimilation supports the relinquishing of those distinguishing characteristics (e.g., linguistic, social, cultural) that mark your identity to become indistinguishable from the dominant society. If any Latinx student in the classroom resents the pressures of assimilation, the self-assertion of one's identity(ies) provides a rhetorical and physical space for these Latinx students—when the moment occurs— to challenge the dominant repression of identity in the interpretative process of a biblical text. In other words, Latinx students can draw confidently from their funds of knowledge (religion, material knowledge, history, and/or economics) to define themselves.[7] When employed in a classroom setting, for instance, these resources become funds of identity for students to define themselves.[8]

My self-disclosure also provides Latinx students an opportunity to determine that they belong in the classroom. Even though I was born in the United States, the notion of a newcomer or guestworker was and is always present and persistent in the rhetoric of the dominantized. The sense of not belonging was real and similar to others over the course of US history who were seen as not belonging, just like many people on the move are experiencing across the globe today. Linked to the issue of self-assertion of identity is the politics of belonging and/or not belonging. Latinx peoples, for instance, were and are seen as temporarily belonging in the country, community, or classroom. Thus, in the classroom, it is important to create a context in which all Latinx students feel and believe that they belong. By drawing on simple and complex experiences in the United States as a Latinx person, I hope to create a lane or a space where Latinx students can connect and engage in a dialectical relationship with certain themes in the biblical text.

---

7. The term *funds of knowledge* refers to the "historically accumulated and culturally developed bodies of knowledge and skills essential for household or individual functioning and well-being" (Moll et al. 1992, 133).

8. The assumption here is that the social world of students is inseparable from their learning experience. The term *funds of identity* is "historically accumulated, culturally developed, and socially distributed resources that are essential for people's [or student's] self-definition, self-expression, and self-understanding" (Esteban-Guitart and Moll 2014, 37).

Allow me to share one specific on how. Along with Adele Reinhartz (2018) in *Cast Out of the Covenant: Jews and Anti-Judaism in the Gospel of John*, I have never been convinced of J. Louis Martyn's expulsion theory (Lozada 2020). At the risk of oversimplification, the theory argues that the Fourth Gospel reflects the traumatic expulsion of the Johannine community from the Jewish community in the years preceding the final edition of the gospel. What is problematic is how Martyn frames this expulsion. He sees the expulsion of the Johannine community as a result of a conflict between Christ-believers and non-Christ (or Jewish) believers. It is not an intra-Jewish debate for Martyn, but rather a debate with Jews and Christians on opposite sides. The result of this debate casts those seen rhetorically as Jewish in the gospel as outsiders and Christ-believers as insiders. This either/or understanding of belonging is not unfamiliar to Latinx and other minoritized students. Latinx students are quite conversant in the politics of identity and belonging. Martyn's expulsion theory—a theory that has shaped Fourth Gospel study for many years—is connected to the question of identity and the politics of belonging. A text such as John, immersed in the question of identity and the politics of belonging (and not belonging), opens a lane for Latinx students to critically think about how they themselves have been used ideologically to name the Other, just as Johannine Jews have served ideologically to mark the Other in the Fourth Gospel. There is no question that Donald Trump and his allies' vituperative rhetoric against immigrants—synonymous these days with Latinx people—is similar to the offensive rhetoric against the Jews in John. Both attacking rhetorical discourses participate in tightening the circle of membership regarding insiders and outsiders.

Know Your History

As a Latinx professor of biblical studies, knowing my own cultural history is important. Over the years, scholars in the field of historiography have helped me understand how history is written, especially the distinction between "what happened" and "that which is said to have happened" (Trouillot 1995). Latinx professors, depending on their Latin American heritage history (even if that history is from the Southwest or California), are familiar with the conquest and colonization history. Without going into too much detail, Latinx peoples have a history that is quite complicated. Depending on where your heritage roots extend, there might be African influences, indigenous influences, Spanish, Portuguese, Jewish,

French, or even Southern European influences. Knowing the history of the roots of our identities, such as the conquest period, the Spanish borderlands, and the colonization beyond the borderlands into the new so-called frontier named Latin America, is necessary in order to understand the various branches that extend across the United States, such as Puerto Ricans, Mexicans, Cubans, Dominicans, Colombians, and the various groups from Central America and beyond. This history or histories help explain the remaking of the United States by Latinxs in politics, the economy, the arts, language, and religion.

Knowing this Latinx history and how this history has been and continues to be written can serve as another entry point into the history of early Christianity and its origins. In a similar way, early Christianity must undergo critical historical analysis. Its roots in Judaism, Hellenism, and the Roman Empire must be studied. Its development and expansion across the Mediterranean world (including northern Africa) and how this expansion remade the Western globe and beyond must be assessed. Just as importantly, the study of how this history is written and imparted in classes must be examined. Early Christianity and its origins, like Latinx history, have often been written with a recognition of empire's material reality but without scrutinizing the historian's own conscious reality. This means that it is easy to speak about how the shadow of the Roman Empire (i.e., New Testament) is present in the narrative text, which is undeniably important. But what is equally important is uncovering those shadows of the empire present in the world that the reader brings or fails to bring to the text, such as social, economic, and cultural imperialism of the United States. The latter is the harder task for sure. Latinx history as it has been traditionally written easily speaks to the Spanish and American colonialism enveloping the border peoples, for instance, but many historians fail to discuss how they have written that history. A good example, in my opinion, of someone who captures that nuance between "what happened" and "that which is said to have happened" is Monica Muñoz Martinez (2018) in *The Injustice Never Leaves You: Anti-Mexican Violence in Texas*. Martinez unearths those silences left out of the narrative of how Latinx borderlanders were murdered by the Texas Rangers in the early 1900s and discusses the actors involved and how the borderlanders' stories have been silenced over the years.

Knowing your history helps in understanding the history of early Christianity and its origins and what this means when reading for early Christian identity(ies). When focusing on the difference between "what happened" and "that which is said to have happened," the results move away from a one-sided historicity and toward a more nuanced, complex history that focuses on how history works for Latinx identities. This pedagogical move in the classroom pushes Latinx students, particularly those coming from religious traditions where critical reasoning is not welcome, to see their early Christian history, just like their own Latinx history, as nuanced and complex—such as seeing Judaism, Hellenism, and early Christianity as diverse rather than homogenous, seeing identities such as Paul's as made up of a variety of cultures, just like their own, and seeing Roman Christianity's role in the colonization of the ancient world as just like what the Spanish and US empires have done in colonizing the Latinx people in the past and present. To be sure, Latinx history is diverse and not the same as early Christianity, but knowing your history can be used to speak self-reflectively from your own politics of location about the similar issues of colonialization and power within our own histories, other histories, and the history of early Christianity and its origins.

Know the Other

For Latinx students with their diverse histories and identities, despite sharing society's projected sense of sameness as Other, it is important to speak from the experience of particularity and to see particularity in the text and others. It is very easy to reify an existing racial (and patriarchal) sense of hierarchy—with whites at the top, blacks on the bottom, and Latinx, Asians, and Native Americans in the middle somewhere—when particularity is not taken seriously in the classroom; this can be espoused by Latinx students themselves and used against Latinx women and transgender students.

In other words, in their quest to belong (nationally speaking), Latinx people can attribute negative stereotypes to others, including themselves at times. Latinx often perceive themselves and other minoritized groups, especially African Americans, as poor, emanating from the inner city, not as academically prepared as others, or limited in English or biblical-language skills. At the same time, they see Asian Americans as wealthy, hard workers, and very smart. In so doing, they operate with a racial hierarchy in the classroom, where they place whites at the top, Asian Americans right under whites, and Latinxs, African Americans, and Native Americans below all others. Nationally speaking, from the point of view of whites, only whites belong, while all others are simply visiting the United States or have earned a contract with the majority to behave as model citizens or minorities, as with the Asian American community (Motomura 2006). Latinx minoritization of themselves and others simply reflects the negative tropes being applied to minoritized groups in the dominant society.

Knowing the particularity of others challenges or resists this mental picturing of others. A tactic I at times employ in the classroom is to show the particularity of the various actors in early Christianity and Judaism. In other words, while textbooks like to provide a clean, homogeneous picture of Christians, the Jewish people, and others, I prefer to try to show how identity is not as clear-cut as the textbooks present the sociohistorical world and its groups. Just as it is today, identity formation in the ancient world was complex, always changing and becoming. For instance, though John is quite anti-Jewish in its rhetoric, its main hero and followers are presented as Jewish. The same can be said for Paul in his discourses on identity. Whereas he was Jewish, he blurred this identity along with many other identities. Knowing the particularity of otherness in the classroom or in the text will influence how well Latinx students will be able to anticipate and understand the future of belongingness. And knowing the Other will also serve as one more entry point into the diverse and ambiguous world of early Christianity and its origins.

The intercultural approach is intentional. Connectivity, the driving postulate, enables us to tap into students' background knowledge and current issues such as identity to understand the subject matter at hand.

Exegesis Paper and the Border Wall

A common requirement in biblical studies courses is the exegesis paper (or what I call the interpretation paper). This is a paper that asks students to demonstrate that they can study (dissect at times) a text critically (and objectively at times) to discover its meaning in the final text or through the many layers behind the final text (such as from the events, individual traditions, collections of traditions, sources, redactions). Engaged in this task, students employ a historical approach and use its tools (e.g., form, source, redaction criticisms). The basic historically oriented task is to reach an informed understanding of a text. An informed reading consists of various steps, such as reading a text several times; reading outside sources about a text; doing research on the sociohistorical situation behind a text; identifying some potential major themes, words, and topics to explore; and asking what purpose is behind the writing of the text, what type of genre the text is, what the text's narrative context is, how the text is shaped or outlined, and how the text relates to the whole of the text. This is all background work that must be done to reach an informed understanding of what the text says, and what it means is the final goal. This background work is also one strongly resembling a historical approach to a text. Other approaches such as literary, sociocultural, rhetorical, and ideological will call on different assumptions, principles, and steps to reach an informed understanding.

How students engage in their research project of a text depends on the question they are asking: historical, literary, or ideological, for instance. The methods or approaches employed will enable students to enter the world behind, in, or in front of a text.[9] At times, questions such as "How does your interpretation have ethical implications for today?" or "Who benefits and who does not benefit from your interpretation?" might be asked. Thus, the interpretation or exegesis paper, traditionally based on a Eurocentric understanding of how to retrieve meaning, does not always connect with Latinx students, or other minoritized students for that matter. Not all cultures understand things the same way across the globe. A text means different things in different cultures, as Kwok Pui-lan (2003) has sharply shown, and retrieving meaning may not be found in the world behind the text but in the stories of the interpreters, as Musa Dube (2016) has illustrated. Understanding this is not an either/or way of teaching or learning. The traditional way of learning should be put into conversation with other ways of learning. Understanding that not all students learn the same way or connect the same way is vital to their learning experience.

A key objective that I aim for in the classroom, as stated above, is to make connections between Latinx students and their life experiences in relationship to what they are learning, such as better understanding the interpretation or exegesis project. Given the proximity of my geographical location to the US-Mexico border, I prefer to draw from this issue—namely, the so-called border wall, which not only affects Latinx students' identities and how they are perceived (not to mention those students on the other side of the wall) but also pertains to all students and their constructions of belonging and not belonging, and the resultant effects on many. My goal is for students to better understand interpreting a text critically by exegeting the border wall as a historical, rhetorical, and ideological product.

---

9. The threefold step is simply for heuristic purposes. By no means am I implying that they do not blend into each other or are completely separate steps.

For this discussion, the border wall is a text. It has a history of development made up of layers of tradition (historical criticism), it has a story (literary criticism), and it represents separation and fear (ideological criticism) for many.

Historical Dimensions

From a historical point of view, the border wall dates back to the nineteenth century (Martínez 2006; Truett 2006). It was a response to Chinese migrants, an attempt to control their movement into the United States for fear of them becoming a public charge. With the Chinese Exclusion Act in 1882 in place, the Bureau of Immigration in 1904 began to place mounted guards at the border, beginning in El Paso, Texas, to restrict entry by Chinese migrants and Europeans looking for a way into the country other than Ellis Island (Truett 2006, 120–25). This buildup at the southern border with mounted guards continued, eventually with a new set of players when military troops were placed there during the First World War period (1914–1918) to reduce undocumented entry and to prohibit the informal flow of goods back and forth between the United States and Mexico (Nevins 2010, 126–29; Grandin 2019, 159–62). The border patrol began on 28 May 1924, through an act of Congress to provide effective control of movement between both countries, mobilizing the mounted guard previously used to restrict the Chinese from entering the United States. To understand the history of the current border wall, it is vital to understand not only these beginnings but also that humans such as the inspectors play the role of a wall, restricting other humans from crossing. In any case, the social imagining of a physical barrier was planted.

It was not until 1993 that the first federal barrier (also known as fencing), or what we call the border wall, emerged as a 23-kilometer or 14.2-mile fence at the crossing point in San Diego, California (Jones 2012, 31). Other crossing points along the southern border soon began having fencing or some sort of barrier, mounting to cover the entire southern border (3,169 kilometers or 1,969 miles). Unlike in the 1890s to 1920s, the fencing is to restrict movement of people from Mexico and Central America principally. The United States' appetite for drugs also created a demand for a more fortified wall, and with the terrorist attacks of 9/11, a heightened sense of security led to a higher and stronger barrier, along with a militarized border (including a virtual border with technology) and an increase of border patrol agents. The pretext was that people from Latin America were (and still are) a security threat to the nation (Jones 2012, 31).

The history of how the wall emerged is complicated. But in my discussion with students on various aspects of this history, students begin to understand that there are many layers behind the signified border wall. As they look for those gaps and contradictions (aporias) in the historical development of the border wall, they can begin to understand how these histories reflect the different points of view at particular moments in history.

Narrative Dimensions

What is the narrative story of the wall? From a literary perspective, the story is made up of a variety of points of view. The border wall present today began with a story of Manifest Destiny, divine mandate, and a notion of exceptionalism. The border wall follows—for the most part— the national boundary between the United States and Mexico. This is the physical boundary that was constructed through the United States' expansionist endeavors in the nineteenth century (1848), which also enabled the United States to acquire certain populations, including Native Americans and Mexicans (Truett 2006, 13–32). Its boundary was not only renegotiated over time, as with the purchase of the Gadsden territory in Arizona in 1853, but was also dictated by nature, with the ebb and flow of the Rio Grande (Truett 2006, 13–32). The story continued with the arrival of new characters over time, such as the mounted guards, the military, and what we call today border patrol agents, but also those seeking crossing to El Norte for economic, ecological, social, and political reasons. Many will try to stop them, but the push they experience in the takeover of their lands by multinational corporations and the pull for their labor so that people can eat well and live in a secure home are both immense. The story of the border wall continues. Now children, mothers, fathers, partners, and families requesting asylum are turned away from the ports of entry along the wall. Once (and still) seen as a security threat, they are also now seen as a public charge, contaminated with COVID-19 (Yong 2020). The story of the wall and how it is told as a unique or exceptionalist story to protect the status quo in the United States involves many features, such as characters, time, points of view, symbolism, and irony. Whether students endorse this story line, resist it, or engage it will have an impact on how to understand the border wall's story.

Ideological Dimensions

As with any literary text, the border wall is a moment of cultural expression. As a cultural expression, it is framed around a binary based on a neo-imperial rhetoric, where one side of the border wall—from the point of view of the United States—is good, moral, free, exceptional (the United States) and the other side is seen as bad, immoral, haters of freedom, and not chosen by God. This binary worldview sees those on the other side of the border wall as threats to the normative way of life in the United States. They (people on the other side) are dehumanized by being called "illegals"—a term employed to cast them in a negative light (Jones 2012, 41–42). They are objects, not humans. The border wall contributes, by creating a divide, to seeing Mexicans, Central Americans, and even Haitians who make their way to the southern border as dirty and diseased immigrants, criminal immigrants, and uncivilized immigrants (42). For these reasons, they are denied entry even when it is done legally through the asylum laws. The border wall is there to protect us from all the dangers (including children and asylum seekers), as one US Customs and Border Protection agent once said during a travel seminar. Today we have border walls all over the world that divide the haves and the have-nots (e.g., Israel/Palestine, India/Bangladesh, United States/Mexico). They signify the geopolitical realism that exists today of nationalism, imperialism, neoliberalism, hypermasculinity, and racialization, to name a few.

This superior/inferior or insider/foreigner division through the border wall influences what people think and how they behave toward those on the other side of the wall. It leads to policies such as family separation, prolonged detention, and deterrence along the US-Mexico border. Many students can easily connect with this issue. They understand the othering that this wall continues to do and the rhetoric that follows to create more unjust policies. If indeed these migrants are made in the image of God, as expressed in the biblical text and throughout the history of Christianity, the tradition is another voice—an ethical voice—that foregrounds the rights and dignity of all persons across the globe seeking safety and a better life.[10]

---

10. For an argument based on the foundation of human rights from a legal perspective, see Koh 2020.

Conclusion

An intercultural pedagogical approach does not focus on what students cannot do but what they can do. It searches for connectivity that students can draw on to create a student-centered emphasis. From experience, Latinx students (like many underserved and racialized students) do face implicit bias. They can be seen and defined by what they cannot do, even in biblical studies courses. My intercultural strategy aims to provide a space to make these students feel valued and empowered through learning their cultures and using their experiences. They are more likely, from experience, to have a sense of belonging that makes learning easier. Drawing on their experiences and history (as discussed above) gives all students a chance to learn another culture, build empathy, and connect parallel cultural stories. For sure, it raises expectations not only for Latinx students but for all. It is a way to increase and support what many colleagues call engagement.

The practices for Latinx students in our biblical studies classrooms, of course, vary. One does not need to become an expert on all cultural groups, but understanding their identities to build connectivity helps to make course materials relevant. My perspectives are not universal or complete. They are particular and in process. Nonetheless, Latinx students these days are bombarded through the political and social media, as well as the rhetoric of political leaders, with the message that they are undesirable, low achieving, and dangerous compared to whites, who belong and are exceptional and safe people. This constant attack on the Latinx psyche can lead many to internalize this negative mental image of themselves. Teachers, especially Latinx teachers, have a crucial role in resisting such negative, untruthful stereotypes. Critically reflecting on what we do with our biblical courses, how we teach and construct the ancient world of the biblical text, and why we teach it will all contribute to dismantling ancient rhetoric and modern-day forms of othering or racialization—both in the classroom and in the community.

Works Cited

Castles, Stephen, and Mark J. Miller. 2009. *The Age of Migration: International Population Movements in the Modern World*. 4th ed. New York: Guilford.

Dube, Musa W. 2016. "The Subaltern Can Speak: Reading the Mmutle (Hare) Way." *JAfRel* 4:54–75.

Esteban-Guitart, Moisès, and Luis C. Moll. 2014. "Funds of Identity: A New Concept Based on the Funds of Knowledge Approach." *C&P* 20:31–48.

Fernandez, Eleazar S. 2014. "Introduction: Birthing Culturally Diverse and Racially Just Educational Institutions: Teaching to Transgress and Transform." Pages 1–20 in *Teaching for a Culturally Diverse and Racially Just World*. Edited by Eleazar S. Fernandez. Eugene, OR: Cascade Books.

Grandin, Greg. 2019. *The End of the Myth: From the Frontier to the Border Wall in the Mind of America*. New York: Metropolitan Books.

Jones, Reece. 2012. *Border Walls: Security and the War on Terror in the United States, India, and Israel*. London: Zed.

———. 2017. *Violent Borders: Refugees and the Right to Move*. London: Verso.

Koh, Harry Hongju. 2020. "Why U.S. Leadership Matters for the Global Defense, Protection and Promotion of Human Rights: An Overarching Human Rights Strategy to Support the 'Globalization of Freedom' Is Needed." *FSJ* 97.5 (June): 32–34.

Kwok, Pui-lan. 2003. *Discovering the Bible in the Non-biblical World*. Eugene, OR: Wipf & Stock.

Lozada, Francisco, Jr. 2017. *Toward a Latino/a Biblical Interpretation*. Atlanta: SBL Press.

———. 2020. *The Gospel of John: History, Community, and Ideology*. London: Bloomsbury.

Martell-Otero, Loida. 2014. "From Foreign Bodies in Teacher Space to Embodied Spirit in *Personas Educadas*: Or, How to Prevent 'Tourists of Diversity' in Education." Pages 52–68 in *Teaching for a Culturally Diverse and Racially Just World*. Edited by Eleazar S. Fernandez. Eugene, OR: Cascade.

Martinez, Monica Muñoz. 2018. *The Injustice Never Leaves You: Anti-Mexican Violence in Texas*. Cambridge: Harvard University Press.

Masuoka, Natalie, and Jane Junn. 2013. *The Politics of Belonging: Race, Public Opinion, and Immigration*. Chicago: University of Chicago Press.

Moll, Luis C., Cathy Amanti, Deborah Neff, and Norma Gonzalez. 1992. "Funds of Knowledge for Teaching: Using a Qualitative Approach to Connect Homes and Classrooms." *TIP* 31:132–41.

Motomura, Hiroshi. 2006. *Americans in Waiting: The Lost Story of Immigration and Citizenship in the United States*. Oxford: Oxford University Press.

Nevins, Joseph. 2010. *Operation Gatekeeper and Beyond: The War on "Illegals" and the Remaking of the U.S.-Mexico Boundary*. New York: Routledge.

Reinhartz, Adele. 2018. *Cast Out of the Covenant: Jews and Anti-Judaism in the Gospel of John*. Lanham, MD: Lexington/Fortress Academic.

Saito, Natsu Taylor. 2019. "Why Xenophobia?" Social Science Research Network. http://dx.doi.org/10.2139/ssrn.3645466.

Salinas, Cristobal, Jr., and Adele Lozano. 2017. "Mapping and Recontextualizing the Evolution of the Term *Latinx*: An Environmental Scanning in Higher Education." *JLE* 18.4:1–14.

Shear, Michael D. 2020. "Leading Homeland Security under a President Who Embraces 'Hate-Filled' Talk. *The New York Times*. 10 July. https://tinyurl.com/SBLPress03111a.

Trouillot, Michel-Rolph. 1995. *Silencing the Past: Power and the Production of History*. Boston: Beacon.

Truett, Samuel. 2006. *Fugitive Landscapes: The Forgotten History of the U.S.-Mexico Borderlands*. New Haven: Yale University Press.

Yong, Ed. 2020. "How the Pandemic Defeated America." *The Atlantic*, 4 August. https://tinyurl.com/SBL03111ap.

Part 3
Reframing Contexts

Seeing Who's Not There:
Velázquez's *Kitchen Maid with the Supper at Emmaus*

Sonja Anderson

For who is greater, the one who is at the table or the one who serves? Is it not the one at the table? But I am among you as one who serves.
—Luke 22:27 NRSV

The Activity and Its Classroom Context

This activity involves viewing an early seventeenth-century Spanish painting of the Supper at Emmaus, comparing it to the biblical text (Luke 24:13–35), and then discussing how biblical interpreters ought to engage with questions of race, class, and gender.[1] I use the exercise in my Jesus, the Bible, and Christian Beginnings course, which I teach at a selective undergraduate liberal arts college in the American Midwest. Students tend to be politically liberal; privately religious if at all; committed to racial, gender, and economic justice; and fairly new to the Bible and its interpretation. Though the college has made impressive gains in student diversity in recent years, the faculty is less diverse, and it is sadly common for a student to find that she is at best one of only two black students in a classroom. Being nonwhite on a majority white campus in the United States can be exhausting and enraging, so it is crucial that instructors make their classrooms places where identity, power, and texts can be engaged critically and with empathy. This can be challenging when a course is about premodern material that does not fit neatly into modern taxonomies, racial or otherwise.

---

1. Described briefly in Anderson 2020. I thank Sofia Barbato for introducing me to this painting.

Jesus, the Bible, and Christian Beginnings enrolls twenty to twenty-five students, meets three times a week for ten weeks, and helps students build skills of close reading, live discussion, and intensive writing and revising. Unlike a traditional Introduction to the New Testament course that marches through the twenty-seven canonical books, this course covers only a selection of New Testament texts in order to make room for ancient noncanonical texts as well as modern biblical interpretation concerned with Christian anti-Semitism, gender and sexuality, and racism and political liberation. Readings include:

	Canonical	
Mark	Matthew	Luke (portions)
John (portions)	1, 2, 3 John	1 Thessalonians
Galatians	Romans (portions)	1 Corinthians
1, 2 Timothy	Titus	Colossians 3:18–4:1
Ephesians 5:21–6:9	Philemon	Revelation
	Noncanonical	
Plato, *Phaedo*	4 Maccabees	Testament of Solomon
Gospel of Thomas	Infancy Gospel of Thomas	Protevangelium of James
Acts of Thecla	Romanos the Melodist, select hymns (Lash 1995)	Martyrdom of Perpetua and Felicitas
Martyrdom of Polycarp	Origen, *On First Principles* (excerpts)	Athanasius, *Life of Antony*

In terms of modern readings, students use Bart Ehrman's (2017) *Brief Introduction to the New Testament* as a textbook but also read abundant secondary material throughout the course. This gives them a decent grasp of the Greco-Roman, Jewish world and of the surprising ways skilled modern readers can arrive at very different, sometimes opposite conclusions about the same text. When we study the Gospel of Mark, for example, I assign Mario DiCicco's (1998) argument that Jesus praises the widow in 12:41–44 for losing her life in order to save it (Mark 8:35); Addison Wright's (1982) argument that Jesus, on the contrary, is lamenting that "she out of her poverty has put in everything she had" (12:44 NRSV) because she has been exploited by those who "devour widows' houses" (12:40 NRSV); and Candida Moss's (2010) article reading the healing of woman with the flow of blood (Mark 5:25–34) in the context of ancient medical theory. During the Gospel of Matthew, students read James Cone (1969) and N. T. Wright (2007) to see how two Protestant theologians grapple with the apocalyptic character of the text. Kate Bowler's (2011) chapter on faith healing in charismatic black churches shows students that the ancient nexus of faith, healing, and medicine that they encountered in Mark 5 continues in the present day. Romanos the Melodist's Byzantine liturgical poetry shows how imagined backstories and dialogues between silent biblical characters enhance and even change what seems to be the plain meaning of a passage (Lash 1995). Students are introduced early, then, to an array of interpretations people give New Testament texts, and they realize that a slight change of emphasis or a shift in context can produce wildly different readings of the same story. (For a fuller list of modern sources I assign, see the works cited.)

The activity I describe here takes place in the fourth week, after students have read Mark, Matthew, parts of Luke, a sixth-century hymn of Romanos the Melodist, and the secondary material listed at the end of this chapter. It is inspired by art historian Jennifer Roberts's (2013) short and profound article "The Power of Patience," describing how she requires her students to spend three hours in a museum looking at a single painting. "It is commonly assumed that vision is immediate," she writes. "But what students learn in a visceral way in this assignment is that in any work of art there are details and orders and relationships that take time to perceive" (40). The instructor should read Roberts's piece and might consider assigning it to students as well. I begin class by projecting Diego Velázquez's seventeenth-century *Kitchen Maid with the Supper at Emmaus* on the screen. I do not reveal the title.

I ask students to spend three minutes looking at the image. That is considerably less than three hours, but after just one minute, students will feel how strange sustained attention is and glance around nervously. Two minutes, and we are still looking. At three minutes, I ask them to write down their answer to two questions: "What do you see?" and "What do you think this painting is depicting?" They then spend five minutes sharing their answers with a neighbor.

Now warmed up, the students join in a whole-class discussion about the painting. They may note the woman's posture, the use of light, the woman's dark skin and the men's light skin. This is a moment when shy

Fig. 1. Diego Velázquez, *Kitchen Maid with the Supper at Emmaus*. Public domain.

or novice students can shine, since describing what one sees is much less intimidating than sharing thoughts on a difficult reading. A consensus usually develops that the woman in the foreground has had a flash of insight or is listening closely to something. Her attention is absorbed by what is in her head or in her ear, so she has turned away from the pitcher she is holding and has stopped in her tracks, looking at nothing.

Asked what is depicted, most students will answer that it is the Last Supper, given the resemblance of the image in the upper left to Leonardo da Vinci's well-known painting. I tell them that they are close and that the scene is biblical, but it is not the Last Supper. A bit more head-scratching, and someone remembers that Luke describes a second supper, similar to the first: the supper at Emmaus, for which the painting is named. I ask someone to read the passage aloud (Luke 24:13–35). The meal scene begins at 24:28:

> As [the two of them] came near the village to which they were going, [Jesus] walked ahead as if he were going on. But they urged him strongly, saying, "Stay with us, because it is almost evening and the day is now nearly over." So he went in to stay with them. *When he was at the table with them, he took bread, blessed and broke it, and gave it to them. Then their eyes were opened, and they recognized him; and he vanished from their sight.* They said to each other, "Were not our hearts burning within us while he was talking to us on the road, while he was opening the scriptures to us?" That same hour they got up and returned to Jerusalem; and they found the eleven and their companions gathered together. They were saying, "The Lord has risen indeed, and he has appeared to Simon!" Then they told what had happened on the road, and how *he had been*

made known to them in the breaking of the bread. (Luke 24:28–35 NRSV, emphasis added)

Now that the students know they are looking at *Kitchen Maid with the Supper at Emmaus* from seventeenth-century Spain, they adjust their interpretations in another round of discussion. There is no woman in the text, at least not explicitly, so who is the woman in the foreground? Was Velázquez taking artistic license and inserting an imagined character into the Bible? Or is that a framed painting rather than a kitchen window in the upper left? Why is the kitchen maid black while Jesus and his companion are white? What was the ethnic makeup of Spain when Velázquez painted this picture? Is she enslaved? Who is sitting with Jesus? Cleopas (24:18) and … ? Is part of the canvas missing, or did Velázquez deliberately omit the second (24:13) disciple? Maybe the viewer is the missing disciple? Or should the viewer identify with the kitchen maid and her epiphany? Would different viewers identify with different figures? Is the kitchen maid more important than Jesus, since she is at the center of the image? I offer students a contemporary interpretation, poet laureate Natasha Tretheway's (2012) poem "Kitchen Maid with Supper at Emmaus, or The Mulata" (full text available in Tretheway 2012 and at https://poets.org/poem/kitchen-maid-supper-emmaus-or-mulata). Tretheway calls the woman an "echo of Jesus at table … his white corona, her white cap." "Listening," writes Tretheway, "she leans into what she knows."[2]

I agree. The kitchen maid indeed "leans into what she knows": the sound of Jesus in the other room, taking bread, blessing it, breaking it, and giving it. She knows this ritual because she has heard it before—at the Last Supper, where she was present and probably unnoticed by those who would later recount the event (Luke 22:14–20). (Caterers and food service workers will recognize the experience of overhearing a great deal from unsuspecting diners.) Moreover, while the disciples require hearing, sight, and perhaps taste and touch before they recognize the risen Jesus, faith for the kitchen maid comes by hearing alone. As a different evangelist says, "Blessed are those who have not seen and yet have come to believe" (John 20:29 NRSV).

I then steer students toward a hermeneutical reflection, comparing Velázquez's style of interpretation to other material we have read. Like the

---

2. My thanks go to Bridget O'Brien for showing me this poem.

Protevangelium of James, Velázquez imported characters and a rich setting into a sparse biblical scene. Like James Cone, he saw race where the text was silent. Like Elsa Támez (1982), he emphasized class difference. Like 4 Maccabees, he inverted a conventional hierarchy of power, gender, and ethnicity. Like Luke's Magnificat, he has "lifted up the lowly" (1:52). And so on. The instructor can keep the discussion going for the duration of class or conclude it here.

What are the outcomes of this exercise? I count seven.

1. Students realize how much they can notice when they slow down and look closely.
2. Students review, synthesize, and apply the course readings with their peers.
3. Students with weaker reading skills can do visual analysis.
4. The task sidesteps students' religious commitments by having them analyze something that is not the Bible.
5. The juxtaposition of image and text shows students how little information is conveyed by the text itself and how much must be supplied by the reader.
6. The image as expanded text sets students up for the weeks to come, when they will encounter expansive riffs on Scripture such as the apocalyptic *Confessions of Nat Turner* (Gray 1831).
7. Students realize that making images of biblical characters—in the mind or on the canvas—involves decisions about race. While race may not have been a category for the biblical authors, it is a category for those of us who now interpret those texts in the midst of a racist political order. Again, to quote Roberts (2013, 42), "Deceleration … is a productive process, a form of skilled apprehension that can orient students in critical ways to the contemporary world."

Though students need not do any additional reading on Velázquez or Lukan women in order to profit from this exercise, instructors may well want more background. In what follows, I offer an overview of some key interpretive issues scholars have noted concerning Velázquez's painting, on the one hand, and women in Luke 22 and 24 on the other. I begin with Luke, because for most biblical scholars, my imaginative exercise immediately raises a textual question: *Could* a woman have been present at the supper at Emmaus and, before that, at the Last Supper?

Women at Luke's Last Supper and the Supper at Emmaus

What did Luke think? In short, we do not know. He does not say that women were present at either meal, but he also does not say that they were not.[3] For the supper at Emmaus, the text is straightforwardly ambiguous. Cleopas (24:18) and a conspicuously unnamed (and ungendered) companion dine with Jesus at Emmaus, and no mention is made of how the meal was prepared (Reed and Matthews 2021, 641–42). No textual obstacle stands in the way of imagining that someone else overheard this meal. But from a narrative standpoint, my interpretation—that the kitchen maid is hearing a voice she's heard before—requires her to have been present at the Last Supper as well. Would the text permit this? Initially, it might seem that it would not: "When the hour came, he sat at table, and *the apostles* with him" (Luke 22:14 RSV; Καὶ ὅτε ἐγένετο ἡ ὥρα, ἀνέπεσεν καὶ οἱ ἀπόστολοι σὺν αὐτῷ).

Does this verse exclude women's presence at the Last Supper? There are two ways to answer the question: (1) figure out whether the apostles could have included women, and (2) figure out whether Luke means and the apostles—and only the apostles—with him.

Could Women Be Apostles?

Could women be among the apostles? Outside the gospels, membership is broad. We have long known, thanks to Bernadette Brooten (1997; Epp 2005; Lin 2020), that Junia was "outstanding among the apostles" along with her partner, Andronicus (Rom 16:7 NIV). Timothy and Silvanus are apostles (1 Thess 1:1, 2:6). Paul is an "apostle of Jesus Christ" (1 Cor 1:1, 2 Cor 1:1, Gal 1:1) and was aware and resentful of other "super-apostles" (2 Cor 11:5). Revelation, too, is suspicious of "those who call themselves apostles but are not" (2:2 RSV). Acts calls Paul and Barnabas apostles (Acts 14:4, 14). Even Jesus himself is called an "apostle and high priest" in Heb 3:1. In short, men and at least one woman, none of them part of the Twelve, are called apostles in New Testament texts outside the gospels.

---

3. On the presence of women at Greco-Roman meals, and their possible presence at Luke's meals, see the discussion and bibliography in Reed and Matthews 2021, 430–34. Of particular importance are Corley 1993; Osiek and MacDonald 2006.

Within the gospels, however, *apostle* never explicitly designates a woman. What led to this discrepancy in early Christian usage? Elisabeth Schüssler Fiorenza (1977) argues that it is in Luke that one can discern a shift from the broader (and earlier) definition of apostle seen above to a more restricted meaning: one of the Twelve, all of whom were men. The selection and commissioning of these twelve men appears in Matthew, Mark, and Luke, and each evangelist calls them apostles:

Matthew 10:1–2 NRSV	Mark 3:13–16 NRSV	Luke 6:12–13 NRSV
"his twelve disciples" = "the twelve apostles"	"those whom he wanted" = "twelve" = "apostles"	subset of "his disciples" = ? "twelve" = "apostles"
Then Jesus summoned *his twelve disciples* and gave them authority over unclean spirits, to cast them out, and to cure every disease and every sickness. These are the names of *the twelve apostles*: (names follow)	He went up the mountain and called to him *those whom he wanted*, and they came to him. And he appointed *twelve*, whom he also named *apostles*, to be with him, and to be sent out to proclaim the message, and to have authority to cast out demons. So he appointed *the twelve*: (names follow)	Now during those days he went out to the mountain to pray; and he spent the night in prayer to God. And when day came, *he called his disciples and chose twelve of them, whom he also named apostles*: (names follow)

What does this tell us about women and apostleship in the gospels? Not much. Only males are listed, but maleness is not listed as a requirement. It is Luke's second volume, Acts, that identifies maleness as essential to membership in the Twelve and therefore in apostleship. Peter, wanting to choose a successor for Judas, says to a large group of brothers (ἄνδρες ἀδελφοί, 1:16):

> "So one of the *men* [ἀνδρῶν] who have accompanied us during all the time that the Lord Jesus went in and out among us, beginning from the baptism of John until the day when he was taken up from us—one of these must become a witness with us to his resurrection."... And they cast lots for them, and the lot fell on Matthias; and he was added to *the eleven apostles*. (Acts 1:21–22, 26 NRSV, emphasis added)

And while Luke is willing to grant the title "apostle" to men who are not part of the Twelve (Paul and Barnabas in Acts 14:4, 14), he never applies it to women. As Schüssler Fiorenza (1977, 138) puts it:

> Luke was aware that women fulfilled the conditions for apostleship. However, he was also aware that according to tradition no women were members of the Twelve. Thus he felt compelled to give the women disciples a preeminent place equal to that of the Twelve (Lk 8:1–3), while not calling them apostles and deemphasizing their resurrection witness (24:11, 34). It becomes apparent that Luke's theological redaction had to formulate maleness as an additional criterion for apostleship because of the peculiar Lukan understanding that the circle of the apostles was coextensive with that of the Twelve.

Perhaps Mark and Matthew were aware of this male-only apostolic tradition, perhaps not. Pauline Christianity, aware of it or not, did not abide by it, as Junia's example at the end of Romans shows. But as for Luke's Last Supper, women's presence will not be found within the phrase "the apostles."

Were Only the Apostles Present at the Last Supper?

The other way to approach the question is to grant that the apostles may well mean the Twelve but insist that Luke thought—and assumed his audience would think—that others were present as well. If this sounds like a stretch, consider the statement, "She delivered her lecture in the classroom, with the senior faculty in attendance." Were only the senior faculty in attendance? Or were students present as well, with the senior faculty's presence noted only because of its significance? Quentin Quesnell (1983) argues along these lines and concludes that women were present at the Last Supper. Quesnell (66) observes that Luke's narrative "gradually builds up a larger and larger group around Jesus," so that "by the time of the arrival at Jerusalem, the group contains at least the Twelve, the Seventy-two, the women (of whom only three are named, but 'many others' noted [8:3]), the mother and brothers of Jesus. Luke thinks the group is large enough to deserve being called 'the entire multitude of his disciples'" (19:37).

Unlike apostles, *disciples* in Luke certainly includes women. Functionally, they play the role of disciples, as Mary does when she sits at Jesus's feet learning from him (10:39). They are also, in a roundabout but undeniable way, called disciples. When the angel tells the women at the tomb to "remember how he told you, while he was still in Galilee, that the Son of Man must be handed over to sinners, and be crucified, and on the third day rise again" (24:6–7 NRSV), the reason they "remember his words" (v. 8) is that they were evidently included among those disciples whom Luke says heard Jesus's passion predictions in 9:22 and 9:44 (Quesnell 1983, 67). Women as apostles in Luke? No. Women as disciples? Yes.

Once in Jerusalem, Jesus plans to "eat the Passover with my disciples" (μετὰ τῶν μαθητῶν μου, 22:11), and after it, the disciples accompany him to the Mount of Olives (οἱ μαθηταί, 22:39). But at the Supper itself, it is the apostles, not the disciples, who are mentioned. Does this mean the disciples were absent? Quesnell (1983, 66) proposes that the reference to "the apostles" may "be no more than a highlighting of one group among the *mathētai* (vv. 11 and 39)," due to the central role the Twelve play at the founding of the church in the opening chapter of Acts.[4] Taken together with Luke's repeated emphasis on women's faithfulness and on the large groups that follow Jesus around, Quesnell is persuaded that this pattern outweighs the single word (*apostles*) on which women's absence at the Last Supper depends. For Quesnell, women's presence is possible because Luke did not mean "and his apostles—and only his apostles—with him."

Not all interpreters have found this argument from silence convincing. Dorothy Lee (2020), for instance, argues that while the *historical* Jesus had women at his Last Supper, Luke does not think he did. Lee observes that, the Last Supper passage aside, Luke uses the term *apostles* rarely and only in reference to the Twelve. There is no reason to think he means it any differently at 22:14. Jesus's promise, moreover, that those present at the Supper will "sit on thrones judging the twelve tribes of Israel" (22:30 NRSV) has greater symbolic heft if addressed to a group of twelve (see especially Lee 2020, 158–59).[5]

In sum, the question of women's presence at Luke's Last Supper cannot be settled exegetically. Luke does not say women are present, nor, if Quesnell is right, does he say they are absent. If we want to treat the biblical text

---

4. Quesnell has *methētai* but means *mathētai*.
5. Quesnell's response to 22:30 is that the number of thrones is not specified in Luke (as it is in Matthew).

as a closed, finished composition, then there is just enough room for the kitchen maid at these meals. There may even be a bit more room if we think not of presence at the table but merely presence within earshot.

On the other hand, there is good ancient precedent for dispensing with the idea of Scripture as a series of fixed, authoritative lemmas that must only be explained or commented on by readers who avoid reading into and otherwise violating the text. As Eva Mroczek (2016) has shown, this is a curiously modern and mostly Christian understanding of the Bible that does not reflect how ancient Jews and Christians conceived of sacred text: as something open, unfinished, and generative of rewritings, supplements, and spin-offs. Consider rabbinic midrash. Or apocryphal texts such as the Testament of Job that provide backstories to famous biblical figures and thereby change the meaning of their canonical counterparts. Or the dramatic metrical homilies of Romanos the Melodist, which pay homage to Scripture by treating it as raw matter from which to build imagined dialogues between imagined characters in imagined scenes. These styles of reading are as old as, and sometimes older than, the sort of exegesis that is commonly taught in churches, seminaries, and graduate programs. I find this more ancient style of scriptural imagination attractive, and I am happy to imagine the kitchen maid at both suppers, essential yet unnoticed by the men she feeds and understands.

Diego Velázquez

What of Diego Velázquez and his time? How have art historians evaluated *Kitchen Maid*? Velázquez was born in 1599 in Seville, the hub of trade in the Spanish Empire (Ayala Mallory 2006; Tiffany 2012, especially 3–22). He apprenticed, beginning at age twelve, under Francisco Pacheco, whose daughter he later married. Velázquez left Seville in 1622 and traveled to Madrid and Italy, eventually coming under the patronage of King Philip IV. He painted numerous genre scenes (paintings that do not portray a particular historical person or event), portraits of court and church officials, and religious works. Perhaps his most famous painting is the mind-bending *Las Meninas* (*The Maids of Honor*, 1656), which shows the child queen Margarita Teresa surrounded by her entourage, with Velázquez to her left painting a portrait and a small mirror on the back wall reflecting back to the viewer the king and queen, who are otherwise not depicted. A prolific and status-seeking artist, Velázquez was finally rewarded with knighthood in 1658. A little over a year later, in 1660, Velázquez fell ill

Fig. 12.2. Diego Velázquez, *Christ in the House of Martha and Mary*. Public domain.

with a fever on the Feast of Saint Ignatius of Loyola (31 July) and died a week later, on the Feast of the Transfiguration (6 August) in Madrid.

Kitchen Maid with the Supper at Emmaus is from his early period in Seville. It hangs in the National Gallery of Ireland and resembles another of his works from the same period, *Christ in the House of Martha and Mary*.[6]

The inverted style of these paintings—everyday objects and foods in the foreground and a small biblical scene in the background—originated in the Netherlands (Tiffany 2012, 108–9). Art historians, most recently Tanya Tiffany (2005), have argued that these inverted scenes prompt the viewer to relate the humble, transitory objects of the foreground to the eternal realities depicted in the background. The relation, however, is not straightforward. A quick reading might say that the background scene above, where "Mary has chosen the better part," serves to denigrate the cooking women in the foreground. Yet, as Tiffany (2005, 442) argues, "the presence of the Lenten still life in the foreground scene also emphasizes the need to join the sacred and the secular by reminding the viewer to honor Christ by heeding the spiritual life even while nourishing the body,"

---

6. A nearly identical work, simply titled *Kitchen Maid* (with no image of the supper), is held by the Art Institute of Chicago.

for it may be that "the toils of the melancholy cook in the painting's foreground will lead to a higher spiritual reward."

Tiffany also considers the ambiguous nature of the background image. Is it a hung painting? A window? This uncertainty heightens the painting's power as a devotional image, for it forces the viewer to consider multiple possible relationships between the two scenes. Such meditation was in fact an increasingly popular religious practice in seventeenth-century Spain, thanks to Ignatius of Loyola's *Spiritual Exercises*, published in 1548 (Tiffany 2005, 442). The *Exercises*, an abbreviated instruction manual for the giver of a retreat, repeatedly call for the retreatant to vividly imagine gospel scenes, converse with the characters in them, and thereby increase in love for God. For instance, in a meditation on the nativity, one would envision

> our Lady, about nine months with child, ... seated on an ass, set out from Nazareth. She was accompanied by Joseph and a maid, who was leading an ox. They are going to Bethlehem to pay the tribute that Caesar imposed on those lands.
>
> This is a mental representation of the place. It will consist here in seeing in imagination the way from Nazareth to Bethlehem. Consider its length, its breadth; whether level, or through valleys and over hills. Observe also the place or cave where Christ is born; whether big or little; whether high or low; and how it is arranged....
>
> This will consist in seeing the persons, namely, our Lady, St. Joseph, the maid, and the Child Jesus after His birth. I will make myself a poor little unworthy slave, and as though present, look upon them, contemplate them, and serve them in their needs with all possible homage and reverence. Then I will reflect on myself that I may reap some fruit.
>
> This is to consider, observe, and contemplate what the persons are saying, and then to reflect on myself and draw some fruit from it. (Puhl 1951, 52–53)

Less happily, a meditation on hell would require one "to hear the wailing, the howling, cries, and blasphemies ... with the sense of smell to perceive the smoke, the sulphur, the filth, and corruption ... to taste the bitterness of tears ... with the sense of touch to feel the flames," and then to "enter into conversation with Christ our Lord" (Puhl 1951, 32–33). Whatever the scene, the vivid imagination of corporeal sensations is required, and the Jesuits recognized that art could foster this. One of Ignatius's companions, Jerome Nadal, composed a book of annotations, or captions, of gospel scenes to accompany the *Exercises*. This volume was richly illustrated by skilled artists and was known to painters like Velázquez. Inverted scenes like *Christ in the House of Martha and Mary* and *Kitchen Maid with the Supper at Emmaus* echo these devotional images and go a step further, inviting the viewer to become a momentary retreatant while puzzling over the connection between the life of Christ and a particular life in the world (Tiffany 2005).

What of our painting? Tiffany (2012, 103–23), again, offers a compelling contextualization of *Kitchen Maid with the Supper at Emmaus*. Seville was a major hub of the slave trade in Velázquez's time, including both white slaves from north Africa, prisoners of war taken by the Ottoman Empire, and *moriscos* as well as black Africans. Velázquez owned and later freed an African slave, Juan de Pareja, who was himself an artist. Slave ownership was common for upper- and middle-class Europeans. Velázquez's father owned slaves, and it may be that the kitchen maid is modeled on one of them. Such enslaved people "formed an integral, but marginal" part of society, but the state of their souls and their capacity for salvation was much discussed by churchmen of the day (105). Tiffany sees Velázquez's painting as part of this discussion. Perhaps he is suggesting to his contemporaries that Africans could receive the light of revelation and that European viewers ought to aid them along that path by offering baptism and catechesis.

I find this a convincing historical interpretation and flinch at the racist paternalism of its artist and probable audience. Taking my cue from the ancient interpreters with whom I am more at home, I prefer to read the image out of its original context and import it into first-century Jerusalem, past historico-literary reconstructions and into the vivid terrain of the scriptural imagination. It seems to me, if I use Ignatius's technique, that I can see the kitchen maid startle as she hears the familiar voice she first overheard in the upper room. She is not invited to the table, and the men's obliviousness to her presence is stunning. But maybe she is busy thinking about the other words she once heard in that upper room: "For who is greater, the one who is at the table or the one who serves? Is it not the one at the table? But I am among you as one who serves" (Luke 22:27 NRSV).

Works Cited

Starred (*) sources are assigned as course readings in the weeks before the activity. Double-starred (**) sources are among those assigned after the activity.

*Alexander, Loveday C. 2002. "Sisters in Adversity: Retelling Martha's Story." Pages 197–213 in *A Feminist Companion to Luke*. Edited by Amy-Jill Levine and Marianne Blickenstaff. New York: Sheffield Academic.

Anderson, Sonja. 2020. "Seeing the Unseen: Art and Politics in the Biblical Studies Classroom." *WCJT* 1.3:123.

Ayala Mallory, Nina, trans. 2006. *Lives of Velázquez: Francisco Pacheco and Antonio Palomino*. London: Pallas Athene.

*Bowler, Kate. 2011. "Blessed Bodies: Healing within the African-American Faith Movement." Pages 81–105 in *Global Pentecostal and Charismatic Healing*. Edited by Candy Gunther Brown. New York: Oxford University Press.

*Brooten, Bernadette. 1977. "Junia ... Outstanding among the Apostles." Pages 141–44 in *Women Priests: A Catholic Commentary on the Vatican Declaration*. Edited by Leonard Swindler and Arlene Swindler. New York: Paulist.

*Cone, James. 1969. "The Gospel of Jesus, Black People, and Black Power." Pages 31–61 in *Black Theology and Black Power*. New York: Seabury.

Corley, Kathleen E. 1993. *Private Women, Public Meals: Social Conflict in the Synoptic Tradition*. Peabody, MA: Hendrickson.

*DiCicco, Mario. 1998. "What Can One Give in Exchange for One's Life? A Narrative-Critical Study of the Widow and Her Offering, Mark 12:41–44." *CurTM* 25:441–49.

*Ehrman, Bart D. 2017. *A Brief Introduction to the New Testament*. 4th ed. New York: Oxford University Press.

Epp, Eldon J. 2005. *Junia: The First Woman Apostle*. Minneapolis: Fortress.

*Fredriksen, Paula. 1999. "God and Israel in Roman Antiquity." Pages 51–73 in *Jesus of Nazareth, King of the Jews: A Jewish Life and the Emergence of Christianity*. New York: Vintage Books.

**Gray, Thomas. 1831. *The Confessions of Nat Turner*. Baltimore: Lucas & Deaver.

**Lash, Ephrem, trans. 1995. *Kontakia on the Life of Christ: St. Romanos the Melodist*. San Francisco: HarperCollins.

Lee, Dorothy A. 2020. "Presence or Absence? The Question of Women Disciples at the Last Supper." Pages 155–76 in *Creation, Matter and the Image of God: Essays on John*. Hindmarsh: ATF.

*Levine, Amy-Jill. 2006. *The Misunderstood Jew: The Church and the Scandal of the Jewish Jesus*. San Francisco: HarperOne.

Lin, Yii-Jan. 2020. "Junia: An Apostle before Paul." *JBL* 139:191–209.

*Moss, Candida R. 2010. "The Man with the Flow of Power: Porous Bodies in Mark 5:25." *JBL* 129:507–19.

Mroczek, Eva. 2016. *The Literary Imagination in Jewish Antiquity*. New York: Oxford University Press.

Osiek, Carolyn, and Margaret Y. MacDonald, with Janet H. Tulloch. 2006. *A Woman's Place: House Churches in Earliest Christianity*. Minneapolis: Fortress.

Puhl, Louis J., trans. 1951. *The Spiritual Exercises of St. Ignatius: Based on Studies in the Language of the Autograph*. Chicago: Loyola University Press.

Quesnell, Quentin. 1983. "The Women at Luke's Supper." Pages 59–79 in *Political Issues in Luke-Acts*. Edited by Richard J. Cassidy and Philip J. Scharper. Maryknoll, NY: Orbis Books.

Reed, Barbara E., and Shelly Matthews. 2021. *Luke 10–24*. WisC 43B. Collegeville, MN: Liturgical Press.

Roberts, Jennifer L. 2013. "The Power of Patience: Teaching Students the Value of Deceleration and Immersive Attention." *Harvard Magazine* (November–December): 40–43.

Schüssler Fiorenza, Elisabeth. 1977. "The Apostleship of Women in Early Christianity." Pages 135–40 in *Women Priests: A Catholic Commentary on the Vatican Declaration*. Edited by Leonard Swindler and Arlene Swindler. New York: Paulist.

*Támez, Elsa. 1982. "Good News for the Poor." Pages 66–74 in *Bible of the Oppressed*. Translated by Matthew J. O'Connell. Maryknoll, NY: Orbis.

Tiffany, Tanya J. 2005. "Visualizing Devotion in Early Modern Seville: Velázquez's *Christ in the House of Martha and Mary*." *SCJ* 36:433–53.

———. 2012. *Diego Velázquez's Early Paintings and the Culture of Seventeenth-Century Seville*. University Park: Pennsylvania State University Press.

Tretheway, Natasha. 2012. "Kitchen Maid with Supper at Emmaus, or The Mulata." Page 27 in *Thrall: Poems*. Boston: Mariner Books. Also available online at https://poets.org/poem/kitchen-maid-supper-emmaus-or-mulata.

*Wright, Addison. 1982. "The Widow's Mites: Praise or Lament? A Matter of Context." *CBQ* 44:256–65.
*Wright, N. T. 2007. "The Mission and Message of Jesus." Pages 31–52 in *The Meaning of Jesus: Two Visions*. By N. T. Wright and Marcus Borg. 2nd ed. San Francisco: HarperOne.

Can the Biblical Subaltern Speak?
A Case for Multiple Historical Criticisms

Haley Gabrielle

Introductory biblical studies courses often do not include minoritized voices on their syllabi, and even when they do, these voices typically are so few as to be nonessential, relegated to the status of optional readings, or segregated into a short block on new ideological criticisms. In order to integrate all critical methods in a just fashion, the authority of *the* historical-critical method must be relativized, and the theoretical rigor of identity-based methods must be validated.[1] *The* historical-critical method is a particular way of doing history, namely, one popularized by mostly male, Protestant, German academics in the eighteenth through twentieth centuries; the strengths and weaknesses of this methodology are tied to its social and historical locations. But there are multiple ways of doing history. One way appears in Gayatri Chakravorty Spivak's (1999) chapter "History" in *A Critique of Postcolonial Reason*; her attention to dominant discourses reveals the problem of the historian's claim of representation and the difficulty of the subaltern's speech.

A case study of Acts 16:16–18 illustrates the value of Spivak's historical method for biblical studies and the existence of multiple historical criticisms. Tracing the dominant discourses surrounding this passage reveals that biblical scholars' claims to represent the subaltern figure in this text are built on the unsteady foundations of exclusivist Christianity or individualist feminism. Both of these approaches obscure our view of her and should prompt us to interrogate our claims as historians to be able to

---

1. By *identity-based*, I refer to methods including but not limited to womanist, *mujerista*, feminist, postcolonial, African American, Asian/Asian American, Majority World, queer, and disability studies criticisms. These methods explicitly or implicitly suggest a particular social identity held by the interpreter practicing them.

represent her satisfactorily. Instructors in biblical studies can improve the equity and inclusion of their classrooms by foregrounding the ideological dimensions and scholarly sophistication of all critical methods and by encouraging their students to explore more than one way of doing history.

The Historical-Critical Method in the Classroom

A high proportion of students are first introduced to the notion of method in biblical interpretation in the introductory biblical studies classroom. But too frequently, students receive the message that *the* historical-critical method is the only legitimate method or at least is the most important method to learn.[2] In some curricula, the message of the sole legitimacy of *the* historical-critical method is communicated when lectures, assignments, and readings only ask students to wrestle with the historical context of the biblical text, and when authors on the syllabus are all of a dominant social location, while their identity is left unmarked. In other curricula, students are led to think that *the* historical-critical method is manifestly the most important method among several. *The* historical-critical method and its unmarked practitioners typically comprise the required readings, while readings that feature identity-based methods and are written by minoritized scholars are offered as merely optional readings. Students may focus on *the* historical-critical method for the vast majority of the time, while ideological hermeneutics are segregated into a short block at the beginning or end of the semester. Even when readings by nondominant scholars are regularly assigned throughout the syllabus, students may not be asked to engage substantively with their content in lectures, discussions, or assessments. The sidelining of identity-based methodologies occurs regularly in a variety of institutions, including those with commitments to inclusion, diversity, and social justice.

---

2. Depending on the theological environment of the introductory biblical studies classroom, the term *historical-critical* may or may not be foregrounded. In a more conservative environment, the critical component of the methodology may be replaced or deemphasized. By referring to *the* historical-critical method, I nevertheless point to the manner in which biblical studies classrooms across the theological spectrum frequently communicate the sense that there is a single historical method (or cohesive set of methods) that allows the interpreter to objectively access the meaning of biblical texts in their original historical context.

The marginalization of scholarship by minoritized authors in the biblical studies classroom makes a profound impact not only on the education of students but also on their well-being. Students are not only less equipped to see and respond to structural oppression and more liable to perpetuate uninterrogated patterns of dominance in their thought. They are also more likely to personally experience such feelings of erasure as shame and anger and to be discouraged from seeing their voices as valuable in theological, academic, and social discussions of the Bible. In her womanist ethical theorization of the cultural production of evil, Emilie M. Townes (2006, 151) expresses the harm of such practices in the classroom:[3]

> i will not rescue the killers
>> who create optional reading lists
>>> that signal to me
>>>> that some actual or alleged scholars really believe
>>>>> that there are optional peoples, cultures, lives, ideas, hopes, realities
>>> and secondary lists are little better
>>>> when they traffic peoples' yearnings and expectations as ideologies and abstractions.

While it may be difficult for instructors to accept and grapple with these realities, our responsibilities to our students and genuine care for them can motivate us to continually reexamine the theoretical foundations on which our syllabi are built.

There are many reasons introductory biblical studies syllabi look the way they do, including the history of the discipline, doctoral education and training, and hiring practices, all of which are informed by patterns of structural injustice. Here I want to focus on a methodological impediment that may still be present for scholars who understand themselves as already working to dismantle such legacies of oppression. I urge us to recognize that *the* historical-critical method is not only one method among many but one *historical* method among many other historical methods. In addition to multiple approaches to the study of a text (e.g., historical, literary, rhetorical, sociological, allegorical), there are multiple approaches to the practice of history itself. Below I briefly outline features

---

3. Townes is reflecting on the following words of June Jordan: "We do not sweat and summon our best in order to rescue the killers; it is to comfort and to empower the possible victims of evil that we do tinker and daydream and revise and memorize, and then impart all that we can of our inspired, our inherited humanity."

of *the* historical-critical method and contrast it with alternative methods of history, with a focus on the method of Spivak.

German Historical Criticism and Spivakian Historical Criticism

The historical-critical method typically refers to a set of mutually supporting exegetical strategies, including history of religions, textual criticism, source criticism, form criticism, redaction criticism, and tradition criticism.[4] These techniques were used in academic settings in the eighteenth through twentieth centuries in Europe and North America; because these methods predominantly originated in Germany, we may refer to the method itself as German historical criticism. The progenitors of this network of methods were white men with the attendant class benefits of university education, and they were frequently supporters and beneficiaries of their nations' colonial activities. Raised and educated in culturally as well as theologically Christian spaces, Christianity was their primary religious frame of reference, in particular Western European Christianity. They frequently held a level of personal commitment to Christ while also maintaining a principled liberty from the institutional church, influenced strongly by Protestant formulations of spirituality.

In this context, a particular way of doing history arose. A primary value in this approach was objectivity, the choice not to bring presuppositions into the scholarly investigation and instead to proceed in a mode of discourse that could be universally agreed on. This approach was understood to contrast with the approach of the church, which ostensibly decided in advance what theology would be found in the biblical text. But it was also understood to contrast with the approach of the irrational subject, who did not have the capacity to come to the same necessary, logical conclusions as the rational subject. A primary goal of this approach was to reconstruct the true history of the biblical text, both the actual course of events that the text claimed to represent and the actual course of events that led to the composition of the text. These events would necessarily have been naturalistic (i.e., not miraculous, though perhaps divinely guided), and this composed text

---

4. *The* historical-critical method has been extensively described and critiqued elsewhere (Weems 1991, 65–66; Segovia 1995; Martínez-Vázquez 2005; Kwok 2005, 61–64, 78–80; Scholz 2017; Foskett 2019), and merely a synopsis of relevant features is given here.

would necessarily have an embedded, decipherable meaning. The end result would be an objective description of the biblical text and of early Christian history that all rational people could agree on. The circle of individuals engaged in this conversation were presupposed to be like the method's progenitors, that is, male (not female), white/European/Aryan (not native, primitive, or Semitic), and neurotypical (not perceiving or processing the world irrationally).

As *the* historical-critical method has been reconsidered in the late twentieth and early twenty-first centuries, some biblical scholars have worked to alter its values and goals to be less exclusionary. While the guild continues to discuss the extent to which it is possible and/or desirable to reform *the* historical-critical method to match our current research and pedagogy, it is important to keep in mind that this method is only *one* of many possible historical methods. Our choices are not only to give up on historical criticism or to reform it; we might make any variety of choices with regard to *German* historical criticism, while at the same time considering other forms of historical criticism.

German historical criticism of the Bible is not the normal or obvious way of doing history but is one socially conditioned tradition of historiography that has a position of dominance in many of our minds and that sits alongside a wide range of other socially conditioned traditions of historiography that have their own goals, merits, and disadvantages. There is not a single, necessary historical criticism, nor is there only one antithesis, but instead there are numerous potential types of and approaches to historical criticism. The past century has seen many modes of historical investigation emerge from distinct cultural moments. Here I briefly survey the approaches taken by Walter Benjamin, Saidiya Hartman, and M. Jacqui Alexander before focusing in depth on the perspective of Spivak.

In 1940, Benjamin wrote the essay "On the Concept of History" as a fleeing German Jewish intellectual who was part of the Frankfurt school. In this text, he proposes an approach to history that attends to power differentials by opposing the narrative arc of the dominant. *Historicism* is his term for the standard methods of history, according to which the surviving pieces of history may be fitted together into a coherent stream that tells the story in such a way as to "sympathize … with the victor" (Benjamin 2006, 391). As an alternative, Benjamin (395–96) articulates the approach of "historical materialism," which instead seizes the elements of history that contain revolutionary possibility.

> To Robespierre ancient Rome was a past charged with now-time, a past which he blasted out of the continuum of history.... [For materialist historiography] thinking involves not only the movement of thoughts, but their arrest as well. Where thinking suddenly comes to a stop in a constellation saturated with tensions, it gives that constellation a shock, by which thinking is crystallized as a monad. The historical materialist approaches a historical object only where it confronts him as a monad. In this structure he recognizes the sign of a messianic arrest of happening.

Taking an event only in its supposedly proper context contains the danger of simply maintaining the received, hegemonic notions of its significance. Rather, Benjamin (2006, 396) advocates a transhistorical reading that challenges dominant metanarratives and aims at achieving "a revolutionary chance in the fight for the oppressed past." Whereas German historical criticism intentionally restricts the significance of a text to its immediate chronological setting, Benjamin's historical materialism aims at linking it to alternative possibilities and futures.

Another approach is found in Hartman's method of critical fabulation. Hartman is an active scholar of African American literature and history, well known for her 1997 book *Scenes of Subjection: Terror, Slavery, and Self-Making in Nineteenth Century America* and her 2008 article "Venus in Two Acts." In this article, she turns to the historical person Venus, an African girl on a slave ship about whom only a few words are said in passing during a legal trial. We know almost nothing about her, or other captive girls and women during the Middle Passage, and what we do know is really "about the violence, excess, mendacity, and reason that seized hold of their lives, transformed them into commodities and corpses" (Hartman 2008, 2). Hartman is caught between two competing impulses: "both to tell an impossible story and to amplify the impossibility of its telling" (11). With critical fabulation, she challenges the conventional practice of history. "I have emphasized the incommensurability between the prevailing discourses and the event, amplified the instability and discrepancy of the archive, flouted the realist illusion customary in the writing of history, and produced a counter-history at the intersection of the fictive and the historical" (12). She will not be able to "resuscitat[e] the girl," but she may be able to "writ[e] a history of present, by which I mean the incomplete project of freedom, and the precarious life of the ex-slave" (13, 4). Unlike German historical criticism's principled distance from the past and its confidence in its abilities of reconstruction, Hartman's counterhistory insists that the past and present are "inseparable" and accepts the possibility and even likelihood of "failure" as one of the qualities of "insurgent, disruptive narratives" (4, 13).

The approach to history taken by Alexander deconstructs the secular framework that undergirds dominant modes of historical scholarship. An Afro-Caribbean scholar who grew up in Trinidad and Tobago and who worked in the United States and Canada, she brought queer, decolonial, and transnational/women-of-color feminist approaches to her scholarship. In her 2005 book *Pedagogies of Crossing*, she describes her experience of being directly contacted by a historical figure through the African-based spiritual practice of possession.[5] Initially, Alexander had been deploying standard historical methods in an effort to learn more about the enslaved woman who was known as Thisbe on the plantation (but who revealed herself as truly named Kitsimba). Alexander analyzed archival documents and struggled with writer's block until finally she worked with a Bakôngo teacher and listened to Kitsimba speak for herself. Kitsimba rebuked Alexander (2005, 295) for her previous scholarly efforts, appearing "diametrically opposed to [Alexander's] research plan of using her body as the ground for an epistemic struggle." Kitsimba denigrated the archive, stating, "What was written in those books was not even a faint shadow of me; it had nothing to do with me" (315). Alexander (315) ultimately realized, "Kitsimba's singular desire was not to have me author her life, but for her to author mine and make public my guarded secrets." Not only does this encounter challenge the conventional exclusion of the supernatural from either the practice of history or the results of it; Kitsimba's voice also reverses the classic power dynamic between historian and historical subject.

I deeply respect all the alternatives to classic history that I have discussed above, but I wish to focus in particular detail on the approach presented in Spivak's (1999) chapter "History" in *A Critique of Postcolonial Reason*, a chapter that is an expanded version of her famous essay, "Can the Subaltern Speak?" (1988). In this late twentieth-century writing, Spivak approaches history from her perspective as an academic trained in the discipline of English most formally but also in the fields of philosophy, history, deconstruction, and postcolonialism, especially postcolonial feminism. She was born and educated in India, and she continued her education and worked as a professor in the United States

---

5. For a similar historical methodology, see Tinsley 2018.

while also working to educate rural, disadvantaged groups in India. The questions she poses about the practice of history are especially aimed at individuals like herself, namely, critical theorists who find themselves, on the one hand, holding positions of relative dominance as members of the academy, and, on the other hand, desiring to be in alliance with subaltern populations.

In standard formulations of history, including German historical criticism of the Bible but also some feminist approaches to history, the job of the historian is to excavate the past. The past is viewed as fundamentally knowable, despite significant gaps in the record, and as accessible to the modern historian, who can perform sophisticated feats of recovery. Even those who are underrepresented in the archive, "the oppressed, if given the chance ... *can speak and know their condition*" (Spivak 1999, 269). This is the presupposition Spivak interrogates most firmly. How adequately is the historian able to represent a figure from the past, in particular, a subaltern informant, especially as exemplified by the so-called Third World woman?

To evaluate this question of representation, Spivak draws on case studies from her own social context: Indian women who appear only fleetingly in the archive. Their poor archival documentation is only one facet of the historian's dilemma, one that academics have developed many techniques of reconstruction to resolve. An even more powerful barrier to understanding is created by the limited frameworks within which the historian can comprehend the positionality of the Indian woman. Modern academics who try to reconstruct the experiences and thoughts of these Indian women will inevitably find that their analysis is dominated either by "patriarchy" or "imperialism" (Spivak 1999, 234). Even postcolonial feminists, such as Spivak herself, searching for a framework in which to make sense of these subaltern Indian women, will still find themselves constrained between the two hegemonic discourses of patriarchy and imperialism, as between a rock and a hard place, both in the sources and in their own minds.

To demonstrate this bind, Spivak draws on a case study of the rani of Sirmur, an early nineteenth-century queen in northern India. As an historical subject, the rani is present in the archives much more than the average individual by virtue of her royal status, but nevertheless only in fragmentary remarks. A major incident in her life, according to the archive, was her sudden decision, after the death of her husband, that she would be a sati; a sati is a "Hindu widow [who] ascends the pyre of the dead husband and immolates herself upon it," a practice that may be succinctly translated as "widow sacrifice" (Spivak 1999, 287). In 1829, the colonial British government banned widow sacrifice, and this incursion of authority may be regarded as one of many instances throughout history of "white men saving brown women from brown men," a power dynamic that upholds imperial and racial power through the appearance of women-friendly politics (285, 287). In the formulation of the colonial British, the sati has been deceived by her backwards and patriarchal culture to do an act of harm to herself; or, if she remains alive, the helping hand of civilizing power has guided her down the best path. Alternatively, in the formulation of the anticolonial "Indian nativist," the sati "wanted to die," or, if she remains alive, she has been deceived by the incursion of foreign dogma (287). Between imperialism and patriarchy, the Hindu widow is limited to two choices (to be a sati or to not be a sati) and two positionalities (to be deceived or to desire the status quo). In fact, the two discourses reinforce each other by means of shutting out any other possibilities; "one never encounters the testimony of the women's voice consciousness" (287). Instead, we find that in the archive a sati "emerges only when she is needed in the space of imperial production" (238).

As Spivak conducts her analysis, she arrives time and time again at the conclusion that there is no pure consciousness buried in the archive, waiting to be found by the historian. In her famous formulation, "the subaltern cannot speak!" (Spivak 1999, 308). By expressing this controversial statement, Spivak's work does not imply that the subaltern cannot literally give voice,[6] since of course they can; instead, it expresses the absolute inadequacy of the historian's ability to hear the subaltern, that is, the impossibility of the subaltern speaking *to the historian*. The silencing of the subaltern is accomplished by the selective recording of the archive, the hegemony of discourse, and even "the liberal multiculturalist metropolitan academy," which falsely purports to be able to represent the subaltern (309). Spivak calls her audience "to acknowledge our complicity in the muting" and to transform our work accordingly (309).

If we cannot unearth the voices of the subaltern from the past and reconstruct their history, what are we to do as academics and historians? Must we simply cease working altogether? As Spivak's chapter illustrates, absolutely not. Having renounced the quest of constructing a coherent

---

6. By *voice*, I mean any kind of communication—not simply speech—including vocalizations, sign language, or body language.

narrative about the rani, Spivak (1999, 207) instead embraces the desire that she would "be haunted by her slight ghost, bypassing the arrogance of the cure." Spivak (304) does believe that a ghost or a trace exists; she "disappears, not into a pristine nothingness, but into a violent shuttling that is the displaced figuration of the 'third-world woman' caught between tradition and modernization, culturalism and development." As we look into the archive, we can witness the displacement of figures between competing hegemonic discourses. We may still carry out the work of reading preserved documents, outlining histories of politics and trade, conducting fieldwork, and developing theoretical apparatuses, but with a different objective and with an acknowledgment of our limitations as particularly situated academics. We would no longer believe ourselves powerful enough—or even subordinated enough—to understand the subaltern; instead, we would trace the violence of the discourses that have blocked out the subaltern's speech. This approach to history may be applied within the context of biblical studies, which I will demonstrate by tracing discourses that prevent us from hearing the voice of a subaltern figure in the text of Acts 16:16–18.[7]

Discourses Displacing the Subaltern Figure in Acts 16:16–18

In the middle of the book of Acts, we encounter a subaltern figure: an enslaved girl,[8] who has a Greek spirit of divination, earns money for her owners through her divinatory work, and resides in a Greek city colonized by the Roman Empire. At this intersection of subjugated identities, she flits in and out of our view. The narrator gives us just enough information that we may come to feel that we have found a toehold with which to climb up and on toward an understanding of her life, voice, and self-understanding.

---

7. Although not referring to it as a method of historical criticism, Kwok Pui Lan (2005, 102–3) has also drawn on this idea from Spivak, analyzing how concepts of home have limited the interpretation of Ruth.

8. This person is not named within Acts. After she is described at some length, she is simply referred to with a female pronoun. Although I considered generating a name for her or choosing one of her many identities with which to consistently refer to her, I have chosen to alternate between titles in order to capture the multiplicity of her identities. The word *slave-girl* (παιδίσκη) suggests but does not guarantee that she is young. Another word for a female slave exists (δούλη), and it does not connote youth, but it also does not guarantee adulthood. My phrasing here takes seriously that the slave-girl may in fact be a young person.

In a time in biblical studies when feminist, womanist, and postcolonial interpretation is flourishing in many circles, important work is being done that attends carefully and compassionately to the Bible in order to assist us with such climbs. But, following Spivak, I want to pause and take a dizzying look down to see what we are standing on. What narratives and discourses are shaping the accounts we give of this individual's subjectivity?

Before we can begin to explore this, I need to complexify slightly Spivak's methodology. For Spivak, it is the two discourses of patriarchy and imperialism that shape *both* the writing of the rani of Sirmur in the archive *and* the modern academic historian's attempts to represent her. Although the archive and the historian are separated in time by nearly two centuries, the forces of patriarchy and imperialism retain sufficient continuity that we may logically use the same two terms to refer to the discourses that impinge on both the archive and the historian. But when we come to the biblical text, we have completely lost the ability to methodologically conflate the two sets of discourses. The discourses controlling the composition of Acts differ monumentally from the discourses controlling biblical interpretation in the twenty-first century, as do the various discourses affecting the reception history of this text in the intervening time. To do a full analysis of the discourses that displace this subaltern figure from our view, we would need to understand all three of these contexts.[9] But for the purposes of modeling Spivak's approach to history as effective for this case study, and also in a way that is potentially replicable in the classroom or as an assignment, I have chosen to focus on the twenty-first-century context, which we may reconstruct and understand most readily. I have surveyed major commentaries that would be easily accessible to students in a theological library. From this survey, I argue that two key modern discourses that restrict us as interpreters from hearing the subaltern figure in Acts 16:16–18 are exclusivist Christianity and individualist feminism.

---

9. Whether or not the slave-girl is a person who actually historically existed is debated in biblical scholarship. The way we would conduct archival work to analyze the first-century context might differ depending on the extent to which we determined that the slave-girl was an existent person, a product of tradition, and/or a literary creation. Such a determination might be influenced, for example, by our assessment of the author of Acts in their capacity as a historian. Regardless, such analysis would still aim at delineating the hegemonic discourses controlling the possible ways of viewing a person of with this set of identities in the first century.

As I engage critically with biblical interpreters, I want to clarify certain key aspects of how I am following Spivak's perspective on history. My critiques of the constraining discourses of exclusivist Christianity and individualist feminism are not meant as critiques of individual scholars; Spivak (1999, 306–11) herself critiques fellow progressive theorists, and even her own family members, not with the goal of calling them *in particular* to account but rather to demonstrate the discursive confines within which we all find ourselves. Similarly, my critiques of these discourses in biblical studies are not meant as critiques of Christianity or feminism as such, and I am not advocating non-Christianity/nonreligion or sexism/patriarchy as an alternative to them. Rather, I am calling attention to how these two discourses compete with each other and imply their own comprehensiveness, blocking out the possibility for alternative understandings to arise. By meditating on these discursive constraints, I dwell on the very real possibility that the subaltern figure in this text cannot speak directly to us today, precisely because hegemonic discourses are blocking our ability to listen to her adequately.

When modern biblical scholars bring our attention to this subaltern figure, we are often prompted by a troubling question: Why does Paul wait many days before exorcising the spirit from the enslaved girl?[10] If the spirit were truly harming the girl, we would expect Paul to exorcise it from her immediately. The delay raises the possibility that the girl was not in fact being harmed by the spirit and that Paul was motivated to perform the exorcism for another reason. The question then arises: Were Paul's motivations appropriate? As biblical interpreters, we find ourselves defending or condemning Paul with the results of our exegesis. Those who see Paul as operating within the paradigms of exclusivist Christianity[11] argue that spirit possession results in the fragmentation of the girl's core identity and that Paul's exorcism of the spirit is a triumph of the Christian God over a demonic spirit. In contrast, those who interpret Paul's action negatively, from the standpoint of individualist feminism, argue that the colonized slave-girl speaks out firmly as a unitary subject and that Paul's exorcism unjustly silences her.

---

10. Commentators who do not seem to find Paul's behavior troublesome also do not attempt coherent reconstructions of the slave-girl's intentions or experience (Munck 1967, 161; Fitzmyer 1998, 583; Holladay 2016, 322–24). One scholar eliminates the delay entirely (Conzelmann 1987, 131).

11. Most but not all of the commentators not only see Paul as operating within this paradigm but agree with Paul and thus align themselves with the paradigm.

Within exclusivist Christianity, which is expressed mostly by male scholars, the possession of the slave-girl results in a splitting of her identity that is harmful, whether because it causes her pain or causes theological confusion. This splitting is sometimes translated into mental illness: "she was possessed by a demon; mentally unbalanced, we would say.... Here is a picture of enslavement—the grip of mental illness, schizophrenia, some 'demon' which holds the victim in bondage" (Willimon 1988, 138). Alternatively, on a theological level, the spirit causes internal division in the slave-girl's relation to God. Although the content of her speech testifies positively to the Most High God, its so-called pagan origin simultaneously issues a challenge to that very God, not because she intends such a challenge but because she "unwittingly" stumbles into the spiritual battle (Wall 2002, 230, 232). The possessed girl is unwell, untrustworthy, and unaware.[12]

Furthermore, these interpreters understand Paul himself to be turning spiritual confusion into spiritual wholeness when he exorcizes the spirit out of the Pythian diviner. One commentator communicates this transformation through the situationally resonant metaphor of slavery and freedom: "chained her whole life to the hell of demon possession, ... now she is free" (Willimon 1988, 139). Any delay that Paul might have had in "cur[ing] her" pales in contrast to the lifelong period of her demon possession—a length of time that is not found in the passage but is added by the commentator (139). Another commentator reads the young woman as having a split spiritual consciousness, predicting—and thus implicitly asking for—this exorcism; Paul's action "fulfill[s] the slave girl's own prophecy: The Most High God saves the lost" (Wall 2002, 232). By far the most common way of expressing Paul's theological motivation is that it is essential for him to not allow a pagan and demonic prophet to continue speaking true words about the Christian God, at the risk of harm to the spiritual purity of the Christian community. "The evil spirit was not trying to draw people to God, but to cause confusion" (Kisau 2006, 1355). "She spoke the truth, but as she carried on doing this for many days, her proclamation hindered rather than helped their ministry" (Venkataraman 2015, 1492). Paul's delay is thus warranted by his need to take time to determine the extent to which the syncretism of the slave-girl was a threat to the church and to potential converts.

---

12. These characterizations are found in the Western commentaries, but not the Majority World commentaries, which instead express the author's and the readers' familiarity with such people in their own communities.

The alternative discourse present in a minority of commentaries is individualist feminism, which is expressed mostly by female scholars and which reclaims the maligned figure of the enslaved Pythian diviner. For individualist feminism, the enslaved prophet is not fragmented, unwell, untrustworthy, or unaware. On the contrary, she is fully capable of having a distinct perspective on Paul as she shouts her prophecy. One interpretation of her speech is as resistance to Paul: "A slave girl, by contrast, refuses to be colonized by Paul, Silas, and their companions. Instead she discloses their identity and agenda as slaves of the Deity who intend to rescue others. Even her naming Paul and his companions as slaves of the Deity exposes them, for it points to the anti-imperializing justification for their travel" (Aymer 2012, 744). In this analysis, Paul appears on the surface to be contesting the oppression of the Roman empire and of enslavement, but in reality, he is establishing a religious empire of his own. By silencing the slave girl, Paul seeks to bring her into a new spiritual domain by force. But her very speech act preemptively resists her future silencing, because it critically exposes the false innocence of imperial Christianity.

Another reading of this figure does not carry as much certainty about her intentions but still carries the assumption that such intentionality exists and is coherent. Her speech act may be either "an expression of her hopes (salvation) or her fears (yet another conquering god)," but it is still a meaningful, deliberate expression of some kind (Burrus 2009, 151). The voice of the young woman may also be imagined to be speaking neutrally, simply "announc[ing] the truth," that Paul is "a man of God," through her "prophetic" ability (O'Day 1998, 400). Regardless of the affect with which each interpreter hears her, the speech that originates from the enslaved Pythian diviner is taken as *her* speech, not the speech of the spirit within her, and as indicating something essential about her internal consciousness.

But just as insistently as the slave-girl works to express herself, Paul works to silence her. In one reading, while the colonized slave exposes the hypocrisy of the Way, Paul "drive[s] out the truth-telling spirit, leaving her enslaved and silenced" (Aymer 2012, 744). For another interpreter, Paul incorrectly perceives the speech of the enslaved diviner as coming not from her but from the Pythian spirit and perceives its ambiguous content as "mockery" (Burrus 2009, 151). Her place in the historical record fares poorly because of Paul's action: "the silenced girl herself evaporates from the text at this point" (151). The reason for Paul's silencing may also be taken in concert with the reason for the implicit silencing by the author of Acts: flat-out sexism. Paul's exorcism has been read as one more example of "Luke's discomfort with the prophetic voice of women in the church" and his subsequent "silencing of women prophets throughout Acts" (O'Day 1998, 400; see also Dinkler 2014, 353). In these commentaries, the word *silence* recurs repeatedly, expressing both literal voicelessness and metaphorical social exclusion. It is all the more striking that this word occurs so frequently given that, while no further speech from the slave-girl is explicitly recorded, there is also no indication that she is unable to say anything anymore but only that the spirit no longer resides within her. As the spirit exits this colonized young woman, these commentators experience the very voice of the slave-girl exiting too.

With these two discursive options, we are left with only two ways of understanding the subjectivity of the Pythian diviner. Either she is a fragmented beneficiary of Paul's divine healing or she is an independent agent whom Paul has unjustly silenced. Again, I reiterate that I am not primarily focused on critiquing the scholarship reviewed above; rather, I am attending to the way that these two discourses disagree with each other and thus appear to exhaust all the possibilities of interpretation between them. The cumulative effect of this discursive production is that it hinders our ability as academic historians to conceptualize sufficiently accurate understandings of this subaltern figure in the biblical text.

Despite the radical differences between these two perspectives, they share many common assumptions. (1) Internal division is inappropriate for the subject, while coherence is valued. We have no room to imagine a subject who is fragmented and who enjoys it, a subject who feels multiple ways about the spirit within her, a subject who feels multiple ways about these curious "slaves of the Most High God." We have no room for a Paul who is something other than a hero or a villain, who perhaps acted without quite knowing why, who perhaps was acted on by the spirit living inside him. (2) The departure of the spirit from the enslaved girl is a monumental change in her life. We have no room to imagine her life outside this encounter with Paul, her daily routines, her intimacies and conflicts, her future life in Philippi. The men who have enslaved her believe that she is radically different because she can no longer make them money with her prophecy (Acts 16:19). Would she have agreed or disagreed about the magnitude of the difference, and on what grounds (emotional, spiritual, economic)? (3) The encounter between the girl and Paul is primarily verbal. We have no room to imagine what her body is doing during those many days that she is shouting after Paul and his companions: whether she walks or crawls, whether she eats or sleeps, whether she laughs or cries, whether her voice changes or always remains the same. (4) The only important characters are the humans. We have no room to imagine the Pythian spirit as an actor in the earthy realm. What did the spirit look like when it left, and where did it go? Was it spiritually connected to the Pythia at Delphi, and if so, how? These many possibilities remain unexplored. Instead, in the language of Spivak (1999, 304), we see this enslaved diviner caught "between … subject-constitution and object-formation." The hegemonic discourses of individualist feminism and exclusivist Christianity would have us believe that they are the only two options, that we can have the slave-girl either as an empowered subject or as a subjugated object.

In the German historical-critical mode, I have not succeeded in my goal as an interpreter if I have not proposed a reconstruction of my own. But in a Spivakian approach to history, detailed reconstruction of what we cannot know is not only impossible but harmful. An equally rigorous approach to history would have us take seriously that this subaltern figure has disappeared "into a violent shuttling" (Spivak 1999, 304). There is no living being waiting in the text to be drawn to the surface and rescued. Her disappearance is no mere accident but an act of violence that reflects the set of power relations within which we are embedded. But the trace of her that remains after this violent collision is not one that lies motionless and easily boxed in. Instead, she is visible in her shuttling, in her continual movement back and forth between each newly born set of hegemonic constraints, constantly spilling over their bounds.

Works Cited

Alexander, M. Jacqui. 2005. "Pedagogies of the Sacred: Making the Invisible Tangible." Pages 287–332 in *Pedagogies of Crossing*. Durham, NC: Duke University Press.

Aymer, Margaret. 2012. "Acts of the Apostles." Pages 734–47 in *Women's Bible Commentary*. 3rd ed. Edited by Carol A. Newsom, Sharon H. Ringe, and Jacqueline E. Lapsley. Louisville: Westminster John Knox.

Benjamin, Walter. 2006. "On the Concept of History." Pages 389–400 in *Walter Benjamin: Selected Writings*. Vol. 4. Cambridge: Belknap.

Burrus, Virginia. 2009. "The Gospel of Luke and the Acts of the Apostles." Pages 133–55 in *A Postcolonial Commentary on the New Testament Writings*. Edited by Fernando F. Segovia and R. S. Sugirtharajah,. London: Bloomsbury T&T Clark.

Conzelmann, Hans. 1987. *Acts of the Apostles: A Commentary on the Acts of the Apostles.* Translated by James Limburg, A. Thomas Kraabel, and Donald H. Juel. Hermeneia. Philadelphia: Fortress.

Dinkler, Michal Beth. 2014. "The Acts of the Apostles." Pages 327–63 in *Fortress Commentary on the Bible: The New Testament.* Edited by Margaret Aymer, Cynthia Briggs Kittredge, and David A. Sánchez. Minneapolis: Fortress.

Fitzmyer, Joseph A. 1998. *The Acts of the Apostles: A New Translation with Introduction and Commentary.* AB. New York: Doubleday.

Foskett, Mary F. 2019. "Historical Criticism." Pages 107–17 in *T&T Clark Handbook of Asian American Biblical Hermeneutics.* Edited by Uriah Y. Kim and Seung Ai Yang. London: T&T Clark.

Hartman, Saidiya. 2008. "Venus in Two Acts." *SA* 12.2:1–14.

Holladay, Carl R. 2016. *Acts: A Commentary.* NTL. Louisville: Westminster John Knox.

Kisau, Paul Mumo. 2006. "Acts of the Apostles." Pages 1323–74 in *Africa Bible Commentary: A One-Volume Commentary Written by Seventy African Scholars.* Edited by Tokunboh Adeyemo. Grand Rapids: Zondervan.

Kwok, Pui-lan. 2005. *Postcolonial Imagination and Feminist Theology.* Louisville: Westminster John Knox.

Martínez-Vázquez, Hjamil A. 2005. "Breaking the Established Scaffold: Imagination as a Resource in the Development of Biblical Interpretation." Pages 71–91 in *Her Master's Tools?: Feminist and Postcolonial Engagements of Historical-Critical Discourse.* Edited by Caroline Vander Stichele and Todd Penner. Atlanta: Society of Biblical Literature.

Munck, Johannes. 1967. *The Acts of the Apostles.* Edited by William F. Albright and Christopher S. Mann. AB. Garden City, NY: Doubleday.

O'Day, Gail R. 1998. "Acts." Pages 394–402 in *Women's Bible Commentary: Expanded Edition.* 2nd ed. Edited by Carol A. Newsom and Sharon H. Ringe. Louisville: Westminster John Knox.

Scholz, Susanne. 2017. "Lederhosen Hermeneutics: Toward a Feminist Sociology of German White Male Old Testament Interpretations." Pages 123–42 in *The Bible as Political Artifact: On the Feminist Study of the Hebrew Bible.* Minneapolis: Fortress.

Segovia, Fernando F. 1995. "'And They Began to Speak in Other Tongues': Competing Modes of Discourse in Contemporary Biblical Criticism." Pages 1–32 in vol. 1 of *Reading from This Place: Social Location and*

Biblical Interpretation in the United States. Edited by Fernando F. Segovia and Mary Ann Tolbert. Minneapolis: Fortress.

Spivak, Gayatri Chakravorty. 1988. "Can the Subaltern Speak?" Pages 271–315 in *Marxism and the Interpretation of Culture*. Edited by Cary Nelson and Lawrence Grossberg,. Urbana: University of Illinois Press.

———. 1999. "History." Pages 198–311 in *A Critique of Postcolonial Reason: Toward a History of the Vanishing Present*. Cambridge: Harvard University Press.

Tinsley, Omise'eke Natasha. 2018. *Ezili's Mirrors: Imagining Black Queer Genders*. Durham, NC: Duke University Press.

Townes, Emilie M. 2006. *Womanist Ethics and the Cultural Production of Evil*. New York: Palgrave Macmillan.

Venkataraman, Babu Immanuel. 2015. "Acts." Pages 1451–1509 in *South Asia Bible Commentary*. Edited by Brian Wintle. Rajasthan: Open Door.

Wall, Robert W. 2002. "The Acts of the Apostles: Introduction, Commentary, and Reflections." *NIB* 10:3–370.

Weems, Renita J. 1991. "Reading Her Way through the Struggle: African American Women and the Bible." Pages 57–77 in *Stony the Road We Trod: African American Biblical Interpretation*. Edited by Cain Hope Felder. Minneapolis: Fortress.

Willimon, William H. 1988. *Acts*. Interpretation. Atlanta: John Knox.

Reflections on Teaching the Bible and Black Lives Matter in a Divinity School

Wilda C. Gafney

ואלה שמות
These are the names ...

—Exod 1:1

I offer my sincere thanks to my former students for their gracious permission to quote their work extensively and anonymously. I have made minimal changes, primarily formatting—that is, italicizing scriptural texts and correcting typos when present.

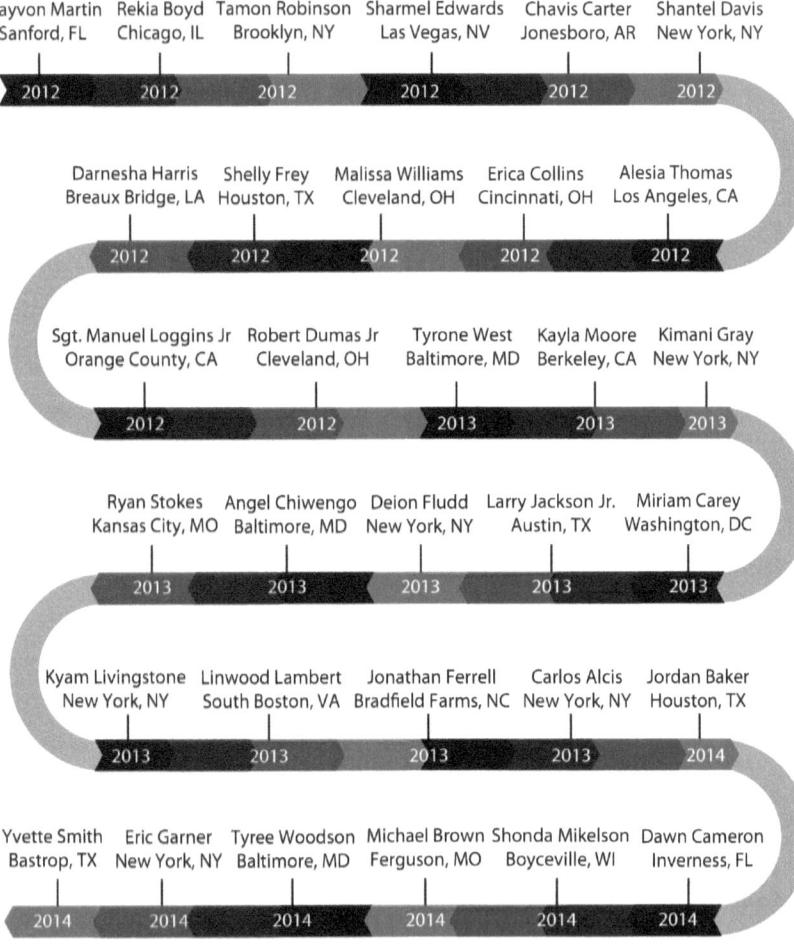

Fig. 1. Black Lives Matter timeline. Source: This timeline was graciously contributed by Tamara Gebhardt, inspired by the Springfield (Illinois) Public Schools Black Lives Matter chart readily available online at https://tinyurl.com/SBL03111at, with additional data from blogger Julian Agabond, https://tinyurl.com/SBL03111aw, and the #SayHerName Campaign In Memoriam page, https://tinyurl.com/SBL03111av.

Reflections on Teaching the Bible 243

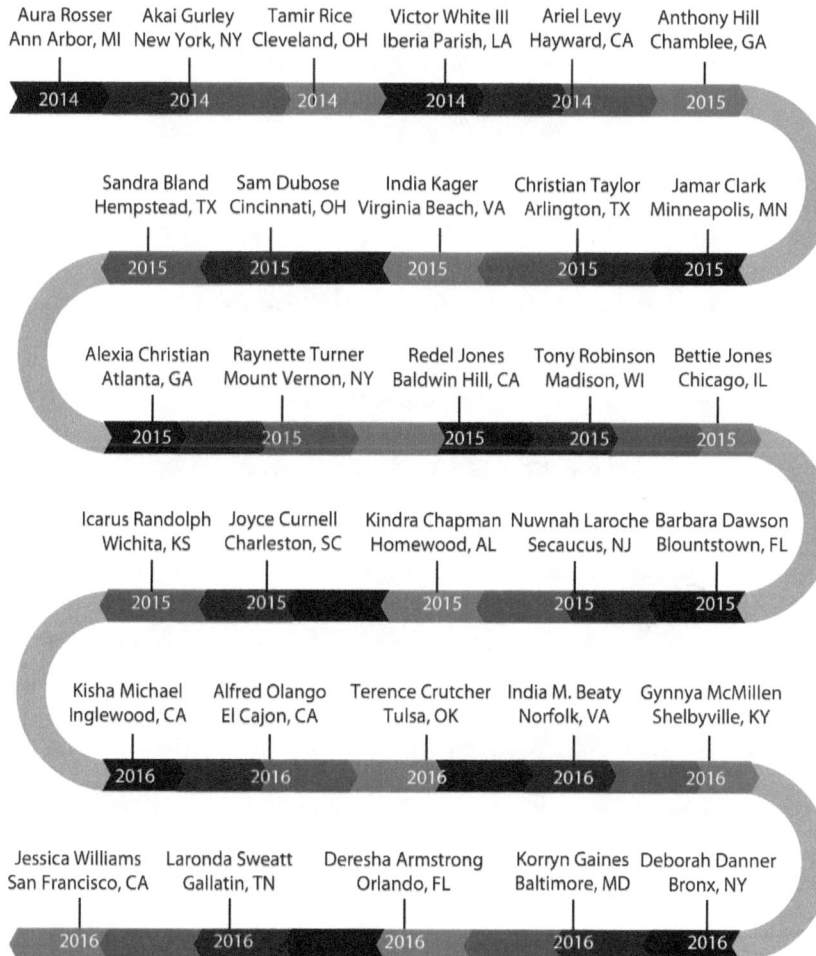

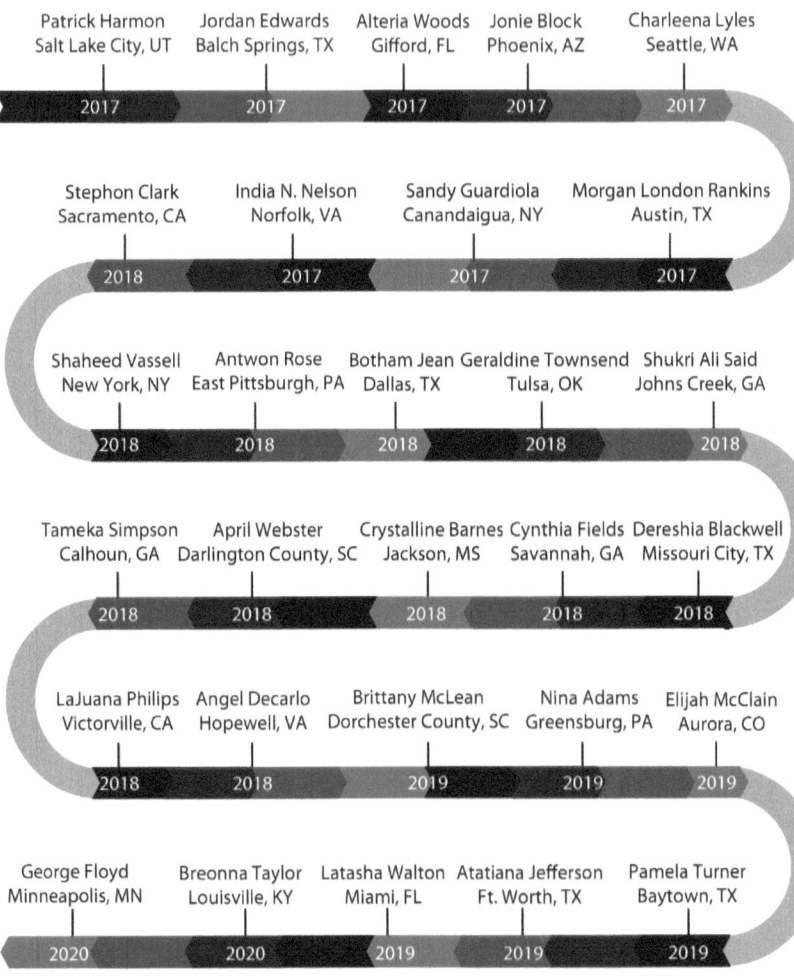

These are not all the names.

—Wilda Gafney, *Womanist Midrash*

Introduction

I moved to Fort Worth, Texas, in the summer of 2014 to begin a new faculty appointment at Brite Divinity School. It was the summer in which Ferguson, Missouri, police officers killed Mike Brown.[1] For many, it was

---

1. I understand all of these killings to have been murders without regard to legal

the summer the Black Lives Matter movement exploded into public consciousness after its earlier coalescence and eruption in 2012 after the killing of Trayvon Martin in Sanford, Florida, in 2012.[2] But for me it was part of a much longer story, the story of being black in America, a story filled with citizen and police violence against black people—rapes, assaults, killings, murders—with little or no sanction.

I became aware of the threat the police pose to black persons on 9 August 1997, when two New York City Police Department officers seized Abner Louima, took him to a bathroom in a police station, and raped him with a broom handle they had broken for the assault. The savagery of the attack, with no concern for being identified, overheard, or interrupted— in uniform, in a police station—has remained with me.[3] While the case against the officers who assaulted Louima was underway, on 4 February 1999, four New York Police Department officers shot Amadou Diallo, who was unarmed, forty-seven times. They were later found not guilty. Diallo's death sparked outrage and upheaval, as did the killing of black women and men, and even children, before and after him. Between 1999 and 2014 my advocacy and activism grew, with certain killings affecting me especially deeply: New York Police Department officers shot Sean Bell fifty times on 25 November 2006, the day before his wedding; Oscar Grant III was shot in the back while lying face down on New Year's Day in 2009 in San Francisco by Bay Area Rapid Transit Police in San Francisco; Aiyanna Stanley-Jones, just seven years old, was shot by Detroit police officers while she was sleeping on 16 May 2010; and Trayvon Martin was executed by a citizen assuming police powers on 26 February 2012.

I brought my memories of the extrajudicial executions of Diallo, Bell, Grant, little Aiyanna, and Trayvon with me to Fort Worth along with those of Rekia Boyd in 2012 and Renisha McBride, Miriam Carey, and Kimani Gray in 2013. Less than thirty days after my arrival, Eric Garner

---

findings. And I intentionally do not name any of the killers, civilian or law enforcement; this work is not about them.

2. Alicia Garza, one of the cofounders of Black Lives Matter (along with Patrisse Cullors and Opal Tometti), articulates the narrative of the movement's founding and rationale in Garza 2014. Patrisse Cullors first posted the hashtag #BlackLivesMatter on Twitter on 14 July 2013, responding to the acquittal of Trayvon Martin's killer.

3. Like womanism, from which I draw in my activism, scholarship, and teaching (and preaching), the Black Lives Matter movement is invested in the well-being of the entire community; lethal shootings are not our only concern.

was strangled to death on a public street by New York Police Department, 7 July 2014. Nineteen days later, police in Beavercreek, Ohio, killed John Crawford on 5 August 2014, and four days later a Ferguson police officer killed Mike Brown and left his body lying in the street for four hours. Five days before Thanksgiving, twelve-year-old Tamir Rice was executed on 22 November 2014 within two seconds of the officer arriving on the scene.

By 2014, it became clear that the extrajudicial shootings and killings of black women were not receiving the same attention in the media and in the black community as were those of black men. In December 2014 the African American Policy Forum and Center for Intersectionality and Social Policy Studies under the leadership of Kimberlé Crenshaw launched the #SayHerName movement, a companion movement to Black Lives Matter. Crenshaw, a lawyer, has some renown for her initial articulation of the ways in which race, gender, class, and other identifying indicators intersect to produce compounded oppressions—giving rise to the term *intersectionality* in 1989.

As I joined others pouring into the streets to protest these killings and other indignities, I reflected on what my own seminary and graduate education offered me to face the moment and concluded it was very little. I looked back on my own teaching, specifically a course on prophetic preaching that drew heavily on the sermons of Martin Luther King Jr. in addition to those of Renita Weems, Cheryl Townsend Gilkes, and Michael Curry. I determined to teach a course that would prepare students to engage the Scriptures authoritatively and contextually, while contemporarily mindful of their originating contexts, to respond to the present moment in and out of the pulpit and in and out of the public square. In spring 2017 I offered The Bible in the Public Square: Interpreting the Bible in the Age of #BlackLivesMatter at Brite Divinity School as an upper-level first master's course.[4] The students were clergy, clergy in formation, and laypersons, and they were diverse in race and ethnicity as well as in gender identity and performance, including queer and nonbinary persons. One was a doctoral student who could not take the class for credit but audited and participated as invited. Most were actively engaged in ministry as pastors, preachers, or religious educators; thus one of my aims was to equip them to preach and teach in their congregations and contexts on the approaching Sunday each week if necessary.

---

4. The course was informally known as "Bible and BLM."

It is important to note that police shootings and killings of black folk continued during this semester as they had the semesters before and would continue to do so, as they continue even now. While not officially determined to have been killed by the police, Sandra Bland's in-custody death in Waller County, Texas, on 13 July 2015 weighed heavily as a harbinger of my individual relative lack of safety. It was followed by a string of rapes and other sexual assaults by an Oklahoma City police officer who preferentially targeted black women and girls.[5] This last brought to the fore something women of my community have always known with regard to the risk police officers hold for our persons. The vulnerability of black women to police violence, sexual and physical, is well documented (Jacobs 2017; Wriggins 1983). During the course of the semester, Jordan Edwards was murdered by an officer in Balch Springs, Texas, on 27 April 2017.[6] Most importantly, this course was meeting while many of its members were actively involved in activism with, as, and as a part of Black Lives Matter.

The aims of the course were to "examine the core claims and commitments of the Black Lives Matter movement in light of the biblical text with an eye to preaching and teaching the scriptures in response to the extra-judicial killings of Black women, men, and children, and subsequent community responses to those killings" and "develop and articulate Black Lives Matter hermeneutic approaches to interpreting the scriptures." The course began with the self-articulated commitments of the Black Lives Matter movement: "to eradicate white supremacy and build local power to intervene in violence inflicted on Black communities by the state and vigilantes. By combating and countering acts of violence, creating space for Black imagination and innovation, and centering Black joy" ("About Black Lives Matter" n.d.).

Specifically, one of the learning outcomes from this course was to give students the ability

---

5. The officer was convicted on eighteen distinct charges against one child and seven women (Miller 2019).

6. Indeed, while preparing this manuscript, Atatiana Jefferson was killed in her home in Fort Worth, Texas, where I am, by an officer firing through the window in front of her nephew in 2019, and since then, there has been the killing of Elijah McClain in Aurora, Colorado, and, in 2020, Brianna Taylor (March) in Louisville, Kentucky; George Floyd (May) in Minneapolis; and Jonathan Price (October) near Wolfe City, Texas.

to define the BLM movement and its aims succinctly and in depth; articulate the justice issues emerging from the BLM movement; engage assigned scripture selections and those of their own choosing to identify texts that can be read or interpreted as speaking to BLM issues, and craft sermons, blog posts, editorials, and other communiqués to respond to BLM concerns raised by assigned reading and current events.

Given the relatively slow pace of the publishing enterprise, there were very few texts available that dealt specifically with the Black Lives Matter movement or its precipitating events.[7] All of the texts were well received with the exception of the Jim Wallis text. I intended this text as a gateway text for seminarians and pastors to begin conversations on race and police violence in primarily white contexts, but while some students found it helpful in this regard, they still thought it was not sufficiently sophisticated for their own use. Others found it too weak in its address to white Christians. Fairly early on there was a recommendation to replace it. Having had at least one semester of an introductory biblical course in either Testament, the students were not new to critical academic studies of Scripture.

The development and articulation of a functional Black Lives Matter hermeneutic by and for each student was my chief aim for the class. I had begun to think through the textual grounds for such a hermeneutic in 2016 when I was invited to the Austin Presbyterian Seminary in Austin, Texas, to give their annual Hesed Lecture under the title "Which Lives Matter?" I presented on the first day of class the early-stage hermeneutic I developed in that lecture as a starting place for the course.

Beginning with the world in which the biblical texts are translated, read, heard, and interpreted, I maintained that the lives that are imperiled and disdained in the text are the ones that matter: the lives that are at risk, the lives that do not matter to those with power in the text, the lives that those on the downsides of the power curve in the texts. In the world that reads the Scriptures and crafts such hermeneutics, those power curves are white supremacy, cisgenderd hetero-patriarchy, and xenophobia, among others. In the United States (and to some degree in the United Kingdom

---

7. The assigned texts were Bailey, Liew, and Segovia 2009; Barber and Wilson-Hartgrove 2016; Douglas 2015; Francis 2015; Lightsey 2015; Wallis 2016. Biblical texts from the Revised Common Lectionary for the coming Sunday were assigned along with a requirement for each student to bring in at least one other text to facilitate sermon preparation for lectionary and nonlectionary preachers actively filling pulpits at the time.

and other parts of Europe, notably France and Germany), those lives are black lives in all their plurality: black women's lives, black queer lives, black trans lives, black Muslim lives, the lives of black disabled folk, and the lives of black folk living with mental illness.

Translating that hermeneutic to the biblical canons was relatively simple on the surface: Israelite lives matter in the Scriptures of Israel. Occasionally other lives matter too. But it cannot be said that all lives matter in the Bible, nor can it be said that of those lives that do matter that they matter equally. While racism does not exist in the Hebrew Scriptures, there is vicious ethnic conflict that can function as an analog for contemporary race-based conflict.

The exercise of this Black Lives Matter hermeneutic was also a womanist praxis. Looking at the full complexity of interwoven effects stemming from different components of identity, we looked for those lives that were at risk, subject to oppression (occupation/colonization), economic exploitation, death, physical and sexual violence, enslavement, relegated to the margins of the text, and/or discounted as disposable, particularly as a result of an intersecting element of identity. The intersecting identities we considered were largely gender and ethnic identity (Israelite/non-Israelite primarily), supplemented by class and economic indicators where available. In addition, we attended to cultural status indicators such as fertility and infertility. In doing so, we regularly read against the text, in which the Israelites and their vulnerability to external imperial powers are the central perspectival subject, to disrupt the normative Christian interpretive practice of reading with the Israelites and coopting that identity to wield against indigenous peoples in colonization, enslavement, and genocide. We progressed from somewhat reductionist "who is oppressed in the text" readings to asking how any text could be read through a Black Lives Matter hermeneutic.

In the following section I present a series of student exegeses with commentary and analysis. The selections were made to demonstrate the diversity of student response and represent the majority of the students across the course of the semester. Both Testaments are represented.[8] Student focus varied between pericopes and individual verses.

---

8. In the course of the semester some students also wrote papers and presented on deuterocanonical texts.

Student Exegesis and Commentary[9]

Exegesis 1: Psalm 116:15

> *Precious in the sight of the SOURCE OF LIFE is the death of their faithful.*[10] That is a verse that I have heard at many [black church] funerals, but a BLM hermeneutic adds a tragic amount of depth to that scripture. If death is supposed to be a precious thing, and I believe that it is, then we can say that so many Black bodies are denied their precious death at the hands of police brutality, state sanctioned violence, and this week literally executions. Perhaps Black congregants will be moved to understand that when a body is left in the street or a killer is suspended with pay or walks with no consequence, death is no longer precious in the way that God created it to be. Maybe as a church we can begin to stand with BLM and fight for the precious death of all even when we do not fight for their lives.

In this case a Black Lives Matter hermeneutic navigates the dissonance between the claims of the biblical text in a simple reading and the lived reality of black people in the United States in particular. It is a hermeneutic of loss. The assurance of the psalm is negated by the recurrent extrajudicial shootings and killings of black people. The losses compound: the loss of life, that life taken through violent means, and the theft of a precious death. In the student's reading, lethal police violence is an interruption of divine intent and the God-ordained cycles of life and death. This theological move enables the writer to name police violence in a womanist way, as in the words of Emilie Townes (2006), a "cultural production of evil."

Exegesis 2: Matthew 5:21–22 and Jeremiah 8:11

> *You have heard that it was said, "Do not call Black people the n-word" and whoever discriminates based on race shall be liable to judgment. But I say to you that if you stay silent in the wake of violence against Black bodies, you will be liable to judgment; and if you suggest that the Black men and women had it coming, you will be liable to their families; and if you say,*

---

9. All of the quoted material in the following section comes from student writing in the course, used with permission. By agreement, they will remain anonymous.

10. The student did not include the text of the verse in their writing. Unless otherwise noted, all translations are my own; I employ gender-fluid language for the divine here, as I did in class.

"*Peace, peace*" *when there is no peace, you will be liable to the hell of fire.*¹¹
Jesus rewrites the text because scripture must be interpreted, and sometimes interpretation must contradict the text.

Engaging in the ancient forms of midrash and rewriting Scripture, the student imitates Jesus, himself a rewriter of Scripture, famously saying in Matthew's Gospel, "You have heard that it was written, but I say unto you." This hermeneutic is a hermeneutic of rebuke, as was its originating text. The student makes at least five hermeneutic moves.

First, the student addresses the use of the common slur wielded against black people, n****r, referring to it as "the n-word," substituting its use for "murder" in the original passage. While the intent may have been to elevate use of the slur to the highest level of offense, drawing on the subsequent rhetorical paradigm in which epithets are equivalent to murder in the passage, it effectually neglects the obvious parallel between murder in the Matthean text and the murders for which the Black Lives Matter movement demands an accounting. It was a missed opportunity to condemn extrajudicial killings as murder in the language of the gospel.¹²

Second, the student separates the judgment from the offense. Whereas in the initial text murder was proscribed and the murderer positioned for legal judgment, in the student's writing, the slur is proscribed, but there is no penalty attached, and judgment is for a new offense, race-based discrimination. The rewritten gospel loses some coherence here. The third move is also with regard to judgment; it is a restatement of the oft-heard refrain "silence is complicity."

The fourth move is perhaps most interesting here. Reading as a womanist collaborator—my term for those who read in solidarity with womanists who are not themselves black women—the student identifies the black community, more specifically the bereaved surviving family members, with the council, the Sanhedrin in the text. Given that self-determination and the well-being of entire community are core womanist values, by

---

11. This student's methodological approach was in conversation with my own womanist midrashic work. While my volume (Gafney 2017) was months away from its release during this semester, the student had read chapter-length essays in which I used the approach.

12. While some might wish to distinguish between those killings that have been adjudged as murder through legal processes and those that have not, the bombastic tone of this passage does not require making that distinction.

identifying the black community as the legal and governing authority in this new gospel, this student removes justice from the hands of the system that has so often failed black women and our communities and lodges it with the violated community. Thus, justice becomes the fruit of an internal community process. However, it is not the murderers who are handed over to the families for justice but those who are silent and complicit and blame the victims for their own deaths. Subsequently, in this novel gospel, as in the world in which it was crafted, justice is still something less than called for by the families, survivors, and communities of murdered black folk.

The fifth and final move was to integrate a portion of Jer 8:11 into Matt 5:22 so that those who "say, 'Peace, peace'" from Jeremiah become "liable to the hell of fire" from Matthew. Lacking is any identification of who it is that is saying "peace, peace" or how those calls are to be understood. Given the upheaval surrounding each shooting or killing, including protest action, which may include deliberate, strategic, targeted disruption, there is no obvious corollary for someone saying "peace" as a status assessment. However, the line can be read as rejecting those who call for peace in the face of social unrest and protest action. The student writing sample did not fully flesh this idea out.

Exegesis 3: Ezekiel 37:12

> *I am going to open your graves and bring you up from your graves.* In what ways might this text be a text of false hope? It seems to place the emphasis on a future resurrection and vindication rather than on justice here and now. Might it be possible to think of the dry bones not as those already dead but as those locked up in oppressive systems under white supremacy, patriarchy, capitalism, etc.? What would it mean for them to be restored to life? The text seems to suggest merely their resurrection, but this is not helpful if the systems killing them are still in place. Their resurrection must represent the destruction of the systems of oppression which resulted in their deaths in the first place.

This student initially employs a hermeneutic of suspicion toward a text and a potential traditional reading, in which it would be invoked as a panacea. In that rejected reading the dead, those killed by police violence, will one day rise (likely in the Christian understanding of resurrection), and that knowledge should bring comfort to their families. It is slaveholding theology and hermeneutics. Instead, this student is reading in solidarity with the broader African American hermeneutical tradition and in rejection of the dominant culture's biblical teaching, which is not only used historically to target the enslaved and other subjugated populations but also propagated in subsequent generations with a focus on suffering in the here and now as a virtue qualifying for a heavenly reward later (see Copeland 2011; Mitchem 2002, 106–11; Townes 1993).

In this student's alternate proposal, the "dead" of the text are black folk living under systemic oppression of a pervasive white supremacy in the American context. In this reading, "restoration to life" would be the transformation of unjust social structures and the larger cultural context. However, this reading does not address the actual dead, those killed by police.

The focus on life is particularly apt in a Black Lives Matter hermeneutic. The aims of the Black Lives Matter movement are not reducible to ending extrajudicial shootings and killings of black and brown and poor folk. As a movement started by black and brown queer women, the movement correlates with womanism in its investment in the flourishing of black people and our communities. "Life" in this context would be nothing short of the complete and utter transformation of American society and policing culture, if not the complete eradication of the latter. The assignment, as a development of an initial hermeneutic, did not allow for the student to develop this thought.

Exegesis 4: Psalm 23

> The biblical text that stood out this week for me was Psalm 23.... The line *you prepare a table for me in the presence of my enemies*, seems to be an outright lie in the context of extrajudicial killings of unarmed Black men. The line *though I walk through the valley of the shadow of death*, was a line that one of my students nearly took offense at, because of how untrue it is.[13] The words of scripture do not always reflect a true reality.... What is the biblical text when it is, or seems to be a lie? When it is simply not true. For whom is this biblical text true?

While this reading provides an opportunity to return to the earlier framing of the course (which includes the content, contexts, and the raison

---

13. Some of the students enrolled in the course were simultaneously engaged in teaching Bible studies that centered the Black Lives Matter movement at their respective congregations.

d'être of the Hebrew Bible), it also gives voice to the grief and anguish that was a regular component of this class.

Exegesis 5: Genesis 4:8

> *Now Cain said something[14] to his brother Abel. And it happened that when they were in the field, Cain rose up against his brother Abel, and killed him.* Throughout the history of our reading, we never ask whether Abel had anything to do with his death. If God favors Abel, that is good enough for us. This makes me wonder why, if we do not hold Abel accountable for his death, why we continue to find African Americans accountable for every bad thing that happens to them?

With this simple question the student holds in sharp relief a conditioned unquestioning stance with regard to the biblical text and the phenomenon of putting a victim on trial for her own assault or murder by questioning her behavior, dress, drug use, previous criminal background, or alleged noncompliant or threatening behavior. Ultimately, what is being questioned is whether the shooting or killing of the black woman or man is really an affront, an offense, a crime. What is not questioned is the authority of the police officer to take and alter the conditions of a human life. In a world in which uncritical formulations of biblical authority are questioned, negated, and transformed—if not outright rejected—by critical engagement, this student argues that the functional absolute authority of police should be every bit as much subjected to the same critical analysis. Yet it is the victim's (or the survivor's) blackness that is suspect; even the multisensory evidence of their bleeding body is made questionable.

Exegesis 6: 2 Samuel 21:9

> *David gave them (the two sons of Rizpah) into the hands of the Gibeonites, and they lynched[15] them on the mountain before the* HOLY ONE.... In [2 Sam 21:8–13] there are clear differentiations of whose lives matter and

---

14. The opening phrase is incomplete, ויאמר קין אל־חבל אחיו ... "Something" both describes and fills the lacuna. NRSV follows LXX, supplying "Let us go out to the field."

15. The semantic range of the Hebrew in this verse includes "hang" and "dislocation" (as in Jacob's hip and thigh in Gen 32:26), and its Arabic cognate, *waqa'a*, includes "falling down." The *hiphil* form in verse 9. connotes execution. The text is a favorite among black women preachers and is widely understood and articulated as a

whose do not. The text threatens the erasure of certain lives entirely in pursuit of the goals of the state, which in today's language likely would have been expressed in terms of "order" or similarly coded racial constructs. The text also offers an opportunity to interrogate the historical events which underly it through the inclusion of a marginalized voice—that of the widowed Rizpah whose sons have been murdered by the state. While it is notable that Rizpah is not actually allowed to speak in this text, her prophetic actions are still able to have a deep impact on the state in ways that one might not expect. Though I will not explore it in depth here, a BLM hermeneutic would also be remiss not to interrogate Merab's absence from the text as five of her sons are impaled on the mountain along with the two sons of Rizpah.[16]

Exegesis 7: Genesis 21:10

Now Sarah said to Abraham, "Cast out this womb-slave[17] with her son; for the son of this slave woman shall not inherit with my son, with Isaac." This BLM hermeneutic seeks to validate the pain of the mothers and the children who are sent away. I don't care what Sarah says. Our children were not created to be cast out and treated like threats or shot down in the streets or incarcerated at alarming numbers. Sarah may not have been Ishmael's mother but Abraham was his father, whether she liked it or not. They call our children bastards and us slave girls, but we have names. We were brought here and oppressed here and it's too late for white America to change their minds about that. Let us hear how we can fight for the lives of our children.

In conclusion, this course was largely successful in that students were able to define the Black Lives Matter movement, relate its history, and articulate its aims in classroom and congregational settings. They were also able to develop and employ their own Black Lives Matter hermeneutic.[18] As

---

lynching in that context. This cultural understanding and this specific translation were both discussed in the class.

16. This student's hermeneutic is fully formed and does not require further comment.

17. I address the translation of אמה (as well as שפחה) in Gafney 2017, 76–77, and women's slavery as sexual and reproductive slavery more broadly in Gafney 2017, 72–84.

18. One student articulated their Black Lives Matter hermeneutic this way: "My Black Lives Matter hermeneutic seeks to interpret scripture in light of the longstanding, foundational historical American tradition of reducing humans who are Black to

expected, the maturity and sophistication of their hermeneutics varied by student. The course will be offered again.

Works Cited

"About Black Lives Matter." N.d. Black Lives Matter. https://tinyurl.com/SBL03111aq.

Bailey, Randall C., Tat-siong Benny Liew, and Fernando F. Segovia, eds. 2009. *They Were All Together in One Place? Toward Minority Biblical Criticism*. Atlanta: Society of Biblical Literature.

Barber, William J., and Jonathan Wilson-Hartgrove. 2016. *The Third Reconstruction: Moral Mondays, Fusion Politics, and the Rise of a New Justice Movement*. Boston: Beacon.

Copeland, M. Shawn. 2011. "'Wading through Many Sorrows': Toward a Theology of Suffering in a Womanist Perspective." Pages 135–54 in *Womanist Theological Ethics, A Reader*. Edited by Katie Geneva Cannon, Emilie M. Townes, and Angela D. Sims. Louisville: Westminster John Knox.

Crenshaw, Kimberlé. 1989. "Demarginalizing the Intersection of Race and Sex: A Black Feminist Critique of Antidiscrimination Doctrine, Feminist Theory and Antiracist Politics." *UCLF* 1:139–67.

Douglas, Kelly Brown. 2015. *Stand Your Ground: Black Bodies and the Justice of God*. Maryknoll, NY: Orbis.

Francis, Leah Gunning. 2015. *Ferguson and Faith: Sparking Leadership and Awakening Community*. Saint Louis: Chalice.

Gafney, Wilda. 2017. *Womanist Midrash: A Reintroduction to the Women of the Torah and of the Throne*. Louisville: Westminster John Knox.

Garza, Alicia. 2014. "A Herstory of the #BlackLivesMatter Movement." The Feminist Wire, 7 October. https://tinyurl.com/SBL03111ar.

Jacobs, Michelle S. 2017. "The Violent State: Black Women's Invisible Struggle against Police Violence." *WMJWL* 24:39–100.

Lightsey, Pamela R. 2015. *Our Lives Matter: A Womanist Queer Theology*. Eugene, OR: Pickwick.

Miller, Ken. 2019. "Oklahoma Court Upholds Sentence for Ex-Cop Convicted of Rape." Associated Press, 1 August. https://tinyurl.com/SBL03111as.

---

sub-human and the variety of ways that the tradition continues to be erected in our present day context."

Mitchem, Stephanie Y. 2002. *Introducing Womanist Theology*. Maryknoll, NY: Orbis.

Townes, Emilie M. 1993. "Living in the New Jerusalem: The Rhetoric and Movement of Liberation in the House of Evil." Pages 78–91 in *A Troubling in My Soul: Womanist Perspectives on Evil and Suffering*. Edited by Emilie M. Townes. Maryknoll, NY: Orbis.

———. 2006. *Womanist Ethics and the Cultural Production of Evil*. New York: Palgrave Macmillan.

Wallis, Jim. 2016. *America's Original Sin: Racism, White Privilege, and the Bridge to a New America*. Grand Rapids: Brazos.

Wriggins, Jennifer. 1983. "Rape, Racism and the Law." *HWLJ* 6:103–43.

"And I Will Give to You, and to Your Offspring after You, the Land Where You Are Now an Alien": Kinship and Land as Devices for Inclusive Pedagogies

Roger S. Nam

Introduction

A theological education commonly begins with the introductory biblical studies class. The placement of such a class is deliberate. Whether in an undergraduate religious studies program or a seminary degree program, a foundational level of competence in biblical studies functions as the base scaffolding of a curricular arc. For universities with religious affiliations, these introductory classes also serve the general curriculum, as an expression of institutional commitments to the integration of faith and learning. In all of these contexts, the introductory Bible course overwhelmingly follows historical-critical approaches (Cornell and LeMon 2016; Reeder et al. 2016).[1] For certain institutions, particularly evangelical schools, theological approaches may supplement the pedagogical methods. In more recent years, social-scientific and ideological approaches are emerging

---

I presented an earlier version of this paper at the 2019 Annual Meeting of the Society of Biblical Literature in the Racism, Pedagogy, and Biblical Studies program unit. I am grateful to Benny Liew and Shelly Matthews for their leadership and initiative in arranging these important conversations. I also warmly acknowledge guild colleagues Roberta Mata, Justine Wilson, and Denise Buell for our spirited discussion, and especially Love Sechrest for her insightful response. All errors and misjudgments are mine alone.

1. See Dale Martin (2008), who laments this dominance of historical-critical methods in introductory classroom texts because of their insufficiency in preparing people for ministry, though he implicitly hints at the problem of monolithic interpretations. For a response to Martin, see Adam et al. 2009.

as potential secondary methods. These approaches have been active in political-religious dialogues for decades, yet their collective emergence in biblical studies is a relatively new phenomenon. In nearly all cases, these approaches do not displace historical-critical approaches but rather supplement them (Cornell and LeMon 2016, 126). The primacy of historical-critical approaches is expected in these introductory courses, as such an approach permeates the biblical studies guild both in its historical trajectory and in current forms of scholarship (Buell 2018).[2] This approach has benefits. The historical-critical approach can guide students into analyzing biblical texts under native contexts, thereby raising the capacities of student interpretive skills. The historical-critical approach also represents the biblical studies guild as a whole.

But the historical-critical approaches in introductory classes represent a particular ideological trajectory. This placement of historical criticism at the center of pedagogical methods has reified a Western dominance on the modern guild of biblical studies. Despite the stated origins of historical approaches as an intentional move toward scientific objectivity and away from dogmatizing theological claims, the historical method undergirded support for theological and political agendas in Western Europe. These historical studies legitimized a colonial ideology, often under the guise of the Christian missionary effort. Not surprisingly, the historical-critical lens continues to reinforce racial marginalization, particularly in the ideal of the Greek origins and promulgation of subtle anti-Semitism (Blount 1995; Byron 2012; Segovia 1998). Despite their claims, historical-critical approaches, like any other method, are also contextual. They belie the approaches' origins and commitment to a Eurocentric reading of the biblical texts. Despite their stated intention to heed original contexts, historical-critical approaches can also promote a Eurocentric application to present contexts. For example, Denise Kimber Buell (2018, 161; see also Buell 2005) has identified a common practice of reconstruction of Christian origins that emphasizes insider/outsider borders with the terms of religion and race as weaponized concepts in weakening the legitimacy of racialized groups.[3] The commitment to a historical-critical pedagogi-

---

2. Buell draws from Heschel 1998; Kelley 2002; Johnson 2004.
3. Buell (2018, 161) writes, "Historical critical approaches to the New Testament in their early articulations have functioned especially as a way for some European Protestants to authorize their own visions of 'true' Christianity over and against both institutionalized forms of contemporary Protestantism and especially

cal approach is a movement, whether intentional or not, in a particular expression of biblical study. As a result, these introductory classes create a homogeneity of interpretation.[4]

Therefore, any inclusive pedagogies must interrogate the nearly exclusive primacy of historical-critical approaches to introductory classes. Such beginning classes are an ideal location to target a decentering of whiteness. Elisabeth Schüssler Fiorenza (2009) argues that the classroom, rather than the setting of guild scholarship, is the critical arena for broader inclusion in the task of biblical studies. She uses the descriptor *emancipatory* to signal the pedagogical ideals of the classroom space. Rather than center on historical-critical methods and their emphasis on objectivity and disinterested interpretation, teachers must recognize that the multivalent lenses of interpretation can be an asset in understanding. This is particularly important for seeking ways in which biblical texts are meaningful to today's lives. For Schüssler Fiorenza, such a movement embodies the *conscientização* of Paulo Freire.[5] As much as historical-critical approaches can construct, they can also deconstruct. Specifically, the introductory biblical studies class can deconstruct previously axiomatic assumptions, often on the nature of biblical texts. Such deconstruction readily opens new vistas of learning.

Consequently, a wholesale elimination of the historical-critical method is not useful nor realistic for most institutional contexts, nor is it even effective as a pedagogical strategy. Rather, scholars should look to other ways to deconstruct white normativity within the historical-critical task.[6] Understanding the complications and that alternative approaches are

---

against Catholicism, not to mention over and against those identified as anything other than 'Christian.'"

4. As Willie James Jennings (2020, 6–7) argues, "Theological education in the West was born in white hegemony, and homogeneity, making it holy and right and efficient—when it is none of these things."

5. The aim of *conscientização* is to "designate a learning process in which groups become skilled at recognizing forms and experiences of social, political, cultural, religious, and economic oppression and dehumanization"; for Schüssler Fiorenza (2009, 16), this recognition is congruent with the aims of biblical studies classrooms.

6. Within the complex palette of power of our academic institutions, we put ourselves at risk when we choose to interrogate whiteness. Consequently, we must intentionally consider a strategic response that is authentic to our teaching personas. We must consider our own vulnerabilities within the institution when we are confrontative. One can think of approaches that are strong, prophetic, and confrontative. One

already supplementing historical-critical approaches (Cornell and LeMon 2016), I wish, in the remainder of my essay, to suggest a very specific plan in which one can interrogate whiteness in the introductory biblical studies course in the spirit of helping our students unlearn. Two dominant themes within the Hebrew Bible can serve as tools for such an interrogation. Specifically, I refer to the themes of kinship and land as devices for pedagogical inclusion.

Ethnography as Pedagogy

Hebrew Bible scholarship has long identified kinship and land as critical tropes within biblical texts across genres, geographic settings, and chronological stages.[7] A single passage can suffice to demonstrate the prominence of these two interrelated themes: the first articulation of the Abrahamic covenant in Gen 12:1–3:

> Now the LORD said to Abram, "Go from your country and your kindred and your father's house to the land that I will show you. I will make of you a great nation, and I will bless you, and make your name great, so that you will be a blessing. I will bless those who bless you, and the one who curses you I will curse; and in you all the families of the earth shall be blessed."[8]

Biblical studies professors should consider the notions of kinship and land that introductory students bring to their interpretation of this passage. In recognizing the patriarchal and agrarian setting of ancient Israel, professors must devise ways to question these assumptions in service of a more

---

can think of approaches that are beguiling, savvy, and subversive. Such approaches are not along a continuum, but I do think that we must intentionally consider how to best interrogate whiteness from our particular contexts. Specifically, the institutional and individual contexts must inform the strategy to interrogating whiteness. The institutional context includes the loci of authority among donors, administrators, faculty, and students. It also entails mission and value; I will note that the implicit values of a university are often unstated and hidden, and they may also be in conflict with the university's explicitly stated mission. The individual context includes the professor's embodied presence as well as agency through formal marks such as tenure.

7. For significant studies on kinship, see Stager 1985; Gottwald 1979, esp. 237–344; on land, see Habel 1993; Davis 2009.

8. Unless otherwise noted, Scripture quotations follow the NRSV.

sophisticated cultural frame to investigate the Bible. Of course, historical-critical pedagogies can service such learning. But introductory students must expand their interpretive imaginations far beyond traditional scholarship. The chronological study of the historical-critical method can be governed by a more ethnographic approach to decenter whiteness and bring tension to reconstructions of historical context. Specifically, I suggest that introductory classes intentionally find spaces where non-Western ideals of kinship and land can challenge hidden assumptions and expand interpretive imaginations.

The usage of ethnographic methods has been extremely limited in biblical studies pedagogy. The nature of biblical studies as a philological discipline in its very core is exclusionary in accord with the limited voices that governed the textualization and redactions of biblical texts. The production of biblical scholarship in written and elite forms in the sanctioned research languages of English, German, and French (and to a lesser extent Modern Hebrew, Dutch, Italian, and Spanish) further signals the restrictions of access to scholarly production. The nature of the historical-critical task reifies these positions in its purported searches for objective interpretations. Until recently, biblical studies scholarship has made limited usage of ethnography. Such a pursuit may have been considered distracting to the interpretive task, and understandably ancient Israel is no longer available for live observation. Because most professors are trained in the historical-critical models, the introductory class often validates a search for objective meaning that typically lies within the limited purview of historical-critical findings. Any attempts to go beyond these viewpoints in classroom settings are often dismissive. Such an exclusivist approach is puzzling, considering the broader goals of biblical studies classes to have outreach beyond the classroom.[9]

Ethnographic pedagogical models, however, can provide a simple and effective strategy to develop a more inclusive pedagogy that gently moves

---

9. Theologians and religious studies scholars are cautious in using ethnography. Within the broader enterprise of theology, critics have rightly accused ethnography as a veiled attempt to maintain colonial structures of earlier theological systems. To this point, in applying ethnographic approach to theology, Todd Whitmore (2011, 185) cautions himself, "Theology has underwritten colonialism, and theological as well as economic aspects of this arrangement ... remain." Other concerns about using ethnography include an overcomparison against distinct cultural systems; see Gustafson 1999 and a different viewpoint in Smith 2013.

students beyond Western frames of biblical interpretation. Unlike the sole method of historical criticism in the spirit of Julius Wellhausen, a broader ethnographic approach resists homogeneity. Principles of ethnography have been emerging more in recent years through social scientific frames. For the introductory biblical studies class, this proposal seeks a modest usage of ethnography. Christian Scharen and Aana Marie Viggen (2011b, 16) provide a working definition:

> Ethnography as a process of attentive study of, and learning from, people—their words, practices, traditions, experiences, memories, insights—in particular times and places in order to understand how they make meaning (cultural, religious, ethnical) and what they can teach us about reality, truth, beauty, moral responsibility, relationships, the divine, etc.

For the introductory class, I suggest ethnography practice to supplement, expand, or perhaps even contest the results of historical-critical methods. Ethnographic pedagogies can broaden understandings of kinship and land to undergird our own readings of a text. Of course, any modern observable culture does not adequately compare to ancient Israel. But I propose a modest usage of ethnography in biblical studies pedagogy. The terminology of kinship and land must be freed from anachronistic assumptions built into the modern reader in subconscious ways that can obfuscate the reading of the text. Specifically, these terms will be seemingly self-explanatory to the introductory student. But the class can nurture an intentional formation of meaning of kinship and land with the understanding that it will be bound within the social systems of the Bible. Consequently, readers must look to cultural systems to access a wider range of meanings.[10] Said cultural systems will not directly replace Westerns norms on kinship and land but will hopefully catalyze a broader potential of interpretation. For example, observations of Melanasian trade cannot adequately compare directly to ancient Israelite exchange, but through studying Melanasia, one could import a better frame for understanding the phenomena (of kinship and land) from ancient Israel, especially considering the limited biblical evidence for reconstructing these themes.

---

10. Despite the modest intent, using ethnography as a pedagogical source also requires caution, particularly in the privilege we invoke as teachers. See Scharen and Vigen 2011a, xx–xxi.

As living cultures can inspire students, this can lead to a greater awareness of the centering of whiteness and its deleterious effects on understanding biblical texts. Through ethnographic practices, one contests whiteness by expanding the voices. This idea of expansive framing has emerged in theological ethnographic research methods (Wigg-Stevenson 2015, 4). The introductory biblical studies classroom becomes less hierarchal and more collaborative, as a greater breath of knowledge shifts expertise to a broader locus of expertise as voices from outside the Western frame are valued as resources of learning (Jennings 2017). Learning can incorporate stories from a heterogeneity of diverse communities alongside the professor's viewpoints. This approach has particular potential considering the significance of kinship and land throughout the Hebrew Bible narrative.

Kinship

One can interrogate assumptions on kinship in an effort to decenter the Eurocentric interpretive lenses. These assumptions are formed throughout our life and reside powerfully in our collective subconscious. Despite many biblical scholars who are embodied as ethnic minorities, their doctoral training and early career development reinforce these Eurocentric perspectives. Thus, assumptions must be identified and examined for their appropriateness for interpretation of biblical texts. The interrogation of such values can free the reader for more productive readings of biblical texts replete with kinship themes. What are notions of family? What is the role that parents bring in the family? What are the roles of power within a family system, and the inputs that shift the dynamic boundaries of power? How is a family system gendered? What is the role of the patriarch? What are the expectations for daughters, and how do those expectations differ from that of sons? What is the significance of blood purity? How does the sibling birth order affect systems of power, and what are the concomitant exceptions? How are family units shifted through natural events of birth/death or of marriage/divorce? What is the role of cousins and second cousins? What is the place of ancestors? What is the place of progeny?

As responsible teachers, we can frame a class to deconstruct students' notions of kinship as they read the biblical text. Kinship has been one of the key subjects in the history of anthropology, whether in political or social organizations (social anthropology) or the symbolic attachments of relationships (cultural anthropology). Modern Eurocentric notions of kinship are highly distinct from the agrarian world of ancient Israel. Many of our present notions of the nuclear family in the West are largely shaped by the Industrial Revolution. One of the social results of the Industrial Revolution was the disembedding of social relationships from our economic transactions. Thus came the rise of capitalism and motivations for profit displacing kinship-based decisions on distribution. Notions of kinship were minimized, and family units were shifted. Another result of the reduction of family systems is the rise of individualism, though, of course, components of this emerged in ancient Israel as well (Halpern 1991; Newsom 2012). The pedagogical approach to themes of kinship need not require a full review of the state of kinship in anthropology, merely an introduction of different ideals of kinship from observable cultures. Challenging notions of kinship prevents anachronistic impositions of modern Western views of kinship on the reading of biblical texts. By engaging a broader set of readers, one can acquire new vistas of the theme of kinship and how it functions in interpretation.

Using ethnography to decenter whiteness is more than a pedagogical tool; doing so follows a growing usage in scholarship in regard to kinship. In one of the seminal works on kinship in Hebrew Bible studies, Lawrence Stager begins in the very first paragraph by quoting from Paul Ricoeur's (1980, 17, cited in Stager 1985, 1) *The Contribution of French Historiography to the Theory of History*, "One must assert that in history the initiative does not belong to the document but to the question posed by the historian." Stager prefaces his article with the admission that the context of the reader is dominant in interpretation and consequently in exploring the archaeology of the family. Therefore, Stager draws from early twentieth-century ethnographies from Palestine to inform his interpretation of domestic dwellings. He then turns to studies of mountain villages in the Zagros to reconstruct everyday family life in relation to material remains. These Middle Eastern ethnographies undergird Stager's interpretation of the mechanics of the multifamily patrilineal household.[11]

---

11. I wonder how much Stager's own context, being born and raised on a Midwestern farm and a first-generation undergraduate at Harvard, created an awareness of his own contextual frame compared to the other students. Perhaps this awareness compelled him to understand the truth in that quote from Ricoeur and to pioneer the use of ethnographic studies to interrogate his own contextual assumptions and articulate a much more sophisticated picture of the family in ancient Israel. I recently asked this very question to one of Stager's doctoral students. Of course, this is speculation, as Stager passed away in 2017. But his former student responded, "I think your guess

We would do well to encourage our students to follow Stager's model in teaching, to recognize the importance of our own reading frames and consequently the disparity between the twenty-first-century Western family and ancient Israel's notions of kinship. It would be good to point out the Eurocentrism in our reading lens, which inhibits a native understanding of the text. Such Eurocentrism embeds all of us who were trained in the legacy of the historical-critical enterprise, which is decidedly rooted in whiteness. In introductory classes, we should teach students that the extended family was the norm. We should teach that the values of these extended families were distributed across deeply patriarchal lines and centered on sons. Marriage was an extension of notions of kinship in that one likely married a distant cousin for economic protections. Our assumptions of family today are very far from our assumptions of family in ancient Israel.

Other scholars on kinship have drawn richly from living models (Hanson 1994). Stager's student David Schloen (2001, 108–16) draws from a broad array of sources to conceptualize the roles of real and fictive kinship in the development of Bronze Age empire. He finds premodern Islamic cities to have had a similar orientation toward kinship hierarchy in Late Bronze Age urban centers. The neighborhood layouts followed clusters of expanded kin, requiring irregular streets and designs. Early ethnographers decried such city plans as chaotic and illogical, though Schloen determines these designs to have been highly functional around a distinct patrimonial ethos and requisite spatial needs for obligations borne out of the patrimonial structure (111). Norm Gottwald's (1979, 237–344) influential *Tribes of Yahweh*, particularly his section on social structure, relies extensively on anthropology to describe the subdivisions of the extended family. Gottwald takes the subdivisions from Josh 7:1–14 and 1 Sam 10:18–21 to name the divisions as tribe, clan, and house. He borrows terms from linguistics, identifying this as an *emic* approach of establishing criteria from the subjects themselves, as opposed to the *etic*

---

might be true. You have realia from the ground (or text on a page, if we were talking about literary analysis) but those things don't speak for themselves—they have to be made sensible within a frame. I think that was his perspective. I can imagine his farm-boy background did make him more sensitive to the frames in which we put things, and he probably found himself in clashes and dialogues with all kinds of Harvard people who did have a very different frame from him, and it made a big difference" (Brian Doak, personal communication, 20 October 2019).

approach of employing external categories (Gottwald 1979, 785 n. 558; see also Pfoh 2010). For Gottwald, the primacy of tribe was foundational for his revolution-settlement hypothesis. The tribal association shared common ancestry even though such ancestry may have been fictionally projected (Gottwald 1979, 334; Fohrer 1981; Perdue et al. 1997; Martin 1989). Although his theories on Israelite origins brought the most attention, his articulation of kinship structures has been the lasting contribution of his volume. Introductory biblical studies courses can emulate such examples of ethnographic study to better understand the biblical values associated with kinship.[12]

Land

The theme of land is deeply tied to kinship. Although this theme does not have its own established division in traditional anthropological studies, the concept of land intersects multiple social scientific fields such as religion, economics, and political power. The direct lens of ethnography in biblical studies has been limited in studies of land. Most studies have been more theological and lacking in ethnologic support (Brueggemann 2002; Habel 1993).[13] Academic discourse of the theme of land in the Bible is especially ideologically loaded due to the contested spaces in the Middle East and claims to religious texts for possession.

Again, modern Western contexts frequently and subconsciously shape our own concept of land. We have assumptions, and we will bring such assumptions subconsciously to a text. But those assumptions are often the result of a colonial Western history. Both literal and figurative colonial movements have displaced notions of land as ancestral heritage. In premodern times, land was tied to economic sustenance, as the land produced crops or fed the animals. Household lands also served as cultic places for worship and burial. Land is a primary component of the covenantal promise. Thus, many large portions of the Hebrew Bible are dedicated to a division of land. This viewpoint of land makes the diasporic narratives of the Bible so devastating. The forced dislocation from ances-

---

12. The ethnography of kinship is also finding development in the field of religious studies (see Thomas, Malik, and Wellman 2017, esp. 1–28).

13. For a Jewish theological approach, with particularly interest in the problem of settlement, see Frankel 2011; for an agrarian approach, see Davis 2009; for a recent anthropological study on land in respect to burial, see Stavrakopoulou 2010.

tral lands alienated peoples from generations of tradition and sustenance. Displaced bodies equated to displaced identities. This view of land made the promise to Abraham so spectacular and the severance of land through the exile event so traumatic. Not only did the Judeans lose their resources for basic sustenance, but they also were permanently detached from their own heritage. Such a traumatic injury through land is difficult to parallel in modern Western culture.

This view of land can interrogate the whiteness of our own assumptions and how they differ from the biblical text. One can consider the transactional aspects of land in modern Eurocentric spaces. Many private and public institutions (including universities and churches) obtained their land through government-sponsored seizure from indigenous communities. In recent years, this land has functioned as a bailout fund for theological education.[14] Land is to be bought and sold and readily transferred across households. Land is also a form of detached investment for individuals. The land provides generationally, but through appreciation and tax incentives. This capitalist understanding of the land contrasts with the concept of land in Israel as a lasting gift to the progeny of Abraham. In its essence, Western capitalism has transformed land into a commodity—a commodity that is to be bought and sold with an aim for profit. Land is no longer tied to kinship. It is a commodity that is readily exchangeable for those who have the means to afford it, a commodity with no ties to heritage or ancestral rights, but whose ownership is a result of colonial expansion for the elite winners of land's commodification.

This is such a vastly different portrayal of land from that in biblical times. Land was a divine inheritance for the people that was allocated according to tribes. Major portions of biblical texts are devoted to the allotment of said land. Even the transactions of land are symbolic and not commodified. Two samples should suffice. In Gen 23:1–10, Abraham purchases the cave of Machpelah from the Hittites as a burial site for Sarah. Abraham precedes the purchase with the admission, "I am a stranger and an alien residing among you" (Gen 23:4). The purchase of a burial lot is not to use the land as commodity, but rather as a place of proper burial for Sarah, and later, befitting the nomadic lifestyle, for Abraham

---

14. One can simply note the many seminaries that are selling properties to maintain cash flow and stave off closures. It is inappropriate to name examples, though it is happening primarily in urban centers with inflated land values—though that is not to say that it does not happen in rural institutions.

himself. The Hittites respond positively, but not out of financial gain; it is simply a matter of honor befitting their declaration of Abraham as "a mighty prince" (Gen 23:6). Abraham proceeds to pay the full price, not out of market exchange but as a function of reciprocal exchange (McDonald 2004). The entire transaction lacks any hallmarks of a market exchange of bargaining. Instead, the transfer of land is a reflex of honor across ethnic lines. Abraham has displayed honor; therefore, he is granted permission to buy the cave of Machpelah, as the Hittites recognize the necessity of a burial space. In return, Abraham reciprocates the honor given him by paying the "full price" for the land even though the Hittites did not request or demand the payment (Gen 23:9).

In another example of the social meaning of land, David purchases the threshing floor of Araunah the Jebusite in 2 Sam 24. David and his servants come and announce their intention to buy the land. Araunah responds in lofty obeisance language by inviting King David to take the land, oxen, and threshing instruments. But when offered this free gift of land, David responds, "No, but I will buy them from you for a price; I will not offer burnt offerings to the Lord my God that cost me nothing" (2 Sam 24:24). So David buys the plot of land for fifty shekels and builds an altar to worship the Lord. This action of David completely defies the assumptions behind modern capitalism and its rule of supply and demand. In this passage, land is not a commodity but bound with the providence of God and the identity of Israel's people. As ancestral land, it is not for sale. Instead, it is deeply integrated into the life and identity of the people. Its purchase is unrelated to any utilitarian function or fiscal gain but comes out of the profound moment of divine encounter. The transaction is especially meaningful as it crosses geopolitical space between Israelites and Jebusites. David and Araunah make the transaction out of devotion to the Lord.

Inclusive Pedagogies, Broader Communities

As we teach introductory classes in biblical studies, we must openly prevent subtle yet powerful tendencies against non-Western views of kinship and land as well as other prominent themes to develop a broader understanding of the contexts of biblical texts. Responsible teaching of introductory biblical studies courses will contest our students' assumed visions of kinship and land that are far different from the biblical world. We can implore readers to turn to non-Western cultures for a more native view of kinship and land. For example, readers from the continents of Africa and Asia can have a much more relevant viewpoint of such tropes. The exclusive frame of modern Western culture impoverishes the capacities of students in our introductory courses to read texts critically. Such perspectives must be identified and challenged.

The ethnographic activity I am suggesting to help interrogate whiteness can affect students' broader learning experiences beyond the introductory biblical studies class. In the introductory class, we have the opportunity to model for our students an expanded imagination on the themes of kinship and land, through which they will discover their own biases as readers so they can appreciate an enhanced understanding of biblical texts by listening to readers from other cultural locations. Thus, the interrogation of whiteness is also an invitation to involve a broader reading community. Instead of forcing readers to analyze the text through the narrow lens of whiteness, non-Western readers are invited to bring their full, authentic selves to the texts. Their viewpoints can then build the capacities of other readers. Inclusion not only shifts the center from whiteness but gives authority to those who can think through themes of kinship and land in non-Western modes. Students from diverse settings are not exclusively taught from a particular historical-critical understanding, but they also become a resource for the broader class by drawing on their own narratives. Whereas academic knowledge is construed as restrictive and exclusionist in accordance with European dominance, the opening of broader resources for learning cultivates belonging. These viewpoints on kinship and land from past and present heritages outside the sphere of whiteness can form the foundation of a more inclusive pedagogy and therefore a more inclusive learning community.

Works Cited

Adam, Andrew K. M., Richard Ascough, Sandra Gravett, Alice Hunt, Dale Martin, Edward Wimberly, and Seung Ai Yang. 2009. "Should We Be Teaching the Historical Critical Method?" *TTR* 12:162–87.

Blount, Brian K. 1995. *Cultural Interpretation: Reinterpreting New Testament Criticism*. Minneapolis: Fortress.

Brueggemann, Walter. 2002. *The Land: Place as Gift, Promise, and Challenge in Biblical Faith*. Minneapolis: Fortress.

Buell, Denise Kimber. 2005. *Why This New Race: Ethnic Reasoning in Early Christianity*. New York: Columbia University Press.

———. 2018. "Anachronistic Whiteness and the Ethics of Interpretation." Pages 149–67 in *Ethnicity, Race, Religion: Identities and Ideologies in Early Jewish and Christian Texts, and in Modern Biblical Interpretation*. Edited by Katherine M. Hockey and David G. Horrell. London: T&T Clark.

Byron, Gay. 2012. "Race, Ethnicity, and the Bible: Pedagogical Challenges and Curricular Opportunities." *TTR* 15:105–24.

Cornell, Collin, and Joel M. LeMon. 2016. "How We Teach Introductory Bible Courses: A Comparative and Historical Sampling." *TTR* 19:114–42.

Davis, Ellen. 2009. *Scripture, Culture, and Agriculture: An Agrarian Reading of the Bible*. Cambridge: Cambridge University Press.

Fohrer, Georg. 1981. "Die Familiengemeinschaft." Pages 161–71 in *Studien zu alttestamentlichen Texten und Themen*. Berlin: de Gruyter.

Frankel, David. 2011. *The Land of Canaan and the Destiny of Israel: Theologies of Territory in the Hebrew Bible*. Winona Lake, IN: Eisenbrauns.

Gottwald, Norman. 1979. *The Tribes of Yahweh: A Sociology of the Liberated Israel, 1250–1050 BCE*. Maryknoll, NY: Orbis.

Gustafson, James M. 1999. "Just What Is 'Postliberal' Theology?" *ChrCent* 16.10:353–55.

Habel, Norman. 1993. *The Land Is Mine: Six Biblical Land Ideologies*. Minneapolis: Fortress.

Halpern, Baruch. 1991. "Kinship and the Rise of Individual Moral Responsibility." Pages 11–107 in *Law and Ideology in Monarchic Israel*. Edited by Baruch Halpern and Deborah W. Hobson. Sheffield: Sheffield Academic.

Hanson, Kenneth C. 1994. "Biblical Theology Bulletin Reader's Guide to Kinship." *BTB* 24:183–94.

Heschel, Susannah. 1998. *Abraham Geiger and the Jewish Jesus*. Chicago: University of Chicago Press.

Jennings, Willie James. 2017. "Race and the Educated Imagination: Outlining a Pedagogy of Belonging." *RelEd* 112 (2017): 58–65.

———. 2020. *After Whiteness: An Education in Belonging*. Grand Rapids: Eerdmans.

Johnson, Sylvester. 2004. *The Myth of Ham in Nineteenth Century American Christianity: Race, Heathens, and the People of God*. New York: Palgrave.

Kelley, Shawn. 2002. *Racializing Jesus: Race, Ideology and the Formation of Modern Biblical Scholarship*. London: Routledge.

Martin, Dale. 2008. *Pedagogy of the Bible: An Analysis and Proposal.* Louisville: Westminster John Knox.

Martin, James D. 1989. "Israel as a Tribal Society." Pages 95–117 in *The World of Ancient Israel: Sociological, Anthropological and Political Perspectives.* Edited by Ronald E. Clements. Cambridge: Cambridge University Press.

McDonald, Nathan. 2004. "Driving a Hard Bargain? Genesis 23 and Models of Economic Exchange." Pages 79–96 in *Anthropology and Biblical Studies.* Edited by Louise J. Lawrence and Mario I. Aguilar. Leiden: Brill.

Newsom, Carol. 2012. "Models of the Moral Self: Hebrew Bible and Second Temple Judaism." *JBL* 131:5–25.

Perdue, Leo, Joseph Blenkinsopp, John J. Collins, and Carol Meyers. 1997. *Families in Ancient Israel.* Louisville: Westminster John Knox.

Pfoh, Emanuel. 2010. "Anthropology and Biblical Studies: A Critical Manifesto." Pages 15–36 in *Anthropology and the Bible: Critical Perspectives.* Edited by Emanuel Pfoh. Piscataway, NJ: Gorgias.

Reeder, Caryn A., Tat-siong Benny Liew, Jane S. Webster, Alicia J. Batten, and Chris Frilingos. 2016. "Response to 'How We Teach Introductory Bible Courses.'" *TTR* 19:143–53.

Ricoeur, Paul. 1980. *The Contribution of French Historiography to the Theory of History.* New York: Clarendon.

Scharen, Christian, and Aana Marie Vigen. 2011a. "Preface: Blurring Boundaries." Pages xvii–xxviii in *Ethnography as Christian Theology and Ethics.* Edited by Christian Scharan and Aana Marie Vigen. New York: Continuum.

———. 2011b. "What Is Ethnography?" Pages 3–27 in *Ethnography as Christian Theology and Ethics.* Edited by Christian Scharan and Aana Marie Vigen. New York: Continuum.

Schloen, J. David. 2001. *House of the Father as Fact and Symbol: Patrimonialism in Ugarit and the Ancient Near East.* Winona Lake, IN: Eisenbrauns.

Schüssler Fiorenza, Elisabeth. 2009. *Democratizing Biblical Studies: Toward an Emancipatory Education Space.* Louisville: Westminster John Knox.

Segovia, Fernando F. 1998. "Pedagogical Discourse and Practices in Contemporary Biblical Criticism." Pages 1–28 in *Teaching the Bible: The Discourse and Politics of Biblical Pedagogy.* Edited by Fernando F. Segovia and Mary Ann Tolbert. New York: Orbis.

Smith, Ted A. 2013. "Troeltschian Questions for 'Ethnography as Christian Theology and Ethics.'" *PM* 6:1–9.

Stager, Lawrence E. 1985. "The Archaeology of the Family in Ancient Israel." *BASOR* 260:1–35.

Stavrakopoulou, Francesca. 2010. *Land of Our Fathers: The Roles of Ancestor Veneration in Biblical Land Claims*. London: T&T Clark.

Thomas, Todne, Asiya Malik, and Rose Wellman, eds. 2017. *New Directions in Spiritual Kinship: Sacred Ties across the Abrahamic Religions*. New York: Palgrave Macmillan.

Whitmore, Todd. 2011. "Whiteness Made Visible: A Theo-critical Ethnography in Acoliland." Pages 184–206 in *Ethnography as Theology and Ethics*. Edited by Christian Scharan and Aana Marie Vigen. New York: Continuum.

Wigg-Stevenson, Natalie. 2015. "From Proclamation to Conversation: Ethnography Disruptions to Theological Normativity." *PC* 1:1–9.

A Pedagogy of Ethnic Prejudice in Matthew 15:21–28

Wongi Park

Faculty who teach at predominantly white institutions encounter several challenges when teaching about racism in a biblical studies classroom. A first challenge is acknowledging the range of assumptions about race, both spoken and unspoken, that students bring into the classroom space. Some may view the topic as having little to no relevance to their personal lives. Some may harbor resentment toward other racial/ethnic groups. Some may believe in the inherent superiority of their own group. Some may think that racism is a thing of the past. All of these different racial/ethnic scripts (Markus and Moya 2010), and many more, may be present in the classroom before the conversation begins.

A second challenge is a general reluctance to talk about racism given the polemical and politicized nature of the subject matter. Toni Morrison (1992, 9–10) captures this point well: "The habit of ignoring race is understood to be a graceful, even generous, liberal gesture. To notice is to recognize an already discredited difference." Some students may prefer not to discuss the topic in public. Others may be hesitant to speak out of the fear of saying the wrong thing at the wrong time. Still others, especially minority students, may not be comfortable talking about their experiences in a majority-white context.

A third challenge, specific to minority faculty, is an implicit questioning of their presence and authority in the classroom. This assumption is often tacit, sometimes overt, but virtually always present with varying degrees of skepticism in predominantly white institution classrooms. Minority instructors may be viewed with disinterest, dismay, or disdain—particularly and perhaps especially when addressing matters such as racism. For this reason, minority faculty should be aware of how these dynamics shape the classroom environment along with the potential impact of negative teaching evaluations (Bonner and Park 2020).

A fourth challenge, specific to a biblical studies classroom, is a fairly widespread belief that Christianity is a universal religion that has nothing to do with the particularities of race and ethnicity. Christianity has broken free of its racial/ethnic ties with Judaism, so goes the dominant narrative, and has become an inclusive religion that transcends race, gender, and class (Buell 2005; Sechrest 2015; Horrell 2017; Park 2019). Based on this way of thinking, emphasizing identity markers of any kind goes against the dominant narrative and the universal, inclusive values it proclaims. Addressing these challenges is a tall order that requires more space than what is allotted here. So, in what follows, my interest is narrow and more focused. Drawing on the story of the Canaanite woman in Matt 15:21–28, I identify pedagogical strategies that may be employed in a biblical studies classroom to alleviate some of the challenges mentioned above.

Overview

The story of Jesus's encounter with a Canaanite woman (γυνὴ Χαναναία, Matt 15:22) presents numerous difficulties. Some commentators bypass these challenges by focusing on the story's miraculous outcome in verse 28 (Edwards 1985; for a critical assessment of white Western readings, see Dube 2000, 157–96). But there are several issues leading up to this point that should not be overlooked. Analyzing how Jesus engages with the Canaanite woman and her daughter proves instructive. His first response is rude; Jesus, as though avoiding a homeless person on the street, ignores her with silence (15:23). His second response is ethnocentric: "I was sent only to the lost sheep of the house of Israel" (οἴκου Ἰσραήλ, 15:24).[1] The woman, undeterred, kneels at his feet for help. Jesus's third response is derogatory and borderline racist: "It is not fair to take the children's food and throw it to the dogs" (τοῖς κυναρίοις, 15:26). Was Jesus prejudiced, ethnocentric, and racist toward the Canaanite woman?

The goal of this paper is to push this reading to its logical conclusion and to consider the pedagogical value of doing so in the biblical studies classroom. However, the average student may be hesitant to accept a reading that acknowledges the possibility of racial and ethnic prejudice in the Bible—much less in the person of Jesus. Hence, the following argument

---

1. All English translations come from the NRSV unless otherwise noted. The Greek text is based on the SBLGNT.

anticipates this objection by performing a close reading of racial/ethnic markers in the text and situating the scene within the narrative tensions of the gospel as a whole. Locating the scene in this way reveals an uncomfortable truth—that what the Judean Jesus displays toward the unnamed Canaanite woman in Matt 15:21–28 is part and parcel of a deep-seated and long-standing tradition of ethnic prejudice in the Bible.[2]

Highlighting Racial/Ethnic Markers in the Text

The first strategy is to show how the politics of race and ethnicity are clearly embedded in the biblical text. This is a good way to begin because students, more often than not, tend to approach the text in a manner that glosses over difficulties. This is also a tendency among traditional Matthean commentaries that follow a religious-theological model of interpretation (Bruner 2004). This reading has the tendency to emphasize the miraculous outcome of the story in Matt 15:28. But there are a few wrinkles leading up to this point.

The best antidote to a quick, cursory reading is to slow down the reading process. A good prompt is to ask students to underline all racial/ethnic markers in the text in light of the following question: What indicators in the text determine whether Jesus displayed ethnocentrism or racism toward the Canaanite woman? The advantage of this prompt is that it allows students to see for themselves how racial/ethnic markers are configured in the biblical text. Students might highlight and underline the text in the following way:

> Jesus left that place and went away to <u>the district of Tyre and Sidon</u>.
> Just then a <u>Canaanite woman from that region</u> came out and started shouting, "Have mercy on me, <u>Lord, Son of David</u>; my daughter is tormented by a demon."
> But he did not answer her at all. And his disciples came and urged him, saying, "Send her away, for she keeps shouting after us."
> He answered, "<u>I was sent only to the lost sheep of the house of Israel</u>."

---

2. In this paper, following Mason (2007), I prefer to translate Ἰουδαῖος as "Judean" to foreground the ethnic dimension of the term rather than the traditional religious and less precise translation "Jew." This choice is informed by a reading of various racial/ethnic markers in the Gospel of Matthew developed below and elsewhere (Park 2019). It also acknowledges the range of variant Judaisms in the early centuries of the Common Era (Hoklotubbe 2021).

But she came and knelt before him, saying, "Lord, help me."
He answered, "It is not fair to take the children's food and throw it to the dogs."
She said, "Yes, Lord, yet even the dogs eat the crumbs that fall from their masters' table."
Then Jesus answered her, "Woman, great is your faith! Let it be done for you as you wish." And her daughter was healed instantly.

The Canaanite Woman from Tyre and Sidon (Matt 15:21–22)

Right off the bat, the story's setting provides the first clue: Matthew's reference to the geographical region in "the district of Tyre and Sidon" (Τύρου καὶ Σιδῶνος, Matt 15:21). Assuming the two-source hypothesis, one can note that Matthew adds "Sidon" to Mark's "Tyre" (Mark 7:24). The phrase "Tyre and Sidon" occurs previously in Matt 11:21–22 in the context of judgment: "Woe to you, Chorazin! Woe to you, Bethsaida! For if the deeds of power done in you had been done in Tyre and Sidon, they would have repented long ago in sackcloth and ashes. But I tell you, on the day of judgment it will be more tolerable for Tyre and Sidon than for you." The animosity implied in these verses is confirmed by Josephus, who says it is well-known that Tyrians were enemies of the Judeans (Josephus, *C. Ap.* 1.13). Tyre and Sidon have pejorative connotations in the Hebrew Bible. Matthew's coupling of this phrase with "Canaanite" recalls a deep-seated enmity that exists between Judeans and Canaanites in the biblical tradition (Davies and Allison 1988–1997, 2:547). A well-known passage exhibiting such enmity is Deut 20:16–18, where God commands the Israelites to annihilate the inhabitants of the land, including the Canaanites.[3] The tension between Tyre and Jerusalem is also well-established in the Hebrew Bible.[4]

---

3. Deuteronomy 20:16–18: "But as for the towns of these peoples that the Lord your God is giving you as an inheritance, you must not let anything that breathes remain alive. You shall annihilate them—the Hittites and the Amorites, the Canaanites and the Perizzites, the Hivites and the Jebusites—just as the Lord your God has commanded, so that they may not teach you to do all the abhorrent things that they do for their gods, and you thus sin against the Lord your God" (see Deut 7:1).

4. Ezekiel 26:1–3: "In the eleventh year, on the first day of the month, the word of the Lord came to me: Mortal, because Tyre said concerning Jerusalem, 'Aha, broken is the gateway of the peoples; it has swung open to me; I shall be replenished, now that it is wasted,' therefore, thus says the Lord God: See, I am against you, O Tyre! I will hurl many nations against you, as the sea hurls its waves."

In Matthew's day the hostility between the two groups culminated during the Judean War (66–70 CE), when many Tyrians killed and imprisoned Judeans (Josephus, *B.J.* 2.478).

A second marker in the text is the ethnic designation attached to the woman as a "Canaanite" (γυνὴ Χαναναία, Matt 15:22). Matthew's ethnic identification of the woman functions as a form of interpellation whereby an individual is marked and singled out on account of their racial/ethnic difference (Mirón and Inda 2000). That is, with respect to Jesus and his disciples—and possibly the Matthean community by implication—she is a non-Judean outsider. The heightened emphasis on the ethnic otherness of the woman can be further appreciated in light of Matthew's redaction of Mark 5:24–30. Here, Matthew specifies the woman's Canaanite ethnicity in contrast to Mark's editorial aside that "she was a gentile [Greek] of Syrophoenician origin" (ἡ δὲ γυνὴ ἦν Ἑλληνίς, Συροφοινίκισσα τῷ γένει, Mark 7:26).[5] Matthew's redaction of "Syrophoenician" is highly significant, especially considering the term is a *hapax legomenon* in the New Testament. Matthew's inclusion of another Canaanite woman in Jesus's genealogy, Rahab (Matt 1:15), provides an important parallel insofar as both women are Canaanites (Gullotta 2014, 331). In this way, Matthew's genealogy hints at a fluidity, flexibility, and fusion of Judean ethnicity that anticipates the tension between particularism and universalism throughout the gospel (McEntire and Park, 2021, 40–41). The editorial change, therefore, is deliberate: Matthew associates the woman with one of Israel's ethnic archenemies (Sparks 2006, 654). In this way, Matthew's account more clearly foregrounds the biblical history of ethnic division.

Jesus Is "Lord" and "Son of David" (Matt 15:22)

The next two markers are subtle and implicit. The Canaanite woman calls out to Jesus using two titles: Lord and Son of David. The third clue, "Lord" (κύριε), signals her faith in Jesus. It is the same confession of faith uttered by the leper (Matt 8:2), Roman centurion (8:8), the disciples (8:25), blind men (9:28), and Peter (14:28). The fourth clue, "Son of David" (υἱὸς Δαυίδ), is a messianic title that is attributed to Jesus by the genealogy (1:1), two blind men (9:27), the crowds (12:33), another two blind men (20:30), and

---

5. For a reading of the Markan account that highlights the intersection of ethnocentrism and sexism, see Liew 1999, 135–37.

the crowds during Jesus's triumphal entry into Jerusalem (21:9). It signifies Jesus's role as king and healer in the Davidic tradition that the "line of David, representing God's rule, will rule forever" (Pss. Sol. 17). Consequently, the use of these titles by the Canaanite woman resembles other confessions of faith both by Judean and gentile disciples in the Gospel of Matthew. She pleads for mercy on behalf of her demon-possessed daughter, though Jesus and his disciples refuse her. The grounds for the refusal are noteworthy.

I Was Sent Only to the Lost Sheep of the House of Israel (Matt 15:24)

The fifth racial/ethnic clue in the text is the phrase "house of Israel" (οἴκου Ἰσραήλ). Based on the quick transition from verse 23 to verse 24, it is unclear whether the woman was present when Jesus answered his disciples. Presumably, she was present based on how she responds in verse 25. In any case, the disciples ask Jesus to send her away, to which Jesus responds: "I was sent only to the lost sheep of the house of Israel" (Οὐκ ἀπεστάλην εἰ μὴ εἰς τὰ πρόβατα τὰ ἀπολωλότα οἴκου Ἰσραήλ). This statement, a double negative in Greek, is one of the clearest utterances of ethnocentrism in the Gospel of Matthew.[6] It is as if Jesus turns to the Canaanite woman and says, "I am not here for you, but for the house of Israel. You are an outsider" (Crowder 2016, 86). The ethnic tension of οἴκου Ἰσραήλ is downplayed in the NRSV translation ("house of Israel"), focusing more on οἴκου as a physical dwelling, and it is omitted entirely from the NIV. By contrast, the CEB translation ("people of Israel") focus on the inhabitants of οἴκου Ἰσραήλ.[7] But since the woman does not belong to the ethnic people of Israel, she is excluded. In fact, the sole reason for Jesus's dismissal of the woman is precisely her ethnic identity and no other reason. It is important to bear in mind that encounters between Jesus and gentiles are an exception to the norm (Gullotta 2014, 335). The anomalous exchange underscores the exclusive character of Matthew's sectarian community. Thus, to the

---

6. See Matt 10:5–6: "These twelve Jesus sent out with the following instructions: 'Go nowhere among the gentiles, and enter no town of the Samaritans, but go rather to the lost sheep of the house of Israel.'"

7. The NIV translation of Matt 15:24 reads: "I was sent only to the lost sheep of Israel." See further Powery 2015, 161.

question of whether Jesus was ethnocentric, the answer is a clear and resounding yes.

Eating the Crumbs That Fall from Their Master's Table (Matt 15:26–27)

The final two racial/ethnic markers in the text are found in verses 26–27, in the concluding dialogue between Jesus and the woman. Unsatisfied with his response, the Canaanite woman kneels before Jesus for help; in so doing, she becomes the only non-Judean to prostrate herself before the Judean Jesus (Powery 2015, 161). At this point, a series of disparaging metaphors are exchanged. Jesus responds in verse 26: "It is not fair to take the children's food [τὸν ἄρτον τῶν τέκνων] and throw it to the dogs [τοῖς κυναρίοις]." In the metaphor Israel represents the children, while the Canaanite woman is one of the dogs. Many commentators soften the force and derogatory implications of the comparison.

Some understand Jesus's metaphor to mean that charity begins at home (Burkill 1967; cited in Davies and Allison, 1988–1997, 2:554). Some point out that Jesus uses the diminutive κυναρίοις (Harrington 1991, 235; Keener 1999, 416). Based on this rationale, M. Eugene Boring (1996, 336) suggests that Jesus is "speaking affectionately of 'puppies.'" Others, however, are far less enamored by the comparison. Regardless of whether κυναρίοις refers to a big dog or a little dog, the Canaanite woman is positioned as "the bitch under the table" (Sawicki 1994, 155, quoted in Jackson 2002, 21). The insult is further compounded in light of Jesus's earlier teaching in the Sermon on the Mount: "Do not give what is holy to dogs [τοῖς κυσίν]; and do not throw your pearls before swine, or they will trample them under foot and turn and maul you" (Matt 7:6). The calculated repetition of the cognate term τοῖς κυσίν in context is unmistakable: Jesus is exemplifying the very thing he said not to do. As Love Sechrest (2018, 293) notes, "A reluctance to cast pearls before swine is essentially a partial restatement of the prohibition of the Gentile mission, as seen in the parallel phrase about giving holy things to dogs."

The Canaanite woman's response is quick, witty, and clever. Without skipping a beat, she retorts, "Yes, Lord, yet even the dogs eat the crumbs that fall from their masters' table" (Matt 15:27). The Canaanite woman plays along with Jesus's belittling metaphor and takes it a step further. With her response, she not only acknowledges Jesus as "Lord" (κύριε) for a second time but also accepts the role of a dog under the table of its master. The Canaanite woman's daughter is healed in the end; however, the underlying depiction of Jesus is rather unflattering. The tension between the ethnocentrism of Jesus's mission and the racialized status quo, while destabilized in this episode, is not fully resolved. To better appreciate this tension, it is necessary to make sense of this encounter in the broader flow and scope of racial/ethnic tensions in the First Gospel.

Contextualizing the Scene in the Gospel of Matthew

A second strategy is to situate Matt 15:21–28 in light of the narrative as a whole. Doing so sheds light on two animating forces that run deep between particularism and universalism throughout Matthew. These forces pull in opposing directions and are embedded in the literary framework at the beginning, middle, and end of the gospel. There are several key moments that showcase a rigid and parochial emphasis on racial/ethnic particularism. In fact, much of Jesus's teaching can be characterized in this way.

The first cluster of examples comes from the Sermon on the Mount. Jesus's teaching is directed to the Judean crowds and disciples (Matt 5:1) and assumes an insider's point of view. In sociological terms this is an emic perspective signaled by the Greek term οἱ ἐθνικοί. The term occurs three times (5:47, 6:7, 18:17) and is typically translated "gentiles." The first occurrence is Matt 5:46–47: "For if you love those who love you, what reward do you have? Do not even the tax collectors do the same? And if you greet only your brothers and sisters, what more are you doing than others? Do not even οἱ ἐθνικοί do the same?" The implication is that those to whom Jesus is speaking to are not, at least from an emic perspective, οἱ ἐθνικοί. Rather, in all likelihood, they are Judeans (Ἰουδαῖος). The contrast between οἱ ἐθνικοί and the language of kinship (τοὺς αδελφοὺς ὑμῶν, 5:47) confirms this point. In other words, Jesus is telling his Judean followers to be better than the gentiles. The pejorative connotation of this verse is not lost on commentators. William D. Davies and Dale C. Allison (1988, 1:559) observe:

> It is odd to find in Matthew condescending words against οἱ ἐθνικοί. How can 5.47; 6.7; and 18.17 be harmonized with such verses as 28.19, which commands Jesus' followers to preach among the Gentile nations? Whether the explanation is wooden, conservative editing, a genuine ambivalence towards the Gentile world, or some other unknown fact, the paradox is not unique to the First Gospel.

A second occurrence is Matt 6:7: "When you are praying, do not heap up empty phrases as οἱ ἐθνικοί do; for they think that they will be heard because of their many words." Again, the inference seems sufficiently clear that οἱ ἐθνικοί functions as a racial/ethnic boundary marker, distinguishing ethnic outsiders from insiders—that is, non-Judeans from Judeans. As Douglas Hare (1993, 66) explains, "The possession of such a prayer would distinguish Jesus's disciples from others. The most noticeable characteristic of the Lord's prayer is its Jewishness." These are two examples of how the term οἱ ἐθνικοί differentiates dialectical relations between two racial/ethnic groups that are clearly demarcated throughout the gospel. In other words, there is a distinctly Judean way to pray; Jesus teaches his Judean disciples not to pray like *this* and not like *them*.

Another relevant example comes from the middle of the gospel, in Matt 18. At this point, the disciples have been called (4:18–22) and sent out (10:1–15), and the ἐκκλησία has been established through Peter (16:18). Now, in 18:15–17, Jesus instructs his disciples how to provide discipline in order to regulate its members:

> If another member of the ἐκκλησία sins against you, go and point out the fault when the two of you are alone. If the member listens to you, you have regained that one. But if you are not listened to, take one or two others along with you, so that every word may be confirmed by the evidence of two or three witnesses. If the member refuses to listen to them, tell it to the ἐκκλησία; and if the offender refuses to listen even to the ἐκκλησία, let such a one be to you as ὁ ἐθνικὸς and a tax collector.

Membership in the assembly is regulated by a principle that maintains the group identity of the ἐκκλησία. Failure to listen on the evidence of two or more witnesses results in exclusion from the ἐκκλησία. The implication, again, seems to be that Jesus and his disciples represent a different kind of group from what is signified by ἐθνικὸς. The description of the group, by definition, is inherently ethnoracial. The identity of the ἐκκλησία is forged in contrast to that which is ethnoracial. In all three examples, Jesus is speaking from within and for a designated group (i.e., Judeans) over against non-Judean gentiles. The racial/ethnic boundary between Judeans and non-Judeans is clearly and consistently delineated.

Another cluster of examples is associated with the term τὰ ἔθνη. The word occurs fifteen times in Matthew and is typically translated "gentiles" to draw a contrast between groups.[8] In the missionary discourse of Matt 10:5–7, Jesus sends out the twelve disciples with the following instructions: "Go nowhere among the ἐθνῶν and enter no town of the Σαμαριτῶν but go rather to the lost sheep of the house of Israel. As you go, proclaim the good news, 'The kingdom of heaven has come near.'" Two racial/ethnic terms are placed in synonymous relation (ἐθνῶν/Σαμαριτῶν) in contrast to the "house of Israel" (οἴκου Ἰσραήλ). Later, in Matt 20:18–19, Jesus predicts his passion: "See, we are going up to Jerusalem, and the Son of Man will be handed over to the chief priests and scribes, and they will condemn him to death; then they will hand him over to τοῖς ἔθνεσιν to be mocked and flogged and crucified; and on the third day he will be raised." The racial/ethnic distinction is heightened and further clarified in these examples. There is a clear boundary between who is and who is not regarded as τὰ ἔθνη. Jesus and his disciples are distinct from gentiles in general and Samaritans and Romans in particular.

A final example occurs at the end of the gospel, in Matt 28:19: "Go therefore and make disciples of πάντα τὰ ἔθνη, baptizing them in the name of the Father and of the Son and of the Holy Spirit." Following the crucifixion and resurrection, Jesus returns to Galilee and commands his Judean disciples to now make disciples of all the gentiles.[9] Only in the final moments of the gospel are gentiles included in Jesus's originally Judean mission. Such is the racial/ethnic framework with which the Gospel of Matthew begins and ends.

What, then, are the implications for understanding Matt 15:21–28? The upshot is that Jesus's mistreatment of the Canaanite woman is rather unremarkable in the scope of the gospel. The overarching framework of Matthew's Gospel suggests a far more insular perspective in relation to Judeans and a far more exclusive stance against gentiles. Simply put, Matthew is not as pro-gentile as many believe (Clark 1947). The basic orientation of the entire narrative, Matt 28:18–20 notwithstanding, is thoroughly Judean in orientation (Sim 2013, 174). The broader context of the

---

8. See Matt 4:15; 6:32; 10:5, 18; 12:18, 21; 20:19, 25; 21:43; 24:7, 9, 14; 25:32; 28:19. Other translations include "nation," "foreign people," or "non-Jewish/Judean."

9. These concluding verses in Matthew are often cited as the most important evidence for a pro-gentile reading of the First Gospel. Other key texts, besides Matt 15:21–28, include Jesus's genealogy as the "son of Abraham" (1:1), the Roman centurion (8:5–13), the parable of the tenants (21:33–46), and the Roman guard (27:54). See, e.g., Gundry 1994.

First Gospel throws Jesus's engagement with the Canaanite woman into sharper relief.

Conclusion

Jesus's encounter with the Canaanite woman is fraught with problematic implications. Clearly, he is rude by ignoring her with silence in Matt 15:23. Then he is ethnocentric by saying his mission is exclusive to οἴκου Ἰσραήλ in verse 24. But is he racist toward the Canaanite woman? If ever there were merit to such a claim, Matt 15:26 would undoubtedly be incriminating evidence. The answer to the question depends on the definition of racism. If a racist is defined as someone who supports racist policies or expresses racist ideas, then Jesus is clearly racist (Kendi 2019, 226). Up to verse 26 in the narrative, Jesus's speech and actions do not depart from but rather reinforce the status quo. There was a diversity of early Judaisms pertaining to the welcome of gentiles, with some Judeans more eager to embrace and others, like Matthew, more ethnocentric and exclusive.[10] Indeed, the primary reason for not helping the woman is precisely on account of her racial/ethnic identity as a Canaanite.

If the narrative had ended at verse 24, there would be no question. Nevertheless, she persisted. The Canaanite woman did all she could for the sake of her daughter. In verse 28, Jesus says: "'Woman, great is your faith! Let it be done for you as you wish.' And her daughter was healed instantly." Jesus heals the woman's daughter and thereby departs from the status quo. As Gail O'Day (2001, 125) observes, "Dismissal of the Canaanite woman would keep things the way they always have been." Still, the fact remains that in order for her daughter to be healed, she must acknowledge her inferior status as a Canaanite. Moreover, the woman's response reinforces existing social hierarchies of Israel over ethnic gentiles, men over women, and humans over animals (Gullotta 2014, 334). While this does not get Jesus off the hook, it highlights the brilliant rhetorical move on the part of the Canaanite woman (Humphries-Brooks 2001, 142). Her response highlights an important Matthean motif of how female disciples have the most intimate knowledge and understanding of Jesus, like the unnamed woman who anoints Jesus for burial in Matt 26:6–13 (Park 2017). In the

---

10. On the diversity of views within Judaism vis-à-vis gentiles, see Fredriksen 2022.

end, Jesus recognizes not only the woman's faith but also his own prejudice in the process.

Acknowledging that Jesus displays prejudice and racism may be a difficult pill to swallow for modern readers. But for a first-century audience, this would not be surprising in light of the long-standing history of tension between Judeans and Canaanites (Duling 2005; Runesson 2011; Sim 2013; Sechrest 2015). The reading advanced here provides a challenge to the dominant narrative that depicts Christianity as a universal, nonethnic entity that is above the particularities of race and ethnicity. But in actuality nothing could be further from the truth. The very beginning of the Jesus movement was located squarely within the racial/ethnic boundaries of divergent, sectarian Judaisms of the first century. The Gospel of Matthew, with its reputation as "the most Jewish gospel" (Hare 2000, 274), is an ideal text to expose this myth. For membership in the Matthean ἐκκλησία was only made possible by virtue of Judean ethnicity or gentile conversion.

Works Cited

Bonner, Layla J., and Gideon W. Park. 2020. "Twelve Strategies for Minority Faculty Teaching Race at Predominantly White Institutions." Social Justice and Civic Engagement Blog, 22 July. Wabash Center for Teaching and Learning in Theology and Religion. https://tinyurl.com/SBL03111ax.

Boring, M. Eugene. 1996. *The Gospel of Matthew*. Nashville: Abingdon.

Bruner, Frederick D. 2004. *Matthew: A Commentary*. Grand Rapids: Eerdmans.

Buell, Denise Kimber. 2005. *Why This New Race: Ethnic Reasoning in Early Christianity*. New York: Columbia University Press.

Burkill, Tom A. 1967. "The Historical Development of the Story of the Syrophoenician Woman (Mark vii: 24–31)." *NovT* 9.3:161–77.

Clark, Kenneth W. 1947. "The Gentile Bias in Matthew." *JBL* 66:165–72.

Crowder, Stephanie Buckhanon. 2016. *When Momma Speaks: The Bible and Motherhood from a Womanist Perspective*. Louisville: Westminster John Knox.

Davies, William D., and Dale C. Allison. 1988–1997. *The Gospel according to Saint Matthew*. 3 vols. ICC. Edinburgh: T&T Clark.

Dube, Musa W. 2000. *Postcolonial Feminist Interpretation of the Bible*. St. Louis: Chalice.

Duling, Dennis C. 2005. "Ethnicity, Ethnocentrism and the Matthean Ethnos." *BTB* 35:125–43.
Edwards, Richard A. 1985. *Matthew's Story of Jesus*. Philadelphia: Fortress.
Fredriksen, Paula. 1991. "Judaism, the Circumcision of Gentiles and Apocalyptic Hope: Another Look at Galatians 1 and 2." *JTS* 42:532–64.
———. 2022. "What Does It Mean to See Paul 'within Judaism'?" *JBL* 141:359–80
Gullotta, Daniel N. 2014. "Among Dogs and Disciples: An Examination of the Story of the Canaanite Woman (Matthew 15:21–28) and the Question of the Gentile Mission within the Matthean Community." *Neot* 48:325–40.
Gundry, Robert H. 1994. *Matthew: A Commentary on His Handbook for a Mixed Church under Persecution*. Grand Rapids: Eerdmans.
Hare, Douglas. 1993. *Matthew*. Louisville: John Knox.
———. 2000. "How Jewish Is the Gospel of Matthew." *CBQ* 62:264–77.
Harrington, Daniel J. 1991. *The Gospel of Matthew*. Collegeville, MN: Liturgical Press.
Hoklotubbe, T. Christopher. 2021. "Civilized Christ-Followers among Barbaric Cretans and Superstitious Judeans: Negotiating Ethnic Hierarchies in Titus 1:10–14." *JBL* 140:369–90.
Horrell, David G. 2017. "Paul, Inclusion and Whiteness: Particularizing Interpretation." *JSNT* 40:123–47.
Humphries-Brooks, Stephenson. 2001. "The Canaanite Women in Matthew." Pages 138–56 in in *A Feminist Companion to Matthew*. Edited by Amy-Jill Levine. Sheffield: Sheffield Academic.
Jackson, Glenna S. 2002. *Have Mercy on Me: The Story of the Canaanite Woman in Matthew 15:21–28*. New York: Sheffield Academic.
Keener, Craig S. 1999. *A Commentary on the Gospel of Matthew*. Grand Rapids: Eerdmans.
Kendi, Ibram X. 2019. *How to Be an Antiracist*. New York: One World.
Liew, Tat-Siong Benny. 1999. *Politics of Parousia: Reading Mark Inter(con)textually*. Leiden: Brill.
Markus, Hazel R., and Paula M. L. Moya. 2010. *Doing Race: Twenty-One Essays for the Twenty-First Century*. New York: Norton.
Mason, Steve. 2007. "Jews, Judaens, Judaizing, Judaism: Problems of Categorization in Ancient History." *JSJ* 38:457–512.
McEntire, Mark, and Wongi Park. 2021. "Ethnic Fission and Fusion in Biblical Genealogies." *JBL* 140:31–47.

Mirón, Louis F., and Jonathan Xavier Inda. 2000. "Race as a Kind of Speech Act." *CS* 5:85–107.

Morrison, Toni. 1992. *Playing in the Dark: Whiteness and the Literary Imagination*. Cambridge: Harvard University Press.

O'Day, Gail. 2001. "Surprised by Faith: Jesus and the Canaanite Woman." Pages 114–25 in *A Feminist Companion to Matthew*. Edited by Amy-Jill Levine. Sheffield: Sheffield Academic.

Park, Wongi. 2017. "Her Memorial: An Alternative Reading of Matthew 26:13." *JBL* 136:131–44.

———. 2019. *The Politics of Race and Ethnicity in Matthew's Passion Narrative*. Cham, Switzerland: Palgrave Macmillan.

Powery, Emerson B. 2015. "'Lost in Translation: Ethnic Conflict in English Bibles'—The Gospels, "Race," and the Common English Bible: An Introductory and Exploratory Conversation." *ExAud* 31:154–68.

Runesson, Anders. 2011. "Judging Gentiles in the Gospel of Matthew: Between 'Othering' and Inclusion." Pages 133–51 in *Jesus, Matthew's Gospel and Early Christianity: Studies in Memory of Graham N. Stanton*. Edited by Daniel M. Gurtner, Joel Willitts, and Richard A. Burridge. New York: T&T Clark.

Sawicki, Marianne. 1994. *Seeing the Lord: Resurrection and Early Christian Practices*. Minneapolis: Fortress.

Sechrest, Love L. 2015. "Enemies, Romans, Pigs, and Dogs: Loving the Other in the Gospel of Matthew." *ExAud* 31:71–105.

———. 2018. "'Humbled among the Nations': Matthew 15:21–28 in Antiracist Womanist Missiological Engagement." Pages 276–99 in *Can "White" People Be Saved? Triangulating Race, Theology, and Mission*. Edited by Love L. Sechrest, Johnny Ramírez-Johnson, and Amos Yong. Downers Grove, IL: InterVarsity.

Sim, David. 2013. "The Attitude to Gentiles in the Gospel of Matthew." Pages 173–90 in *Attitudes to Gentiles in Ancient Judaism and Early Christianity*. Edited by David C. Sim and James S. McLaren. London: Bloomsbury.

Sparks, Kenton L. 2006. "Gospel as Conquest: Mosaic Typology in Matthew 28:16–20." *CBQ* 68:651–63.

Contributors

Sonja Anderson
    Assistant professor of Religion, Carleton College, Northfield, Minnesota

Randall C. Bailey
    Andrew W. Mellon Professor of Hebrew Bible Emeritus, Interdenominational Theological Center, Atlanta, Georgia

Eric D. Barreto
    Frederick and Margaret L. Weyerhaeuser Associate Professor of New Testament, Princeton Theological Seminary, Princeton, New Jersey

Denise Kimber Buell
    Cluett Professor of Religion, Williams College, Williamstown, Massachusetts

Greg Carey
    Professor of New Testament, Lancaster Theological Seminary, Lancaster, Pennsylvania

Haley Gabrielle
    PhD candidate in New Testament studies, Emory University, Atlanta, Georgia

Wilda C. Gafney
    Right Rev. Sam B. Hulsey Professor of Hebrew Bible, Brite Divinity School, Fort Worth, Texas

Julián Andrés González Holguín
    Associate professor of Old Testament, Church Divinity School of the Pacific, Berkeley, California

Sharon Jacob
: Visiting professor of New Testament and Postcolonial Studies, Claremont School of Theology, Claremont, California

Tat-siong Benny Liew
: Class of 1956 Professor in New Testament Studies, College of the Holy Cross, Worcester, Massachusetts

Francisco Lozada Jr.
: Charles Fischer Catholic Professor of New Testament and Latinx Studies, Brite Divinity School, Fort Worth, Texas

Shelly Matthews
: Professor of New Testament and Director, Carpenter Initiative on Gender, Sexuality and Justice, Brite Divinity School, Fort Worth, Texas

Roger S. Nam
: Professor of Hebrew Bible, Candler School of Theology, Emory University, Atlanta, Georgia

Wongi Park
: Assistant professor of New Testament, Belmont University, Nashville, Tennessee

Jean-Pierre Ruiz
: Associate professor of theology and religious studies, St. John's University, Queens, New York

Abraham Smith
: Professor of New Testament, Perkins School of Theology, Southern Methodist University, Dallas, Texas

Kay Higuera Smith
: Professor of biblical and religious studies, Azusa Pacific University, Azusa, California

Modern Authors Index

Adam, Andrew K. M. 259
Agamben, Giorgio 64–65
Aguirre, Adalbert, Jr. 115
Ahmed, Sara 9, 44–46, 48, 56, 122–23
Aichele, George 64
Alcoff, Linda Martin 17
Alexander, Loveday C. 219
Alexander, M. Jacqui 13, 229
Allison, Dale C. 278, 281–82
Althusser, Louis 3
Anderson, Benedict 81, 88
Anderson, Sonja 205
Anderson, Victor 54
Anidjar, Gil 52
Aponte, Edwin David 146
Appiah, Kwame Anthony 17
Arnimesh, Shankar 85
Ayala Mallory, Nina 215
Aymer, Margaret 141, 236
Back, Les 44
Badiou, Alain 62
Bailey, Randall C. 1, 25–26, 30, 33–34, 36–39, 123, 125, 146, 248
Baird, William 124
Baldwin, James 9, 56
Banerjee, Sikata 87, 92
Baranowski, Shelley 173
Barber, William J. 248
Barrios, Richard 159
Barthes, Roland 6
Bartlett, Katharine T 69
Benjamin, Walter 13, 227–28
Bauman, Zygmunt 61
Bell, Derrick 113–15
Bennett, Harold V. 30

Bernasconi, Robert 45–47
Bieber, Florian 81, 91
Bigott, Luis Antonio 72
Blount, Brian K. 260
Blum, Edward J. 4
Bonilla-Silva, Eduardo 117–18
Bonner, Layla 275
Bordas, Juana 126
Boring, Eugene, M. 281
Bowens, Lisa M. 148
Bowler, Kate 207
Bowles, Samuel 119
Boyles, John H. 2
Brett, Mark G. 135
Briggs, Laura 2
Brodkin, Karen 57
Brooten, Bernadette 211
Brown, Kevin 114
Brueggemann, Walter 268
Brunner, Frederick D. 277
Buell, Denise Kimber 4, 43–44, 52–54, 122–23, 135, 260, 276
Bultmann, Rudolf 173–74
Burke, Daniel 83
Burke, Sean D. 141
Burkill, Tom A. 281
Burnett, Fred 63
Burrus, Virginia 236
Butler, Judith 72
Byrd, Jodi A. 17
Byron, Gay L. 2, 5, 17, 43, 48, 135, 212
Calderón, Dolores 122
Callahan, Allen Dwight 89
Carillo, Ellen C. 8
Carroll, Joseph 136

Carter, J. Kameron	4, 47, 53, 63, 65, 75	Ellis-Petersen, Hannah	85
Case, Karen A.	44	Eng, David L.	3, 6
Castles, Stephen	191	Entin, Joseph	3, 5
Cave, Sydney	51	Epp, Eldon J.	211
Ceballos, Manuela	63	Esteban-Guitart, Moisès	187, 191
Chatterjee, Partha	90	Fanon, Frantz	81
Cho, Sumi	115	Feagon, Joe R.	114, 117, 121, 127
Chuh, Kandice	18	Felder, Cain Hope	30
Clark, Elizabeth, A.	51	Fentress-Williams, Judy	126
Clark, Kenneth W.	284	Ferguson, Roderick	1–3, 5–7, 16
Cone, James	207, 210	Fernandez, Eleazar S.	190
Conzelmann, Hans	140, 234	Fields, Karen E.	4
Cooper, Brittney	111	Fields, Barbara J.	4
Copeland, M. Shawn	253	Fishbane, Michael	10, 66
Corley, Kathleen E.	211	Fisher-Steward, Gayle	62
Cornell, Collin	259–60, 262	Fitzmyer, Joseph A.	234
Cornell, Drusilla	70	Fohrer, Georg	268
Cosgrove, Denis	125	Foskett, Mary F.	226
Cox, Daniel	159	Foucault, Michel	4–6, 65–66
Crenshaw, Kimberlé	115, 245	Francis, Leah Gunning	248
Crowder, Stephanie Buckhanon	286	Frankel, David	268
Daniel, Joseph	82, 84	Frankenberg, Ruth	48
Dantley, Michael	182	Frankovic, Kathy	101
Davies, William D.	278, 281–82	Freeman, Alan D.	114
Davis, Clayton A.	112	Fredriksen, Paula	219, 287
Davis, Ellen	262, 268	Friedland, Valerie	91
De La Torre, Miguel A.	146	Frow, John	124
Deleuze, Giles	88–90	Frye, Matthew Jacobson	52
Delgado, Richard	114, 117–18, 121	Gafney, Wilda C.	67, 244, 251, 255
Derrida, Jacques	2–5	Gamboa, Suzanne	87
DiCicco, Mario	206	Gardner, John	6
Dinkler, Michal Beth	237	Garrett, Susan R.	88
Dixson, Adrienne D, 115.	114	Garza, Alicia	245
Donaghue, Erin	83	Gillborn, David	115
Douglas, Kelly Brown	248	Gilman, Sander	52
Du Bois, W.E.B.	39	Gintis, Herbert	119
Duling, Dennis C.	286	Goldberg, David M.	4
Du Mez, Kristin Kobes	86	Goldberg, David T.	61
Dube, Musa W.	49, 125, 196, 276	González Holguín, Julián Andrés	65, 68, 70, 73
Duclos-Orsello, Elizabeth	3, 5	Gorsline, Robin Hawley	44
Dunbar, Ericka	33	Gotay, Samuel Silva	103–4
Durkin, Joseph T., SJ.	104	Gottwald, Norman K.	165, 262, 267–68
Edwards, Richard A.	276		
Ehrman, Bart D.	206		
Eliav-Feldon, Miriam	43	Grandin, Gregg	197

Modern Authors Index

Gray, Thomas 210
Grossman, Joanna L. 69
Guattari, Félix 88–90
Gullotta, Daniel N. 279–80, 285
Gundry, Robert H. 284
Gustafson, James M. 263
Habel, Norman 262, 268
Haddad, Samir 2
Hall, Stuart 69
Halpern, Baruch 266
Hammett, Dashiel 156
Hanson, Kennith C. 267
Hare, Douglas 283, 286
Harney, Stefano 15
Harper, Shaun R. 116
Harrington, Daniel J. 281
Harris, Cheryl 120
Harrison, Faye V. 15
Harrison, Peter 47
Hartman, Saidiya 15, 228–29
Harvey, Paul 4, 44
Haynes, Stephen R. 26
Hegel, Georg W. F. 172
Heschel, Susannah 4, 50, 63, 142, 260
Hickman, Jared 47
Hidalgo, Jacqueline M. 49, 146, 175
Hill, Rebecca 3, 5
Hill Collins, Patricia 27
Hockey, Katherine M. 135
Hodge, Caroline Johnson 4
Hoklotubbe, T. Christopher 277
Holladay, Carl R. 234
Horrell, David G. 135, 142, 276
Horsley, Richard, A. 124
Hughes, Langston 36
Humphries-Brooks, Stephenson 285
Hunter, Ian 124
Ince, Jelani 112
Inde, Jonathan Xaviere 279
Inoue, Asao B. 8
Isaac, Benjamin 43
Iser, Wolfgang 124
Iverson, Susan VanDeventer 115–16
Jacobs, Michelle S. 246
Jackson, Darrell D. 114
Jackson, Glenna S. 281
Jennings, Willie James 4, 7–8, 47, 135, 141, 261, 265
Johnson, Sylvester A. 4, 50–52, 260
Johnson-DeBaufre, Melanie 48
Johnson Hodge, Caroline 4, 135
Jones, Reece 190, 199
Jones, Robert P. 159, 198
Jordan, June 7, 15–16
Junn, Jane 188
Keener, Craig S. 281
Kelley, Shawn 6, 50, 67, 72, 75, 118, 135, 171–73, 260
Kendi, Ibram X. 285
Kerr, Clark 6–7
Khan, Arshad Afzal 85
Kidd, Colin 4, 47, 117
Kim, Yung Suk 4
Kim-Cragg, HyeRan 4
King, Martin Luther, Jr. 126
King, Philip J. 125
Kisau, Paul Mumo 235
Koh, Harry Hongju 199
Kondo, Dorinne 18
Kurz, William S. 140
Kutsko, John F. 136
Kwok, Pui-lan 196, 226, 232
Ladson-Billings, Gloria 115
Lahiri, Jhumpa 1, 18
Lalruatkima 55–56
Lash, Ephrem 207
Laughter, Judson C. 119
Laytner, Arson 69
Ledesma, Maria C. 116, 121
Lee, Dorothy A. 214
LeMon, Joel M. 259, 260, 262
Levenson, Jon 64
Levine, Amy-Jill 220
Lewis, Oscar 123
Liew, Tat-siong Benny 1, 2, 6, 123, 146, 248, 279
Lightsey, Pamela R. 248
Lim, Swee Hong 66
Lin, Yii-Jan 211
Lincoln, Bruce 47

Lipsitz, George	44	Mitchem, Stephanie Y.	253
Livingstone, Josephine	142	Molina, Natalia	118
Lloyd, David	1, 3	Moll, Luis C.	187–88, 191
Lluveras, Lauren	97	Monge, José Trias Monge	100
London, Norrel	3	Moore, Stephen D.	6
Long, Burke O.	6	Moran, Joe	125
López, Iris	99	Morrison, Toni	275
Lorde, Audre	53	Moss, Candida R.	207
Lowe, Lisa	16–17	Moten, Fred	15
Lozada, Francisco, Jr.	189, 192	Motomura, Hiroshi	195, 197
Lozana, Adele	187	Moxnes, Halvor	51
MacDonald, Margaret Y.	211	Moya, Paula M.	287
Mahn, Jason A.	86	Mroczek, Eva	215
Mailloux, Stephen	124	Munck, Johannes	234
Malak, Asiya	268	Murry, Linda O.	126
Marable, Manning	125	Nasrallah, Laura	135
Markus, Hazel R.	275	Navorro-Rivera, Juhem	159
Martell-Otero, Loida	190	Negrón-Muntaner, Frances	97
Martin, Clarice	125, 141	Neuman, Gerald E.	100
Martin, Dale	259	Nevins, Joseph	197
Martin, James D.	268	Newsom, Carol	266
Martínez, Juan	136	Newton, Richard	123
Martinez, Monica Muñoz	193	O'Day, Gail R.	236–37, 285
Martínez, Vanessa Lina	178	Olender, Maurice	47
Martínez-Vázquez, Hjamil A.	226	Omi, Michael	5
Mason, Steve	277	Osiek, Carolyn	211
Masuoka, Natalie	188	Pandey, Neelam	85
Matthews, Shelly	211	Park, Gideon W. *See* Park, Wongi	
McCann, Erin	107	Park, Wongi	4, 6, 275–77, 279, 285
McCoskey, Denise Eileen	43	Patel, Vimal	47
McDaniel, Dennis	85	Patton, Lori D.	115–16
McDonald, Nathan	270	Perdue, Leo	268
McElhinney, J. M.	105–6	Pérez Huber, Lindsay	174, 178
McEntire, Mark	279	Perkinson, James	47
McIntosh, Peggy	44, 86	Perry, Imani	119
Meeks, Wayne A.	124	Pfoh, Emmanuel	270
Melamed, Jodi	16	Pierce, Chester M.	116
Merwin, Ted	66	Pinarski, Phil	123
Meyers, Marvin	54	Pittman, Amanda Jo	2
Mignolo, Walter	63	Pixley, Jorge V.	64
Miller, Ken	247	Powell, Mark Allan	182
Miller, Mark J.	191	Powery, Emerson B.	67, 135, 280–81
Mills, Charles W.	33	Prothero, Stephen	73
Mirón, Luis F.	279	Puhl, Louis J.	217
Miscall, Peter	64	Quesnell, Quentin	213–14

Ragland, Alice	111, 122	Silbermann, Abraham M.	34
Ramachandran, Sudha	82, 84–85	Sim, David	284, 286
Rancière, Jacques	1	Smith, Abraham	37, 111
Ransby, Barbara	111, 122	Smith, Andrea	117
Rasmussen, Birgit Brander	4	Smith, Jonathan Z.	53
Ray, Victor E.	116	Smith, Lillian	39
Reed, Barbara E.	211	Smith, Mitzi J.	4
Reeder, Caryn A.	259	Smith, Ted. A.	263
Reid, Melissa Renee	60	Solórzano, Daniel G.	116
Reinhartz, Adele	192	Sparks, Kenton L.	279
Rhodesia, Deborah L.	69	Spivak, Gayatri Chakravorty	17, 223–24, 229–34, 238
Rice, Gene	30		
Richardson, Elaine	111, 122	Spöhrer, Markus	159
Ricoeur, Paul	266	Stager, Lawrence E.	262, 266–67
Roberts, Jennifer L.	207, 210	Stavrakopoulou, Francesca	268
Roediger, David R.	52	Steele, Claude M.	11–12, 151–55
Rojas, Fabio	112	Stefanic, Jean	114, 117–18, 121
Román, Ediberto	100–101	Stevenson, Bryan	121
Rosenbaum, Morris	34	Sue, Derald W.	115
Rousseau Anderson, Celia K.	115	Szanton, David	3
Runesson, Anders	286	Támez, Elsa	210
Russo, Vito	159	Tannehill, Robert	140
Sadler, Rodney S. Jr.	4, 79, 125, 135	Tate, William	115
Said, Edward	173	Tatum, Beverly Daniel	2
Saito, Natsu Taylor	189	Taylor, Edward	115–16
Salinas, Cristobal, Jr.	187	Thandeka	44
Santos, Boaventura de Sousa	16	Thiong'o, Ngũgĩ wa	2
Savarkar, Vinayak Damodar	82–84	Thomas, Todne	268
Sawicki, Marianne	281	Tiffany, Tanya J.	215–18
Scharen, Christian	264	Tillman, Linda	182
Schloen, J. David	267	Tinsley, Omise'eke Natasha	239
Schüssler Fiorenza, Elisabeth	53, 135, 212–13, 261	Townes, Emilie M.	225, 251, 253
		Tretheway, Natasha	209
Sechrest, Love L.	135, 276, 281, 286	Trouillot, Michel-Rolph	192
Segovia, Fernando F.	1, 123–24, 146, 226, 248, 260	Truett, Samuel	197–98
		Tupamahu, Ekaputra	142
Seth, Sanjay	3	Ulfgad, Håkan	89
Shah, Pankaj	85	Venator-Santiago, Charles R.	100
Shankar, Soumya	83–84	Venkataraman, Babu Immanuel	235
Sharad, Arpita	84	Vessey, Mark	47
Sharma, Arvind	82	Viggen, Aana Marie	264
Sharpe, Jenny	3	Villalobos, Manuel	141
Shear, Michael D.	189	Viswanathan, Gauri	3, 52
Sherwood, Yvonne	6	Vitali, Ali	107
Scholz, Susanne	226	Wagenheim, Kal	102–4

Wagenheim, Olga Jiménez de Wagenheim	102–4
Wall, Robert W.	235
Wallerstein, Immanuel	63
Wallis, Jim	248
Walsh, Richard	64
Ware, Vron	44
Warren, Michael	86
Warrior, Robert Allen	38, 64–65
Weems, Renita J	38, 226
Wellman, Rose	268
West, Cornell	113, 115
Whalen, Carmen Teresa	99
Whitmore, Todd	263
Wigg-Stevenson, Natalie	265
Willimon, William H.	235
Wilson, Brittany	141
Wilson-Hartgrove, Jonathan	248
Witherington, Ben	141
Wilder, Craig Steven	2
Wimbush, Vincent L.	10, 17, 55–56, 108–9
Winant, Howard	5
Wing, Adrien Katherine	115
Wolf, Z. Byron	83
Wolf, Hans Walter	28
Wooden, Ontario S.	116
Worthington, Bruce	62
Wriggins, Jennifer	246
Wright, Addison	206
Wright, N.T.	207
Yamada, Frank	9, 54–55
Yancy, George	1, 45, 53
Yong, Ed	198
Yosso, Tara J.	116
Zamudio, Margaret M.	115, 118–19, 121
Ziegler, Joseph	43
Zurcher, Anthony	83

Subject Index

1619 Project, 17
9/11, 197
A Night with the King, 36
Abe, Shinzō, 91
Abram/Abraham, 30, 33–34, 38, 255, 262, 269–70, 284
Acts, 13, 49, 135, 140–41, 163, 178, 182, 184, 211–14, 223, 232–33, 236–37
aesthetics, 63, 172–74
affirmative action, 120–21
Afghanistan, 82
Africa, African, 17, 25, 27–33, 51, 123, 140, 218, 271
   Africana studies, 116, 125
   Afro-Caribbean, 229
African American, 26, 30, 36–37, 47, 51, 67, 68, 86–87, 99, 111, 113–14, 116, 118, 121, 125, 136, 141, 175, 179, 194, 223, 228, 246, 252, 254
   hermeneutics, 50
age, 61
agency, 45, 65, 143, 164, 178, 238, 263
America. *See* United States
anachronism, 76, 264, 266
   anachronistic whiteness, 9, 14, 43–44, 53
anamnesis, 10, 68
ancestors, 27–28, 30, 54, 56, 265, 268–70
Anderson, Tanisha, 122
ancient Near East, 9, 32, 68, 125
anthropology, 124, 265-8
anti-Semitism, 33, 45, 173–74, 195, 206, 260
apocalypse, apocalypticism, 10, 89, 207, 210, 215

apostle, 211–14
Arabia, 29, 83
Aram, Aramean, 30–31
archaeology, 35, 40, 266
art, 13, 35–37, 40, 69, 74, 98, 101, 105, 125, 162–63, 205–18
   music, 126
Aryan, 227
Asian, Asian American, 1, 9, 33, 39, 48, 83, 118, 121, 123, 125, 136, 175, 180, 188, 194–96, 223, 271
   hermeneutics, 50, 125
assessment. *See* grading
assimilation, 1, 62, 88–89, 90–93, 191
Association of Theological Schools, 136
astrology, 146
asylum, 184, 198–99
Austin Presbyterian Seminary, 248
authority, 2, 5, 9, 48–49, 54–55, 62–63, 67, 119, 176, 178, 212, 215, 223, 231, 246, 252, 254, 262, 271, 275
Babri Masjid, 84
Babylonian Empire, 30
Bangladesh, 82, 199
barbarian, barbarism, 102
Baumgartner, Jack, 162
Bell, Sean, 245
belonging, 7–11, 39, 52–54, 83, 85–86, 90–92, 152, 191–92, 195–96, 200, 271
bias, 7, 15, 29, 117, 125, 200, 271
Black, Blackness, 6, 15, 26–39, 47, 61, 64, 66, 71, 87, 106, 109, 111–12, 115–16, 120–23, 127, 136, 140–41, 145, 151–53, 175, 188, 194, 205, 207, 209, 218, 241, 242, 245–55

Black, Blackness (cont.)
and Latinx, 145
of biblical characters, 33, 35–36
studies, 7, 125. *See also* Africana studies
Black History Month, 33
Black Lives Matter, 14, 76, 111–12, 121–22, 127, 188, 241–42, 245–51, 253, 255
Black Youth Project, 122
Bland, Sandra, 122, 247
Blyden, Edward, 51
border, 12, 32, 44, 55, 87, 141, 143–44, 148, 187–90, 193, 195–99, 260
militarized, 197
US-Mexico border wall, 187–200
Boyd, Rekia, 122, 245
Brexit, 91
Brite Divinity School, 188–89, 244, 246
Brown, Michael, 112, 127, 244, 246
Buddhism, 83, 124
Bull, John, 101–2
Bynum, Wanita, 36
canon, 3, 5–6, 9, 37–38, 47, 49, 54, 72, 123, 167, 206, 215, 249
capitalism, 10, 62, 65, 69, 74, 88, 119, 252, 266, 269–70
Carey, Miriam, 245
cartography. *See* maps.
Cain and Abel, 68, 70, 254
Canaan, Canaanite, 26, 38–39, 68, 104, 278–79
Canaanite woman, 14–15, 276–81, 284–86
Catholicism, 52–53, 104–5, 145–46, 188, 261
Central America, 193, 197, 199
China, Chinese, 16, 83, 99, 121, 197
Christianity, 4, 34, 52–53, 56, 63, 65, 173, 192, 212–13, 215, 226, 234–35, 260–61, 276. *See also* Catholicism; church; Protestant
among minorities, 54, 81–83
and empire, 85–86, 91, 236
Christian anti-Semitism, 206
Christian identity, 4

Christian interpretation of scripture, 123, 249
Christian nationalism. *See* nationalism
Christian triumphalism, 16
Christian universality, 15
cultural dominance of, 83, 86
early, 9, 43, 46–56, 63, 70, 189–90, 193–5, 205–6, 212, 227, 260
evangelical, 73, 86–87, 107, 175–76, 259
exclusive. *See* exclusivity
missionary. *See* missionary, missionizing
muscular, 87
white, 248
church, 28, 31, 36, 63, 67, 73–74, 76, 138, 165, 176, 182–83, 215, 226, 269. *See also* Christianity
Black church, 35, 207, 250
white church, 180
citizenship, 3, 10, 81–85, 91, 93, 101, 144, 245
"model citizen," 194
civil rights, action, era, movement, 2, 6, 36, 113–14, 119–20, 124, 183–84
civilization, 4, 51, 99, 102, 105, 107, 123, 231
uncivilized, 51, 123, 199
class, 13, 39, 45, 63–64, 68–69, 71, 91, 101, 114, 117, 120–21, 154, 167, 179, 180–81, 188–89, 194, 205, 210, 218, 226, 246, 249, 276
classification. *See* taxonomy
colonialism, colonization, 2–3, 7, 10–11, 13, 16–17, 28, 30, 44, 51, 64, 68, 71, 97, 99–100, 102–5, 107, 109, 125, 139, 143, 147–48, 171, 176, 189, 192–94, 226, 231–32, 234, 236–37, 249, 260, 263, 268–69
colorblindness, 75, 86, 112, 119–20
community, 7, 15, 18, 55, 63, 65–66, 69, 70, 72–73, 81, 88, 121, 138–43, 145, 147–8, 156, 160, 165–66, 168, 187, 189–92, 235, 245, 247, 251–53, 265, 270–71, 279–80

community (cont.)
   Black, 246–47, 251–52
   classrooms as, 18
   ecclesial, religious, 65, 68, 73, 139, 165–66, 235
   indigenous, 269
   interpretive, 55, 64, 165–66
   Latinx, 126, 144–5, 188
   minoritized, oppressed, 65, 135, 138, 148, 178, 188–89
compassion, 10, 66, 70, 72, 74, 87, 233
conscientização, 261
constructionism, 117
conversion, 28, 51–52, 286
countermemory, 68, 70
counterstory, 67, 121, 125, 183, 228
Cover, Robert, 113
COVID-19, 83, 116, 188, 198
Crawford, John, 246
creation story, 9, 31, 54–55, 64
critical fabulation, 13, 228
Critical Race Theory, 11, 111, 113, 115–19, 121, 177
critical reading, 67, 238, 254
Cuba, 74, 98–109, 189, 193
Cullors, Patrisse. *See* Khan-Cullors, Patrisse
cultural contextualization, 124
cultural hermeneutics, 189
curriculum, 4–6, 11, 14, 16, 47, 56, 62–63, 116, 124–25, 151, 153, 156, 175, 224–25, 259
Curry, Michael, 246
Cush, Cushite (Kushim), 29–31, 34
Da Vinci, Leonardo, 162, 208
Dalrymple, Louis, 98–109
decolonialism, 13, 71, 229
deconstruction, 14, 62, 82, 90, 135, 229, 261, 265
dehumanization, 10, 39, 63–64, 87, 138, 199, 261
Diallo, Amadou, 245
diaspora, 107–8, 268
disability, 8, 179–80, 223, 249
   criticism, 223

disciple, 181, 209, 212–14, 277, 279–80, 282–85
diversity, 2, 5–6, 8–10, 49, 56, 61–64, 66, 68–69, 72–73, 89–90, 93, 115–16, 138, 143–44, 146–47, 151, 154, 165–66, 183, 188, 194–95, 205, 224, 246, 249, 265, 271, 285
doctoral studies, 47–48, 50, 147, 174, 225
Downes v. Bidwell, 100–101
drugs, 118, 197, 254
ecocriticism. *See* environmentalism
ecology. *See* environmentalism
economy, economics, 2, 8, 44, 61–63, 65, 71, 74–75, 81, 91–92, 119, 148, 180–81, 183–84, 188, 191, 193, 198, 205, 237, 249, 261, 263, 266–68, 270
exploitation, 249, 261
Edwards, Jordan, 247
Egypt, 28–31, 34–35, 38–39, 125
embodiment, 2, 9–10, 12, 43–45, 49, 55, 66, 73, 138, 145, 262, 265
Emmaus, 13, 205, 207–11, 216, 218
empire, 10, 17, 33, 68, 88–90, 92, 139, 141, 193, 236, 267
   American, 85, 194
   Babylonian, 30
   Bronze Age, 267
   divine, 88
   Greek, 33
   Indian, 3
   language of, 89–92
   Ottoman, 218
   Persian, 33
   religious, 236
   Roman, 35–36, 43, 89, 193, 232, 236
   Spanish, 194, 215
Enlightenment, 117, 124, 171, 173–74
environmentalism, 64, 70, 86, 198
epistemology, 5, 16, 63, 142, 148, 171–75, 229
Ephesians, 34–35
equality, 11, 26–27, 64–65, 90, 111, 114–15, 117, 119–20, 123
Erdoğan, Recep Tayyip, 91
essentialism, 6, 53, 68–69, 118, 120, 124

Esther, 25, 28, 33, 36
ethnicity, 5–6, 9, 14–16, 31, 43, 49–50, 52–53, 55–56, 97, 136–37, 140, 142, 156, 167, 180, 187, 209–10, 246, 249, 264–5, 270, 276–77, 279–86
ethnocentrism, 15, 27, 276-7, 279–82, 285
ethnography, 14, 263–68, 271
Ethiopia, 17, 25, 30–31, 33–34, 37, 48
  Ethiopian eunuch, 135, 140–2,
  Ethiopic, 162
Eurocentrism, 4, 14, 25, 29, 33-34, 37, 39–40, 62, 125, 174, 196, 260, 265, 267, 269
Europe, 16, 28, 30–36, 39–40, 44, 48–53, 62, 89, 102, 109, 117, 125, 136, 141, 171–72, 175, 179–81, 193, 197, 218, 249, 226–27, 260, 271
  Europeanizing, 9, 30
  post-Europe, 76
  proto-European, 33–34
evangelism, 39–40, 168
evil, 68, 225, 250
exceptionalism, 6, 63, 91, 198–200
exclusion, exclusivity, 7–8, 17, 72, 76, 84, 87, 121, 223, 227, 229, 233–35, 237–38, 263, 271, 283–85
  Christian, 13
exile, 54–55, 143, 269
existentialism, 61, 76, 171–74
Exodus, 27–29, 38, 64, 126
  plagues, 38
extrajudicial killings, 87, 112, 121, 127, 137, 193, 244–47, 250–55
Ezra-Nehemiah, 26
Farrakan, Louis, 33
family, 1, 35, 65, 121, 154, 178–80, 187, 234, 265–67. *See also* kinship
  multifamily households, 266
  separation, 199
femininity, 65, 67, 87–88
feminism, feminist, 13, 44–45, 49, 55–56, 70, 121–23, 167, 223, 229–30, 233–34, 236, 238
  black feminism, 122

feminism, feminist (cont.)
  criticism, hermeneutics, 50, 123
  individualist, 234, 236, 238
  white feminism, 121
Ferguson, Missouri, 112, 138, 244, 246
fertility, 249
film, 12, 36–37, 74, 156–61
Fiske, John, 102
Floyd, George, 86, 127, 247
foreignness, foreigner, 26, 87, 91, 100, 189, 199, 231
form criticism, 29, 124, 195, 226
Freire, Paulo, 261
Garner, Eric, 245
Garza, Alicia, 111
Gebhardt, Tamara, 242
gender, 9, 13, 25, 32, 44–45, 48, 50, 53, 56, 64–68, 71, 81, 87-88, 140–42, 145–46, 156–58, 161, 179–80, 187–88, 190, 205–6, 210–11, 213, 227, 234, 236, 246, 249–50, 265, 276. *See also* femininity; masculinity; transgender
  criticism, 177
  of God, 67
genealogy, 6, 33, 50, 63, 171–2, 279, 284
gentile, 34, 54, 68, 180, 279–86
geography, 4, 12, 16, 27, 30–33, 125, 140, 178, 187, 196, 262, 278. *See also* maps
Germany, 50, 52, 91, 124, 173, 223, 226–28
Ghana, 32
Gibeonites, 38, 254
Gilkes, Cheryl Townsend, 246
Gilliam, Victor, 102–3
gospel, 5, 15, 35–37, 49, 54, 106–7, 109, 126, 139–41, 162, 173, 192, 206–7, 211–12, 217, 251–52, 277, 279–86
grading, 6–8, 12, 152, 154–65, 161, 224
graduate studies, 29–30, 47, 50, 123, 153, 188, 164, 215, 246
Grant, III, Oscar, 245
Gray, Kimani, 245
Great Commission, 36–37
Greco-Roman context, 16, 182, 206, 211, 232

Greece, Greek, 33, 40, 52–53, 91, 137, 172, 193, 232, 260, 279
Green Pastures, 37
Guam, 98
guns. *See* violence control, 87
habituation, 45–46, 50, 73, 122–23
Hadassah, 36
Hagar, 33, 38, 255
Hall, Mya 127
Ham, curse of, 26, 33, 38
Harnack, Adolf von, 51
Hawai'i, 98–109, 136
"Hays Code," 159
HBCU, 29–30
healthcare, 207
heathen, 51–52, 123
Hebrew Bible, 9, 34–36, 61–76, 126, 176, 254, 262, 265–6, 268, 278
heresy, heretic, 52–55
Herodotus, 140
hermeneutic of suspicion, 252
hierarchy, 6, 13, 68–69, 91–92, 118–20, 180, 194, 210, 265, 267, 285
Higgenbotham, A. Leon, Jr., 113
historical criticism, 13–14, 53, 62, 91, 159, 163, 174–75, 184, 195–97, 218, 223–28, 230, 232, 238, 259–64, 267, 271
historical materialism, 13, 227–28
historiography, 192, 227–28, 266
history, 2, 10–12, 26–28, 35, 37, 44, 46, 48, 51, 54–55, 61, 63, 68–69, 71, 113, 117, 120, 124, 144, 168, 174, 182, 188–94, 197–200, 223–31, 233–34, 238
  cultural history, 192
  prehistory, 167
Hinduism, 10, 13, 82–87, 124–25, 230–31
Hispanic, 101, 125, 136, 187–88
Hispanic Theological Initiative, 147
homogeneity, 49, 62, 88, 90, 93, 125, 135, 142, 147, 194–95, 261, 264
Holocaust, 69
Hosea, 29–30, 65
housing, 120, 276

Hughes, Langston, 36
hybridity, 68, 144–47
identity, 4, 13, 17, 28, 43, 62, 64–65, 68–70, 82–86, 90–93, 121, 139–41, 144, 146–48, 154, 156, 172, 174, 177–79, 181, 183, 187–88, 190–6, 205, 224, 232, 234–36, 246, 249, 270, 276, 280, 285
  collective identity, 178, 283
  identity-based methodology, 223–24
  national, 93
  politics, 192
ideological criticism, 49, 67, 118, 196–97, 223, 259
ideology, 2, 67, 74, 76, 81, 85, 92, 104, 109, 115, 125, 137, 171, 173–74, 176–77, 189, 192, 196, 224–25, 260, 268
  colonial, 260
  gender, 87
  liberal, 119
  nationalist, 3
  political, 10, 82
  racist, racial, supremacist, 10, 66, 85, 91, 117, 119, 142, 171
Ignatius of Loyola, 216–18
immigration, 1–2, 52, 72, 81, 87, 91, 105, 121, 144, 183, 189, 192, 197, 199
  "illegal," 199
imperialism, 13, 68, 88, 90, 92, 141, 193, 199, 230–31, 233, 249
  imperial Christianity, 236
incarceration, 121, 183, 255, 279
inclusion, 8, 14, 62, 76, 92, 116, 143, 153, 187–88, 224, 255, 259, 261–63, 270–71, 275–76
India, 1, 3, 10, 13, 25, 33, 51–52, 81–87, 91–92, 199, 229–31
indigeneity, 2, 125, 144, 175, 187, 198, 249, 269
infantilization, 1, 105
inheritance, 46, 48, 50, 53–54, 122–23, 226, 255, 269, 278
injustice, 62, 68–69, 126, 138–39, 148, 182, 199, 225, 234, 237, 253

insider/outsider, 10, 26, 52, 82–83, 148, 181, 189, 192, 199, 260, 279, 280, 282–83
intercultural approach, 12, 187, 189–90, 195, 200
interpretation, 9–10, 13–14, 25–31, 33–34, 37, 40, 43–57, 61–76, 82, 88, 91–92, 108, 119, 123, 141–42, 146, 153–54, 157–68, 172–83, 190–91, 195–96, 205–7, 209–11, 214–15, 218, 223, 232–38, 246–51, 255, 259–66, 277, 281
   public interpretation, 157
intersectionality, 18, 44–45, 121–22, 141, 182, 246, 249
Islam, 16, 48, 51, 83–85, 249, 267
   Islamophobia, 33, 45
Ishmael, 33, 255
Israel, 28–31, 33–34, 38–39, 63, 65, 68–70, 183, 199, 214, 249, 262–70, 276–81, 284–85
   as African, 37
Jainism, 83
Japan and Japanese American, 9, 54–55, 91, 125
Jesus, 4–5, 15, 27–28, 33, 35–36, 54, 73, 86–87, 106, 126, 162–63, 173–74, 179–81, 205–6, 208–9, 211–14, 217, 251, 276–86
   whiteness, 4
Jim Crow, 44, 120
John of Patmos, 10, 88–90, 92, 126
John the Baptist, 12, 162–63, 180
Juan de Pareja, 218
Judah, Judean, 28–31, 39, 269, 277–86
Judaism, Jews, Jewishness, 3, 33–34, 48, 51–53, 63, 68–69, 121, 142, 171–74, 180–81, 183, 188, 192–95, 206, 215, 227, 268–69, 276–7, 279, 283–86
   as proto-Europeans, 34
justice, 66, 69–70, 101, 121–22, 137, 139, 175, 182–84, 205, 248, 252. *See also* injustice; social justice
#JusticeforAllBlackWomenandGirls, 122
#JusticeforReka, 122
Khan-Cullors, Patrisse, 111, 245

King, Jr., Martin Luther, 126, 246
kinship, 14, 259–71, 282. *See also* family
Kipling, Rudyard, 102
knowledge production, 5–6, 8, 11–12, 16, 52, 63, 67, 75, 125–26, 171–84, 187, 191, 271
Korea, 125
labor, laborers, 8, 39, 64, 72, 99, 118, 120–21, 183–84, 191, 194, 198, 209
Lancaster Theological Seminary, 151, 153, 156, 161, 163–64
land, 14, 31–32, 38–39, 71, 83–84, 100, 102–3, 120, 126, 148, 217, 259–71, 278
   father/motherland, 83–84
   holy, sacred, 31–32, 82–85, 125
   homeland, 37, 106, 109
language, 3, 8, 10, 25, 48, 65, 82, 88–93, 102, 104, 107–9, 123, 144, 193, 231, 263
   bilingualism, 122
   cultural dominance, 89
Last Supper, 208–14
Latin America, Latin American, 64, 74, 125, 143–64, 175, 187, 192–93, 198
   interpretation, 50
Latinx, latino/a, 11–13, 48, 64, 74, 116, 120–21, 123, 126, 135–36, 140, 143–47, 171–84, 187–96, 200
   and black, 145
   Chicana, 178
   hermeneutics, 49–50, 125
Lazarus and the rich man, 182
legal system, 44, 61, 64, 114–15, 118, 145, 182, 199, 228, 244–45, 2515-2
legalism, 173
LGBTQ+, 13, 25, 49, 61, 87, 125, 153, 158–60, 167, 189, 223, 229, 246. *See also* queer studies; sexuality; transgender
   hermeneutics, 49
liberalism, 16, 114, 119–20, 205, 231, 275
   neoliberalism, 15, 199
liberation, 28–29, 61–62, 64–68, 70, 72–73, 115, 124, 138, 206
   theology, 64

Lincoln, Abraham, 107
literacy, 105
literary criticism, 16, 174–76, 184, 196–98, 218, 225, 267, 282
Louima, Abner, 245
lynching, 126, 254–55
Maccabees, 210
Magnificat, 180, 183, 210
Maltese Falcon, The, 156–63
"Manifest Destiny," 102, 109, 198
maps, 9, 11, 31, 37, 40, 103, 124–25
marginalization, 5, 10, 50, 56, 61, 63, 73, 85-86, 137–38, 178, 180–82, 189, 190, 218, 225, 249, 255, 260
Martin, Trayvon, 111, 245
Martyn, J. Louis, 192
Marxism, 8, 114, 119
masculinity, 86-87, 160, 119, 160, 199, 213
materiality, materialism, 76, 228. *See also* historical materialism
McBride, Renisha, 245
mental illness, 88, 235, 249
Mercado, Walter, 145
meritocracy, 114, 119
Mexico/an, 12, 83, 118, 120–21, 144, 189, 190, 193, 196–99
Michelangelo, 35
microaggression, 116, 121
Middle East, 32, 125, 266, 268
midrash, 10, 66, 215, 251
migrant, migration, 70, 99, 144, 167, 183, 188–89, 197, 199
minoritization, 1, 6–7, 11–13, 16, 49–50, 55, 119, 135–36, 139, 142, 151–52, 176, 178–79, 181, 190, 192, 194–96, 223–25
    minoritized interpretation, 50, 56, 146–74
minority, 5, 10, 50, 56, 62, 82–87, 116–19, 121, 147, 152, 236, 265, 275
    model minority, 194–95
    religious, 83–85
missionary, missionizing, 5, 28, 44, 51–52, 103–8, 260, 284

modernism, 176–77
modernity, 17, 61, 65–66, 71–72, 76, 85, 124, 176–77, 232
Modi, Narendra, 83, 85, 91
moriscos, 218
Morris, David, 162
Movement for Black Lives, 111–13, 121, 127
Muhammad, 33
mujerista criticism, 223
multiculturalism, 47, 62, 69, 75, 231
Muslim, Moslem. *See* Islam
Nadal, Jerome, 217
Nag Hammadi, 9, 54–55
narrative criticism, 32, 124, 211
nationalism, 10, 38, 51, 81–82, 84, 87–89, 91–92, 199
    black, 114
    Christian, 10, 17, 85–87
    religious, 10, 81–82, 85–86, 88, 90–93
    white, 10, 85–87, 139
Native American, 2, 48, 64, 99, 100, 116, 120–21, 125, 125, 175, 188, 194, 198
    hermeneutics, 125
    reservation schools, 120
native, nativism, 105, 107, 227, 231, 260, 267, 270
    language, 88, 91, 104
neurotypical, 227
neutrality, 10, 67–68, 71, 114–15, 117, 123–24, 147, 171, 173, 176, 224, 226–27, 236, 260–61, 263
New Deal, 121
nonviolence, 87
Obama, Barack, 83
objectivity. *See* neutrality.
oppression, 10–11, 17, 30, 62, 65, 67–69, 76, 83, 102, 109, 112–13, 117–18, 120, 124, 138, 141, 148, 225, 227–28, 229–30, 236, 246, 249, 252, 255, 261
    internalized, 27, 30, 37
    of diversity, 63
    systemic, 225, 252–53
orientalism, 3, 63, 171–72
orthodoxy, 9, 53, 145

other, othering, otherness, 1–2, 10, 12–13, 34, 38–39, 63, 72, 83, 87, 90, 108, 141, 190, 192, 194–95, 199–200, 279
outside, outsider. *See* insider/outsider
paganism, 40, 235
Pakistan, 82,
Palestine, 83, 125, 199, 266
Parsiism, 83
particularity, particularism, 15, 138–39, 144, 171–72, 190, 194–95, 276, 279, 282, 286
patriarchy, 13, 28, 63–64, 87, 141, 194, 230–34, 248, 252, 262, 265, 267
patriotism, 83
Paul, 35, 37, 49, 126, 194–95, 211, 213, 234–37
Peter, 182–83, 212, 279, 283
phenomenology, 9, 44, 122, 124
Philippines/Filipino, 98–109, 179–81
philosophy, 2, 37, 46–47, 65, 67, 70, 76, 108, 171, 176–77, 229
Pieter Bruegel the Elder, 162
pluralism, 82, 116
poesis, 10, 66
police, policing, 72, 85–86, 112, 121–2, 137–38, 245, 148, 181, 244–48, 250, 252–54. *See also* extrajudicial killings; legal system
politics, 1, 5, 8, 10, 18, 29–30, 43, 47, 49–50, 52, 61–70, 72, 76, 81–92, 98, 102, 104, 111–13, 118–20, 124, 139, 141–42, 168, 183, 189, 193–94, 198, 200, 206, 210, 231–32, 260–61, 265, 268, 275, 277
   of belonging, 91–92, 191–92
   political cartoon, 98–109
   political exegesis, 64, 66, 69, 76
positivism, 176
postcolonialism, 27, 70, 75–76, 92, 167, 223, 229–30, 233
   feminism, 229–30
postmodernism, 66, 70, 76
postracialism, 114–15
poverty, 71–72, 107, 119, 123, 182, 206, 271

power, 1–7, 11–12, 16, 27, 65, 68, 71, 92, 104, 107, 112, 115–16, 148, 176, 179, 182, 194, 205, 210, 227, 229, 238, 265, 268
   and whiteness, 76, 92
   colonial, 30, 44, 139, 143
   disciplinary, 4, 6
   economic, 63, 74
   gendered, 65
   imperial, 89–90, 139, 231, 249
   in biblical texts, 248–49
   institutional, 2, 74, 261
   local, 247
   of people of color, 141
   of racism, 118, 120, 231
   over knowledge, 3. *See also* knowledge production
   social, 179
prejudice, 2, 27, 74, 117–18, 275–77, 286
privilege, 8, 27, 45, 63, 76, 85–86, 92, 114, 117–18, 120–22, 124, 181, 187, 264
primitive, primitivization, 105, 227
prison. *See* incarceration
property rights, 119–20
Protestant, 52–53, 103, 104–6, 145, 223, 226, 260
Reformation, 124
psychology, 27, 65, 67, 117–18, 124, 152
Puerto Rico, Porto Rico, 6, 10–11, 97–109, 143–45, 188–89, 193
purity, 3, 34, 36, 52, 63, 231, 235, 265
queer studies, 13, 25, 125, 159, 223, 229. *See also* LGBTQ+
race, 11, 53, 154
racialization, 7, 9, 11–12, 17, 44–45, 48–49, 51–53, 63, 65–67, 71, 76, 83, 117–18, 121, 135, 137, 140, 142, 171–72, 174, 179, 189, 199–200, 260, 282
racism, 2, 4, 10–11, 27, 45, 61, 64, 68–69, 72, 74–76, 97, 101–9, 114–15, 117–20, 172, 275, 285
   differential, 118
   in biblical studies, 9, 11, 14, 26, 67–76, 139, 142, 249
   linguistic, 10, 91–92

racism (cont.)
   scientific, 27
   structural, systemic, 2, 11, 27, 67, 75, 112, 114, 151, 188
Ramjanmabhoomi movement, 84
Rashi, 34, 36
reader-response criticism, 124
reception history, 55, 69, 233
redaction criticism, 167, 195, 226
refugee, 83
representation, 5, 16, 50, 56, 68, 76, 81, 159, 162, 175, 223, 230
resistance, 16, 18, 63, 68, 70, 72, 75, 86, 121, 195, 199–200, 236, 264
Revelation, Book of, 10, 88, 92, 126, 211
rhetorical criticism, 196, 225
Rice, Tamir, 246
Romanos the Melodist, 207, 215
Rome, Roman Empire, 27, 35–37, 40, 43, 53, 88–89, 126, 141, 182–3, 193–4, 228, 232, 236, 284
rural, 121, 230, 262, 265, 268–69, 265
Ruth, 25, 36, 232
Samaritan, 280, 284
Sanders, Bernie, 97
Sarah/Sarai, 34, 255, 269
sati, 230–31
savage, 105, 245
#SayHerName, 122, 242, 246
segregation, 17, 120, 223
   desegregation, 116
separate but equal, 120
secularism, 13, 82, 216, 229
seminary. *See* theological education
Sermon on the Mount, 281–82
sexual assault, 245, 247, 249,
sexuality, 25, 45, 105, 118, 141, 145, 156–61, 188, 206. *See also* LGBTQ+
sexualization, 34, 38–39
Shakespeare, 98
Shepard, Matthew, 127
Sherman, Thomas, 104
Sikhism, 83
sin, 37, 174
skin color, 36, 43, 46, 92, 106, 207

slavery, 2, 7, 13, 16, 26, 28, 30–31, 33, 37–39, 43–44, 51, 56, 65, 67, 116, 123, 148, 209, 217–18, 228–29, 232–38, 249, 252–53, 255
social justice, 12, 182, 184, 224
social location, 12, 26, 124, 153, 165, 167, 177, 180, 224, 230, 271
social media, 72, 111, 121, 200
social sciences, 124, 182, 259, 264, 268
Society of Biblical Literature, 8, 10, 25–26, 35, 48–50, 56, 108–9, 123, 135–37, 139, 147, 151, 174–75, 187, 259
   Status of Women in the Profession Committee, 50
   Underrepresented Racial and Ethnic Minorities in the Profession Committee, 50
sociocultural criticism, 124, 196
sociology, 115, 225, 282
source criticism, 195, 226
Spain, 98, 100, 103–5, 109, 193–94, 209, 215, 217
Stanley-Jones, Aiyana, 122, 245
#StayWoke, 111. *See also* wokeness
stereotypes, 12, 37, 67, 118, 123, 151–52, 160, 194, 199–200
   threat, 152–53, 157, 161
stigma, 181
subaltern, 13, 69, 223, 229–34, 237–38
subjectivity, 6, 11, 43, 45, 62, 66, 68–69, 71–72, 86, 90, 102, 143, 148, 176, 189, 226, 229–30, 233–34, 237–38, 249
suffering, 10, 62–63, 68–72, 74, 122, 253
supersessionism, 54, 63
supremacy, 81, 85–86, 90–93
   linguistic, 8
   religious, 10, 82, 84, 86
   white, 8–9, 16–18, 28, 34–37, 39–40, 44, 71, 91–92, 114–5, 142, 247–48, 252–53
syncretism, 145, 235
Table of Nations, 33, 38
tax, taxation, 100–1, 117, 182, 269, 282–83
taxonomy, 27, 117, 172, 205

Taylor, Breonna, 127
technology, 7, 197
testimonial, 177–79
testimonio, 12, 171, 177–79
textualization, 10, 66, 263
theological education, 7, 29–30, 61–63, 72, 125, 135–37, 139–40, 147, 151, 165, 174, 190, 215, 241, 246, 259, 261, 269
theology, 53, 55, 61, 64–65, 67–68, 73, 87, 138–39, 146, 154, 168, 188, 207, 224–26, 235, 250, 252, 259–60, 263, 265, 268, 277
Third World, 230, 232
tokenism, 63
Tometi, Opal, 111
Transfiguration, 27–28, 48, 112, 216
transgender, 112, 159, 194, 248
translation, 9, 17, 25–26, 36, 54, 66–67, 163–64, 167, 248, 255, 277, 280, 282–83
transnationalism, 13, 229
trauma, 74, 105, 113, 192, 269
triumphalism, 16
Trump, Donald, 83, 86, 91, 97, 107–8, 138–39, 189, 192
Turkey, 91
Turner, Henry McNeal, 51
Turner, Nat, 210
Uncle Sam, 98–109
undergraduate studies, 47, 50, 175–76, 188, 205, 259, 266
United Kingdom, 3, 33, 35, 44, 49, 99, 102, 231, 248
British Museum, 35
United States, 1–5, 9–12, 14, 25–26, 31, 33, 39, 44, 47–50, 52–56, 66–67, 73, 81–87, 91–92, 97–109, 113, 115, 118–20, 124, 126, 136, 144–45, 156, 159, 175, 180, 183, 187–91, 193–94, 197–99, 205, 229, 245, 248, 250, 253, 255
military, 2, 102–4, 108, 112, 197–98
Supreme Court, 100–1, 114
universal religion, 15, 51, 53, 276, 282, 286

universalism, universality, 69, 119, 123, 147, 200, 226, 276, 279, 282
University of the Incarnate Word, 188
urban, 26, 66, 120, 267, 269
Velásquez, Diego, 13, 205–18
violence, 17, 65–67, 70, 72, 84–85, 111–12, 122, 139, 193, 228, 232, 234, 238, 245, 247, 248–50, 252
Wabash Center, 151
Weems, Renita, 246
Wellhausen, Julius, 264
Wells, Ida B., 126
West, Western, 3, 5–6, 9–10, 12, 14, 17, 32, 63, 67, 71, 108, 119, 125, 172–74, 176, 193, 226, 235, 260–61, 264–9, 276. *See also* Europe
cultural dominance, 1, 8, 10–17, 62–63, 68, 118, 126, 191, 224, 226, 253, 260, 271
Williams College, 175
Williams, Jesse, 111
womanism, 14, 125, 167, 223, 225, 233, 245, 249–51, 253
women, 28, 47, 50, 61, 64–65, 112, 178–9, 184, 207–16, 231, 237, 276–79, 285. *See also* Canaanite woman
biblical, 210–14, 237
enslaved, formerly enslaved, 7, 228, 255
Indian, 13, 230
minoritized, 178
of color, 13, 105, 112, 122, 137, 175, 189, 194, 229, 231, 245–47, 249–55
women's studies, 115
"White Man's Burden," 102–3, 107
white, whiteness, 1–18, 29, 33–37, 39–40, 43–48, 52–54, 56–57, 61, 63, 66, 68, 71–72, 76, 86, 91–92, 113, 117–18, 120–24, 145, 151–52, 177, 180–81, 187–88, 194, 227, 248, 252–53, 261–63, 265–67, 271, 275
as normative, 55, 64, 72, 116, 122, 261, 264, 266–67, 271
critical white studies, 120
of biblical characters, 35–36

white, whiteness (cont.)
   passing, 145
wokeness, 111–12, 127. *See also* #Stay-Woke
World War II, 9, 54–55, 142
xenophobia, 61, 64, 248
Zimmerman, George, 111

www.ingramcontent.com/pod-product-compliance
Lightning Source LLC
Chambersburg PA
CBHW021935290426
44108CB00012B/845